Personnel Management in Government Agencies and Nonprofit Organizations

Personnel Management in Government Agencies and Nonprofit Organizations

Fifth Edition

Dennis L. Dresang
University of Wisconsin, Madison

PEARSON
Longman

New York   San Francisco   Boston
London   Toronto   Sydney   Tokyo   Singapore   Madrid
Mexico City   Munich   Paris   Cape Town   Hong Kong   Montreal

To Maxine

Editor-in-Chief: Eric Stano
Executive Marketing Manager: Ann Stypuloski
Production Manager: Denise Phillip
Project Coordination, Text Design, and Electronic Page Makeup: Pre-Press PMG
Cover Design Manager: Wendy Ann Fredericks
Cover Designer: Kay Petronio
Cover Photo: Harry Nowell/Age Fotostock America, Inc.
Senior Manufacturing Buyer: Dennis J. Para
Printer and Binder: Courier Corporation/ Westford
Cover Printer: Phoenix Color Corporation

Library of Congress Cataloging-in-Publication Data

Dresang, Dennis L.
    Personnel management in government agencies and nonprofit organizations / Dennis L.
    Dresang.
    —5th ed.
        p.   cm.
    Revised ed. of: Public personnel management and public policy
    Includes bibliographical references and index.
    ISBN 0-205-61679-8
    1. Civil service–Personnel management.   I. Dresang, Dennis L. Public personnel
    management and public policy.   II. Title.
JF1601.D7 2007
352.6—dc22
007038894

Please visit our website at www.ablongman.com

ISBN 13: 978-0-205-61679-4
ISBN 10:   0-205-61679-8

4 5 6 7 8 9 10—V013—15 14 13 12

Contents

Preface

Previous editions of this book focused on personnel management in government. The expansion to include nonprofit organizations responds to the growth of nonprofit organizations and governments' increased reliance on these organizations for work that public employees had traditionally completed. The absence of profit as a goal and yardstick certainly presents human resource managers in government and non-profit organizations with similar challenges. Likewise, governments and nonprofits share missions that are social, educational, and service-oriented. On the other hand, constitutional provisions and the dynamics of the electoral process uniquely empower and constrain governments. Throughout the book, the similarities and differences of government agencies and nonprofit organizations are discussed, especially as they relate to personnel management.

Another distinctive characteristic of this text is that the primary audience is defined as those who have responsibilities for supervising and managing people. Few individuals will actually have careers as specialists in personnel management. Almost every professional and manager in a public agency or nonprofit organization, on the other hand, will have responsibility for hiring, developing, disciplining, and managing other employees. Most readers of other texts or of previous editions of this one have had to translate messages directed at personnel specialists into relevant lessons for the more general concerns of achieving agency productivity and responsiveness. Now, no more eavesdropping.

It is time to refocus this text. A central theme of Reinventing Government, Total Quality Management, continuous improvement, and other management reform efforts since the early 1990s, is to improve governance by decentralizing and devolving responsibilities. Agency managers have acquired increased discretion. They also have increased responsibility for the technical tasks of personnel management. In some jurisdictions there have been significant cutbacks in the central offices that did position analyses, recruitment plans, examination development, employee training, and compensation administration. Agency managers now need to do these tasks. With these developments in mind, this edition continues to explain the tasks and techniques of personnel management functions.

Personnel specialists, who increasingly are fewer in number and provide consultation rather than control, will still find this text relevant and valuable. The tools and techniques of the field are described in detail. Although these are presented in the context of more general management responsibilities, human resource specialists can learn from these discussions what they need to assist line managers. And in the process they will have acquired a better understanding of the perspective of those they will be or are serving.

This edition, even more than previous ones, is based on experiences as well as scholarship. I have been able to supplement my own experiences in managing personnel with a rich diversity of lessons learned from a large number of elected executives, agency managers, union officials, attorneys, and employees. I am grateful to all of them. In addition, I would like to thank the following reviewers who provided comments and suggestions that were invaluable in the development of this edition: Chris Hamilton, Washburn University; Mike Mast, Grand Valley State University; Debra Moore, Southern Illinois University.

I dedicate this work to my wife, Maxine Austin, who shares my concern that those who provide us with public services work with their employees in ways that everyone finds productive, satisfying, and supportive.

DENNIS L. DRESANG

Chapter 1

Introduction

Personnel Management in Government Agencies and Nonprofit Organizations

The work of governments and almost all nonprofit organization is labor-intensive. To provide the services, implement the policies, and enforce the regulations of government, it takes people—and lots of them. Likewise, most nonprofits offer services, analyses, and consultation—the kinds of knowledge-based activities that requires able, dedicated individuals. If human resources are central to the work and the success of an organization, then the tasks of attracting, compensating, evaluating, disciplining, motivating, and developing quality employees are obviously critical.

A challenge that is common to personnel management in both governments and **nonprofit organizations** is that profit is neither a goal nor reward for employees, individually or collectively. The policy premise for the official designation of an organization is that they exist for public purposes—charity, education, social welfare, culture, religion, and the like. Section 501 of the federal Internal Revenue Service Tax Code recognizes these organizations and provides them with tax-exempt status. They may not pay dividends on profits or distribute income to members and if they dissolve, their assets must be given to another nonprofit organization. In addition, both governments and nonprofit organizations are severely limited in the kinds of political activity in which they may engage.

Government agencies and nonprofit organizations come in a wide variety of sizes and shapes. Some, like the federal departments of Defense, Health and Human Services, and Homeland Security and state departments of health and human services, transportation, and natural resources, have thousands of employees, millions of dollars, and several units performing many different tasks. Nonprofit organizations like the YMCA and YWCA, Boys and Girls Clubs, and Nature Conservancy similarly have hundreds of employees, millions of dollars, and numerous branches throughout the country. At the other extreme are agencies in federal, state, and local governments with less than a handful of employees with a narrow scope of responsibilities and nonprofit organizations that are literally run out of someone's home with a few part-time workers and perhaps some volunteers.

The employees that are the focus of this book number in the millions and are in a wide variety of occupations. Federal government workers include investigators and program analysts, postal workers and immigration authorities, scientists and accountants,

1

spies and soldiers. State governments hire receptionists and computer programmers, social workers and prison guards, game wardens and highway engineers, purchasing agents and tax auditors, physicians and attorneys, budget analysts and building maintenance crews. Local governments employ police officers and teachers, civil engineers and librarians, pathologists and sanitation workers, recreation directors and parking lot attendants. Nonprofit organizations include many of the same specialties— accountants and lawyers, social workers and environmental engineers, receptionists and policy analysts.

This book is for anyone interested in how people work in government and non-profit settings, but especially for those who direct and manage others. Virtually all managers and professionals in these agencies have responsibility for directing other employees. In order for these **managers** and supervisors to do their jobs effectively, they need to know the laws, rules, procedures, and techniques of public personnel management. They need to know what motivates workers and how to match organizational needs with individual talents and interests.

This book explains the prescriptions and the restrictions of personnel management that applies to government and 501 organizations, and, importantly, the policy rationale for this framework. In addition, the text draws upon lessons from the fields of organizational behavior, industrial psychology, and industrial sociology to provide an understanding of how individuals behave in organizations. In short, the scope of this book includes concern for both the generic issues of human behavior in organizational settings and the specific needs of public sector **accountability** in a democracy. Throughout the book, distinctions between the generic nature of personnel management and the specific requirements and characteristics of government and nonprofit organizations will be explained.

Most personnel management is done as part of the work of heading an agency or office or of being a senior analyst, accountant, engineer, librarian, social worker, police officer, or other professional. Medium- and large-scale jurisdictions do hire staff who specialize in employment testing, compensation, training, affirmative action, and collective bargaining. Most of these offices were down-sized in the 1990s and much of this work delegated to agency managers.

Although the central perspective of this book is that of the *manager*, the substance of the individual chapters is the core tasks and functions of different personnel *specialists* and *technicians*. Those pursuing careers as specialists in personnel obviously will find that this book informs them about their field. Because of the managerial focus, this text will also sensitize specialists to the needs and concerns of their primary customer (i.e., public agency managers).

Managers, particularly in the public sector, must meet multiple objectives. This chapter introduces the generic objectives of productivity and satisfaction and then the specific public policy concerns of accountability. Subsequent chapters provide more in-depth discussions and more detailed explanations.

LEARNING OBJECTIVES OF THIS CHAPTER

- Secure an overview of the scope of activities included in personnel management in government and nonprofit organizations

- Understand the major ingredients of human productivity in organizations
- Appreciate the different personal needs that jobs meet for individuals
- Understand the various kinds of demands that a representative democracy makes on personnel management in government and nonprofit organizations

PRODUCTIVITY

A basic responsibility of all those with leadership responsibilities is to be sure the job gets done. Team leaders, committee chairs, agency heads, and chief executive officers must use the formal authority and informal influence they have so that the people under them work creatively and energetically to accomplish organizational goals. The fundamental ingredients of productivity are presented in Figure 1.1. Managers need staff that is competent *and* works hard. It does little good to have people with skills if they are too lazy or distracted to apply what they know. What may be even worse is to have energetic but incompetent people. There is nothing like correcting lots of errors! Managers are—or should be—involved in the personnel tasks of defining what skills are needed and who should be hired and/or retained. A daily challenge for managers is ensuring that employees apply their skills and abilities.

In part, working hard is dependent on environmental factors: Effort is dependent on motivation. Environment can facilitate or obstruct work, it rarely contributes in a positive, long-term way to productivity. Cleanliness and safety, for example, remove disruptions that interfere with production. But there is a limit to how clean or safe a place can get and, therefore, how much additional effort to clean or to protect will in turn lead to more productivity.

The quest for strategies managers might use to motivate their workers has been a long and rather frustrating one. In large part, the frustration is due to the dubious assumption that there is a single approach that will fit all employees and all organizations. It is important to learn that a job is inherently important for some. For others, work is a necessary part of living. This difference is amoral and to recognize it is not to judge it. Research suggests that individuals who work in relatively low-skilled, routine jobs tend to have something other than their job as the main subject of concern in their lives. Professionals, on the other hand, tend to consider their work as a central part of their own identity. For them, achievements in their work are of vital importance to personal satisfaction and self-esteem.[1]

As will be explained in more detail in Chapter 5, effective management depends on recognizing and acting on what motivates employees. Professionals generally

SKILLS   +   EFFORT   = PRODUCTIVITY
(Determined by   (Motivation–potentially
organizational   positive force–and
needs)   Working Conditions–
                        potentially negative force)

FIGURE 1.1   The Fundamentals of Productivity.

respond well to managerial approaches that empower them, whereas those doing more routine work value participatory opportunities less and sometimes even regard them as manipulative. Incentives for professionals to do well lay in the accomplishments themselves and the recognition of those accomplishments. For those doing more structured tasks, incentives come in more immediate and tangible forms.

One cannot say that everyone should or should not consider his or her employment as something that is intrinsically of personal value and satisfaction. To do so is presumptuous. Instead, managers need to recognize and to accept the different personal value systems of their employees and to pursue work motivation in ways that relate to these value systems.

Productivity is a concern of personnel management regardless of whether the organization is public, private, or nonprofit. Managers in government have additional issues that must be addressed.

GOVERNMENT SETTING

Although there are many similarities between personnel management in a private business or nonprofit organization and a government agency, there are also some distinct and important differences. The most obvious traits unique to the public sector are the links to legislative institutions and the electoral process.

Legislators differ in fundamental ways from stockholders. The former are accountable to the voters; if elected officials hope to repeat their success at the ballot box, they must act publicly and in accord with voter preferences. Legislators seek a wide variety of policy objectives, whereas stockholders are concerned primarily with the financial health of their company. As representatives of particular constituencies, elected officials pursue special concerns that vary considerably over time and from one official to another. Legislators are more involved in oversight than stockholders are in a private company. This is true even for part-time legislators in local and state governments. Constituent casework, legislative hearings, and the budget process all draw elected officials into the scrutiny and direction of public agencies.

In the 1980s and 1990s, a heightened interest in combating alcohol and other drug abuse reminded public employers of another difference between them and their private sector counterparts. The U.S. Constitution restricts how governments can treat citizens. Thus, when governments take action to identify drug abusers, including government employees, they must not violate constitutional rights to privacy, self-incrimination, and the like. Private employers, however, are not bound by the Constitution and have more options as they deal with drug abuse among their employees. Chapter 3 contains a discussion of how public employees' needs are balanced with public employers' rights.

The legal framework within which personnel management in public agencies must operate is not always unique. Government regulations concerning labor relations and equal employment opportunities apply to all but the smallest of firms. The explanation in Chapter 4 of social representation policies and the steps taken to minimize employment discrimination applies equally to public, private, and nonprofit organizations.

NONPROFIT SETTING

The requirements and restrictions specified in the federal tax code for nonprofit organizations provide a setting for personnel management that has some similarities to government, but without the demands of electoral politics and a legislature. By their very nature, nonprofits typically have a mission of public or community service. The goal may be to provide healthy development for young people, to ensure safe, affordable housing in a community, to preserve wilderness areas, to promote a rural lifestyle, or to inform the public of the nature of a particular illness. Nonprofits are distinct from governmental agencies in that they do not have the authority or responsibility of enforcing laws and regulations. They do not make and sell goods and services, like private businesses do. On the other hand, nonprofit organizations increasingly contract with governments to run programs that public agencies could or did do. Nonprofits sometimes partner with governments and businesses to pursue common objectives. But, to retain their tax-exempt status, nonprofit organizations must not in essence take on the character of a profit seeking business.

The prohibition against lobbying or engaging in partisan political activity is sometimes clearer in concept than it is in practical situations. Nonetheless, this restriction is a serious concern for nonprofit organizations and affects personnel management. As is the case in government agencies, steps must be taken to ensure that employees do not in substance or appearance engage in politics as members of the organization, but this must be balanced with the rights that individuals have as citizens under the First Amendment.

The challenges and opportunities of relying on volunteers are associated more with nonprofit organizations than with government agencies or private businesses. Obviously, the discussions in future chapters of employee motivation, discipline, compensation, and the like need to include the issues raised by having volunteers in a workforce.

PERSONNEL SPECIALISTS

Personnel specialists in the public sector have formed a professional association, the International Personnel Management Association, which is devoted to establishing principles and practices that meet the varying needs of government agencies and, increasingly, of nonprofit organizations. One example is the efforts of the profession in the 1970s to develop job-related criteria for the selection process. Although the criteria for selecting someone to fill a vacancy were always supposed to be job-related, this was frequently not the case. Psychological research cast doubts on the validity of certain examinations, educational requirements, and experience standards used to screen job candidates.[2] Evidence was brought to courts to show that some employers placed educational requirements on jobs as devices to make most minority group members ineligible for positions.[3] As a result, personnel professionals have made major efforts, individually and collectively, to reexamine the selection criteria and techniques used to screen candidates to determine whether or not they can do the job. These efforts respond equally to affirmative action concerns and to the demand for competent employees. Done correctly, they will meet the needs of agencies, employees, customers, and society in general.

Unfortunately, professionalism does not always mean the development of ways to provide high-quality service. The use of tools and techniques can become a preoccupation. Specialists can become so concerned with creating categories, procedures, and routines that they lose sight of the major objective of their efforts. An approach misses the primary goal if it is thorough and detailed but too time-consuming and complicated to meet the needs of either employees or agency managers.

Figure 1.2 illustrates common combinations of the various influences on public personnel management. The focus in this illustration is on how these influences relate to the selection of public employees. A similar diagram could be constructed for other tasks of personnel management.

At the center of Figure 1.2 is the ideal public personnel management system. Here, the balance of influences provides for a selection process that (1) is merit oriented and takes full advantage of professional techniques for identifying competent workers, (2) pursues affirmative action goals to secure a **socially representative workforce**, (3) maintains accountability to the public through its elected representatives, and (4) provides incumbent employees with satisfying career opportunities. Deviations from this ideal can be instances where one of the four major demands on public personnel management dominate. The domination of politics, for example, results in a patronage system of selection. A stress on the need for minority representation can lead to a quota system and reverse discrimination. A fascination with professional techniques can lead to a neglect of the service goals that those techniques

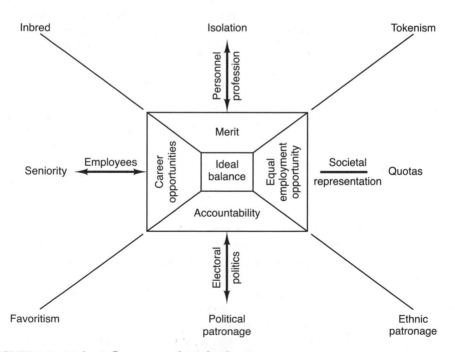

FIGURE 1.2   **Major Influences on the Selection Process.**

were designed to achieve and the emergence of a time-consuming, cumbersome, and rigid system. A selection process that aims to provide career opportunities to employees at the expense of other needs and values is a process that over-emphasizes the value of seniority.

Two or more influences, rather than just one, can dominate selection systems that suffer from imbalance. There are, of course, other possible combinations than those included in Figure 1.2; those in the figure are the most common. Also, Figure 1.2 has been constructed to illustrate the influences most directly juxtaposed to each other: professionalism and politics, on the one hand, and affirmative action and seniority principles, on the other. Where politics and societal representativeness dominate, ethnic or minority patronage is likely to occur. The domination of politics and employee concerns may lead to favoritism. The combination of professional techniques and criteria with a concern for affirmative action will probably lead to tokenism, whereas an overemphasis on employee careers and professional techniques will result in a relatively static, inbred workforce.

Political change has been key to the establishment of the policies that direct personnel activities in government. The next chapter discusses the history of political change and public personnel management policies, with an emphasis on the civil service, which includes most government employees. Before looking back to understand the foundation of current policies, it might be useful to consider the challenges of changes ushering in the twenty-first century.

Diversity

The laws prohibiting discrimination in employment apply equally to government and nonprofit organizations. Increasingly, managers have workforces that are diverse. The percentage of women who are employed has been increasing and, despite some continued obstacles, women are found in senior positions and in professions once reserved for men. The population of the United States is becoming more diverse ethnically, and so also are its employees. Race continues to be an emotional political issue. Managers, thus, must be alert to potential conflict among employees based on gender or ethnicity and must deal with a wide array of personal and family situations that need to be accommodated.

Intergovernmental Relations

Relations between federal, state, local, and tribal governments have gone through a number of stages since the birth of the United States. The rhetoric of the late 1990s suggested that state, local, and tribal governments might have a wider scope of authority and responsibility and the federal government less. On the other hand, policy makers in Washington seem intent on preempting the authority of state, local, and tribal officials to determine social policies and economic regulations. The thrust of concerns over homeland security has been to increase federal involvement in state and local governance. Likewise, state governments feel obliged to favor home rule but simultaneously establish state policies and standards through preemptions and mandates. Many of the federal and state restrictions and directives affect personnel management. Some of these rules and regulations directly shape how employees are selected or compensated or disciplined. Others may complicate or simplify how managers supervise their staff.

Contracting

Contracting out for services rather than employing staff is not new, but it has increased significantly since the 1990s. Even before the attack on Iraq in 2003, there were more than four times as many people working on federal contracts than as federal employees.[4] Overall, 17 percent of the national civil labor force in the United States are government employees and 22 percent work under contracts with federal, state, and local governments. Many of those contracts are with nonprofit organizations. Some of the contracts are for personnel management activities, such as recruitment, training, and compensation administration. Other contracts are for government responsibilities ranging from welfare administration and prisons to environmental analysis and toll roads. Clearly the increase in the number and the size of nonprofit organizations is due in part to government contracting. For managers in nonprofits, one implication is the set of provisions in contracts that place restrictions on human resource management—similar to intergovernmental requirements. For managers in government, part of contract administration is negotiating and monitoring personnel policy requirements and also dealing with morale issues when employees fear their job is being or might be outsourced.

BOX 1.1

PERSONNEL MANAGEMENT ACTIVITIES

Job analysis
Human resource planning
Performance appraisal
Testing
Selection
Employee training and development
Discipline and dismissal
Counseling
Labor relations
Communications
Research and evaluation
Wage and salary administration
Benefits and services
Political rights and constraints
Equal employment opportunities
Quality improvement

Technology

Technological advances have had some of the most profound impacts on organizations. Assembly lines, for example, determined how work would be defined and assigned. Computer technology has redefined some jobs and generated the need for new types of specialists. There is now the possibility of employees performing some tasks at sites remote from the traditional office. A concern that has emerged is privacy and electronic access to information about employees. Taking advantage of computer technology and ensuring only appropriate usage obviously require new approaches toward personnel management.

Worker Participation

The idea of involving employees in organizational decision making is not new, but the emphasis since the 1990s has been substantially different. Likewise, the approaches are new. Traditional forms of worker participation in management are collective bargaining and organizational development. In both cases, workers are empowered. Collective bargaining is an adversarial model in which workers and management negotiate an agreement on how they will work together and relate to one another. Organizational development, and similar approaches, assume workers and managers can agree on common objectives and then work cooperatively together, in nonhierarchical forms, to reach those objectives. Total Quality Management (TQM)—also known as Quality Management and as Continuous Improvement—is a more recent approach, which has become widely used as a strategy in both government and nonprofit agencies. Although TQM does not empower workers, it solicits and values their information and insight on production processes and ways of meeting consumer needs. Employees participate in teams in the discussions leading to decisions, but managers retain the authority and responsibility to make the decisions.

Regardless of the specific approach, employee participation models challenge managers and pose important questions to traditional systems of personnel management. The focus on groups and teams, for example, runs counter to traditional emphases on evaluating, rewarding, training, and sanctioning employees as individuals. Employee empowerment places some conscious constraints on how managers manage.

The changes described above are real and have prompted concern.[5] They are beyond the kind of speculation that warrants only a footnote. The background and the implications of these and other developments will become integral parts of the chapters that follow.

PLAN OF THE BOOK

This text is about personnel management, written primarily from the perspective of those who have responsibility for hiring, directing, disciplining, developing, and motivating employees in public agencies and nonprofit organizations. In most cases, personnel management is only one of several responsibilities that people in senior and mid-level positions have. The most basic responsibility of managers is to get the job done, as efficiently and as effectively as possible. Productivity, in other words, is a key concern.

However, productivity is not the only concern of those who manage personnel. Chapters 2 through 4 contain discussions of the policy issues that also form the substance of personnel management. Chapter 2 is about the civil service and thus uniquely related to government. Chapters 3 and 4 are about constitutional rights, restrictions on political activity, and social diversity, topics that relate to nonprofit organizations as well as public agencies. Chapter 5 returns to productivity—a generic subject—and discusses in some detail the relevant theories and research findings. How agencies organize to allocate responsibility for meeting the various policy objectives of personnel management is explained in Chapter 6.

The three key analytical components of personnel management are

1. organization
2. position
3. individual

The goal is to match organizational needs with individual strengths and interests. Thus, it is essential to analyze what the organization requires in order to define jobs or positions and then to identify the relevant knowledge, abilities, and behaviors of employees and applicants for employment. In Chapters 7 through 10, the techniques used to examine organizational needs, positions, and individuals are presented. Included in these chapters are discussions of the policy and managerial implications of how jobs and people have been defined.

The remainder of the book focuses on specific managerial functions and concerns, such as employee assistance and development, discipline, compensation, and conflict resolution. In each of these chapters, the discussion includes managerial approaches and philosophies, relevant laws and regulations, and public policy issues. Again, these are concerns to both government agencies and nonprofit organizations.

Public personnel management lends itself to learning-by-doing. At appropriate places throughout the book, exercises and case studies are included. The case studies present managerial problems that need resolution. The exercises are more technical in nature. They describe how to analyze jobs, design examinations, or evaluate performance. Personnel specialists—in those organizations and jurisdictions that have these positions—spend most of their time doing the work described in the exercises. Managers are involved in at least some steps and would benefit from understanding the overall intent and nature of the analyses or processes upon which the exercises are based. Where there are no personnel specialists, agency managers may have to conduct job analyses and write position descriptions themselves. Especially in these cases, a broad understanding is much better than simply being able to follow a recipe.

SUMMARY

A core objective of personnel management is to facilitate productivity in organizations. This requires attention to how work in an organization is structured and to how one might motivate employees. These tasks in government and nonprofit organizations are constrained by the nature of public organizations. Governments must be accountable to whomever is elected to office and they must abide by the provisions of statutes and constitutions. Nonprofit organizations must operate within the restrictions that accompany tax-exempt status and, of course, their own respective charters.

Increasingly, personnel management is the responsibility of leaders within organizations, not just human resource specialists. This provides agency managers with discretion and opportunities, but also requires an understanding of the relationships between work, employees, and public policies.

DISCUSSION QUESTIONS

1. What role does your job and career (or prospective job and career) have in defining your identity and your self-esteem? What about for others that you know well? Does the link between self-esteem and a job change with the job?
2. What is common in human resource management in government, nonprofit, and private organizations? What is different?
3. Is it important for managers within the same organization to balance organizational goals, personal needs, professional concerns, and political rights in a consistent manner? If so, what are some approaches toward providing consistency?

Case Study:
Susan M. and Personnel Management

Susan M. took a deep breath as she entered the office. She was both scared and excited about her new job. Susan just completed a masters degree program in public policy and had been hired by a nonprofit organization to fulfill the terms of a new state government contract to promote a significant increase in the number of providers of child care.

In order to help welfare recipients who were parents meet work requirements, the state was taking steps to ensure there were sufficient opportunities for getting child care. Susan had a sister who struggled to find good care for her two children when she had to go back to work after her husband suddenly abandoned the family. The cost, the availability, and the quality of care all were major problems. The frustrations that Susan's sister faced added incredible stress to an already traumatic situation. The pain of this experience was a major reason why Susan went to graduate school and wanted to pursue a public service career. No wonder Susan was excited about the contributions she might be able to make in her new job.

A challenge was going to be to reorient her nonprofit agency from being a service provider to one that encouraged the emergence and development of other providers. She was confident that she was inheriting a staff of very good, competent people. The concern was whether they would share her enthusiasm for encouraging an increase in the opportunity for low-income parents to get quality care for their children.

After about five weeks on the job, Susan concluded that she could count on support from everyone, but enthusiasm from only some. The social work professionals and paraprofessionals felt rejuvenated by the change in the organization's role. They relished the idea of being catalysts and problem solvers. The support staff—one clerical person and a management information specialist—was certainly not hostile to the idea, but in group and individual meetings they seemed more concerned about implications for workload than anything else. The clerical worker was, for example, a prominent leader in a community youth sports program. In a discussion about making some changes in office hours to provide more flexibility for staff, she objected and said she would have to find another job. It was immediately clear that her concern was that the changes might limit her involvement in the youth program. Susan wanted her to stay since she was very skilled and had the advantages of having been with the agency for almost 20 years. Susan agreed to a schedule that met the clerical's needs.

Another challenge was to get the support of the legislators on the committees responsible for services to children and families. Susan wanted to use their links to community leaders and she wanted to be sure that the contract would get renewed at the end of the current three-year limit. Three years would not provide adequate time. Of special importance was the chairperson of the Senate committee, who also was the senator elected from Susan's district. The senator believed the role of government was to provide for public health and safety. He did not support an active or entrepreneurial role for Susan's agency. Other members of the Senate committee favored the developmental role that Susan was pursuing.

Elections are seven months away, and the main opponent running against Susan's senator stated at a recent forum that he regarded an increase in child care slots as key to the success of welfare reforms. It appears that the race is very close. Susan would obviously like the challenger to win and certainly plans on voting for him. Likewise, a member of Susan's staff supports the challenger and is doing so by helping with the campaign. Susan talked to the staff member and urged an almost total reduction in campaign involvement. Susan pointed out that there are risks if the incumbent wins reelection and in any case there are restrictions on the involvement of nonprofit organizations in electoral politics. The staff member was irate, charging that Susan was, in effect, making her employees second-class citizens and accusing Susan of not having a genuine commitment to the new mission of the agency.

Susan was learning to balance the issues that are integral to personnel management in a nonprofit organization—organizational goals, professional concerns, personal needs, and political rights.

QUESTIONS

1. How important is it to get enthusiastic support, as opposed to just support, from everyone on the staff?
2. Is there a danger in setting a precedent by meeting the demands of one employee for a change in work schedule?
3. Do you agree that Susan acted appropriately by asking the politically active staff member to curtail involvement in the campaign?

GLOSSARY

Accountability Concern that employees and organizations are pursuing the goals for which they were established

Manager Someone with responsibility for directing the human and financial resources of an organization to pursue organizational goals

Nonprofit organizations Educational, social, and religious organizations established to serve public interests and limited by Internal Revenue Service regulations as a condition of receiving tax-exempt status

Socially representative workforce Extent to which employees reflect the different groups in society, based on race, ethnicity, gender, and national origin

SOURCES

Heclo, H. (1977). *Government of strangers.* Washington, DC: Brookings Institution.
Classic discussion of the relationships between political officials and career civil servants.

Kettl, D. F., Ingraham, P. W., Sanders, R. P., & Horner, C. (1996). *Civil service reform: Building a government that works.* Washington, DC: Brookings Institution.
Brief but insightful statement of personnel management issues in the federal government that concerned the administration of President Bill Clinton.

Muchinsky, P. M. (1990). *Psychology applied to work* (3rd ed.). Pacific Grove, CA: Brooks/ Cole.
Useful introduction to industrial and organizational psychology.

Thompson, F. J., ed. (2003). *Classics of public personnel policy* (3rd ed.). Belmont, CA: Thompson.
As the title implies, this is a collection of important, classic essays on various personnel policies.

NOTES

1. W. C. Freund and E. Epstein, *People and Productivity* (Homewood, IL: Dow Jones-Irwin, 1984).
2. D. J. Peterson, "The Impact of *Duke Power* on Testing," *Personnel* 51, no. 2 (February 1974): 30–37; J. P. Wanous, "Effects of a Realistic Job Preview on Job Acceptance, Job Attitudes, and Job Survival," *Journal of Applied Psychology* 58, no. 1 (1973): 327–332.
3. U.S. Supreme Court, *Willis S. Griggs, et. al.* v. *Duke Power Company,* March 8, 1971.
4. Guy Peters and John Pierre, "Governance Without Government? Rethinking Public Administration," *Journal of Public Administration Research and Theory* 8 (1998): 223–254.
5. Richard C. Kearney and Steven W. Hays, "Reinventing Government, The New Public Management and Civil Service Systems," *Review of Public Personnel Administration* 18, no. 4 (Fall 1998): 55–67.

Chapter 2

The Development of the Merit System

Conflict and compromise are the parents of the contemporary system of personnel management for most government employees. That system is frequently referred to as a merit system, emphasizing the principle that people are hired and fired because of their ability to complete assigned tasks, rather than on the basis of their ties to a political party or because of their sex, age, or race. Yet, the fundamental reason for the establishment of the merit system was not so much a concern for ability as it was a triumph of educated, English-speaking whites over political machines based on patronage linkages to new-immigrant communities. Many recent changes in the merit system are also best understood as part of larger political struggles. Likewise recent challenges to the merit system are a part of political conflict.

This chapter is the first of four presenting the basic public policies that shape personnel management in government and nonprofit organizations. While Chapters 3 to 5 discuss policies that apply generally, this chapter focuses on the civil service or merit system, which covers most employees working for administrative agencies in the executive branches of federal, state, and local governments. Employees in the legislative and judicial branches are not included in the merit system, nor are the relatively few leadership positions in the executive branch that political appointees fill.

The decision to use merit instead of political patronage as the basis for appointing people to most positions in the executive branch was a fundamental policy choice. This chapter presents an historical overview of how and why merit principles were adopted. Table 2.1 summarizes the development of major public personnel management policies by the size and scope of government and by the increased complexity of society generally. Whereas at one time much of what government did was clerking, now it interacts with diverse and complex forces and with sophisticated technologies. Agency managers at all levels of government increasingly need highly skilled professionals, technicians, and paraprofessionals. Machines can do the routine.

The demand for people with distinct specialties and sophisticated skills poses a challenge to more than personnel management. The dependence on experts has generated a concern for the democratic nature of public policy making and for political accountability in the United States. Managers need to balance the requirements for competence with the demands for accountability to the electorate. This chapter

TABLE 2.1 DEVELOPMENT OF PUBLIC PERSONNEL MANAGEMENT IN THE UNITED STATES

	Period	Benchmark
1789–1829	Government by gentlemen: The guardian period	Inauguration of Washington
1829–1883	Government by the common man: The spoils period	Inauguration of Jackson
1883–1906	Government by the good: The reform period	Pendleton Act
1906–1937	Government by the efficient: The scientific management period	New York Bureau of Municipal Research
1937–1955	Government by administration:	Report of the Brownlow Committee . The management period
1955	Government by shared power: Professionals	Report of the Second Hoover Commission
1959	Unions:	Wisconsin law mandating collective bargaining
1972	Minorities and women:	Extension of 1964 Civil Rights Act to state and local governments
1978	Public managers:	Carter Civil Service Reform Act
1980	Contractors:	Reagan privatization efforts
1992	Customers:	National Performance Review

Source: The first five periods have been identified by Frederick C. Mosher, *Democracy and the Public Service* (New York: Oxford University Press, 1968), 54–55.

LEARNING OBJECTIVES OF THIS CHAPTER

- Understand the historical background to current merit system (or civil service) policies and concerns
- Know the dynamics of the rise and fall of patronage in government employment
- Appreciate the implications of the growth of government, professionalism, unionization, and diversity
- Understand contemporary challenges to civil service and professionalism

GEORGE WASHINGTON AND HIS MEN OF CHARACTER

Despite the rhetoric about rule by the people that accompanied the American Revolution, the initial governments of the United States were ruled by the upper classes. The wealthy, the literate, and the landowners among the colonials led the revolution itself, and it was not surprising to see these same faces in the newly independent government. When George Washington assumed the presidency, he looked to those with whom he plotted against British rule. Loyalty to the new Constitution, which at that time was regarded as a highly political and controversial document, was essential for appointment by Washington to a government position.

In addition to loyalty, Washington looked for fitness of character. Family backgrounds, formal education, honor, and esteem measured this.[1] Except for educational attainment, these traits were based almost entirely on reputation. Character and competence were regarded as closely linked. The elite in the new country was small enough so that the application of these criteria was feasible. Good letters of recommendation written by prominent politicians impressed Washington, and he was the first to give special recognition and job preference to military veterans. To help assess the reputation of candidates and to share the opportunity to make patronage appointments, Washington worked with members of the Senate. This was the informal beginning of the tradition of **senatorial courtesy**, wherein a president does not appoint someone to a position unless the senators from the candidate's home state have given their approval.

Working with senators in making appointments also had two practical political effects. Washington wanted to maintain a geographic balance to provide representation from the various states in the union. Systematically seeking suggestions and recommendations from members of the Senate helped to accomplish this goal. Second, many of the appointments required confirmation by the Senate. By involving senators at an early stage in the selection process, Washington developed advocates and supporters for his decisions.

One of the early issues was whether or not the president had the right unilaterally to dismiss someone whose appointment had to be confirmed by the Senate. In other words, did dismissal, like confirmation, require Senate approval? As Van Riper described it: "Though the direct evidence is scanty, the great debate on the removal power may have turned more on confidence in President Washington than the constitutional theories and fine-spun arguments of our early legislative leaders."[2] The conclusion of Congress, supported by the Supreme Court and referred to as the **decision of 1789**, was to endorse the concept of removal as a prerogative of the president. Despite the lack of restrictions, Washington fired only seventeen federal employees during his tenure as president.[3]

Another fundamental principle established during the first years of the republic was the recognition that employees should be treated in accordance with the level of their responsibilities. Federal employees who were high-ranking policy makers and managers usually served at the pleasure of the president. Workers with low-level or specialized skills, such as clerks, customs employees, surveyors, and postal employees, on the other hand, were commonly regarded as serving for indefinite periods and dismissable only for cause.[4]

As Washington left office and others followed, the principles of personnel management that he had established continued. This was particularly true of the administration of John Adams. When Thomas Jefferson assumed office in 1801, a new political party came to power and questions about continuity inevitably emerged.

Confronted with a workforce appointed by the Federalists and intent on bringing into government some of the Republican Party loyalists, President Jefferson saw the need for change. Yet, like other executives, he was also concerned that there be some continuity and stability. To resolve these differing needs, Jefferson promulgated the doctrine of "equal division of the offices between the parties." He dismissed some officials, counted on some turnover, appointed Republican supporters to vacant positions, and retained many of the current Federalist employees to achieve a rough balance. This practice was accepted without challenge and followed by Jefferson's successors.[5] When using competence as a criterion for selection, Jefferson, like Washington and Adams, looked to the well bred and the well educated.

In short, the personnel needs during the first years of the Republic were a blend of political loyalty and individual competence. The former was defined in partisan terms and the latter in educational attainment and personal reputation. Traditions were established specifying that the public workforce should be representative (geographic and partisan) and chief executives should have the right to select their own management and policy-making team. Although there were no legal definitions of job security, clearly those at the lower and middle levels of the federal bureaucracy could have a higher expectation of long-term employment than those at the very top. Few things were done systematically, but they were done well. In his history of the civil service in the United States, Van Riper wrote:

> That the personal and partisan interests of political realists of the caliber of most of the Founding Fathers and their associates should be accompanied by administrative expertise, intelligence, and a high sense of responsibility to the country at large was indeed fortunate. Not only was a new nation placed on firm political foundations, but also its early civil service was established with a reputation for integrity and capacity that is remembered to this day.[6]

ANDREW JACKSON AND SPOILS

President Andrew Jackson is commonly identified as having introduced the spoils system to the United States. Jackson did, in fact, claim that he was bringing to Washington a new element in U.S. politics. Jackson successfully appealed to a newly enfranchised segment of the electorate, white males who did not meet the previous tests for owning property and/or earning above a stated level of income. He campaigned against the old order and identified with the newly expanding frontiers of the United States.

Nevertheless, to picture Andrew Jackson as a king of patronage eager to sweep out the old crowd and replace them with his own supporters is an exaggeration. Jackson swept out of office no more than Thomas Jefferson did when he led a new political party into the White House. Both replaced incumbents in about 20 percent of the senior positions. As Table 2.2 demonstrates, the change in the background of top administrators, as measured by fathers' occupations,[7] was only moderately different in Jackson's administration than in the Adams and Jefferson administrations. Still over half of the senior civil servants came from families with fathers who had high-status occupations and almost all others were sons of artisans, teachers, shopkeepers, and the like. The inauguration of Jackson did not bring pioneers off the frontier and into Washington offices.

Jackson's rhetoric did convey the impression that he was interested in rewarding his supporters, although here too the common image is misleading. The brash statement, "To the victor belongs the spoils!" often attributed to Jackson, was actually the

TABLE 2.2 PRIMARY OCCUPATIONS OF FATHERS OF SENIOR-LEVEL CIVIL SERVANTS (PERCENT)			
Occupation	Adams (N = 100)	Jefferson (N = 104)	Jackson (N = 129)
High-ranking			
Landed gentry	22	29	21
Merchant	22	13	17
Professional	26	19	15
Middle-ranking			
Artisans, proprietors, farmers, teachers, sea captains, shop or tavern keepers	23	25	39
Unknown	7	15	8
Total	100	100	100

political slogan of Senator William L. Marcy of New York.[8] In his inaugural address, Jackson made a reference to the need to appoint faithful people, but he did not request the resignations of existing federal employees. One of his boldest statements spoke more to the issue of competence than to loyalty:

> The duties of all public officers are, or at least admit of being made, so plain and simple that men of intelligence may readily qualify themselves for their performance; and I can not but believe that more is lost by the long continuance of men in office than is generally to be gained by their experience.[9]

Clearly one could—and people did—deduce from this statement that Jackson favored a relatively short tenure of office and discounted the need for anything other than basic skills and knowledge. The record indicates, however, that he did not base his own personnel actions on this principle.

Officials in local governments, not the federal government, began the use of **patronage** to build and maintain political machines. State and local politicians, especially in New York and Pennsylvania, relied on bloc voting by groups of recent European immigrants and used patronage appointments as rewards for those able to deliver blocs of votes.[10] The widespread, visible use of spoils in the federal government came with the election of President Abraham Lincoln. Confronted with the challenges of a civil war and with the needs for building and stabilizing his new political party, Lincoln felt compelled to use his appointive powers aggressively and strategically. His primary concern was for maintaining unity, rather than for securing competence. Of a total of 1,639 presidentially appointed positions, Lincoln fired and then replaced 1,457.[11] A similar proportion of lower-level positions also changed hands.

Patronage during the Lincoln administration was so prevalent it became the source of popular joking. It was said, for example, that the retreat of the Union army at the Battle of Bull Run had nothing to do with the performance of the Confederates. Rather, the retreat was a reaction to the announcement that there were three vacancies in the New York Customs Office.

Patronage power is a valuable prize. During the last half of the nineteenth century, fearsome political battles were waged over the control of patronage appointments. The impeachment proceeding against President Andrew Jackson was over this issue. In the aftermath of Lincoln's assassination, Johnson confronted a hostile Congress and factions of the Republican Party with which he was at odds. He used his appointive powers to combat Congress and to rid himself of many of Lincoln's people, only to enrage his opponents all the more. In 1867, Congress passed the Tenure of Office Act in an effort to secure a greater role in the appointive process. The act specified that those appointed with the advice and consent of the Senate could only be removed from office with the Senate's approval. Johnson defied that act, was impeached by the House of Representatives, and survived only when the Senate acquitted him by one vote.

The issues that divided President Johnson and Congress were wider than this personnel item. Likewise, the personnel controversies during the administrations of Presidents Grant and Hayes were intermingled with other issues.[12] The government badly bungled the task of Reconstruction after the Civil War. The postwar period was one of the sorriest chapters in the country's history. The economy and society were on the threshold of technological breakthroughs, and the frontier was fully extended to the Pacific Ocean. Yet conflict, corruption, and incompetence paralyzed government. The potential of the country seemed strangled by the selfish greed of the operators of political machines.

THE MERIT SYSTEM AND MACHINE POLITICS

The ingredients that led to the demise of the **spoils system** included a tough political battle against **political machines** and between Americans of Anglo-Saxon heritage and newly arrived immigrant groups from countries that did not speak English. A sense of idealism combined with reaction to a murder generated change. At the forefront of the reform movement was a group of prominent eastern personalities, some of whom attacked the patronage system as the jugular of the political machines and some of whom had been active abolitionists who saw spoils as yet another means of curtailing individual freedom.[13] Reformers "wished to return to the attitudes of the good old days before Jacksonian democracy and the industrial revolution—days when men with their background, status, and education were the unquestioned leaders of society."[14]

A number of **civil service** reform associations emerged to make the arguments for change. The first of these was organized in New York in 1877. These associations united in a single organization, the National Civil Service Reform League in 1881.

The league learned that the British were also concerned with civil service reform and sent one of its members, Dorman B. Eaton, to England to meet with Sir Stafford Northcote, Sir Charles Trevelyan, and John Stuart Mill, who were members of a commission charged to design the changes. Part of the motivation for reform in Great Britain was, like in the United States, a concern about the emergence of a new political force. The upper classes felt threatened by a mercantilist, commercially based class that was growing increasingly wealthy and able to purchase the land, titles, and status that had traditionally been a matter of birthright. Their solution was to base civil service employment on merit and then define merit in terms of formal education and performance on examinations. Thus, entrance at the lowest level required an elementary school education and a relatively high score on a competitive examination, at the middle level a secondary school education and an examination, and at the senior level a university education and an examination. In the British context educational opportunities were not universally available, so the implications of the reform were to restrict entrance to the upper levels of the civil service to the upper classes in society.[15]

Eaton returned with the British merit concept and worked with Senator George H. Pendleton, a Democrat from Ohio, who had—independently of the activities of the National Civil Service Reform League—been drafting legislation to end the spoils system. Like previous efforts, however, this work seemed to have little chance for success. Those in a position to act were those benefiting most from the spoils system.

The setting for considering reform changed drastically when Charles J. Guiteau, an ardent supporter of the spoils system, fired a bullet into the head of President James A. Garfield. Guiteau was a disappointed office seeker who felt he had a right to a federal appointment because of his support for the Garfield-Arthur ticket. There is also some evidence that Guiteau might have been suffering from a mental illness. At the time it appeared that out of revenge, and hoping that he would have better luck with Vice President Chester A. Arthur, a noted practitioner of spoils, Guiteau assassinated Garfield. In so doing, Guiteau handed the reformers the dramatic event they needed to rally support for their cause.[16] The spoils system and the existing operations of government were now squarely linked with evil. Republican incumbents could not shake off identification with the evils of spoils and suffered severe losses in the 1882 congressional elections. The lesson was clear. In 1883, with very little debate, Congress passed the Pendleton Act, thereby establishing the **merit system** for government employment in the United States.

The essential features of the Pendleton Act, which continue to be the criteria for defining a merit system, are

1. Entry through open, competitive examinations
2. Prohibition against using political party identity as a criterion for appointment to or retention in a position
3. Existence of a bipartisan, independent commission to act as a watchdog, ensuring compliance with merit system principles

As was the case with the British reforms, "merit" is a misnomer. The primary objective was to destroy machines, not to get top talent in government jobs. Civil service selection relied on a single examination that tested an applicant's use of English. Examinations were not tailored to measure an individual's fit for a particular job. The single, standard civil service exam disadvantaged non-English speaking immigrants and had social effects parallel to how education requirements screened for class in the British "merit" system.

The spread of the merit system to other jurisdictions in the United States took place in spurts. New York and Massachusetts, which supplied much of the leadership in the civil service reform movement, adopted merit systems immediately after the federal government. There was little further activity at the state and local levels until the Progressive movement attacked political machines in the Midwest in the early 1900s. For most other state and local governments, it took federal government mandates before changes were made.

The major asset of the federal government has been money. This was first used in the 1940 Social Security Act, which included a provision that those state officials administering funds granted under the act must be employed under a merit system. This provision has become common in federal programs. Most states complied by establishing merit systems for all their employees. The response of seven states was to construct two separate personnel systems: a merit-based system for employees working with federal funds, and a looser system that allowed for patronage for employees not hired with federal money.

The passage of merit system legislation was not the panacea that many of the reform advocates had expected. Initially, the new laws covered only a minority of positions. The Pendleton Act authorized the president to establish a **Civil Service Commission** and to designate which positions, if any, were to be covered by the act. There were no mandates to the president. In fact, President Arthur did appoint a commission, but he placed only 10.5 percent of the federal positions under the civil service.[17]

In some jurisdictions, the formal adoption of a merit system was little more than a symbolic gesture. Cook County in Illinois was the first county government to adopt a civil service ordinance, yet, primarily through the extensive use of "temporary" and "acting" appointments, Cook County became notorious as one of the strongest patronage-based political machines in the country. Similarly, Massachusetts, the second state to adopt the merit system, developed a reputation for patronage appointments.[18]

MERIT AND THE CONSTITUTION

The U.S. Supreme Court has to some extent made the legislative history of outlawing patronage moot by ruling that hiring or firing individuals in the public sector on the basis of partisan affiliation is, for most jobs, unconstitutional.[19] The basic principle is that patronage personnel practices violate First Amendment protections of freedom of expression and association. The Fourteenth Amendment applies these protections to state and local government employees.

In *Elrod* v. *Burns* (1976), the Court ruled that a Democrat newly elected as Sheriff of Cook County could not dismiss employees in the department because they were Republican loyalists. To do so would violate their First Amendment rights. The Court said that party identification could be a basis for dismissal only if the position had policy making responsibilities.

Branti v. *Finkel* (1980) allowed the Court the opportunity to be more specific about the exception that might be made for policy making positions. The Rockland County, New York, legislature appointed a Democrat (Branti) as public defender. He then dismissed Aaron Finkel and Alan Tabakman, both Republicans, from their positions as assistant public defenders, arguing that they had policy making responsibilities.

The Court did not allow these dismissals, again citing the First and Fourteenth Amendments to the U.S. Constitution. The six to three majority opinion of the Court stated that the policy making responsibilities had to be of a *partisan* nature in order to justify a partisan based dismissal. The Court used admittedly easy illustrations to make the point. Justices noted that a football coach and a speechwriter both make policy decisions. Partisanship is not relevant for the former but is for the latter. Assistant public defenders are apparently more like football coaches than speechwriters.

In *Rutan et al.* v. *Republican Party of Illinois* (1989), the Court dealt with appointments instead of dismissals. Governor James Thompson, a Republican, had issued an executive order proclaiming a hiring freeze throughout Illinois state government. The executive order stipulated that no exceptions to the freeze would be made without the governor's explicit approval. The five individuals who brought suit represented instances of initial hires, promotions, transfers, and recalls. They demonstrated that exceptions to the freeze were allowed only if the individuals being considered for appointments had been active in the Republican Party. None of the positions involved partisan-related policy making responsibilities and the Court ruled that the First and Fourteenth Amendments had been violated.[20]

The operational distinction between positions that may be filled through political appointment and those that are covered by merit system principles is essentially statutory. Legislatures designate which positions are available for elected executives to appoint whomever they wish. A president, governor, county executive, mayor or other political official may fill these posts with friends, relatives, political supporters, or Nobel Prize winners. The criteria—and the consequences—are the responsibility of these politicians. It is certainly conceivable that a legislature may abuse the authority to determine which positions are political appointments and which are civil service, but there has not been litigation on this since the Court decisions.

The constitutional restrictions placed on patronage practices are of fundamental significance. They do not, however, make civil service legislation meaningless. Court rulings do not specify the standards and procedures that must be followed to adhere to merit system principles, and courts do not have the supervisory responsibility or capacity to ensure compliance. Courts essentially determine what is acceptable, not what is desirable. Legislative and executive actions are necessary to establish a more complete public policy.

The Pendleton Act can be credited with ushering in a new era in public personnel management in the United States. Political identity was formally rejected as a criterion for the selection, promotion, and retention of those employees who were not part of the management and policy making team of chief elected officials.

In part, the acceptance of the merit system concept was acceptance of Woodrow Wilson's basic argument that there is and should be a basic distinction between politics and administration. Woodrow Wilson was a reform advocate and served as president of the National Civil Service Reform League before he was elected as President of the United States. He contended that politics involved values, conflict, and compromise and the output of politics was public policy. Administration, on the other hand, was technique, process, and science. The task of administration was to implement public policy.[21] On this foundation, the scientific management movement attempted to build on the separation of politics and administration begun by the merit system.

SCIENTIFIC MANAGEMENT AND EFFICIENT GOVERNMENT

Bureaus of municipal research acted as the primary agents to encourage **scientific management** in government. Private philanthropy funded these bureaus, which existed outside the boundaries of government. The most active and visible one was the New York Bureau of Municipal Research, established in 1906. Behind much of the work done by these institutions was the basic assumption that there were no essential differences between the public and private sectors.

The central legacy of the scientific management era (discussed further in Chapter 5) to contemporary personnel management is position classification. The pioneers of industrial engineering suggested that organizations define the duties and responsibilities of positions in accordance with what was determined to be the single most efficient way of accomplishing their goals. Those positions with like duties and responsibilities then could be grouped together for a common selection process, training program, efficiency evaluation, and compensation.

Whereas a major attraction of position classification in the private sector was the opportunity to develop systems of efficiency ratings and productivity incentives, in the public sector the primary push was for equitable compensation. Governments, with their wide varieties of agencies, found, for example, that clericals in a unit collecting taxes received one salary, whereas clericals in a corrections department or a public health office were paid at different rates. There was a belief that all clericals working for the same government should be compensated at the same level. When Congress passed the Classification Act of 1923, it was responding to pressures for standardized wages as well as efficiency in government.[22] State and local jurisdictions followed. Commitment to the principle of equal pay for equal work at this time was prompted by a concern for general order and standardization not by any concern for discrimination.

The emphasis on specialization during this period fostered the rise of a number of new professions. Personnel management is itself an example. Hitherto, personnel work was clerical work that focused on keeping records and processing paychecks. The demands of scientific management and position classification, plus the requirements of the merit system, meant that people were needed to conduct job analyses, classify positions, develop examinations, design training programs, and establish compensation systems. Like other emerging professions, personnel specialists sought autonomy and independence so that they might establish their own standards and monitor their own behavior. Fortuitously, by law, civil service commissions and personnel boards had autonomy and independence and provided an important measure of protection for personnel professionals. Political forces might require compromises with professional standards, but at least there was an opportunity to use merit system laws and personnel board/civil service commission policies and rulings to develop and articulate standards.

As government confronted the complex challenges of the Depression, the New Deal, and two major wars, the faults of scientific management became visible. The identification of the single best way of accomplishing a task was a quixotic mission. Jobs and technology changed more quickly than could be accommodated by position classification systems. The dichotomy between politics and administration and the unity of public and private sector administration were both built on false assumptions.

President Franklin D. Roosevelt sought a new approach and turned to the Brownlow Committee for suggestions.

THE NEW DEAL AND PUBLIC MANAGEMENT

The response of the political system to the Great Depression was to define a positive, initiating role for government in social and economic problems. Although that role had never been totally absent, it did not have the emphasis and legitimacy that came with the electoral mandate Franklin D. Roosevelt brought with him to the White House. Government joined private businesses as an entrepreneur. Sometimes government worked with private enterprises. Sometimes government acted as if it were a private enterprise, in public works projects and regional development schemes. In addition, government took major steps toward assuming responsibility for the welfare of individual citizens. These new roles led to an expansion of the size, scope, and complexity of government.

It soon became apparent that the proliferation of government agencies and public goals required a managerial capacity that did not exist in government. To address this need, President Roosevelt appointed the Committee on Administrative Management. Louis Brownlow chaired this committee. Other members of the committee were Charles E. Merriam and Luther Gulick. The report of the **Brownlow Committee** stressed the need to centralize administrative power in the federal government and enhance the managerial competence of the presidential office. As a means of implementing this general recommendation, the committee urged that personnel management be more closely integrated with general presidential management. In some ways their proposals were a forerunner of the Carter reforms of 1978. Brownlow and his associates suggested that the Civil Service Commission be replaced by an agency headed by a single administrator who would work directly with and serve at the pleasure of the president. President Roosevelt failed to get congressional approval for all of the recommendations but did follow the spirit of the proposed reforms as much as possible. Although he did not get a single administrator in charge of a personnel agency, the Civil Service Commission did take on more personnel management functions, such as selecting new employees and hearing appeals of disciplinary actions. Agency heads were responsible for the day-to-day management of personnel.

Beginning with the New Deal, professionals were relied on to provide direction to new and old government agencies. These professionals were needed by chief executives both because of their substantive knowledge and for their sympathy with the policy directions of the government. The careers of specialists and professionals were not limited to government service, and the civil service system could not easily accommodate them. The political executive route, typical for patronage appointments, was not appropriate either. Yet, the need for these people was real, and they had to be squeezed in somehow. The Brownlow Committee and the president recognized this, but they were not able to resolve it. Thus, a legacy of this period was recognition of management needs and the discomfort of not being able to provide adequately for those needs. There were no major organizational or policy reforms.

SPECIALIZATION AND PROFESSIONALISM

In the aftermath of World War II, the growth of professionals in government reached major proportions and posed fundamental challenges to public personnel management. During the course of the war, technological breakthroughs occurred and new specializations emerged in a wide variety of fields. Government itself became a major employer of professional and technical specialists. By the end of the 1950s, 36 percent of all professionals in the country were working in government. Since 1960, over one-third of all government employees have been professionals or technicians.[23]

One of the implications of the increased professionalization of the public service was to remove personnel selection one step further from agency managers and supervisors. The merit system, with its requirements for open recruitment, examinations, and certification in order to avoid patronage and favoritism, already took personnel selection partially away from managerial authorities. Professions further restricted the choices of appointing authorities by requiring licenses, certification, and/or the satisfaction of certain educational and apprenticeship requirements for membership. Questions about job relevancy were resolved not by the employer but by the profession itself. Professional standards heavily influence how positions are defined and work is structured. Frederick C. Mosher expressed the concern this way:

> They (the emergence of professions and the professional composition of public agencies) are challenging, modifying, or overturning the most central—and most cherished— principles associated with civil service reform in this country: equal opportunity to apply and compete for jobs; competitive examinations for selection and (sometimes) promotion; "the job's the thing"; equal pay for equal work; neutral and objective direction and control of the personnel system.[24]

Another implication of the growth of professions within government has been the resurrection of the politics-administration dichotomy. The issue had never completely gone away, but it gained new life when professionals claimed political interference whenever their judgment was questioned or ignored. Professionals are valued precisely because their judgment is well informed, yet their disdain for political officials added new dimensions to long-standing tensions. The antipathy between politicians and civil servants is commonplace and worldwide.[25] A profession, almost by definition, typically seeks autonomy and a status that commands deference.[26] The mixing in a common arena of a political official pursuing the mandates of the ballot box and a professional expecting to dominate in the policy-making process is bound to generate conflict and distrust. There are likely to be frustrations, too, because the politician and the professional need each other.

Two events in the period following World War II exacerbated the tension between politicians and professionals: McCarthyism and the election of President Dwight D. Eisenhower. The witch-hunting of Senator Joseph McCarthy hit educators and the State Department hardest, but the concern for loyalty among employees and applicants for employment pervaded the entire public sector. In retrospect, it is clear that this Cold War hysteria was not well founded and at times trampled basic individual rights. At the time, it was a cause for citizens and some elected officials to suspect government employees. Loyalty oaths, discussed more in the next chapter, were widely required.

The election of General Eisenhower to the White House raised issues of patronage and the relationship between career civil servants and political officials. Republicans had not had the opportunity to make federal appointments in more than two decades. They regarded the federal bureaucracy as a creature of the Democratic Party and therefore not to be trusted. Indeed, before leaving office, President Harry Truman used his authority under the Pendleton Act to extend civil service status to large numbers of political appointees.

Although President Eisenhower accepted the size and scope of the federal government, thereby providing bipartisan endorsement of the New Deal changes, he was anxious to make alterations in the civil service system. In 1955, he issued an executive order establishing **Schedule C**, a group of 900 positions designated for political appointments. These positions had some policy responsibilities but were at relatively low levels in the federal bureaucracy. President Jimmy Carter extended Schedule C appointments to mid-level policy positions and almost doubled the original number. President Eisenhower also tried to secure congressional approval for a Senior Executive Service that would have provided a pool of top-level managers that could be moved rather freely from one position and agency to another.[27] Jimmy Carter succeeded in establishing a Senior Executive Service.

RE-THINKING MERIT

Frustrations with the limitations imposed by the merit system have prompted some political officials to consider alternatives. Sometimes the frustrations are with trying to establish new directions and a different agenda in the face of resistance from professionals and from government employees who have the kind of First Amendment job protection provided by the *Elrod* v. *Burns* and *Branti* v. *Finkel* cases previously described. Sometimes elected officials are simply seeking patronage to reward their supporters, as was more common prior to the passage of the Pendleton Act. Attacks on the merit system have been both open and subtle.

A rather blatant attempt to undermine the merit system led to one of the articles of impeachment levied against President Richard M. Nixon. A Congressional investigation conducted in the aftermath of the Watergate scandal concluded that the Civil Service Commission under President Nixon had engaged in three major types of abuses:

1. Commissioners made political referrals that resulted in preferential treatment for certain job applicants.
2. The commission operated a "special referral unit" that helped manipulate merit procedures to make political appointments.
3. High-ranking Civil Service Commission officials knew of personnel abuses and did nothing about them.[28]

A major feature of the 1978 federal civil service reforms was the replacement of the Civil Service Commission with two bodies: the Office of Personnel Management, which is headed by someone who serves at the pleasure of the president and acts as a personnel management arm of the president; and the Merit System Protection Board, which has an independent and bipartisan status and acts as a watchdog and appeals agency to ensure compliance with the basic principles of civil service.

President George W. Bush expressed his concerns with the constraints of civil service when he proposed the establishment of the Department of Homeland Security after the attacks of September 11, 2001. The President argued that the procedures designed to protect employees and candidates for employment from the vagaries of politics had the effect of obstructing an agency that needed to hire and fire employees in a manner that ensured national security. Wholesale changes were not adopted, but some of the objectives were met by creating numerous temporary jobs that did not have the restrictions and protections of civil service.

In 2007, President George W. Bush and, especially, Attorney General Alberto Gonzales generated debate and discussion about principles of merit and political appointments when eight U.S. Attorneys, who are appointed by the President with the advice and consent of the Senate and serve at the President's pleasure, were dismissed for apparently political reasons. On the one hand, there was surprise when both Republican and Democratic lawmakers cried foul, since these are political appointments. Why should it matter whether individuals were losing their jobs because they were too vigilant in pursuing corruption by Republicans and not energetic enough in pursuing the misdeeds of Democrats? The concern of critics was that the professional responsibility of a prosecutor is to focus on crime, regardless of who the criminal is, and that the judicial system depends on impartial and competent work by U.S. Attorneys.

Efforts to avoid the merit system extend beyond the federal government. Georgia passed a law that ended the civil service system for their state government, effective July 1, 1996. The intent was not to reinstate political patronage. The Supreme Court cases described prohibit that. But the central personnel office served as more of a consultant to managers than as a watchdog and enforcer of regulations and managers had more flexibility. The fears of employees that they would be treated more arbitrarily and have less job security were not realized and, in fact, most managers and employees agreed that there were no major changes in personnel management practices. Florida and Texas followed Georgia's lead, but on a more limited basis.[29]

In contrast, Kentucky experienced an apparent attempt to return the state to patronage hiring and firing. On May 11, 2006, a grand jury indicted Governor Ernie Fletcher on three counts for allegedly creating an illegal operation to reward political supporters with jobs. Testimony by several current and former state employees described instances where hires, promotions, transfers, demotions, and firings were based on political identities. The Governor took the Fifth Amendment. A court ruled that Governor Fletcher could not be tried while in office and, prior to a bid for reelection, the Governor agreed to a settlement where he acknowledged that the evidence indicated wrongdoing and prosecutors dropped charges against him.

CONTRACTING: THE NEW PATRONAGE?

There are obvious reasons why governments contract with private businesses and nonprofit organizations, rather than establish new agencies or hire new civil servants.

There may be a temporary need for workers to complete a particular project. Economies of scale may mean that a vendor can do a job with less expense and more expertise than a government agency. Expertise in some fields has a short life-span and it may make more sense to contract with current experts than to count on existing employees keeping up with technological and scientific advances.

Scandals in state governments and the federal government point to another obvious reason for contracting: to reward campaign contributors. As pointed out in Chapter 1, there has been a significant increase in government contracting. While it is obviously difficult to measure how much of the increase is linked to the hunt for campaign cash and how many of the contracts are going to vendors because of campaign contributions, the rise in scandals related to contracting seems more than coincidental.[30] No bid contracts are especially vulnerable to being interpreted as political payoffs. Even when contracts are bid, there is an appearance—and perhaps substance—of a quid pro quo.

SUMMARY

Public personnel management in the United States has grown from a clerical task to a multifaceted set of responsibilities. A selection process that had been informal and relied on a person's general social reputation is now a series of steps designed to avoid consideration of politics and to emphasize job requirements and individual abilities. The creation of the merit system was a response to what might be regarded as excessive politics. The merit system does not, however, resolve the questions about how to balance professionalism and accountability.

The effort to provide public sector managers with fewer restrictions and more tools and discretion represents a shift in emphasis more than a major departure from earlier concerns about abuses and potential abuses. Worries about patronage, favoritism, discrimination, and exploitation continue, and many of the rules and regulations designed to prohibit these evils still limit what managers can do. The desire is to have government work more effectively and efficiently. In part, this means more flexibility for managers; in part, it means being responsible for achieving certain goals and outcomes, as well as complying with a body of laws and restrictions. This development is both exciting and challenging. To make wise decisions and informed choices, it is essential that managers understand the policies and the principles of public personnel management. The next chapters explain the policies fundamental to the management of human resources, for governments and for nonprofit organizations.

DISCUSSION QUESTIONS

1. What are the implications of the battle between patronage and merit system reform for contemporary public personnel management? Is the battle over?
2. To what extent does professionalism pose a challenge to politicians? How can we ensure both professional standards and political accountability?

3. What are circumstances when contracting is appropriate? Are there situations where contracting is inappropriate?

GLOSSARY

Brownlow Committee A task force President Franklin D. Roosevelt appointed that recommended strengthening the managerial capacity of the presidency, in part by placing personnel management directly under the control of the president

Civil Service Those positions in government that are filled and retained in processes that prohibit the consideration of partisan affiliation or support for an elected official

Civil Service Commission A federal agency established by the Pendleton Act of 1883 to serve as a watchdog to prevent political patronage in the civil service. This commission was replaced in 1978 by the Office of Personnel Management and the Merit System Protection Board. Some state and local governments continue to have a civil service commission

Decision of 1789 The endorsement by Congress of the principle that the President may remove those whom he or she appoints to positions without having to get the advice and consent of the Senate, as is required for confirming the appointments

Machine politics An approach toward elections that is hierarchically controlled and relies heavily on securing votes—usually in neighborhood blocs—based on a quid pro quo of jobs and services for votes

Merit system A policy of prohibiting the hiring of people based on their partisan affiliation or their support of a candidate for elective office. (Note that this term does *not* mean rewarding individuals because of excellent performance.)

Patronage The treatment of jobs, contracts, and similar benefits as goods to be given to political supporters of parties and elected officials

Schedule C A set of positions established by President Dwight D. Eisenhower that were explicitly available to the president for political appointment

Scientific management An assembly-line approach toward organization and supervision that assumes there is a single best way of doing something and defines jobs accordingly

Senatorial courtesy A tradition that the president will not appoint someone to a position unless the senators from the nominee's home state approve

Spoils system The practice of giving jobs to those who support victorious candidates in an election

SOURCES

Cooper, P. J. (2002). *Governing by Contract*. Washington, DC: Congressional Quarterly Press.
   Review of the development and expansion of contracting by government and discussion of the issues this raises.

Freedman, A. (1994). *Patronage: An American tradition*. Chicago: Nelson Hall.
   Analysis of the history of patronage hiring in the United States, with an emphasis on Chicago and three Midwestern states. Includes discussion of the U.S. Supreme Court cases that found patronage to be unconstitutional.

Ingraham, P. W., & Rosenbloom, D. H., eds. (1992). *The promise and paradox of civil service reform*. Pittsburgh: University of Pittsburgh Press.
   Essays that describe the Carter civil service reforms and evaluate their implementation.

Pfiffner, J. P., & Brook, D. A., eds. (2000). *The future of merit: Twenty years after the civil service reform act.* New York: Oxford University Press.
Research assessing the effects of the Carter civil service reforms and projecting future trends.

Van Riper, P. P. (1958). *History of the United States civil service.* Evanston, IL: Row, Peterson.
The most extensive historical analysis of the federal civil service through the early 1950s.

NOTES

1. Frederick C. Mosher, *Democracy and the Public Service* (New York: Oxford University Press, 1968), 57.
2. Paul P. Van Riper, *History of the United States Civil Service* (Evanston, IL: Row, Peterson, 1958), 14–15.
3. Carl R. Fish, *The Civil Service and the Patronage* (New York: Longman, Green, 1935), 13.
4. Mosher, *Democracy and the Public Service,* 58.
5. Van Riper, *History of the United States Civil Service,* 58.
6. *Ibid.,* 27.
7. The use of father's occupation as an index of social status is sexist and would be misleading if used today, but this measure is valid for the period included in Table 2.2.
8. Van Riper, *History of the United States Civil Service,* 30.
9. James D. Richardson, ed., *Messages and Papers of the Presidents,* vol. 2 (New York: Bureau of National Literature and Art, 1905), 449.
10. Fish, *Civil Service and the Patronage,* 79–104.
11. *Ibid.,* 170.
12. Van Riper, *History of the United States Civil Service,* 60–95.
13. Jay M. Shafritz, *Public Personnel Management: The Heritage of Civil Service Reform* (New York: Praeger, 1975), 26–32.
14. Ari Hoogenboom, *Outlawing the Spoils: A History of the Civil Service Reform Movement, 1865–1883* (Urbana: University of Illinois Press, 1961), 197. See, also, Wilbur Rich, *The Politics of Urban Personnel Policy: Reformers, Politicians, and Bureaucrats* (Port Washington, NY: Associated Faculty Press, 1981).
15. John A. Armstrong, *The European Administrative Elite* (Princeton: Princeton University Press, 1973).
16. Hoogenboom, *Outlawing the Spoils,* 2136–2137.
17. According to Van Riper, in *History of the United States Civil Service,* pp. 97–98, Republicans supported the Pendleton Act both out of a concern for electoral support and as a way of retaining jobs for Republican appointees should the Democrats win. Although the president, under the act, has authority both to place and remove positions from civil service coverage, the political pressures would almost inevitably be against removal.
18. Van Riper, *History of the United States Civil Service,* 298–304.
19. Yong S. Lee, *Public Personnel Administration and Constitutional Values* (Westport, CT: Quorum, 1992).
20. *Rutan, etal.* v. *Republican Party of Illinois* (1989); Anne Freedman, *Patronage: An American Tradition* (Chicago: Nelson-Hall, 1994).
21. Woodrow Wilson, "The Study of Administration," *Political Science Quarterly* 2 (June 1887): 197–222.
22. Van Riper, *History of the United States Civil Service,* 477–524.
23. James M. Buchanan, "Why Does Government Grow?" in Thomas E. Borcherding, ed., *Budgets and Bureaucrats: The Sources of Government Growth* (Durham, NC: Duke University Press, 1977), 3–18.

24. Mosher, *Democracy and the Public Service*, 124.

25. Hugh Heclo, *A Government of Strangers* (Washington, DC: Brookings Institution, 1977); Guy Benvenisti, *The Politics of Expertise*, 2nd ed. (San Francisco: Boyd and Fraser, 1977).

26. Mosher, *Democracy and the Public Service*, 124.

27. Van Riper, *History of the United States Civil Service*, 477–524; Patricia W. Ingraham, James Thompson, and Elliot Eisenberg, "Political Management Strategies and Political/Career Relationships: Where Are We Now in the Federal Government?" *Public Administration Review* 55, no. 3 (May/June 1995): 263–273.

28. Committee on Post Office and Civil Service, U.S. House of Representatives, *Final Report on Violations and Abuses of Merit Principles in Federal Employment* (Washington, DC: Government Printing Office, 1976). See, also, Richard P. Nathan, *The Plot that Failed: Nixon and the Administrative Presidency* (New York: Wiley, 1975).

29. Jonathan Walters, *Life After Civil Service Reform: The Texas, Georgia and Florida Experiments* (White Plains, NY: IBM, 2002); R.L. Facer, "Reinventing Public Administration: Reform in the Georgia Civil Service," *Public Administration Quarterly* 22, no. 1 (1998): 58–73.

30. See reports of Inspectors General in the federal government, the reports of state audit bureaus and newspaper stories. See, also, J. G. Brudney, S. Fernandez, J. E. Ryu, and Deil Wright, "Exploring and Explaining Contracting Out: Patterns Among the American States," *Journal of Public Administration Research and Theory* 15, no.1 (2005): 19-36; W. C. Lawther, "Privatizing Personnel: Outsourcing Public Sector Functions," in Steven W. Hays and Richard C. Kearney, eds., *Public Personnel Administration: Problems and Prospects*, 4th ed.(Upper Saddle River, NJ: Prentice Hall, 2003); P. J. Cooper, *Governing by Contract* (Washington, DC: Congressional Quarterly Press, 2002).

Chapter 3

Ethics, Rights, and Responsibilities

Employment in a public bureaucracy is a privilege. With a government job comes a steady income, authority, and, in many societies, a relatively high level of prestige. Public sector employment also places certain restrictions on its workforce. In a monarchy, loyalty to the royal family is a prerequisite to government employment. Dictators or military governments that run countries demand support. In democracies with competitive political parties and a commitment to protect certain basic individual freedoms, however, the expectations and requirements of loyalty are not obvious.

Similarly, those employed in nonprofit organizations enjoy certain privileges and must abide by some limitations. The law that provides tax exempt status for nonprofit organizations recognize and encourage the charitable and public service missions of these organizations. But, these laws also aim at preventing nonprofit organizations from becoming an appendage of a political party. Employees of nonprofits, of course, enjoy the same basic rights to participate in the political process as other citizens. However, these employees must also abide by a set standard of ethical and legal behavior consistent with the organization's mission and public policies towards nonprofits.

This chapter is concerned with the ethical standards, rights and responsibilities of employees in government agencies and nonprofit organizations. Managers, of course, have these rights and responsibilities themselves. In addition, they must take care to uphold the rights of their employees while at the same time ensuring that the work of their agencies gets done.

Courts, as well as legislatures and chief executives, have been active in defining restrictions on public employee behavior on and off the job. Public policies in this area involve balancing the individual liberties enjoyed by government and nonprofit workers as U.S. citizens and the requirements of the political system in this country. How the proper balance is defined affects the ways these employees may and may not participate in electoral politics. The balance of rights and responsibilities also affects the behavior and image that these employees must maintain in the community.

LEARNING OBJECTIVES OF THIS CHAPTER

- Know what kinds of political activities are allowed for employees in government agencies and nonprofit organizations

- Understand whether conversation in the office among these employees is subject to any restrictions
- Know how to handle potential conflicts between an individual's job responsibilities and economic interests
- Understand when limits can be placed on employees' grooming standards, sexual activity, and drug use.
- Appreciate the personal liability that managers have in upholding the rights of their employees

POLITICAL NEUTRALITY: GOVERNMENT EMPLOYEES

A rationale for limiting the partisan political activities of government and nonprofit employees is to thwart the development of political machines. An additional concern that relates especially to government employees is the need to have these individuals work effectively regardless of which political party prevails at the ballot box. Note that this concern applies to civil service positions, not those designated for political appointment nor those in the legislative branch. There political loyalty trumps other considerations. The traditions and rules of state and federal courts, like civil service regulations, provide for a professional staff that can work effectively regardless of who is on the bench.

The policy of **political neutrality** for government employees is part of an English tradition. The British concern for a civil service able to serve any government can be explained in two ways. The traditional explanation notes that the major political parties in England have significantly different ideologies and draw support from different socioeconomic classes. A major source of stability in the midst of sometimes radically different political philosophies is a government bureaucracy that provides expertise in the policy-making process and implements adopted policies. This is an argument that has been applied to parliamentary countries like the Fourth Republic of France and contemporary Italy in an even more forceful manner.[1] A more contemporary justification is that political neutrality is a means of providing protection for senior civil servants and other professionals, thus enabling them to contribute their expertise in whatever government might be elected.[2]

Although political neutrality was a prominent feature of the Pendleton Act of 1883, the idea was not new. As early as 1802, President Thomas Jefferson issued a circular encouraging federal government employees to refrain from heavy involvement in partisan political activities. As a matter of personal preference and as a strategy for survival, many employees were very supportive of the principle of noninvolvement. The Pendleton Act reasserted the need for this principle, but did not give it the same force of mandate that the act gave to merit criteria for selection. Political neutrality was clearly encouraged and expected but not firmly translated into law.

In 1896, President Grover Cleveland ordered all federal employees to avoid any campaign activity, either for themselves or for others. This was too broad an edict. It made federal employees second-class citizens and quickly became apparent that it was unenforceable. Nine years later, President Theodore Roosevelt made another attempt. He issued Executive Order 642, restricting the political activities of classified federal civil servants. They were barred from campaigning and soliciting contributions in partisan elections, but they could run for offices in local, nonpartisan races. Between 1907, when the order was issued, and 1939, the Civil Service Commission issued more than 3,000 rulings clarifying and interpreting President Roosevelt's edict. As frequently happens, the Executive Order was a forerunner to a law passed by Congress.

Hatch Acts

The 1939 Political Activities Act, often known as the **Hatch Act**, is the fundamental statutory base for the restrictions of public employees throughout the United States. In large part, the Hatch Act provided a statutory basis for Executive Order 642, of 1907, and the 3,000 Civil Service Commission rulings related to it.

In 1940, Congress extended coverage to state and local employees whose salaries were funded, in whole or in part, by federal money. Subsequent to the federal action, all but a few states passed what were referred to as "little Hatch Acts," which placed state and local civil servants under the same restrictions as federal and federally funded employees.[3]

The Hatch Acts approached the goals of a politically neutral civil service from two perspectives: On the one hand, there are provisions protecting individual employees from political pressures and harassment, and, on the other hand, there are stipulations prohibiting civil servants from using their positions and offices to give advantage to any particular candidate or party. Related to the latter is a ban on civil servants themselves running as candidates on a partisan ticket. There are generally no restrictions on involvement in local, nonpartisan elections, and, of course, civil servants may vote.

The secret ballot alleviates some of the most direct and crude forms of pressure on government employees. Most of the effort of the Hatch Acts focuses on the solicitation of campaign funds. Classified employees may not be coerced into contributing, and there may be no solicitation of campaign contributions at government offices.

With few exceptions, voluntary contributions are recognized as a form of free expression and therefore protected by the First Amendment to the U.S. Constitution. As one might expect, there inevitably are instances in which political officials make it known that they expect a voluntary contribution and imply repercussions if these contributions are not forthcoming. Although such pressures could be brought to the attention of enforcement authorities, the nature of the evidence and/or the enforcement process may discourage complaints.

The United States is generally much more stringent than other countries about letting civil servants take a leave of absence, without pay, to run as candidates for elective offices. With few exceptions, civil servants in the United States who want to run for an office must resign their position. The exceptions are when the office is part time and nonpartisan, such as many school board, town council, and county board positions. Also, the federal government allows its employees to get fully involved in local politics, including partisan contests, in communities where most people are federal civil servants. These communities are in the Washington, D.C., area and in some parts of Alaska, Georgia, and Washington. In no case, of course, may employees run for an office that might involve a conflict of interest with their civil service job.

The restrictions of most state "little Hatch Acts" focus on the most visible and active forms of campaigning and, without exception, prohibit campaigning during work hours. There are some jurisdictions, however, that do not even allow attendance during off-work hours at political meetings or active involvement on bond or referendum issues.

In 1947, the U.S. Supreme Court addressed the potential conflict between the Hatch Act and the Constitution. In *United Public Workers of America* v. *Mitchell*, the Court reasoned that the First Amendment rights were not absolute and the Hatch Act represented a reasonable set of restrictions for a legitimate public policy objective. During the same term, the Court in *Oklahoma* v. *United States* ruled that the federal government could extend the Hatch Act provisions to state and local government employees supported by federal money. The Court noted that states did not have to accept federal funds and could therefore avoid the restrictions that went along with those funds.

In 1973 the Hatch Act withstood yet another challenge. This time the effort was to persuade the Supreme Court that the law was too vague and therefore unconstitutional. The Court did not agree.[4]

After two decades of failed attempts, public employees who were unhappy with the restrictions and ambiguities of the Hatch Act were successful in amending it. Table 3.1 lists major features of the Hatch Act as amended in 1993. Most federal

---

TABLE 3.1   MAJOR PROVISIONS OF THE HATCH ACT

Prohibited Political Partisan Activities

- May not solicit, accept, or receive political contributions from the general public, except under specifically defined circumstances
- May not coerce another employee to make a political contribution
- May not solicit personal services, paid or unpaid, from a business or corporation
- May not participate, even anonymously, in phone-bank solicitations for political contributions
- May not display partisan buttons, posters, or similar items or participate in partisan political activity on federal premises, on duty, or while in uniform

---

Permitted Political Partisan Activities

- May contribute money to political organizations and attend political fund-raising events
- May solicit, accept, and receive political contributions for the multicandidate committee of a federal labor or employee organization from an employee who is not a subordinate and who belongs to the same federal labor or employee organization
- May give a speech at a fund-raiser, as long as the speech does not include an appeal for political contributions
- May serve as an officer or chairperson of a campaign or political fund-raising organization, as long as activities do not include the personal solicitation, acceptance, or receipt of political contributions
- May participate fully, including being a candidate or officer and soliciting, accepting, and receiving political contributions, in local nonpartisan elections
- May accept and receive political contributions in local partisan contests in specific communities designated by the Office of Personnel Management
- May display partisan bumper sticker on private automobile when used occasionally for official business, but must cover bumper sticker if it is used recurrently for official business

---

employees may now hold office in a political party, work for candidates in a partisan campaign, solicit votes, and distribute campaign literature as long as these activities are done outside of work hours and work facilities. These reforms do not affect the little Hatch Acts although many states made changes to follow the federal model.

Union Activity

The Hatch Acts focus on individuals. The restrictions on a single employee's political activity do not apply to employee organizations. Public employee unions, at all levels of government, have established **political action committees** (PACs). Through these committees, union members can decide which candidates they will support and which referenda issues they will back. Like with PACs organized by businesses, farmers' organizations, and other unions, members can contribute money and energy to candidates and parties. This method of participation is only available to union members, and PAC activity, of course, is not allowed on the job. Nonetheless, PACs do provide an important way of contributing to partisan campaigns, despite Hatch Act restrictions. Public school teachers have been particularly effective in participating in electoral politics through their union.

The ability of public employees to influence the outcome of elections raises a concern about basic democratic principles. Accountability may become circular. Public employees and their elected officials are supposed to be accountable to the electorate. If political executives are beholden to government employee PACs, then, in a sense, public employees are their own bosses.

This scenario is too simplistic and too alarmist. Gerard S. Gryski found that the differences between the political activity of union and nonunion federal employees were not so great as to suggest that public employee PACs mobilize much additional effort. He concluded:

> The data showed union people to be relatively more active politically, and serious union members to be considerably more active politically, than casual union members. . . Nevertheless, at the most general level it seems clear that increased unionization of the government service is not likely to alter drastically or perhaps even significantly the current balance of power in the political system.[5]

According to Gryski's study, public employees in general vote at rates 20 to 25 percent higher than the electorate as a whole. Unionized federal workers have a voting rate that is even higher than their nonunionized co-workers (89 percent to 83 percent). But, the difference between the two rates is only marginal.

A study of state- and local-government employees in Michigan provides additional support for Gryski's general conclusion that the political activity of government workers has only a modest impact on election results. The study examined voting behavior on a statewide referendum to limit government spending and taxation. When compared to the general electorate, public employees had a turnout rate that was about 20 percent higher than the general electorate, and public employees opposed lower spending limits at a rate that was also about 20 percent higher. Public employees, however, constituted only 17 percent of those who voted.[6] It is easy to exaggerate the electoral power of public employee unions. One can, however, imagine situations in which public employees can have a major impact in a local election or provide the winning margin in a close election.

In 2007, public employee unions in California lobbied hard to influence the selection of the head of the state's personnel system—someone they would meet at the bargaining table. Despite the considerable political power of the unions, they were not successful. In short, although the concern about possible circular account-ability is real, there is evidence that there is a gap between fear and reality.

FREE SPEECH

Loyalty Oaths and Security Clearances

There are times when public employees who express opposition are revolutionaries, subversives, and traitors. Traumatic times in a country's history almost inevitably produce concerns and suspicions about the loyalty of those in a position to sabotage governmental operations. The years immediately after the Revolutionary War and the period of the Civil War clearly were such periods. It was relatively easy during these times to take action against government employees whose loyalties were in question. Whereas there may well have been abuses and false accusations, few doubted the need to be concerned and to take action.

In the aftermath of World War II, amidst the tensions of the Cold War and the fears of Russian expansion, the United States again was concerned about the loyalty of its public employees. In 1947, with Executive Order 9835, the Federal Bureau of Investigation was ordered to conduct security checks on all current and prospective federal employees. Thus was launched the first comprehensive federal loyalty program.

In addition to the concern about loyalty, the Department of Defense and other agencies concerned with national defense sought to identify those who posed a security risk. Security risks include people who might reveal secret information because they are vulnerable to pressures and/or prone to indiscretion. Loyalty, in other words, is primarily a matter of ideology. Security, on the other hand, is con-cerned with the likelihood of being forced or tricked into helping those who seek to overthrow the government or defeat the country militarily. Between 1947 and 1953, 557 persons were dismissed because they did not pass a loyalty or security investigation.

Since the mid-1950s, investigations of individual trustworthiness have been conducted only for those positions directly concerned with national defense and foreign policy. Homeland security was added in the aftermath of the attacks on September 11, 2001. Except for the Departments of State and Defense, the Cen-tral Intelligence Agency, and the Nuclear Regulatory Commission, which perform their own security checks, all investigations are completed by the federal Office of Personnel Management. The FBI is invited to participate only when there are alle-gations or suspicions of disloyalty.

There have been serious abuses of security investigations and loyalty oaths. Politi-cal demagogues, like the late Senator Joseph McCarthy, can use the issue of disloyalty to promote their own careers. McCarthy flung accusations of communist sympathy very carelessly. Zealous investigators probed aspects of individual lives unrelated to any job responsibilities. Individuals and groups intent on denying public employment opportunities to certain people generated suspicions of disloyalty to accomplish their goals. Mere accusation frequently ruined careers and destroyed social relationships.

In 1960, the U.S. Supreme Court started finding many of the loyalty oaths to be unconstitutional. The first case was *Shelton* v. *Tucker* (1960), in which an Arkansas **loyalty oath** requiring a declaration that one had never been a member of any of a long list of organizations was struck down. The specific case involved membership in the National Association for the Advancement of Colored People. The Court found the list to be irrelevant and the loyalty oath to be an abridgment of First Amendment rights. Other loyalty oaths were set aside because they were too vague or violated equal protection of the laws by singling out one particular group of citizens or employees.

In response to concern that loyalty and security investigations had become unwieldy and extended unjustifiably into the private dimensions of lives, the Civil Service Commission (now Office of Personnel Management) established an interagency study group and in 1968 issued standard criteria to guide investigators. Behind the criteria is the fundamental principle that the inquiries be job-related. Questions about behavior patterns can be asked only if a strong connection to job responsibilities can be demonstrated. The use of polygraph tests, for example, is now limited to a relatively narrow range of purposes.

Although homeland security concerns have resurrected fears of dire consequences if critical employees are not sufficiently vigilant, there seems to be recognition that a failure to preserve basic civil liberties would in itself subvert the political system of the United States. Loyalty oaths are still required for some public sector jobs, but they generally are no longer vague and far ranging. **Security clearances** are still required for those who must deal with sensitive material. Occasional spy cases keep the concerns alive. But the security checks are related to a position's responsibilities rather than to general issues.

Positions on Public Issues

Political activity is not confined to partisan conflict or even nonpartisan campaigns for office. Some of the most important issues to a community are settled by referenda, and some of the most significant political activity is directed at causes rather specific candidates. Through decisions on cases dealing with public employee participation in this kind of activity, the courts have provided some guidelines on the proper balance between public needs and individual rights outside the context of the Hatch Act and partisan politics.[7]

Pickering v. *Board of Education* (1968) established the fundamental principles. This case arose from a conflict in Illinois, when a public school teacher (Pickering) was fired for writing to a local newspaper a letter criticizing the school board for placing too much emphasis on athletics. Pickering argued the importance of basic academic subjects and urged voters to turn down an upcoming bond referendum for new athletic facilities. The Illinois courts upheld Pickering's dismissal, accepting the contention that employees have an obligation to accept the policy choices of their employer and that Pickering was being disruptive. The U.S. Supreme Court reversed this decision and ruled for Pickering. The Court stated that it is essential to maintain a balance between the rights of public employees as citizens and the interests of public employers in providing services. In order to set aside individual rights, the Court argued, it is necessary for public employers to show that their ability to function properly and provide effective services is seriously threatened. This could be demonstrated in five different areas:

1. The effect on managerial direction and discipline
2. The effect on harmony among co-workers
3. The breach of relationships, which require personnel loyalty and confidence
4. The effect on job performance
5. A disruptive impact on the functions of the agency, including an undermining of public confidence

The Court was not persuaded that this case posed a threat to any of the above and ordered that Pickering be reinstated. The Court had opportunities in 1972 and 1974 to apply this formula for determining the proper balance between the rights of public employees and the needs of management. In *Donohoe* v. *Staunton* (1972), the Court was presented with a case where a chaplain of a state mental hospital was fired after he publicly criticized the hospital's program. The Court saw no evidence of ill effects on patients as a result of the critique and saw virtue in a public policy debate on the program. It ordered that the chaplain be reinstated. On the other hand, in *Smith* v. *United States* (1974), the Court was persuaded that a clinical psychologist working in a veteran's administration hospital was disturbing patients by wearing a peace button and opposing U.S. military activity in Vietnam. He became at least partially ineffective in his work, especially with those returning from Vietnam. The Court upheld the dismissal of the psychologist.

In a 1987 case, the Court dealt with casual conversation in the office and added a step in the analysis of nonpartisan free speech cases for public employees. Ardith McPherson, a probationary employee in the office of Constable Rankin, reacted to the report of an assassination attempt on President Ronald Reagan by saying to a co-worker, "Shoot, if they go for him again, I hope they get him."[8] Another employee overheard this and reported the incident to the Constable, who then fired McPherson. The Supreme Court regarded this as a violation of McPherson's right of free speech and ordered her to be reinstated, and, importantly, provided a two-step process for managers, employees, lawyers, and judges when considering First Amendment rights of public employees:

1. Determine whether the statement is of public concern. If the comment is about something private, such as another employee's demeanor or behavior, or something outside the public arena, such as how well a local team has been playing, then constitutional protections do not apply.
2. Apply the *Pickering* **balance test** if, as in this case, the statement is about a public sector concern.

RESTRICTIONS ON NONPROFIT ORGANIZATIONS

Public policy limiting the political activities of nonprofit organizations is found primarily in the rules of the Internal Revenue Service and circulars issued by the federal Office of Management and Budget. As a condition of maintaining tax exempt status, there are limits both on lobbying and campaigning, and the penalties for violation are the removal of tax exempt status and fines. The penalty for government workers, on the other hand, is disciplinary action, including dismissal.

IRS rules allow lobbying—attempts to influence legislation or, in the states that allow this, lawmaking through initiative or referenda—if it is confined to issuing reports of research and analysis or to testifying at public hearings. The rules on campaigning are very restrictive. Nonprofit organizations and their staff may not participate in any campaign on behalf of or in opposition to "any candidate for public office."[9] Note that, unlike the prohibitions that apply to government employees, the scope of restrictions that apply to nonprofit organizations include both partisan and nonpartisan contests. It is also noteworthy that penalties for noncompliance can be levied both against the organization and its managers. (These provisions do not apply to a special class of political organization, established under Section 527 of the Internal Revenue Service Code, which qualify for limited federal tax exemption.)

Religious institutions that are 501(c)(3) organizations are more strictly limited in their political activities, both lobbying and campaigning, than are other nonprofit organizations. There has been lax enforcement of this distinction in the IRS Code, although the visible increase in the involvement of churches in electoral politics since the mid-1990s has prompted more review by the IRS.

RELIGION

Neither nonprofit organizations nor government agencies are supposed to discriminate against employees on the basis of their religion. There are some obvious and understandable exceptions when job responsibilities require someone to be a member of the clergy or have a similar religious qualification. Government managers have an additional obligation. They must maintain, in substance and appearance, the principles of separation between church and state.

The Supreme Court in *Sherbert v. Verner* (1963) addressed a fundamental principle when it ruled that government agencies should not put their employees in a position where they have to choose between their religion and their employment. Following this ruling and the passage of the 1964 Civil Rights Act, which included a prohibition against discrimination on the basis of religion, the Equal Employment Opportunity Commission promulgated rules that all employers must make **reasonable accommodations** to the religious needs of their employees. The term reasonable accommodations is, of course, open to interpretation.

In a 1986 case, the Supreme Court indicated that employers, not employees, have the primary right and responsibility to determine what was a reasonable accommodation in a specific situation. In *Ansomnia Board of Education v. Philbrook* (1986), the dispute involved a fundamentalist Christian who argued that he needed at least six days of leave for religious observances. The school district had a contract with the teachers' union that provided for three days of leave for religious observances and another three for personal reasons. Philbrook thought it was reasonable for him to have at least six days for religious purposes and three for personal if he arranged and paid for a substitute for the additional days. The school district considered reasonable accommodation as one in which any leave beyond that provided for in the contract be unpaid. In part, the district was concerned that Philbrook or someone else in a similar situation could make money if he or she were on paid leave and then found a substitute for less than their salary and benefits. In addition, in order to be certain that all teachers, including those who were temporary, were qualified, the district insisted that it, not a teacher, obtain the substitute. Writing for the majority, Chief Justice William Rehnquist explained that ruling in favor of the school district was an acknowledgment that the district had designed an accommodation that was reasonable. Importantly, the Court stated that it is the employer, not the employee, who needed to take the lead in balancing agency needs with employee rights.

In 1993, Congress passed the Religious Freedom Restoration Act, which was intended to limit the authority of federal, state, and local governments to restrict religious expressions and practices.[10] The act, which does not apply to nonprofit organizations, stipulated that a government had to show a compelling interest in order to prohibit a person's exercise of religion and that government had to take the least restrictive measures possible to pursue that interest. In *Boerne* v. *Flores* (1997), however, the U.S. Supreme Court struck down the act as an intrusion on the authority of the courts and state and local governments.

In August 1997, two months after the *Boerne* v. *Flores* ruling, President Bill Clinton issued executive guidelines instructing federal agency managers to let their employees wear and display religious symbols, conduct prayer meetings, and otherwise practice religion in the workplace as long as agency productivity is not diminished and there is no appearance of government endorsement of any particular faith. The White House encouraged state and local governments to take similar actions to clarify and expand the religious allowance for public employees. Legally, employers still are required to make reasonable accommodation, and they have wide discretion in determining what is reasonable.

WHISTLEBLOWING

Whistleblowing represents another issue of the right to freedom of expression. This term refers to instances when an employee reveals information to the press, legislators, or higher authorities, about illegal and improper activities within an agency. Whistleblowing is somewhat distinct from freedom of expression in that employees use information specifically available to them as employees and the allegations of impropriety relate to operational activities rather than broad public policies.

Although there have been instances of whistleblowing throughout history, the dramatic events leading to the threatened impeachment and then resignation of President Richard Nixon made visible some of the issues involved in employee-initiated information. One of President Nixon's major concerns was the series of leaks of information about improper behavior and abuse of authority in his administration that got to the press and to Democrats in Congress. In response, President Nixon established a "plumbers unit" to identify the sources of the leaks so that he could retaliate. The plumbers themselves engaged in illegal activity, using unauthorized wiretaps and burglarizing offices to secure evidence. Leaks about the plumbers contributed to the case for impeaching President Nixon.

In the 1978 Civil Service Reform Act, President Jimmy Carter responded to the Nixon abuses by including provisions to protect the right of employees to blow the whistle on improper behavior by government agencies and officials. Federal law now states that federal employees are protected from reprisals if they reasonably believe that information they reveal is evidence of (1) a violation of a law, rule, or regulation; or (2) mismanagement, gross waste of funds, abuse of authority, or a danger to public health or safety. Following cases of whistleblowing in corporations—made particularly visible by a movie detailing a chemical company's efforts to cover up its pollution and the effects on public health—Congress passed the Sarbanes-Oxley Act of 2002 extending **whistleblower** protection to organizations outside government. That law provides criminal penalties for those who retaliate against whisteblowers.

Whistleblowing rights are not absolute. They do not apply if the information that would be used is specifically protected by law. In other words, whistleblowers may not use classified information, which is considered secret for national defense and security purposes, nor may they use data covered by legislation designed to protect rights to privacy for individual citizens. Some states have also enacted laws protecting whistleblowers. They, too, exempt confidential information to ensure privacy rights. Exemptions, although necessary, create some ambiguities. There may be debates about whether something is appropriately classified or included under the provisions of the Privacy Act.

A legitimate concern of managers is that an employee about to be disciplined might fabricate a charge of abuse or mismanagement and then seek whistleblowing protection to stop any potential disciplinary action. Whistleblower laws anticipate this scenario by prohibiting any disciplinary action while the charges are investigated, but do not continue the protections if the charges cannot be supported. In order to discourage frivolous or mischievous charges, some jurisdictions levy penalties against whistleblowers whose allegations are without foundation.

In fact, the record indicates that whistleblower protections appear to be more ineffective than they are excessive. A study of 161 whistleblowers found that 62 percent had lost their jobs, 11 percent had their responsibilities and/or their pay reduced, and all but 5 percent suffered some other form of retaliation.[11] To add insult to injury, whistleblowers spent an average of $28,166 each to defend themselves.

In the first decade after the passage of the Carter Civil Service Reforms, the Merit System Protection Board received slightly more than 200 whistleblowing cases per year. The board ruled only five times that agencies retaliated illegally against whistleblowers. Although it is possible that there simply are few legitimate whistleblowers and there are many who try to use whistleblower protection to thwart actions based on poor performance or some other legitimate reason, the numbers are so dramatic they cast a shadow of serious doubt on the effectiveness of the protections.

Congress was certainly skeptical. In 1989, it passed the Whistleblower Protection Act, which removed the Office of Special Counsel from under the Merit System Protection Board and gave the office authority to prevent federal agencies, temporarily, from demoting or firing a whistleblower. In addition, the 1989 act provides protection in cases where retaliation is a factor in an adverse personnel action. Originally, whistleblowers had to show that retaliation was a significant determinant. States have also amended their laws to try to make protections more meaningful.

In *Garcetti* v. *Ceballos* (2006) the U.S. Supreme Court restricted whistleblower protection to public discourse and ruled that the First Amendment did not apply to disagreements within the office on what the agency should do. Ceballos disagreed with his colleagues and his superior that available evidence justified arresting a particular suspect. When he persisted in voicing his dissent in staff meetings and other internal settings, Ceballos was disciplined. He cried foul, but the majority on the Court did not agree that he was engaged in whistleblowing and therefore could not be disciplined. It is possible that the distinction between disagreeing and whistleblowing may not always be clear and this ruling may discourage some employees from speaking out.

CODES OF ETHICS FOR PUBLIC AND NONPROFIT EMPLOYEES

There is an expectation that all employees, regardless of where they work, will be honest and hard-working. Expectations are particularly high for nonprofit and public organizations. Some organizations have written statements designed to set standards for their employees. Professions typically have their own code of ethics that speak to the quality of their work and the access they will provide to those in need of their expertise. Professionals, in other words, may be guided both by an employer-specific statement as well as that of their professional association.

In addition, nonprofit organizations and government agencies have a special need to avoid **conflicts of interest**. Government must have the trust of the people it governs. Citizens should feel confident that their taxes and their officials are working for public, not private, interests. Nonprofit organizations likewise need those who provide funds or volunteer time to believe that contributions are being used for the mission of the organization and not for enriching businesses in which nonprofit managers have personal investments.[12]

As the public and private sectors of our society become more intermingled, chances increase that there will be conflicts between the responsibilities of government employees in their jobs and the economic investments and activities of these employees off their jobs.[13] It is all but inevitable that those who work in government and in nonprofit organizations are going to be making decisions that could benefit companies or land in which they or people close to them have an interest. Links—real or imagined—between campaign contributions and agency spending pose a special and growing concern in government.

As in the cases of free speech, there must be a proper balance between the rights of individuals and the needs of managers. Few would disagree, for example, that someone who has the responsibility for letting a contract for printing some brochures and who is also the owner of a printing firm bidding for the contract has a serious conflict of interest and should not participate in the decision making. The fact that its owner is a government employee or an executive in a nonprofit organization will inevitably lead to suspicions of pressure and influence if the employee's firm gets the contract. If a substantial proportion of that individual's responsibilities require contracting with printers, then perhaps either the government position or ownership of the firm should be relinquished. Most would also agree that the same conflict would arise if it were the staff member's spouse or a close relative who owned the printing firm.

But, what if the issue were purchasing word processing equipment and the employee was one of the thousands of stockholders in company manufacturing this equipment? The order for a single office or agency is not likely to be of such magnitude that an individual stockholder would receive a noticeable benefit. What about the investments made by staff members who have purchasing and contracting responsibilities in mutual funds, where the portfolio includes many firms and the contents of the portfolio may change frequently? Even if an order might have an impact on the profits of a firm whose stock is in the portfolio, it is unlikely that the employee would be aware of it. Are we prepared to say that government purchasing officers and their counterparts in nonprofit organizations may not hold personal investments of any size in any firm with which their agency might do business? Are those restrictions necessary in order to be certain that funds are used properly?

The standards applied to employees in the public sector are different from those applied in the private sector. The integration of related businesses and economic activities is regarded as appropriate and even desirable in the private sector, but can be a conflict of interest in the public. Providing special discounts and services to friends and business acquaintances is common in the private sector but unethical and even illegal in government. The differences in the two sets of standards are real, but they can be exaggerated. Scandals involving bribes, kickbacks, and payments for goods and services that were never provided reflects poorly on both the government or nonprofit employees and the private firms that were in collusion.

One of the most difficult problems facing government agencies and nonprofit organizations—and, importantly, their employees—is avoiding the appearance as well as the substance of impropriety. Appearance, like beauty, is in the eye of the beholder. Yet, appearance is consequential.

There are a number of approaches to deal with the appearance of a conflict of interest. In the aftermath of the Watergate scandal that forced President Nixon from office, governments at all levels sought to restore public confidence by both promulgating codes of ethics and sponsoring seminars and workshops on these codes. For the most part, these codes were statements of broad principles. The federal government provides an example. In Executive Order 11222, issued by President Carter in 1978, federal employees were told they must avoid any action that might result in or create the appearance of:

1. Using their office for private gain
2. Giving preferential treatment to any person or group
3. Impeding government efficiency or economy
4. Losing independence or impartiality of action
5. Making government decisions outside of official channels
6. Affecting adversely public confidence in the integrity of government

Managers must use common sense and good judgment in applying these principles to specific situations. That is imprecise and can be frustrating, but the alternative of being very specific about what constitutes a conflict of interest or improper behavior is usually even less desirable. It is difficult to anticipate all of the situations that should be avoided, and by trying to do so one is likely to focus attention on what specific situations are and are not permissible, rather than to uphold the general principle.

A federal policy, embodied in an executive order, is to discourage employees from incurring debts. There is a fear that a debt to a particular individual or organization will make the employee vulnerable to pressure from the creditor. In addition, knowing that federal salaries are not subject to garnishment, employees might be reckless with their finances and use their status as federal workers to hide from creditors. This is, in other words, a concern both about ethical behavior and about the image of the government. Thus, federal employees are instructed that they must meet just financial obligation when there is a court judgment or an overdue tax bill. Employees who accumulate substantial, outstanding debts are subject to disciplinary action, although the initial response is to provide financial counseling.

Another approach to maintaining the appearance and substance of ethical conduct of employees is the **disclosure** of financial interests. This is common in nonprofit organizations and governments at all levels.[14] Senior officials must reveal their financial assets. According to the Ethics in Government Act of 1978, for example, federal employees with a pay rate equal to or higher than a GS-16 level and those who are in confidential and policy-making positions must disclose their financial interests. In addition, during the first two years after leaving federal employment, individuals may not represent or be employed by an organization closely related to the work and responsibilities they had as a federal employee. Someone who had been on the staff of the Federal Communications Commission (FCC), in other words, is barred from employment with a radio station or television network immediately after leaving the FCC. Nor could such a person represent a media organization in a hearing before the FCC during the first two years after being on the staff.

A long-standing practice in the courts has been for judges with current or past connections to litigants who appear before them to refuse to participate in deciding the case. Administrators who must make purchases or negotiate contracts for their agencies follow a similar practice. In some cases where the administrator's expertise is essential, nonparticipation makes little sense. Instead, the decision-making process will include several officials who share authority and responsibility. Disclosure would be essential in such a situation.

Given the importance and prevalence of private ownership and investment in our economy, it is inevitable that conflicts of interest—in substance and appearance—will arise. Although it is possible to limit and monitor these conflicts through codes of ethics and financial disclosures, mechanisms must exist for handling those instances where potential conflicts still arise. The provision and administration of appropriate mechanisms is sometimes the responsibility of a special board or commission. More frequently, this is a task of managers. Managers are expected to help avoid major problems and scandals by ensuring that employees are familiar with and comply with general ethical standards and specific laws and regulations.[15]

Some basic features follow for a process for managing conflict of interest problems.

Definitions and Criteria for Determining Potential Conflicts of Interest

It is of fundamental importance to establish who is included—the employee, spouse (or equivalent), family members, and so forth. In addition, it is important to identify the threshold beyond which a potential conflict is so small as to be insignificant. Thresholds can be set according to a percentage of ownership in an enterprise or a dollar level of the transaction. In many cases, especially for professional and managerial positions, it is important to state the amount of time outside of working hours that an employee can pursue economic activities without generating concern about a possible conflict of interest. Finally, managers must restrict the use of equipment and facilities for activities related to outside interests. Commonly, there is a total ban on such usage.

Review and Decision Process

Ideally, employees would use the spirit and letter of the criteria for determining when a conflict of interest problem occurs to monitor and report their own activities. There are obvious defects in a self-reporting system, thus there are often ways in which managers gather information on the outside interests of employees. There are few ways of doing this systematically and comprehensively without violating rights of privacy. Some use income tax returns as an information source. Most rely on complaints and allegations from members of the public, the press, and other employees. Whatever the source of information, a process is commonly established for determining whether, in fact, a conflict of interest does exist and, if so, what should be done about it. If there is a special ethics board or commission, the matter is referred to them for a decision. If there is no such body, then the usual procedure is for the immediate supervisor to make a determination and have that decision reviewed by the agency head. The most serious conflict of interest problems are likely to involve senior-level officials, so the agency head and even the chief executive usually play a direct and active role.

Appeal Procedure

As is discussed in more detail in Chapter 11, it is critical to allow employees an opportunity to appeal decisions that adversely affect their rights and interests. That opportunity, in most cases, is available in the courts, but both our judicial system and sound personnel management policies suggest that an appeals opportunity should exist within the established personnel management system. Most frequently, this means that, if there is no special ethics board or commission, appeals on ethics cases will follow the same procedures and guidelines that apply for disciplinary cases, even though these are not strictly the same as a disciplinary issue.

It should be noted that the previously described criteria and procedures apply primarily to cases of economic conflicts of interest. Other behavior that might be labeled unethical, such as favoritism and sexual harassment, are regarded as disciplinary matters.

RIGHTS TO PRIVACY

Societal standards place some restrictions on the private social lives of public employees. What is permitted and prohibited changes with society itself. In the first years of the republic, for example, public school teachers could be dismissed for not attending church or for courting, drinking, smoking, and not being properly clothed. During the Depression, some public and private organizations hired only single women, on the grounds that men were supposed to be the major breadwinners and the place of married women should be at the stove, laundry tub, and bassinet.

Private sector employers and nonprofit organizations can insist that their workers follow certain life styles, such as not smoking, as long as they do not discriminate on the basis of race, sex, age, disability, and country of origin—the subject of the next chapter. Government is more limited, since the Constitution prohibits government from taking away basic rights of citizens, including public employees.

Consistent with its rulings in freedom of expression cases, the Supreme Court has stated that a government employee can be disciplined because of social behavior only if there is a harmful effect on job performance. This principle was first established in *Norton* v. *Macy* (1969). Norton, who was an employee of National Aeronautics and Space Administration (NASA), was arrested in the early morning hours near the Washington Monument when he picked up another male in his car. The Washington, D.C., police only gave Norton a traffic summons, but NASA pursued the matter further. During interrogation, Norton admitted to homosexual preferences. NASA dismissed Norton, but the Supreme Court voided this action. The Court took note of a recent award to Norton for outstanding performance in his job and said that NASA failed to show "some ascertainable deleterious effect on the efficiency of the service." Without meeting this test, public employers cannot take action against employees for private social behavior.

The Court, however, applied the basic principles of the *Norton* v. *Macy* ruling to law enforcement officers in a way that is more restrictive of employee rights. In *Kelly* v. *Johnson* (1976), for example, the Court rejected the contention that individual police officers had a right to any hairstyle they wanted. The court understood that hairstyle did not affect performance of the tasks assigned to officers. However, the Justices considered it appropriate for police departments to promulgate grooming regulations as part of required uniforms.

In 1985, the Court went further in distinguishing law enforcement personnel from other public employees when it upheld the dismissal of two unmarried officers for having sexual intercourse with one another. In *Wisenhunt* v. *Amarillo* the police chief defended the dismissals by arguing that members of his force had to abide by the highest of community standards in order to maintain public respect for the department as a whole. He acknowledged that the sexual activity occurred while the officers were off duty and their relationship had no noticeable effect on their individual job performances. Nonetheless, his concern for the general reputation of the department prompted the firings.

DRUG TESTING

Managers may want to have a drug-free workforce and they may pursue this goal with required drug testing if the organization is private or nonprofit. Public sector managers, however, face some constitutional barriers. Tests for drugs require urinalysis. To ensure that urine samples are identified with the right person, the test administrator must watch the person being tested urinate. Inasmuch as the **Fourth Amendment** prohibits the government from engaging in unreasonable search and seizure, public employers must justify the requirement that employees provide urine samples, especially while being observed. Also, since the issue is the use of illegal substances, the **Fifth Amendment** protections against self-incrimination apply to requiring drug testing in the public sector.

Fourth and Fifth Amendment prohibitions, like other constitutional provisions, are not absolute. What might otherwise be an unreasonable search and seizure becomes reasonable if there is a basis for suspecting someone of breaking a law. Where there is evidence beyond that generated by a general protocol like mandatory, random drug testing, then there is no self-incrimination.

In addition, the Supreme Court ruled in 1989 that constitutional protections could be set aside if significant safety and security concerns were at stake (*Skinner* v. *Railway Labor Executives Association*). The specific issue here was an agency rule that required drug testing of any employee involved in a railroad accident. The Court considered the rule itself as fair notice to employees, thus not requiring a search warrant, and recognized the need to get urine samples immediately after an accident in order to run a valid test.

During the same 1989 session, the Court provided for another circumstance in which testing could be required (*National Treasury Employees Union* v. *William Von Raab, Commissioner, U.S. Customs Service*). The union objected to the Customs Service program of requiring drug testing for employees who were involved in drug interdiction, who carried firearms, or who had access to classified material. The Court believed that the requirement for a high level of employee integrity and credibility justified the testing. The association of illegal drugs with corruption and organized crime obviously weighed heavily here.

The Court, to sum up, has not approved the required testing of government employees on a random or wholesale basis. There must either be a valid reason to suspect that an employee has been using drugs or a concern that the public would be endangered if the individual's behavior or judgment was affected by drugs.[16]

PRIVACY AND NEW TECHNOLOGIES

New technologies pose challenges to managers as they balance privacy rights of employees with the needs of an agency. To what extent, for example, should managers monitor the email communications of their employees? Should DNA testing and information about a person's genetic makeup be used in hiring decisions or in assigning work? Clearly one can imagine someone using email for private correspondence not related to work. Also, it might be useful to know if someone is genetically vulnerable to certain diseases or work conditions before placing them in a position that might place them at risk. Or is it?

The principles derived from court cases on other privacy issues suggest three basic questions that need to be asked before a manager intrudes on the privacy of employees:

1. Is the proposed monitoring reasonable? The court includes in its consideration of reasonableness whether prior notice is given to employees before certain behavior patterns or personal traits are inspected.
2. Is there a compelling interest? Does a manager really have to monitor email or to administer a genetic test in order to get the agency's work done?
3. Are the incursions job-related? Again, the burden of compromising employee privacy must be met by a significant and relevant need of the agency.[17]

If the above questions can be answered affirmatively, managers would seem to be safe in using computer technology and DNA testing. The lessons of the past are that we start with the protection and safeguarding of individual rights, but these rights are not absolute. They may be set aside if there is a legitimate agency need to do so.

The above describes legal mandates for government managers. These mandates might be treated as guidelines or suggestions for nonprofit organizations. Managers in the latter have more discretion here and can adapt to the particular size, mission, location, and culture of their organizations.

LIABILITY OF GOVERNMENT EMPLOYEES

What if, as a manager, you violate an employee's right to privacy or freedom of speech and association? Can you be sued and are you liable personally for your actions? The answer is that it depends.

Until the 1970s, the United States provided all public employees with absolute immunity from civil suits. This was based on the British tradition that one cannot sue the throne. The idea of providing immunity from suits has never been applied to profit or nonprofit organizations. In a number of rulings, the U.S. Supreme Court recognized that government officials might abuse their authority and deny constitutional rights or statutory benefits to individual citizens. To try and keep this from happening, the Court adopted the concept of **qualified immunity**.[18] The Court ruled that public employees enjoyed personal immunity from suits only if they were acting within their sphere of responsibility and complying with what a reasonable person should know about the law.

In *Harlow* v. *Fitzgerald* (1982), the Court took action to prevent a flood of frivolous or misguided lawsuits against government employees. In this ruling, the Court said that suits against public managers and workers had to go through two steps. In the first step, a judge would determine if there was immunity by asking whether a) the official was acting within his or her sphere of responsibility and b) the official violated a law that a reasonable person would have known. If the answer to the first question was positive and/or if the law would not have been known by a reasonable person, then the judge would grant immunity and dismiss the case.

If the case is not dismissed, it goes to trial where the questions are whether indeed the official violated the rights of the plaintiff and whether the individual acted with malice or recklessness. Malice is the more serious charge. A judgment on motives is critical in awarding damages.

In short, it is critical that managers know and respect the constitutional and statutory rights of the people they supervise. Managers have personal liability if they fail to protect these rights.

SUMMARY

Contemporary civil servants would rebel if they had to accept the restrictions placed on their predecessors. Employees of nonprofit organizations would chafe at the managerial practices common in earlier times.

The trend toward the recognition and protection of the individual rights of employees is recent. This trend is reinforced by personal liability that managers have in upholding these rights. The reforms that established the merit system, while providing more security for those working for government, included the principle of civil service neutrality and the concomitant prohibitions of many forms of participation in partisan politics. The provisions of the Internal Revenue Service code for tax exempt organizations were written with a sensitivity to the political machines that emerged after the Civil War. A response to Watergate, to corporate scandals, and to the increased intermingling of the private and public sectors of the economy has been the promulgation of new codes of ethics and limitations on the economic activities of public employees, in order to avoid both the substance and appearance of conflicts of interest.

Although there has been a liberalization in the restrictions on the political, social, and economic activities of government workers and nonprofit organization employees, there are still important limitations. The emphasis is to strike a balance between the sometimes competing logic of individual rights, agency needs, and public trust. This is, of course, a fundamental issue for democratic societies as they define relationships between citizens, their government, and service organizations.

DISCUSSION QUESTIONS

1. Are public and nonprofit employees second-class citizens? How would you weigh the restrictions placed on their political activities and the special protections they enjoy?
2. Does the balance test used to determine limits of free speech and expression for public and nonprofit employees favor managers, employees, or neither?
3. Are managerial and professional employees held to higher standards than workers who have lower level positions? Answer this with specific reference to conflicts of interest regarding economic and social or private activities.
4. What procedures would you suggest for minimizing violations of political, economic, and social restrictions on employee behavior?

Case Study:
Employee Rights and Responsibilities

As you arrive at your office this morning, you are surprised to see Jan there waiting anxiously for you. You are early, and Jan actually is scheduled to be on vacation today. She is obviously very concerned.

Jan follows you into your office and closes the door. In a nervous voice, she tells you that when she and her family were checking into a hotel upstate last night to begin their vacation, she saw Terry, her boss in the purchasing office, leaving the registration desk with Kim, the owner of the major office supply company in the county. The two of them walked hand-in-hand to the elevator. Later in the evening, Jan saw Kim and Terry emerge from the same room and go to the hotel swimming pool.

Jan says she didn't sleep all night. The county is about to solicit bids for new contracts. Obviously, one option is to renew the contract with Kim's firm, even though a number of county agencies have complained about the quality of some of the supplies and about delays in delivery. Jan is worried about what she saw at the hotel and the implications for the contracting process. She is also concerned about her own position under Terry's supervision.

You are the head of the county's Department of Administration, which includes the purchasing office. Obviously, you want to protect the integrity of the bidding process—both in substance and appearance. Kim is known as a major contributor to the county executive's campaign treasury, and there already have been rumors and whispers about preferential treatment. You do not think this is true and, in fact, you disagree with those who think that the quality of service provided by Kim's firm has been poor. The firm is clearly one of the best in the community. Nonetheless, if Kim and Terry have developed a romantic relationship, that inevitably will add to the rumors and suspicions.

An additional concern that you have is Jan's credibility. You know that there has been tension for some time between Jan and Terry. Two weeks ago, in fact, Terry met with you about Jan's continued performance problems. Terry was developing a plan of close supervision with specific expectations as a basis for deciding what, if any, actions need to be taken regarding Jan's future in the department.

You have some decisions to make:

1. What do you say, immediately, to Jan?
2. What are your options in dealing with Terry and what are your plans for resolving this situation?
3. What legal rights or protections, if any, does Terry have?
4. What will you do to respond to Jan's fears that she is vulnerable to retaliation by Terry?
5. With whom, if anyone, will you share this situation?
6. Do you think it would be good to promulgate some general rules or guidelines in response to this situation?
7. Does the gender of Terry and of Kim make any difference to how you proceed?

GLOSSARY

Balancing test Principle emerging out of U.S. Supreme Court cases that the individual liberties of public employees protected by the Constitution are not absolute and must be balanced against the requirements of their government jobs

Conflicts of interest Instances when employees have an economic or personal tie that might prompt them to exercise their official authority or discretion in order to serve themselves

Disclosure Practice of having individuals who help make decisions that commit funds to reveal their economic interests and ownerships as a way of dealing with potential conflicts of interest

Fifth Amendment Provision of U.S. Constitution that prohibits the government from forcing someone to incriminate themselves

Fourth Amendment Provision of U.S. Constitution that prohibits government from unreasonable search and seizure, which restricts the authority of public employers from taking urine samples of employees for drug testing

Hatch Acts Laws passed in 1937 (federal) and 1940 (state and local employees using federal funds) that prohibit civil servants from engaging in many partisan political activities. Most states have their own versions of the Hatch Act. In 1993, Congress enacted amendments to the Hatch Act for federal employees

Loyalty oath An affirmation by an employee or prospective employee that he or she is a patriot and not engaged in any activity to overthrow or subvert the government

Political action committees Formally recognized bodies associated with employee unions and other organizations that may, within certain restrictions, collect money from members and disperse to political candidates and campaigns

Political neutrality Principle that career employees in government need to keep from being identified with any particular political party so that they can serve effectively regardless of who is elected

Reasonable accommodation Requirement that managers must do all that is reasonably possible to meet certain needs (religious in this chapter) of individual employees, without sacrificing the work and mission of the agency

Security clearance An investigation and evaluation to certify that an employee or prospective employee does not have a background that includes some liability that would make them vulnerable to pressures to share secret information or do something else that might threaten the country

Whistleblower An employee who discloses instances of illegal, wasteful, or abusive activity in an agency or organization to a higher authority, legislators, or the press

SOURCES

Copper, T. (1991). *An ethic of citizenship for public administration.* Englewood Cliffs, NJ: Prentice-Hall.
Discussion of ethics in public administration that emphasizes the concept of citizenship to guide decision making.

Gortner, H. F. (1995). *Ethics and public personnel administration.* In S. W. Hays, & R. C. Kearney, eds., *Public personnel administration: Problems and prospects* (3rd ed.). Englewood Cliffs, NJ: Prentice-Hall, pp. 273–288.
Discussion of the role of personnel specialists and offices in promoting ethical behavior of public employees.

Rosenbloom, D. H. (1971). *Federal service and the Constitution.* Ithaca, NY: Cornell University Press.
  Historical analysis of the political rights of federal government workers.

Lee, Y. S. (1992). *Public personnel administration and constitutional values.* Westport, CT: Quorum Books.
  Explanation of court cases and legal issues regarding the rights and restrictions that apply to public employees.

NOTES

1. B. Guy Peters, *The Politics of Bureaucracy: A Comparative Perspective* (New York: Longman, 1978), 52.
2. John A. Armstrong, *The European Administrative Elite* (Princeton, NJ: Princeton University Press, 1973).
3. Karl T. Thurber, Jr., "Big, Little, Littler: Synthesizing Hatch Act-based Political Activity Legislation Research," *Review of Public Personnel Administration*, 8, no. 1 (Winter 1993): 38–51.
4. *U.S. Civil Service Commission* v. *National Association of Letter Carriers* (1973) and *Broadrick* v. *Oklahoma* (1973).
5. Gerard S. Gryski, "Unionized Federal Employees and Political Participation." Paper presented at the meeting of the American Society for Public Administration, Phoenix, AZ, April 12, 1978.
6. Edward M. Gramlich and Daniel L. Rubinfeld, "Voting on Public Spending: Differences Between Public Employees, Transfer Recipients, and Private Workers," *Journal of Policy Analysis and Management* 1, no. 4 (1982): 516–533.
7. Kathryn Eisenhart, "The First Amendment and the Public Sector Employee: The Effect of Recent Patronage Cases on Public Sector Personnel Decisions," Review of Public Personnel Administration 18, no. 3 (Summer 1998): 58–69.
8. *Rankin* v. *McPherson* (1987), 322.
9. Internal Revenue Service Code 4955.
10. David C. Wyld, "*Bessard* v. *California Community Colleges* and the Religious Freedom Restoration Act: Implications for Public Administration," *Public Personnel Management* 26, no. 2 (Summer 1997): 273–288.
11. James S. Bowman, "Whistle Blowing: Literature and Resource Material," *Public Administration Review* 49, no. 1 (January/February 1989).
12. Ralph Clark Chandler, "Deontological Dimensions of Administrative Ethics, Revisited," Public Personnel Management 28, no. 4 (Winter 1999): 505–514.
13. Donna Holmquist, "Ethics—How Important is it in Today's Office?" Public Personnel Management 22, no. 4 (Winter 1993): 537–544.
14. Elizabeth Schmidt, "How Ethical Is Your Nonprofit Organization?" www.Guidestar.org article 827 (October 2004).
15. Harold F. Gortner, "Ethics and Public Personnel Administration," in Steven W. Hays and Richard C. Kearney, eds., *Public Personnel Administration. Problems and Prospects*, 3rd ed. (Englewood Cliffs, NJ: Prentice-Hall, 1995), 273–288; Gary B. Brumback, "Institutionalizing Ethics in Government," *Public Personnel Management* 20, no. 3 (Fall 1991): 353–366.
16. Frank J. Thompson, Norma M. Riccucci, and Carolyn Ban, "Biological Testing and Personnel Policy: Drugs and the Federal Workplace," in Carolyn Ban and Norma M. Riccucci, eds., *Public Personnel Management: Current Concerns—Future Challenges* (New York: Longman, 1991), 156–172.

17. Don A. Cozzetto and Theodore B. Pedeliski, "Privacy and the Workplace: Future Implications for Managers," *Review of Public Personnel Administration* 16, no. 2 (Spring 1996): 21–31.
18. David H. Rosenbloom and Margo Bailey, "Public Employees' Liability for 'Constitutional Torts'" Norma M. Riccucci, ed. *Public Personnel Management. Current Concerns, Future Challenges* 4th edition (New York: Longman, 2006).

Chapter 4

Diversity

A powerful anecdote is a story about how someone got a job because they were African American, female, or handicapped. Heads shake in disgust and dismay about the unfairness. Some warn about disaster if we keep favoring women and minorities and sacrificing competence. Women and minority group members, on the other hand, have mixed feelings—supportive of the principle that competence should not be sacrificed, defensive about steps that correct historic patterns of discrimination, and frustrated that the anecdote itself continues to be told, takes on a life of its own, and evokes such a negative reaction.

Although it seems that everyone has an anecdote to tell, the aggregate picture continues to show that white males without handicaps have the best chance of landing a job and getting promotions and favorable assignments. Despite allegations that the impact of the civil rights movement was **reverse discrimination**, the most important effect has actually been to focus personnel management on what is needed to get the job done rather than on traits associated with racial and gender stereotypes.

Competence has always been essential in employment decisions, but it has never been the sole criterion for the selection and advancement of employees. The United States, like other countries, has maintained a concern for the social identity of government workers. At times, these policies have been exclusive. As late as 1913, for example, women were barred from working for the post office and from taking most civil service examinations.[1] Prior to the passage of the 1964 Civil Rights Act, it was common for newspapers to run job vacancy advertisements for men only, for women only, for whites only, and for colored people only. Because of the 1964 Act, managers in any organization with 15 or more employees must follow policies that are inclusive and base decisions primarily on job-related criteria.

The 1964 Civil Rights Act, as passed initially, covers private sector (profit and nonprofit) employers. Governments were included later. In 1972 amendments to the Act, Congress extended coverage to include state and local governments. The federal government included its own civilian agencies when it passed the 1978 Civil Service Reform Act of President Jimmy Carter. In 1995, Congress included the legislative branch under the commitment to nondiscriminatory employment. In short, now all employers, other than those with small workforces, are covered.

Executive Orders in the federal government and some state governments explicitly cover organizations who do work under contract with government. Here there is no threshold related to the number of employees. Executive Order 11246, signed by President Lyndon B. Johnson in 1965, which amended an Executive Order issued by

President Dwight D. Eisenhower in 1953, required anyone with a contract of $10,000 or more in a single year to refrain from discrimination in employment decisions on the basis of race, gender, religion, or national origin. Executive Order 11246 also requires plans and efforts to achieve diversification, thus going beyond simply not discriminating.

LEARNING OBJECTIVES OF THIS CHAPTER

- Understand the rationale for nondiscrimination in employment
- Identify patterns and trends of the social profile of workers in the public sector
- Trace the development of public policies through legislation and court rulings regarding social representation
- Understand what special efforts managers may and may not make to hire, retain, and promote individuals in order to have a diverse workforce

THE CONCEPT OF REPRESENTATIVE BUREAUCRACY

There is more to the concern for the social identity of government officials than the raw power of politics. Representation is fundamental to the theory and reality of a democracy. Although legislatures are the primary institutions providing for representation of the populace, they are not the only bodies expected to draw from the governed. In some jurisdictions, judges, sheriffs, and village clerks are elected. In virtually all jurisdictions, there is concern about who is appointed to public positions.

J. D. Kingsley first used the term **representative bureaucracy** in his 1944 study of Great Britain. Kingsley adopted a moderately Marxist perspective as he analyzed the social background of senior-level civil servants in England: "The view of the Civil Servant as a disinterested assembler of facts simply will not stand examination."[2] He assumed that individuals acted in accordance with the values and interests of whatever class they belonged to and argued that government bureaucracy was an instrument of the class represented by most of the higher level civil servants. For Great Britain, this meant control of the bureaucracy by the upper classes.

Writing a few years later, Reinhard Bendix presented a portrait of senior-level civil servants in the United States that was much more heterogeneous than the English counterpart.[3] Bendix was not really interested in the representativeness of U.S. bureaucracy but in whether or not there was an administrative class that might threaten democracy in the United States. Because of the heterogeneity of top administrators, he concluded with a sigh of relief that there was not such a class.

Norton E. Long went a step further. After noting diversity among administrators and a comparatively high homogeneity among legislators, Long declared that "the bureaucracy now has a very real claim to be considered much more representative of the American people in its composition than the Congress."[4] Long had disdain for the legislature. He not only thought of it as deficient because of what he considered its dominance by lawyers, he thought it was weak and irresponsible because of petty partisanship. Long argued that the bureaucracy should increase its representative character by building in a "loyal opposition" to participate in the deliberations on public policies. Even without this, Long took great comfort in the combination of expertise and representativeness that existed in the bureaucracy.

The concept of a representative public bureaucracy, then, denies the separation of politics and administration that Woodrow Wilson described and prescribed in his classic essay.[5] It accepts a vital policy-making role for administrators, and it emphasizes the importance of administrators who are both competent and represent societal values.

There is a fundamental flaw in this reasoning. Although it is conceivable, for example, that a Mexican American who is a U.S. attorney will be partial to Mexican Americans, it is equally plausible that such an individual would be careful to establish a record of professionalism and impartiality. Indeed, Mexican Americans might be relatively disadvantaged as they deal with people trying to make the point that they are not partial to their own ethnic group. Moreover, for most of what U.S. attorneys would do, a Mexican-American background would be irrelevant. The irrelevance of social background would be even clearer if the position were a forest ranger, an accountant, a statistician, or many other types of jobs. Is there an African-American way of being a highway engineer, a female type of architect, or a handicapped approach to contract administration?

This is not to say that there are no circumstances in which social background makes a difference. The missions of some nonprofit organizations and some government agencies suggest the need for hiring people who have the same gender or racial identity as those being served. Women administrators of programs for battered women or rape victims would seem to be sensitive to issues that men might not. Perhaps more importantly, victims of rape and domestic violence might feel more comfortable being cared for by women. Minority professionals working in youth programs would probably implicitly serve as role models and help ensure responsiveness to the needs of minority youth.

Sally Coleman Selden studied public loan programs and found that administrators tended to favor recipients with whom they shared the same gender and/or ethnic identity.[6] Sylvester Murray and his colleagues conducted a survey to gauge the extent to which minority public administrators define their role as advocates for minority interests. They found that 71 percent strongly agreed that they should act as advocates.[7] Survey participants acknowledged, however, that their positions and responsibilities did not always give them an opportunity to pursue concerns of the minority community.

In *Democracy and the Public Service,* Frederick C. Mosher makes a useful distinction between passive and active representation.[8] **Active representation** refers to an expectation that individuals will press for the interests of those whom they represent, whereas **passive representation** concerns the degree to which administrators collectively mirror the composition of the total society. Although some may be dismayed that there is only a modest amount of active representation based on class background, there are dangers to efficiency and democracy when administrators take it on themselves to make unilateral decisions about which public policies should be pursued.[9] Agencies would be shapeless like amoebas if, in an extreme case, everyone ran in a different direction. The lines of accountability to the electorate are most direct and effective to elected officials, not civil servants, and although oversight and direction by legislative bodies is imperfect, it does minimize the insularity and power of the bureaucracy. In any case, there is empirically very little of what Mosher calls active representation.

Passive representation is not, on the other hand, as inconsequential as it may initially appear. As Mosher puts it: "While passive representativeness is no guarantor of democratic decision-making, it carries some independent and symbolic values that are significant for a democratic society."[10] If the social backgrounds of administrators are similar to the pattern of differences in the society as a whole, an agency is regarded as having a **balanced workforce** and there is a strong indication of an open personnel system and equal opportunity for members of various groups to secure employment. An organization with a balanced workforce is not an alien body. African Americans, Mexican Americans, women, and handicapped persons in visible positions in the public bureaucracy serve as role models to others from their respective groups who might aspire to government careers. The symbols of passive representation, in short, can have a substantive effect on both individual mobility patterns and general support for the government.

Not everyone agrees that government should make an effort to have a representative bureaucracy. In *Affirmative Discrimination,* Nathan Glazer complains that an approach classifying people as members of groups violates some of the basic tenets of U.S. democracy that assert the importance of individual rights.[11] It is the pursuit of group interests at the apparent sacrifice of a particular individual that evokes so much emotion when stories (authentic or apocryphal) are told of someone getting a job because they are African American or female.

WHO IS REPRESENTED

Politics defines what groups should be represented in the public bureaucracy. Societal concerns, reflected in part in the political discourse, define the criteria for diversity in nonprofit and government organizations. As pointed out in Chapter 2, states and regions have served as part of the selection criteria in the federal bureaucracy since the beginning of the Republic. George Washington's concern for geographic balance led to the senatorial courtesy convention, and the Pendleton Act gave statutory sanction to the tradition that civil servants in the national government come from all parts of the country. During these periods, society and public policy did not include race or gender as a salient part of workforce diversity.

A major thrust of politics in the mid-twentieth century was to seek an end to formal and informal means of discrimination on the basis of race, national origin, sex, handicap, and age. The achievements of the 1960s and 1970s were not the first steps against discrimination, however. In the aftermath of the Civil War, the federal government began hiring African Americans. In 1867, Solomon J. Johnson became the first recorded African-American civil servant in the federal government. His employment reversed the principle embodied in a law passed in 1810 that said one had to be a free white person in order to work for the government.[12]

The post–Civil War laws had, however, a habit of getting turned on their heads or having only short lives. In 1870, Congress passed a statute designed and intended to give women greater equality. It stated:

> Women may, in the discretion of the head of any department, be appointed to any of the clerkships therein authorized by law, upon the same requisites and conditions, and with same compensations as are prescribed for men.[13]

Paradoxically, this statute was later interpreted to emphasize the discretion of the appointing officer rather than the principle of equal treatment for women. As late as 1919, women were excluded from 60 percent of all civil service examinations. Positions open to women were primarily clerical in nature and virtually all positions were in the lowest ranks of the bureaucracy.

African Americans temporarily benefited not only from post–Civil War legislation but also from the establishment of the merit system. In 1883, at the time the Pendleton Act was passed, there were 620 African Americans in the federal government. In 1892, there were 2,393. The gains African Americans made were soon followed by severe setbacks. The administrations of Presidents Taft and Wilson were particularly harsh. In 1914, there were massive dismissals and demotions of African Americans, and for the first time all job applicants had to submit photos. In the 1920s, the federal government established separate work areas and separate eating and toilet facilities to segregate African Americans from whites. As pointed out earlier, want ads in newspapers had separate columns for jobs available to individuals based on gender and on race.

In the 1960s and 1970s, African Americans and women insisted on an end to exclusion and discrimination. Latinos, the handicapped, and the elderly made their demands in the afterglow of successes by African Americans and women and are now included in what are referred to as **protected classes**, that is, those groups covered by statutes prohibiting discrimination. The relevant statutes are discussed later in this chapter.

Sexual orientation is another characteristic on which discriminatory treatment in employment is prohibited. The U.S. Supreme Court, not Congress, made the key federal policy decision. In *Norton* v. *Macy* (1969), discussed in Chapter 3, the Court said that the Constitution protected public employees from being dismissed because of their sexual orientation. Subsequent to this decision, the now defunct Civil Service Commission and then the Office of Personnel Management both advised federal managers to avoid discrimination against lesbians and gay men.[14] As of the beginning of the twenty-first century, 19 states and almost 150 municipalities specifically prohibited discrimination on the basis of sexual orientation in all employment decisions, not just dismissals.[15]

While current policy generally includes lesbians, gay men, and bisexuals in employment, the issue of representativeness is somewhat different from other categories. In part because sexual orientation is not an obvious and visible trait and is not recorded, we have no way of measuring whether the diversity of a public workforce on this characteristic matches the diversity of society generally. The limitations of measurement have an impact on what managers can do.

MEASURES OF DIVERSITY

The measurement used in academic analyses and in casual discussions is—where possible—to compare the social backgrounds of employees with the social backgrounds of the general society. If the patterns are similar, the workforce is judged to be representative.

The achievement of a workforce that replicates the backgrounds of society generally presupposes not only open hiring practices, but also equal access to educational and other opportunities to prepare for jobs. It also assumes an absence of gender- and race-based stereotypes. If women constitute 50 percent of the population but, because of traditional sex roles and restricted opportunities, comprise only 5 percent of society's civil engineers, then one can hardly expect employers to have women in half of its civil engineer positions. Although the ultimate goal may be a totally integrated and socially balanced workforce in all ranks and occupations, agency managers have had to meet less-demanding standards. The ultimate goal is a very demanding yardstick. Public policy and legal standards for measuring diversity are more grounded in what is currently feasible to achieve.

Standard 1: Those Qualified in the General Workforce

To implement the 1964 Civil Rights Act, the Equal Employment Opportunity Commission (EEOC) initially adopted the standard that the proportion of women, minorities, and handicapped employed in a particular occupational category in an agency should equal the percentages these groups constitute of those in the general workforce with the necessary qualifications. According to these guidelines, for example, if only 5 percent of the qualified civil engineers in the country are women, then employers are expected to retain women in approximately 5 percent of their civil engineer positions.

The EEOC further restricted the measurement of diversity according to the geographic area from which agencies could reasonably be expected to draw new employees. For most positions a region or a metropolitan area was used, although for some highly technical or professional positions, this meant that the potential pool was nationwide.

There is, of course, a problem with this approach. If the expectation that 5 percent of the civil engineers in an organization are to be women is satisfactory because only 5 percent of all civil engineers are women, then there is little incentive for increasing the proportion of qualified women engineers. Employers could, in effect, pass the buck to families and educational institutions when pressed about modest efforts to hire members of minority groups, women, and the handicapped. In a sense, there is the classic chicken-egg dilemma: Which comes first, the opportunity or the qualified individual?

Standard 2: Those Who Apply

In 1978, the EEOC adopted a different standard for measuring compliance with equal employment opportunity policies. It adopted the standard that the Office of Federal Contract Compliance (OFCC) in the Department of Labor used in contracts with nonprofit and business organizations.

The litmus test of this measurement is a comparison of the selection rate for a particular class of people and the selection rate for those outside of that class. The formula for testing probable sex bias would be

$$\frac{\text{Selection rate for women}}{\text{Selection rate for men}} \times 100 = \underline{\hspace{2cm}}$$

Thus, if 25 women applied and three women were selected, the dividend would be 0.12, and if 45 men applied and 15 were selected, the divider would be 0.33. Using these figures in the formula, the result would be 36 percent. According to the guideline, if the selection rate for the protected class is less than 80 percent of the rate for those not in that class, then there is evidence of probable discrimination. In this example, there clearly is an indication of discrimination.

Whereas this standard is not tied to the current supply of qualified individuals, relying on applicants also has its limitations. If an employer wanted to take minimal steps to satisfy this standard, a strategy would be to discourage the number of applications from women, minorities, and the handicapped and then be sure that a relatively high proportion of these groups who did manage to apply were selected. Efforts to limit the number of applicants from particular classes could appear unintentional. Recruitment efforts could be passive and minimal, and those who showed interest in applying might be discouraged and treated brusquely. One might imagine a result in which three African Americans would apply and two would be selected, whereas 65 whites would apply and 30 would be selected. This process would do little to achieve diversity in the employer's workforce, but the comparison of selection rates would surely look good.

THE RECORD

We can use social divisions among the general population as our yardstick for determining whether or not we have a representative bureaucracy. This is the yardstick used by Kingsley, Long, Mosher, and the other scholars cited earlier. Parity between the social identities of civil servants and the population they serve is the long-term objective of open-access selection, and using this measurement provides cues to governments, families, schools, and other social institutions involved in career preparation. A review of where we are in relation to where we want to be is important for the design of programs and strategies for pursuing the ultimate goal.

The EEOC began collecting statistics in 1973 on the composition of workforces by gender and race. It should be recalled that 1972 is the year when the 1964 Civil Rights Act was amended to apply to state and local government.

The record of the public sector since 1972 shows a steady increase in the proportions of employees who are women and members of minority groups. The percent of women working for state and local governments increased from 38 percent in 1973 to 48 percent in 2003. In the federal government, the increase for the same period was 37 percent to 47 percent. Minorities likewise rose. African Americans, for example, rose from 6 percent to 12 percent during this period and Latinos from 5 percent to 11 percent.

The EEOC does not distinguish between nonprofit and for-profit organizations in its analyses and reports. Trends in the private sector generally are similar to those in the public sector and in 2003 women were employed in 48 percent of the jobs, African Americans in 14 percent, and Hispanics in 11 percent.[16] These are aggregate numbers that indicate general progress in diversifying workforces.

These numbers, however, mask differences in job occupations and in particular in distribution throughout levels of the organization. Using 2000 census data, the EEOC reports, for example, that 80.4 percent of clericals are women and only 12.8 percent of those working in crafts are women. Although almost half the general workforce are women, only 35.9 percent are in managerial positions. Similarly, African Americans are concentrated primarily in service positions (23.6 percent) and scarce in professional positions (7.0 percent). While African Americans make up 14 percent of those employed, they represent only 6.8 percent of the managers. Hispanics are primarily in labor jobs (24.3 percent) and few are professionals (4.0 percent). They fill only 3.1 of the managerial jobs, even though they represent 11 percent of those who are employed.[17]

The concern about the lack of progress in achieving balanced representation at the top has led to the suspicion that there is a **glass ceiling**, or **sticky floor** (i.e., an artificial, nonjob-related barrier to the advancement of women and minority employees). Governments at all levels established task forces in the early 1990s to determine whether such barriers existed and, if so, what might be done to overcome them. The glass ceiling issue is discussed in greater detail in Chapter 11 on employee development.

The patterns of continued imbalance, despite progress, suggests that charges of reverse discrimination are born more out of fear than fact and in some cases more out of opposition to diversity than concern about unintended consequences. The attainment of social representation throughout the workforce requires more than general policies of nondiscrimination. If the policy objectives of the 1964 Civil Rights Act had been attained, the profile of the current public workforce would be more socially representative than it is. An individual entering elementary school when the Civil Rights Act was passed in 1964 could have earned a masters degree and have had over 30 years of progressing through the ranks to a relatively senior position as we near 2010. The evidence is that not many women or minority group members have had that success. Clearly, a need continues for avoiding discrimination and achieving diversity in the workplace.[19]

BOX 4.1

IMPORTANT FEDERAL LAWS AND COURT CASES ESTABLISHING EQUAL EMPLOYMENT OPPORTUNITY POLICY

Title and Date	Major Provisions
1964 Civil Rights Act, Title VII	Prohibits discrimination in employment in the private sector on the basis of race, color, religion, sex, or national origin. Establishes the Equal Employment Opportunity Commission (EEOC) to implement the act.

BOX 4.1 (*Continued*)

1971 *Griggs, et al.* v. *Duke Power*	Affirms the authority of the EEOC to issue guidelines that assume discrimination if an employer's workforce is unbalanced and that require job-related and valid selection processes.
1972 Equal Employment Opportunity Act	Extends provisions of 1964 Civil Act Rights Act to local and state governments and covers all employers with 15 or more employees.
1973 Vocational Rehabilitation Act	Encourages and assists employers so they will hire handicapped persons.
1974 Age Discrimination Act	Prohibits discrimination on the basis of age.
1978 *University of California* v. *Bakke*	Declares that hiring and admissions quotas to achieve a balanced workforce or student population violate equal protection rights under the Fourteenth Amendment.
1979 *Weber* v. *United Steelworkers*	Permits affirmative action programs to train and promote minorities, as long as other routes to advancement are available to nonminorities.
1981 *Texas Department of Community Affairs* v. *Burdine*	Establishes a three-step procedure for determining whether an employer is guilty of discrimination.
1984 *Cleveland Firefighters Local* v. *Stotts*	Prohibits layoff procedures that give special protections to employees on racial basis.
1986 *Wygant* v. *Jackson (MI)*	Prohibits a labor agreement that allows board of education to lay off some white teachers with more seniority before minority teachers of less seniority in order to maintain racial balance.
1987 *United States* v. *Paradise*	Supports court-ordered quota system as mechanism for enforcing desegregation decree in face of refusal to implement court rulings to end a discriminatory practice.
1987 *Johnson* v. *Transportation Agency of Santa Clara, CA*	Permits consideration of gender as a factor in making promotions when candidates are about equal.
1989 *Wards Cove Packing Co.* v. *Atonio*	Requires plaintiff to identify employment practice responsible for disparate impact on members of protected classes.
1989 *Martin* v. *Wilks*	Allows a challenge to a consent decree by white males who were not a party to the original decree.
1990 Americans with Disabilities Act	Orders employers to make reasonable accommodation to needs of disabled person unless doing so causes undue hardship on the employer.
1991 Civil Rights Act	Overturns *Wards Cove* and *Wilks* cases, establishes limits on damages, and repeats ban on quotas.

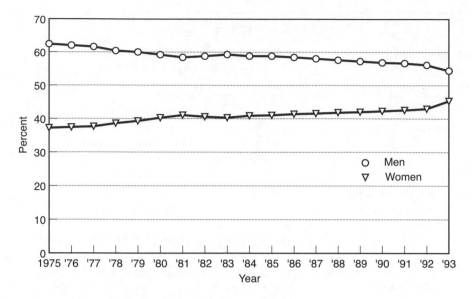

FIGURE 4.1   Men and Women in State and Local Governments.
Source: Equal Employment Opportunity Commission, *Job Patterns for Minorities and Women in State and Local Government* (Washington, DC: Government Printing Office, 1993), ix.

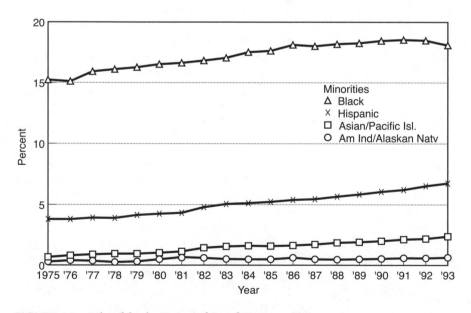

FIGURE 4.2   Minorities in State and Local Governments.
Source: Equal Employment Opportunity Commission, *Job Patterns for Minorities and Women in State and Local Government* (Washington, DC: Government Printing Office, 1993), ix.

THE LEGAL MANDATES

Affirmative Action and Reverse Discrimination

The public policy of achieving a diverse workforce has been accompanied by an ongoing debate about how aggressive employers should be in pursuing diversity and about how concerned we need to be about the effects of this policy on white males. **Equal employment opportunity** is the minimal approach, which is to avoid discriminatory practices. The limitation is that this is a passive posture, which accepts the adverse effects of past or current discrimination elsewhere in society. **Affirmative action** is the term used to refer to aggressive methods of correcting injustices. This is supposed to be a temporary effort that will last only as long as remedies are needed. Reverse discrimination refers to instances where white males are disadvantaged by efforts to achieve diverse representation.

Laws and court rulings have been clear and consistent: reverse discrimination and **quotas** are illegal.[20] The only exception is the rare instance when a court mandates a quota system when an employer persists in refusing to comply with orders to correct discriminatory employment practices. The clear legal mandate is for equal employment opportunities. The more proactive affirmative action policy is not legally mandated but may be pursued in order to achieve diversity after a history of discrimination—but still only as long as it does not exclude white males from consideration.[21]

The fundamental legislative statement is Title VII of the 1964 Civil Rights Act. The act is broad in scope. Other titles prohibit discrimination in housing, public accommodations, and other areas of life. At the time of its passage, in fact, discrimination in employment was not a major focus of attention. Likewise, discrimination on the basis of sex was not a major concern of Congress. Representative Howard Smith of Virginia proposed adding gender as a discriminatory category in an effort to make the bill seem so broad and impractical that it would not get enough votes to pass. The strategy backfired. The House passed the amendment on a 168 to 133 vote and the Senate agreed to keep this provision.[22] Gender-based as well as race-based discrimination was outlawed. According to the 1964 act, it is unlawful for an employer

> to fail or refuse to hire or to discharge any individual, or otherwise discriminate against any individual with respect to his [sic] compensation, terms, conditions, or privileges of employment, because of such individual's race, color, religion, sex, or national origin.[23]

As mentioned previously, the 1964 Act was amended in 1972 to extend coverage beyond the private sector to state and local governments. The federal government is covered by a provision in the 1978 Civil Service Reform Act that reads as follows:

> All employees and applicants for employment should receive fair and equitable treatment in all aspects of personnel management without regard to political affiliation, race, color, religion, national origin, sex, marital status, age, or handicapping condition, and with proper regard for their privacy and constitutional rights.[24]

The scope of the federal Civil Service Reform bill is broader than that in the 1964 Civil Rights Act. Age and handicap were not included in the 1964 legislation, but they were added later. The 1974 Age Discrimination Act outlaws discrimination against persons 40 or more years old. The 1990 Americans with Disabilities Act requires employers to make reasonable accommodation to enable persons with disabilities to work. All states and major cities have local laws that overlap to some extent with federal legislation. In addition, 19 states and about two-thirds of the major cities prohibit discrimination because of criminal record or sexual orientation.[25]

The Eleventh Amendment to the U.S. Constitution limits the extent to which state and local governments are liable under the federal laws prohibiting discrimination. The Eleventh Amendment generally does not allow suits against state and local governments without their consent. In *Kimel et al.* v. *Florida Board of Regents* (2000), the U.S. Supreme Court ruled that individuals charging discrimination based on disability could not sue state and local governments. The following year, *University of Alabama* v. *Garrett* (2001), the Court applied the same immunity in cases of age discrimination. The Court essentially followed a principle that there is not necessarily a legally available remedy when for some reason a person or organization breaks a law. The Court, in both of these cases, however, was clear that while it was prepared to extend Eleventh Amendment immunity in cases of age and disability, it was not applying this to cases that involve gender, race, religion, or national origin. The kind of discrimination cited in the 1964 Civil Rights Act is considered to violate more basic rights.

The 1964 legislation established the **Equal Employment Opportunities Commission (EEOC)** to ensure the implementation of Title VII of the Civil Rights Act. The EEOC was to establish guidelines for fulfilling the public policy objectives embodied in the legislation, receive complaints of noncompliance, monitor employer activity, and bring legal suits against violators. The creation of the EEOC was critically important. Here now was an agency whose sole mission was to combat discrimination in employment. This agency had in its arsenal the very powerful authority to promulgate rules and to prosecute cases in court.

Job-related Criteria

The first major court ruling involving the 1964 Civil Rights Act and the authority of the EEOC was *Griggs, et al.* v. *Duke Power Company* (1971). After the passage of the 1964 legislation, Duke Power Company formally ended its policy confining African Americans to low-paying, low-skilled jobs. The company then established a new screening procedure for middle- and high-level jobs. The procedure included a requirement that applicants have a high school diploma and pass a standardized test on general vocabulary, knowledge, and aptitudes. This was not a screening process that examined individuals according to how prepared they were to do any particular job. Because of the social circumstances in the South, the requirements of a high school diploma and certain scores on a standardized test had the effect of making most African Americans ineligible for consideration for anything but the low-level jobs. A group of African Americans, adversely affected by this change in company policy, initiated legal action.

The U.S. Supreme Court supported the EEOC and the plaintiffs. In explaining its decision, the Court established two fundamental principles:

1. The 1964 Civil Rights Act allows legal action based on effects, without having to prove intent.   Intent is difficult to establish. If there is evidence that a manager did not want to hire someone because of his or her race, religion, gender, or age, the evidence can, of course, be used in court. The *Griggs* ruling allows an individual to present a case based on the effects of a particular practice, regardless of whether the intent of using the practice was to discriminate.

2. Examinations, required credentials, and other screening devices must be job-related.   *Griggs* specified how employers could defend themselves against the charge that a practice, whether or not intended, was discriminatory. The Court said that if the practice was a "business necessity," then it could be used even if it had the effect of screening out members of a protected class. Managers do not have to hire people who lack the skills and abilities to do the job. If certain minority groups have not had the opportunity to get the education genuinely needed to do a particular job, then a manager would not have to lower the qualifications even if not doing so disadvantaged minorities.

Disparate Impact and Disparate Treatment

In applying the policies and principles of nondiscrimination, the Court has developed the concepts of **disparate impact** and **disparate treatment**. The former is when an employment practice has an effect on an entire category of employees or applicants for employment. The *Griggs* case, for example, is about criteria used that kept almost all African Americans from holding senior-level positions in the company. In this and similar cases, a class-action suit is filed and the court ruling affects all applicants or employees of the race or gender that filed the suit.

Disparate treatment, in contrast, is when an individual is treated unfairly because of gender, race, religion, or other protected trait. Individuals make complaints and pursue litigation when the issue is a charge of disparate treatment. They must show that "but for" their race or religion or gender, they would have received more favorable treatment in the hiring, promotional, or other employment decision that was made. Only the individual pursuing a disparate treatment case benefits directly from a favorable ruling. Others may benefit indirectly if the case prompts an employer to change a particular practice or procedure.

Sometimes, disparate treatment cases involve the possibility of mixed reasons for why an individual was not hired or promoted or otherwise favored. The Supreme Court considered such a case when it ruled in *Price-Waterhouse* v. *Hopkins* (1989). The evaluations the partners (all of whom were men) made in this accounting firm of a woman they were considering for promotion included positive and negative performance appraisals. In addition, there were some sexist judgments. One evaluation criticized her for being "too masculine" and said she should dress and act more femininely. Some of the other evaluations relied similarly on sexual stereotypes. The Justices indicated that the use of sex-based traits that were not job-related when making employment decisions was unlawful. However, they also recognized that it was quite possible that Ms. Hopkins would not have been promoted to partner even if there were none of the gender issues present. They ruled that in order to prevail, an employee must demonstrate that the discriminatory criterion was the *predominant* reason for the treatment received.

Congress disagreed with this application of the laws. In the 1991 Civil Rights Act, legislators included a provision which specifies that in mixed-motive cases, an employee or applicant for employment need only show that discriminatory criteria were a *contributing* factor in order to win. The 1991 act, however, somewhat limits the liability of employers in these cases. If an employer can demonstrate that the same decision to hire, promote, fire, and so forth would have been made even if there had been no inappropriate use of race or gender as a factor, then the employer would have to pay monetary damages and attorney's fees but would not have to hire, promote, or reinstate the individual.

Burden of Proof

The Supreme Court has elaborated on the criteria and processes for determining when employment practices are discriminatory. In *McDonnell Douglas Corporation* v. *Green* (1973) and even more clearly in *Texas Department of Community Affairs* v. *Burdine* (1981), the Court summarized and reaffirmed the lessons of previous decisions. A three-step process is to be followed:

1. A prima facie case of discrimination is established.   In a disparate impact case, this usually means showing that discrimination seems apparent when using the EEOC selection ratio standard or comparisons between the employer's workforce and the proportion of qualified individuals who are in protected classes.

A **prima facie** case of discrimination in a disparate treatment case typically requires some evidence that *but for* an individual's race or gender, given how other employees or applicants have fared, the individual lodging the complaint would have benefited from an employment decision.

2. The employer must provide evidence that legitimate, job-related, nondiscriminatory reasons were used in the decision.   Employment practices that result in the exclusion of women, minorities, or members of other protected classes can be defended if they are job-related.

3. Those making the challenge must prove that the reasons offered by the employer were actually a pretext for discrimination.   This can be done by showing that the practice is not job-related and/or that other well known, nondiscriminatory approaches are available to meet the employer's needs. In short, the task here is to show that the employer's defense offered in step two is **pretextual**, i.e., not a credible reason for discriminating.

The *Burdine* standards and processes were temporarily modified when the Supreme Court ruled in *Wards Cove Packing Company, Inc.* v. *Frank Atonio* (1989).[26]

Congress responded to this ruling by passing the 1991 Civil Rights Act, which included statutory endorsement of the *Burdine* process, thereby overturning the Court.

Quotas and Reverse Discrimination

Another provision of the 1991 legislation was language making it clear that employers could not use quotas as a way of hiring or retaining a diversified workforce. While this clause responded to a political demand, it was redundant. The U.S. Supreme Court had already ruled that neither the 1964 Civil Rights Act nor the U.S. Constitution allowed for quotas. The first critical case on quotas was *University of California Regents* v. *Bakke* (1978).

Allan Bakke, a white male, applied to the University of California–Davis Medical School. In the system used to rank applicants, he scored slightly below those admitted through the general admissions process but above some African Americans who were admitted through a process established to fill four positions reserved for minority group members. The U.S. Supreme Court was bothered by the exclusiveness of the quota system. The Court made the obvious observation that a quota system intended to grant preference to a disadvantaged group operates on the same principles as an exclusionary system that seeks to preserve advantages for the already advantaged. Instead of saying, "Blacks need not apply," for the positions in question, UC-Davis was in essence saying, "Whites need not apply." The Court ruled that racial quotas to achieve representation were in violation of the Constitution.[27]

The Supreme Court did sanction racial quotas in the extraordinary case where a public employer, the Alabama Department of Public Safety, refused for nine years to comply with a federal court order to end discrimination against African Americans. In order to enforce its own ruling, the district court, in 1981, required the state to promote one qualified African American for every white officer it promoted. This requirement applied to any rank with less than 25 percent African Americans. Note that this unusual use of quotas was to implement a court order, not legislation, and the state was to promote *qualified* officers, whether white or African American. The U.S. Supreme Court upheld this specific use of quotas in *United States* v. *Paradise* (1987). Other public employers that had to use quota systems because they refused to obey court orders included agencies in Milwaukee, Wisconsin; Buffalo, New York; and Birmingham, Alabama.

Employer Protections

Although the primary purpose of the 1964 Civil Rights Act and the legislation that followed was to end discrimination and to ensure employment opportunities for people without regard for age, handicap, race, gender, or religion, legislators and justices have been careful to recognize and protect the need of public agencies and private businesses for competent and committed human resources. Beginning with the *Griggs* ruling, courts have accepted the requirements of the job and the organization as a defense of what seems to be a pattern of discrimination. In addition, the term **bona fide occupational qualification (BFOQ)** is used formally and explicitly to recognize when a job is limited to individuals of a specific gender or race or religion. Examples of such jobs are chaplains and prison employees who must conduct body searches. Courts construe the BFOQ narrowly and the burden of proof for a BFOQ claim is on the employer.

Some nonprofit organizations have explicit and broad coverage under BFOQ principles. Sections 702 and 703 of Title VII of the 1964 Civil Rights Act included provisions that permit religious organizations to give preferential treatment to hiring members of their respective religions, even if the job duties are not 0religious in nature. In court cases that tested issues beyond hiring, the Salvation Army successfully defended paying women less than men doing ministerial work on the grounds that the relationship between a religious organization and its clergy was exempt from the 1964 Civil Rights Act's prohibitions against employment discrimination.[28]

The Americans with Disabilities Act (ADA) also affirms the right of managers to get the work of their organizations done while pursuing policies designed to balance workforces. The ADA balances the mandate that employers provide "reasonable accommodation" with the explicit provision that makes it clear organizations do not have to suffer "undue hardship." Reasonable accommodation is also the standard for balancing job requirements and an employee's religious practices, as explained in Chapter 3. Admittedly, reasonable accommodation and undue hardship are not terms of precision and they invite case-by-case judgments. Managers should, however, be skeptical of those who advise timidity in the face of potential confrontation. The policy is to achieve equal opportunities and diversity without sacrificing quality of service or the efficiency of operation.[29]

Affirmative Action

President Lyndon B. Johnson explained affirmative action by using an analogy of a race in which one runner was in shackles and eating a poor diet while the other was exercising to stay in shape and eating well. Equal opportunity would be to place both runners at the same starting line and then letting them race to a common finish line. Affirmative action would be to remove the shackles from the one runner and help him or her get in shape before starting the race.[30]

In *United Steelworkers* v. *Weber* (1979), the Court upheld the legality of affirmative action programs, as long as they focus on getting everyone ready to run the race, rather than excluding some from even running. United Steelworkers and Kaiser Aluminum agreed to train African-American employees at a plant in Louisiana so that they might be better prepared to compete for higher-level jobs. Brian Weber, a white male, claimed that he was denied access to the training program simply because of his race. Admittedly, the program to which Weber objected was a special effort to upgrade the skills of African-American employees, but the program did not guarantee promotions to participants and the program was not the only route to securing advancement within the company. The Court concluded that when Congress passed the 1964 Civil Rights Act, it sanctioned—even though it did not mandate—race-conscious affirmative action programs. This upward mobility program did not violate Weber's constitutionally protected rights, and it was allowed to continue.

The Court ruled in 1987 that managers seeking to diversify their workforces have the discretion to use race or gender as a factor when considering candidates with similar scores. The Santa Clara County Transportation Agency promoted a woman, Diane Joyce, to a position of road dispatcher. Paul Johnson, who had scored 2 points more than Joyce in a promotional examination sued, charging that he was denied the job because he was male. The county justified its decision on the grounds that the 2-point difference was insignificant and that Joyce's promotion helped correct an imbalance in social representation in that job category. The agency managers were, moreover, acting under an affirmative action plan that authorized consideration of gender as a factor in making promotions to positions that had traditionally been sex-segregated. At the time of the promotion decision, women filled none of the 238 skilled craft positions. In *Johnson* v. *Transportation Agency, Santa Clara* (1987) the Court agreed with the county and noted that the agency did not have a quota system excluding men from consideration.

The University of Michigan was sued in two cases that allowed the Court to develop further the limits of affirmative action.

In *Gratz* v. *Bollinger* (2003) the Court considered the Wolverine's approach to undergraduate admissions. The University of Michigan had a point system for admitting applicants. Points were awarded for high school grade point average, ACT/SAT scores, extra-curricular activities, and—important here—racial status. The Court ruled that the effects of using racial status in this point system were to disadvantage and to exclude in a systematic way based on their ethnic identity. In *Gutter* v. *Bollinger* (2003), the Court considered and approved the admissions approach that the University of Michigan Law School used, which considered race and gender of applicants in order to reach a goal of having a diverse student body, but reviewed all candidates on a case-by-case basis. The lesson, in other words, is that schools and employers may take steps to achieve diversity, but these steps may not include a systematic way that favors or disadvantages individuals because of their race or gender.

DIVERSITY PLANNING

Almost all employers with more than 2,000 employees have specific plans for diversity and sometimes a separate office that is responsible for affirmative action policy development and implementation. The Supreme Court decisions discussed in this chapter provide principles that define the following appropriate diversity plans:

1. The plan is designed to end any existing patterns of segregation.
2. The plan is a conscious effort to remove the effects of past discrimination.
3. The plan does not exclude white men from job or promotional opportunities.
4. The plan is a temporary measure.

Two basic functions of affirmative action offices are reporting and planning. To comply with federal regulations the Equal Employment Opportunity Commission has issued, employers must compile records on the social composition of their workforces and on the backgrounds of applicants. If there were no records, no one inside or outside the agency would be able to determine if there were apparent patterns of discrimination.

The reporting function includes monitoring the behavior and decisions of managers. This almost inevitably causes tension between managers and central staff, primarily because the latter focus on the goal of having a diverse workforce whereas managers have responsibility for multiple goals.

Diversity planning is an effort to specify objectives, strategies, and timetables so that the goal of a socially representative workforce does not get lost amidst all of the tasks and responsibilities of managers. Explicit statements of the direction in which an organization is headed will, it is hoped, make more certain that behavior conforms to goals. Affirmative action officers typically do not have the authority to force compliance. They rely heavily on the process of formulating plans and on the existence of plans to generate the thought and support among managers necessary for implementation.

Typically, diversity plans include the following:

1. Identification of where the workforce is unbalanced and what the major problems are
2. Recruitment strategies to attract applicants in areas where there are shortages of women, minorities, and handicapped workers
3. Programs for training, mentoring, transferring, and developing existing women, minorities, and handicapped employees
4. Efforts to make the workplace environment supportive for a diverse workforce
5. Training designed to inform supervisors about relevant laws and to educate them about the principles and issues of affirmative action
6. Goals and timetables for securing a more diverse workforce

Because of the heavy reliance on cooperation and voluntary compliance in making the plan a reality, central human resource or affirmative action offices seek participation by managers in the construction of the plan. Managers can help make sure that plans are realistic. Also, through their participation, managers can better understand and identify with the provisions of the plan.

Increasingly central offices serve as consultants and work with agency managers to foster change in organizational culture to ensure hospitable and supportive work environment for diverse workforces. Managers typically hire new employees occasionally, but they work daily within a culture that succeed or fail, stay or quit.[31] Key ingredients to effective management of a diverse workforce are clear support from the top, participation and sensitivity from co-workers, and genuine respect for all employees.[32]

TABLE 4.1 EXECUTIVE BRANCH (NON-POSTAL) EMPLOYMENT BY GENDER, RACE/NATIONAL ORIGIN, DISABILITY STATUS, VETERANS STATUS, DISABLED VETERANS

	1982–1992					
	1982	1984	1986	1988	1990	1992
TOTAL (SEPTEMBER)	2,008,605	2,023,333	2,083,985	2,125,148	2,150,359	2,175,715
Gender						
Women	788,868	809,095	861,182	897,099	927,104	945,546
Percentage of women	39.3	40.0	41.3	42.2	43.1	43.5
Men	1,219,737	1,214,238	1,222,803	1,228,049	1,223,255	1,230,169
Percentage of men	60.7	60.0	58.7	57.8	56.9	56.5
Race/National Origin						
Non-Minority	1,524,598	1,520,445	1,542,203	1,557,793	1,562,846	1,570,812
Percentage of non-minorities	75.9	75.1	74.0	73.3	72.7	72.2
Total Minorities	484,007	502,888	541,782	567,355	587,513	604,903
Percentage of minorities	24.1	24.9	26.0	26.7	27.3	27.8
Black	311,131	317,875	339,770	350,052	356,867	360,725
Percentage of blacks	15.5	15.7	16.3	16.5	16.6	16.6
Hispanic	89,967	95,580	105,191	109,566	115,170	120,296
Percentage of Hispanics	4.5	4.7	5.0	5.2	5.4	5.5
Asian/Pacific Islander	49,043	56,018	62,137	70,032	76,312	81,522
Percentage of Asian/Pacific Isl.	2.4	2.8	3.0	3.3	3.5	3.7
Am. Indian/Alaska Nat.	33,866	33,415	34,684	37,705	39,164	42,360
Percentage of Am. Ind./Ak. Nat.	1.7	1.7	1.7	1.8	1.8	1.9
Disability						
Disabled	124,381	126,214	128,123	132,317	140,169	153,197
Percentage of disabled	6.9	6.9	6.6	6.6	6.9	7.4

(*Continued*)

TABLE 4.1 (CONTINUED)

| | 1982–1992 | | | | | |
	1982	1984	1986	1988	1990	1992
TOTAL (SEPTEMBER)	2,008,605	2,023,333	2,083,985	2,125,148	2,150,359	2,175,715
EEOC specified disab.	18,271	20,324	22,424	23,652	24,619	25,896
Percentage of EEOC spac. disab.	1.0	1.1	1.2	1.2	1.2	1.2
Not disabled	1,667,061	1,715,955	1,801,530	1,861,080	1,897,843	1,923,856
Percentage of not disabled	93.1	93.1	93.4	93.4	93.1	92.6
Not identified	217,163	181,164	154,332	131,751	112,347	98,662
Percentage of not identified	10.8	9.0	7.4	6.2	5.2	4.5
All Veterans	N/A	761,082	730,703	681,571	641,469	612,631
Percentage of veterans*		37.7	35.1	32.1	29.8	28.9
Vietnam era veteran	N/A	315,328	352,241	362,734	364,358	347,901
Percentage of all veterans		41.4	48.2	53.2	56.8	56.8
Non-Vietnam era veterans	N/A	445,754	378,462	318,837	277,111	264,730
Percentage of all veterans		58.6	51.8	46.8	43.2	43.2
Nonveterans	N/A	1,257,261	1,353,185	1,443,509	1,508,810	1,510,787
Percentage of non-veterans*		62.3	64.9	67.9	70.2	71.1
Disabled veterans						
All disabled veterans	N/A	92,177	91,797	90,087	89,918	90,752
Percentage of all veterans		12.1	12.6	13.2	14.0	14.8
30%+Disabled vets	N/A	20,854	25,398	27,191	28,908	30,323
Percentage of disabled vets		22.6	27.7	30.2	32.1	33.4
Percentage of all veterans		2.7	3.5	4.0	4.5	4.9

N/A = Data Not Available

*Army and Air Force National Guard Bureaus are excluded from percentage calculations of veterans and non-veterans.

Source: U.S. Office of Personnel Management, Central Personnel Data File.

TABLE 4.2 EXECUTIVE BRANCH EMPLOYMENT OF TOTAL, WOMEN, AND MINORITIES BY WHITE-COLLAR OCCUPATIONAL CATEGORY, *1982–1992*

Employment by PATCO Category

	1982		1984		1986		1988		1990		1992	
	Number	%	Total Number	%	Total Number	%	Total Number	%	Total Number	%	Total Number	% Total
Occupational Category												
Professional	352,672	22.2	371,223	23.1	388,367	23.2	415,545	23.9	463,576	26.0	484,566	26.6
Administrative	413,044	26.0	440,089	27.4	472,990	28.2	508,063	29.2	512,204	28.8	548,397	30.1
Technical	351,297	22.1	348,187	21.7	359,035	21.4	373,294	21.5	388,534	21.8	415,883	22.8
Clerical	429,538	27.1	406,581	25.3	415,309	24.8	401,047	23.1	373,768	21.0	322,073	17.7
Other	40,415	2.5	40,147	2.5	40,540	2.4	40,962	2.4	42,792	2.4	50,796	2.8
Total White-Collar Women	1,586,953	100.0	1,606,227	100.0	1,676,241	100.0	1,738,911	100.0	1,780,874	100.0	1,821,715	100.0
Occupational Category												
Professional	91,349	25.9	101,139	27.2	112,887	29.1	128,083	30.8	156,294	33.7	170,416	35.2
Administrative	128,282	31.1	147,078	33.4	166,819	35.3	188,657	37.1	196,062	38.3	218,737	39.9
Technical	158,128	45.0	165,031	47.4	178,684	49.8	193,084	51.7	211,540	54.4	233,553	56.2
Clerical	363,448	84.6	348,209	85.6	354,567	85.4	340,836	85.0	316,573	84.7	273,947	85.1
Other	3,272	8.1	3,255	8.1	3,296	8.1	3,759	9.2	4,903	11.5	9,022	17.8
Total W-C Women*	744,479	46.9	764,712	47.6	816,253	48.7	854,419	49.1	885,372	49.7	905,675	49.7
Minorities												
Professional	46,610	13.2	51,822	14.0	58,599	15.1	66,885	16.1	80,666	17.4	87,852	18.1
Administrative	68,255	16.5	78,692	17.9	87,594	18.5	98,152	19.3	103,143	20.1	115,670	21.1
Technical	88,619	25.2	92,208	26.5	100,276	27.9	108,828	29.2	118,816	30.6	133,078	32.0
Clerical	132,314	30.8	133,601	32.9	147,598	35.5	151,268	37.7	146,466	39.2	129,190	40.1
Other	11,620	28.8	11,486	28.6	12,250	30.2	12,849	31.4	13,753	32.1	17,866	35.2
Total W-C Minorities*	347,418	21.9	367,809	22.9	406,317	24.2	437,982	25.2	462,844	26.0	483,656	26.5

*% based on total white collar.

Source: U.S. Office of Personnel Management, Central Personnel Data File.

SUMMARY

There are strong public policy mandates to end discrimination in employment and to achieve workforce diversification. These mandates apply to all but the smallest of employers. A socially representative staff indicates openness and access to employment, and to educational and career opportunities in general. For many, the pattern of social backgrounds of civil servants, at all levels, is an important determinant of how they will feel toward government and toward a particular organization.

Part of the conflict in the pursuit of a diverse workforce is over how aggressive managers should be. Should the standards of affirmative action or equal employment apply? Does the concern go beyond compliance with legal mandates to the active pursuit of a goal?

An implication of a diverse workforce, no matter how attained, is that managers will be challenged to support and motivate their employees. The traditional assumptions of a homogeneous set of workers no longer apply. Chapters that follow explain ways in which diversity can be recognized and adjustments made.

Public personnel management policies seem full of misnomers. In Chapter 3 it was noted that merit most directly means a prohibition against partisan patronage rather than competence or abilities. In fact, the so-called merit system was installed to provide an advantage to white, English-speaking groups. Similarly, the term affirmative action has fostered misunderstanding. The laws and Court rulings certainly do not sanction reverse discrimination, and, while there have been improvements in the social representation of public workforces, imbalances remain. Ironically, the efforts to avoid continued discrimination have emphasized merit more than anything else. The primary defense against charges of bias is that personnel decisions and activities are based on what the job requires. The next chapter discusses productivity, which is a presumed outcome from a workforce that is hired according to job requirements rather than partisanship or prejudice.

DISCUSSION QUESTIONS

1. What are the benefits of having a diversified workforce that reflects the social characteristics of the population generally?
2. Is it OK to insist that only women be hired by an organization providing service and support to victims of domestic violence or rape?
3. The federal statutes do not list lesbians and gay men along with women, racial minorities, and the like as protected against employment discrimination. What are the implications of this?
4. What, if anything, limits a manager who is eager to diversify his or her workforce?
5. Describe what you project will be the social profile of employees in a given organization (your choice) in ten years. What should a manager do to be supportive of such a workforce?

GLOSSARY

Active representation   The pattern when an individual represents a group by consciously seeking group members' opinions and advice and then trying to influence policies accordingly

Affirmative action Positive, proactive steps, taken on a temporary basis, to correct the effects of past discriminatory practices

X **Balanced workforce** A situation in which employees in an agency have the same distribution of social backgrounds as found in the public generally

Bona fide occupational qualification (BFOQ) A job requirement that allows excluding members of a certain gender or race, even though usually that would be a prohibited discriminatory practice

Disparate impact A discriminatory practice that affects an entire category of employees or applicants for employment

Disparate treatment An instance of discrimination that affects a particular individual

Equal employment opportunity A situation in which there is no discrimination on prohibited grounds

Equal Employment Opportunity Commission (EEOC) The federal agency authorized to ensure implementation of the 1964 Civil Rights Act and similar legislation by promulgating rules based on the statutes and adjudicating disputes that arise when applying the laws

Glass ceiling A pattern in an organization in which women and minorities do not progress or rarely progress beyond a certain level

Passive representation The idea that an individual represents the group to which he or she belongs because they naturally share the values and perspectives of the group and will apply them when making or implementing policy

Pretextual A defense, which is not credible, that tries to explain why a pattern of discriminatory treatment has occurred

Prima facie A case that on the surface seems like discrimination has occurred

Protected classes Those categories or groups identified in the statutes as having legal status in discrimination lawsuits

Quota A predetermined percentage or ratio used to select candidates for employment, training, or a similar opportunity

Representative bureaucracy A public workforce that has the same pattern of gender, race, and similar characteristics as the society as a whole

Reverse discrimination Adverse treatment of white men, based on their race and gender

Sticky floor Another term for glass ceiling

SOURCES

Glazer, N. (1975). *Affirmative discrimination: Ethnic inequality and public policy.* New York: Basic Books.
An articulation of the philosophical concerns about affirmative action and what the author regards as an all but inevitable process leading to reverse discrimination.

Ocon, Ralph. (2006). *Issues on gender and diversity in management.* Lanham, MY: University Press of America.
A review and discussion of the broad scope of concerns organizations face about diversification of their workforces.

Rosenfeld, M. (1991). *Affirmative action and justice: A philosophical and constitutional inquiry.* New Haven, CT: Yale University Press.
A defense of affirmative action based on an examination of U.S. political and constitutional principles.

Whalen, C., & Whalen, B. (1985). *The longest debate: A legislative history of the civil rights act.* New York: Mentor Books.
A detailed explanation of the political and legislative history of the 1964 Civil Rights Act.

NOTES

1. David Rosenbloom, *Federal Service and the Constitution: The Development of the Public Employment Relationship* (Ithaca, NY: Cornell University Press, 1971), 124.
2. J. Donald Kingsley, *Representative Bureaucracy* (Yellow Springs, OH: Antioch Press, 1944), 275.
3. Reinhard Bendix, *Higher Civil Servants in American Society* (Boulder: University of Colorado Press, 1949).
4. Norton E. Long, *The Polity* (Chicago: Rand McNally, 1962), 71–72.
5. Woodrow Wilson, "The Study of Administration," *Political Science Quarterly* 2 (June 1887): 197–222.
6. Sally Coleman Selden, *The Promise of Representative Bureaucracy: Diversity and Responsiveness in a Government Agency* (Armonk, NY: M.E. Sharpe, 1997)
7. Sylvester Murray, Larry D. Terry, Charles A. Washington, and Lawrence F. Keller, "The Role Demands and Dilemmas of Minority Public Administrators: The Hervert Thesis Revisited," *Public Administration Review* 54, no. 5 (September/October 1994): 409–417.
8. Frederick C. Mosher, *Democracy and the Public Service* (New York: Oxford University Press, 1968), 12.
9. For a strong and exaggerated statement of this point, see Victor A. Thompson, *Without Sympathy or Enthusiasm: The Problem of Administrative Compassion* (Tuscaloosa, AL: University of Alabama Press, 1975).
10. Mosher, *Democracy and the Public Service,* 13.
11. Nathan Glazer, *Affirmative Discrimination: Ethnic Inequality and Public Policy* (New York: Basic Books, 1975).
12. The law specifically addressed the employment of mail carriers, but the requirement was applied throughout the federal government. See David H. Rosenbloom, *Federal Equal Employment Opportunity: Politics and Public Personnel Administration* (New York: Praeger, 1977), 52.
13. U.S. Revised Statutes, no. 165, U.S. code (1964 ed.), vol. 5, 33 (July 12, 1870); originally U.S. Statutes at Large, no. 16,250.
14. Charles W. Gossett, "Lesbians and Gay Men in the Public Sector Work Force," in Carolyn Ban and Norma M. Riccucci, eds., *Public Personnel Management: Current Concerns, Future Challenges,* 2nd ed. (New York: Longman, 1997), 123–138.
15. Roddrick A. Colvin, "Improving State Policies Prohibiting Public Employment Discrimination Based on Sexual Orientation," *Review of Public Personnel Administration* 20, no. 2 (Spring 2000): 5–19.
16. U.S. Equal Employment Opportunity Commission, *Characteristics of Private Sector Employment* www.eeoc.gov/stats/jobpat
17. *Ibid.*, 14–16.
18. Bonnie G.Mani, "Gender and the Federal Senior Executive Service: Where is the Glass Ceiling?" *Public Personnel Management* 26, no. 4 (Winter 1997): 545–558.
19. Robert Gest, "Gaining Practical Insights from Experience: Reflections on Cases of Racial Discrimination in the Federal Service," *Review of Public Personnel Administration* 20, no. 1 (Winter 2000): 54–67.
20. Michel Rosenfeld, *Affirmative Action and Justice: A Philosophical and Constitutional Inquiry* (New Haven: Yale University Press, 1991).
21. R. A. Lee, "The Evolution of Affirmative Action," *Public Personnel Management* 28, no. 3 (Fall 1999): 393–408.
22. Charles and Barbara Whalen, *The Longest Debate: A Legislative History of the Civil Rights Act* (New York: Mentor Books, 1985), 117.

23. U.S. Civil Rights Act, 1964, Section 702(a)(1).

24. U.S. Civil Service Reform Act, 1978, Title I, Section 2301(b)(2).

25. Equal Employment Opportunity Commission, *Personnel Testing and Equal Employment Opportunity* (Washington, DC: Government Printing Office, 1970), 134.

26. The Court majority said that the presentation of a prima facie case must include the practice or practices that are responsible for the statistical disparities in the employer's workforce. The employer then, as in *Burdine,* has the burden of justifying the challenged practice(s) as necessary to get competent employees. As part of showing that the justifications are pretextual, plaintiffs can offer alternative ways of meeting the employer's needs without incurring a disparate impact on women, minorities, or other protected classes. The *Wards Cove* modification, in other words, increased substantially the burden of work for the plaintiffs.

    In 1989, the Court issued a number of rulings interpreted as hostile to the general goals of equal opportunities. The *Wards Cove* decision was included in this list. Another was *John W. Martin, et al.* v. *Robert K. Wilks et al.* (1989). In this case, the Court sided with white firefighters in Birmingham, Alabama, who argued that they should not be subjected to a consent decree to which they were not a party. The specific consent decree to which they objected was agreed to as a result of 1974 litigation over racial discrimination in hiring and promoting employees. The decree established promotion goals in the fire department that allegedly disadvantaged whites. Thus, although the Court was making it harder for women and minorities to litigate (*Ward Cove* decision), it opened the door for whites and men to object to consent decrees between employers and women and/or minorities. The 1991 Civil Rights Act overturned this ruling also.

27. *University of California Regents* v. *Bakke,* 98 S.Ct. 2733; 57 L.Ed.2d 750 (1978), V.B.

28. Williams, Gzant, "Rank and File: Former Salvation Army Officer Charges that Charity's Policy on Pay for Married Couples Violated her Civil Rights," *Chronicle for Philanthropy* XII, no. 7 (January 27, 2000): 25–26; Joan Pynes, "Human Resource Management in Nonprofit Organizations," Carolyn Ban and Norma Riccucci, eds., *Public Personnel Management: Current Concerns, Future Challenges,* 3rd ed. (New York: Longman, 2002), 243–254.

29. Pan S. Kim, "Disability Policy: An Analysis of the Employment of People with Disabilities in the American Federal Government," *Public Personnel Management* 25, no. 1 (Spring 1996): 73–88.

30. Lyndon Johnson, *Lyndon B. Johnnson: Public Papers of the Presidents of the United States, 1965, Book II* (Washington DC: Government Printing Office, 1965), 636.

31. Frederick A. Miller, "Strategic Culture Change: The Door to Achieving High Performance and Inclusion," *Public Personnel Management* 27, no. 2 (Summer 1998): 151–160; Matti F. Dobbs, "Managing Diversity: Lessons from the Private Sector," *Public Personnel Management* 25, 3 (Fall 1996), 351–368; Steve Ballard and Gayle Lawn-Day, "Affirmative Action in Municipal Government: Anatomy of a Failure," *Review of Public Personnel Administration* 12, no. 3 (Summer 1992): 5–18.

32. Audrey Mathews, "Diversity: A Principle of Human Resource Management," *Public Personnel Management* 27, no. 2 (Summer 1998): 175–186; Gill Robinson Hickman and Ann Creighton-Zollar, "Diverse Self-Directed Work Teams: Developing Strategic Initiatives for 21st Century Organizations," *Public Personnel Management* 27, no. 2 (Summer 1998): 187–200.

Chapter 5

Productivity

It is perhaps too obvious that organizations exist—or should exist—to accomplish goals and objectives. It is equally obvious that human resources are key to productivity. People are the providers of services, the enforcers of regulations, the analysts, and the problem-solvers. A central concern of personnel management, therefore, is how to ensure a productive workforce.

The challenge to managers is to translate the mission of their respective agencies into jobs and then to have those jobs completed by able and energetic people. An essential responsibility of managers is to facilitate the work of their staff by providing an environment that is supportive and free of distractions.

Once upon a time, scholars and practitioners believed that all workers, jobs, and organizations were essentially similar. We now know—or should know—better. Research, often testing a theory for increasing productivity through a single approach, finds that there are important differences in job responsibilities and worker motivations. For some, the most important reward of work is the compensation that enables the employee to meet living expenses and to pursue other interests. Obviously, this is not relevant for volunteers, who are often critical resources as workers and board members for nonprofits and as workers and committee or commission members for governments. Whether or not compensation is involved, social relationships among co-workers may be important, either inherently or as part of the general work setting.

Others find the job itself rewarding:

- Teaching a child
- Improving air quality
- Planning the development of a new neighborhood
- Helping a single parent get a job
- Solving a crime
- Preserving a marsh

Whether a job is necessary or satisfying—or has elements of both—is a difference among workers and volunteers that is neither good nor bad, but it is important for a manager to know.

Fortunately, there are some patterns to suggest how managers might approach people in their agencies. Members of boards and commissions, as well as professionals, tend to identify closely with their jobs and to get satisfaction primarily from doing their jobs well. Workers in routine jobs, on the other hand, usually regard something outside of work as most important to them. Employees in these positions are concerned about the demands of work, about relations with co-workers, and about pay and benefits. Volunteers doing routine tasks are usually motivated by social relationships or see these positions as an opportunity for networking. Obviously, these are general patterns and there are exceptions. In addition, some positions are best classified as paraprofessional and do not always easily fit in one of the other categories. Nonetheless, the distinctions are important and suggestive for managers grappling with the issues of productivity.

LEARNING OBJECTIVES OF THIS CHAPTER

This chapter discusses the key tasks of human resource management that relate to productivity:

- Design jobs and workflow
- Recruit, develop, and retain competent workers and volunteers
- Motivate employees and volunteers to work hard
- Provide an environment that facilitates able, energetic work
- Evaluate the efforts of employees and volunteers
- Make any necessary changes in response to evaluations

The general formula in Figure 1.1 presents the general outline for this chapter. Subsequent chapters cover in detail the subjects introduced here:

- Understand the importance of how jobs are designed and how work is organized
- Appreciate the significance of recruiting, developing, and retaining skilled, competent workers
- Know what motivates employees to work hard
- Understand the components of work settings and the contributions of the work environment
- Know the roles that evaluation plays

JOB DESIGN

The bottom-line responsibility of managers is to accomplish the mission or missions of their agency. In many situations, that may involve first discovering or clarifying that mission. Elected officials and their appointees play a primary role in defining the missions and agendas of government agencies, but that is often through interaction with career officials. Board members of nonprofit organizations, likewise, work with their managers to define and re-define goals and objectives. These interactions, in both settings, can be riddled with conflict or fueled by cooperation.

Total Quality Management and reengineering approaches used in the 1990s rely on customers to define what quality means in the products and services of an organization. In the public sector, the vagueness and ambiguity of legislatively defined missions often invite administrators to work with customers to more specifically define missions. In some contentious policy areas, it is not always clear who the primary customer is. The selection of, for example, home owners, developers or environmentalists is obviously consequential.

The details and dynamics of how agency missions are and should be established are discussed in other literature.[1] The relevant personnel management task that flows from the agency mission is **job design.** If the mission is to deliver the mail, then there must be jobs to receive mail, sell stamps, sort and transport mail to local post offices, and then sort and deliver the mail to the intended recipients. These jobs require the support of individuals who purchase supplies, keep records, and supervise staff.

The establishment of jobs is part of the foundation for the classical theory of organizations as espoused by the German sociologist, Max Weber. He viewed bureaucracies as structures that identify and arrange the specialized assignments that need to be complete if the organization is to achieve its goals and objectives.[2] Whoever occupies a given position in an organization is responsible for the tasks assigned to that position.

The work of Frederick W. Taylor begun in the 1870s and 1880s is consistent with Weber's theory and had a major impact on approaches and practices used in personnel management. Taylor conducted experiments in the steel industry in the Midvale and Bethlehem plants and developed what he called the "principles of **scientific management.**"[3] His major focus was the analysis of work, and he believed one could scientifically determine the single best way of designing jobs in order to accomplish organizational goals. He advocated the systematic observation, classification, and tabulation of job activities and then the design of tasks according to the motions and capacities of humans and equipment. His major contribution was assembly line technology. Taylor's emphasis was in an extreme way on tasks rather than employees:

> Now one of the very first requirements for a man who is fit to handle pig iron as a regular occupation is that he shall be so stupid and so phlegmatic that he more nearly resembles in his mental makeup the ox than any other type. The man who is mentally alert and intelligent is for this very reason entirely unsuited to what would, for him, be the grinding monotony of work of this character.[4]

Although scientific management has been widely criticized and new approaches have emerged, Taylor was successful at increasing efficiency and productivity in organizations where he applied his principles. His work left important legacies. Positions, defined in terms of job duties and responsibilities, determined as a result of systematic analysis of work, continue to be the fundamental building blocks of most public organizations. Those who manage agencies typically inherit already defined jobs that reflect someone's decisions about how to structure work in order to accomplish goals and fulfill missions. Much of personnel management consists of recruiting, hiring, transferring, supervising, evaluating, training, and promoting individuals so they fit existing position descriptions.

While managers need to define and redefine jobs with the agency mission foremost in mind, how duties are assigned has important implications for how employees identify with their work. Jobs designed in accordance with the assumptions of assembly line technology do not always fit the needs of individuals. Professionals who intrinsically identify with organizational goals need facilitation more than they need direction from a detailed job description. The achievement of efficiency and accuracy in an assembly line depends on individuals doing what they are told to do—no more, no less. Professionals who focus on problem solving and goal achievement, on the other hand, need more general direction and then the opportunity to exercise discretion and creativity. A common feeling of professionals, in fact, is to get frustrated with those who refuse to do something that is not specifically and explicitly in their job description.

Individuals who invest their self-esteem in their jobs need room for growth. This applies to volunteers, as well. They need to be able to take on more responsibility and to be recognized for their individual contributions and achievements. Managers who design jobs that accommodate these needs are able to reward and reinforce these employees and volunteers and to obtain the services of a highly motivated and effective staff member. Positions defined in detail are incompatible with these needs. Research confirms the benefits of allowing for growth and flexibility in jobs that involve more than routine work.[5] Nonetheless, position descriptions, which define expectations and boundaries that are important for some employers and positions, perhaps to a fault, continue as basic building blocks for general management.

Chapter 6 presents a thorough description and discussion of how personnel management systems and practices have traditionally structured positions. Managers will probably find that traditional practices fit the routine jobs well. On the other hand, managers who rely on the commitment and creativity of good professionals are likely to be frustrated with the rigidities of predefined jobs.

ABILITY

Common sense tells us that ability is a fundamental ingredient for getting a job done. Expert work requires expertise. For very good reasons, managers prefer energetic workers and employees who get along with one another. But these traits assume ability as well. It does not help much if someone is congenial but incompetent. An employee who is hard working but makes mistakes, in fact, can be a major liability. There will be lots of errors to correct! Better that the error-prone be lazy!

The need for able employees is obvious, and the concern that ability may rank below other criteria is serious. In the private sector, the concern is whether family ties or personal favoritism might be more important than skills and experience. In the public sector, as discussed in Chapters 2 and 4, the anxiety is that competence might be sacrificed because of patronage or favoritism. Clearly that is not the intent of public policies and is done at the risk of waste and inefficiency.

EFFORT

The need for effort is just as clear as the need for ability. It matters little how competent an employee or volunteer is if he or she does not work hard.

The first major attack on Taylor's scientific management was over the issue of worker effort. Managers brought industrial consultants Vannevar Bush and Joseph Baker to the Hawthorne Works plant of Western Electric Company in Chicago, after the managers had made unsuccessful attempts to improve productivity by applying the principles of scientific management. The fear at Hawthorne Works was that they misunderstood scientific management. Bush and Baker confirmed that jobs were well designed and employees were hired with the skills needed to do the work assigned to their respective positions. These consultants concluded that human motivational factors might be critical and called in some social scientists, specifically Professor Elton Mayo of the Harvard Business School and some of his colleagues.

Indeed, research indicated that productivity increased when workers acted as a team and cooperated spontaneously.[6] This research is credited as the beginning of the **human relations school** and the study of **industrial sociology.** The goal of the human relations approach is to design the work environment, orient supervision, and otherwise shape organizations so that employees and volunteers have high morale and a positive attitude about their jobs and about co-workers. This attitude will, the theory posits, prompt high levels of effort.

As a result of the human relations studies and findings, companies took steps to focus on the health and happiness of their workers. Companies tried everything from sponsoring bowling and softball teams to the establishment of company towns, in which the company provided for the health and recreational needs of workers and their families within a community setting. Employee Assistance Programs, which offer individualized care and treatment programs for troubled employees and some-times their families, are a contemporary example of the human relations approach.

Motivation Theory

A central figure in **motivation theory** is Abraham H. Maslow. He reasoned that human needs are multiple and that individuals work to satisfy those needs in a specific sequence.[7] He also noted that noneconomic needs are important to people. This hierarchical sequence is shown in Figure 5.1. Maslow asserted that movement from the lower two categories through the upper three takes place over a lifetime. Some people never satisfy the higher order of needs.

There is no empirical evidence that either confirms or disproves Maslow's theory.[8] In part, concepts like self-actualization and recognition needs are too vague to determine the extent to which they have been met. Another problem with Maslow's work is that the sequence of the needs could be somewhat reordered and still be logical. Some needs may be so interactive that it would not be accurate to even place them in a sequence. The relationships between self-esteem and attach-ment to others certainly seem more interactive than sequential.

Despite the lack of verification of Maslow's hierarchy of needs, it has considerable intuitive appeal. His thinking has had great influence on personnel management. Min-imum wage and due process laws address the physiological and security needs identi-fied by Maslow, although in fact these components of personnel systems have their origins more in public policies than in scholarly theories. Other personnel management practices more directly draw from Maslow and other theorists. Job enrichment and

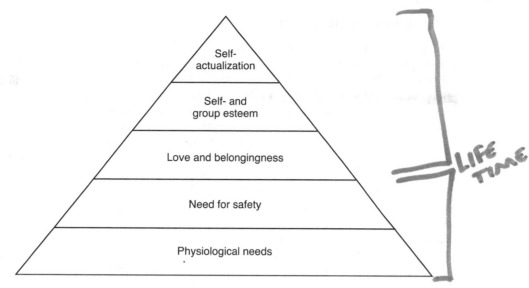

FIGURE 5.1   A Graphic Representation of Maslow's Hierarchy of Needs.

participatory management are, for example, based on a recognition of aspirations for interesting and fulfilling work and for sharing and interacting with others.

Douglas McGregor formulated a dichotomy of assumptions about human motivation that contrasted the traditional approach of management with what Maslow's theory suggests.[9] McGregor labeled the traditional view **Theory X,** which considers the average individual as someone who inherently dislikes work and avoids it if possible. Thus, according to this view, most people must be coerced, controlled, directed, and threatened into working. **Theory Y,** on the other hand, characterizes work being as natural as play or rest. Work itself is a source of satisfaction. Theory Y argues that individuals can identify their own ego and self-fulfillment needs with the goals of an organization. McGregor contends that managers who assume workers are lazy and need to be controlled will in fact destroy their natural inclinations to seek satisfaction and fulfillment in work, whereas managers who empower and guide their employees will enhance and build on worker energy and enthusiasm.

McGregor's theories are more prescriptive than descriptive, and they assume that a single approach could be applied to all employees in any given organization. As will be shown later in this chapter, empirical evidence supports the view that there are individuals and there are jobs that are nicely described by each of the theories. Theory X generally describes those in routine jobs and Theory Y those in professional jobs. It should be noted, as well, that there is evidence to suggest that orientations to work—and especially to public and community service—vary from one generation to another, depending on national and world events.[10] Also, a study of federal employees found a slightly higher public service orientation among women, minorities, and those with higher levels of education.[11] Motivation, in sum, follows some patterns, but is complex and requires managers to learn what prompts the individuals in their own respective organizations.

Participatory Management

The positive view of worker motivation in Theory Y is the foundation of the **participatory management** theories. Rensis Likert is among the most prominent scholars who have contributed to this school of thought.[12] Likert observed that people tend to work in small groups, whether those groups are structured formally or emerge informally. He based his theories and prescriptions on the premise that work groups are the optimal unit for harmonizing the objectives of the larger organization with the needs and desires of individuals. Productive organizations, he argued, are based on effective groups. Thus, management leadership and personnel policies should facilitate and encourage work groups by involving them in the running of the organization. Warren Bennis further developed and advocated for this perspective. He boldly predicted the eventual demise of hierarchical organizations, replaced by internally democratic ones.[13]

The establishment of quality work circles and other forms of participatory management became associated with the economic success of Japan in the 1970s and 1980s.[14] Ironically, the Japanese success generated positive visibility for an American management consultant, W. E. Deming, and his approach to quality improvement, Total Quality Management (TQM).[15] Deming initially found a more receptive audience for his ideas in Japan than in the United States but by the late 1980s had developed an enthusiastic and devoted following in his own country.

Total Quality Management

Total Quality Management, although associated with earlier approaches to participatory management, is significantly distinct. Likert, Bennis, and others argue for empowering employees and involving them in management decisions as a way of getting them to identify organizational goals as their own. Japanese management is touted as linking individuals within the factory or firm into a familial collectivity where everyone is committed to a common welfare.[16]

TQM, however, does not advocate empowering workers, but instead values workers for the information they can provide about the production process. Factory employees working with materials, machinery, and the like know the details and nuances of how things work and don't work. Front-line employees and volunteers in service industries, such as government and nonprofit organizations, are face to face with clients and customers and have a good understanding of the problems and the successes of providing certain programs and applying given rules. Managers responsible for making decisions about when and how to improve a process can use the information and the wisdom of these front-line people. In short, for TQM the primary objective behind the establishment of work groups is information, not motivation.

The link between motivation and production for TQM lies more in employee performance evaluation than it does in participatory management. Deming argues that the evaluation of individual workers has a negative effect on motivation and productivity. Evaluations are inevitably more threatening than they are rewarding. Moreover, productivity almost invariably is the result of group, not individual, activity, and so traditional performance evaluation uses the wrong unit of analysis. Deming stresses that one should look at systems, not people, to improve productivity.

This perspective challenges traditional public personnel management policies and procedures, which have utilized individual performance evaluations. In Chapter 8 this subject is discussed in greater detail.

A limitation of all of the participatory management approaches is the assumption that everyone wants to be involved in affecting the work flow or work environment. As mentioned previously, individuals relate differently to their jobs. Professionals are likely to invest themselves in their work so that they do value playing some role in managerial decision making.[17] Workers for whom their jobs are not the central part of their identities and their lives, on the other hand, do not fully appreciate the opportunity to participate in managing their organizations. Some, in fact, resent doing what they regard as the job of managers.[18] A problem, in short, is in treating all individuals and all occupations alike.

Multiple Sources of Satisfaction

A basic assumption in motivation theory and the human relations approach to organizations is that satisfaction prompts effort. The question then is, what produces satisfaction? The Hawthorne experiments focused on working conditions. Maslow looked at human needs. McGregor examined leadership style. Participatory management considers empowerment the key, and TQM cautions against individual performance evaluations as a negative motivator. All of these theories implicitly or explicitly regard employees as having similar orientations toward work and toward their work setting.

Social psychologists Daniel Katz and Robert L. Kahn developed a model that outlines several relationships between organizational factors and individual motivations.[19] They treated organizations generically, without regard to whether they were private, public, or nonprofit, and identified four types of organizational incentive systems that are linked to different motivations. Table 5.1 presents a useful summary of the organizational incentives and worker motivations and the impact of each pattern on productivity.

The first organizational feature Katz and Kahn considered is legal compliance, which rests on an acceptance by workers of the legitimacy of the organization and its rules and/or on a recognition of the organization's ability to force compliance. Rules can be a basis upon which an organization appeals to other needs and incentives. Rule-oriented organizations are appropriate when tasks are routine and errors can be costly, but a preoccupation with rules tends to sacrifice creativity and innovation.

Katz and Kahn identify four types of instrumental rewards that organizations can provide to their members:

1. General system.   These are rewards that come through membership itself and usually increase with seniority. Retirement programs, vacation and sick leave, and cost-of-living increases in wages are examples. The expectation is that these rewards would encourage employees to continue their employment with an organization. Productivity benefits if there is minimal turnover and an organization can use the experience of its workers.

2. Individual rewards.   Pay, promotions, development opportunities, and other rewards linked to individual performance fit this category. The assumption here is that individual performance can be somehow identified and measured and that individuals

TABLE 5.1 MOTIVATIONAL PATTERNS, REWARDS SYSTEMS, AND ORGANIZATIONAL BEHAVIOR OUTCOMES

Incentive/Motivational Pattern	Type of Behavior Produced
Legal Compliance	Internalized acceptance of authority or minimally acceptable quantity of work can reduce legitimacy of organization rules and/or absenteeism external force can be used to compel compliance
Instrumental Satisfaction	Minimal quantity and quality of role performance
General-systems reward	Reduction in turnover and absenteeism
Individual rewards	Possible increase in productivity
	Possible reduction in turnover and absenteeism
Approval of leaders	Possible decrease in turnover and absenteeism
	Possible increases in productivity (or possible decreases)
Approval of peers	Possible decrease in turnover and absenteeism
	Possible increases in productivity (or possible decreases)
Self-Expression	High productivity
	Decreases in absenteeism
	Self-concept, identification, and intrinsic satisfaction with the work or job itself
Internalization of Organization Goals	Increased productivity
	Spontaneous and innovative behavior
	Reduced turnover and absenteeism
	Value expression, self-identification with goals of organization

Source: Based on Daniel Katz and Robert L. Kahn, *The Social Psychology of Organizations* (New York: John Wiley & Sons, 1966), 347–366.

value the rewards. Victor Vroom's expectation theory is based on the links between the salience of the reward and preferred performances.[20] The issues and approaches toward performance evaluation and compensation will be discussed in further detail in later chapters.

3. Approval of leaders. This is essentially a kind of individual reward. Katz and Kahn might well have included approval of leaders in the category described above. In order for the approval of leaders to have a positive effect on productivity, workers must value the approval of their leaders and leaders must be able to make meaningful distinctions among individual performances. If performance is not or cannot be measured, then leaders may be accused of favoritism and/or arbitrary behavior when they express approval. This can demoralize employees and volunteers and decrease rather than increase productivity.

4. Approval of peers. As is approval of leaders, this is a form of individual reward and to be effective, employees and volunteers must value the approval of their peers and believe that their peers are capable of identifying when performance warrants their approval. If such students of organizations as Mary Parker Follett are right, there is inevitably at least implicit conflict between workers and managers, and approval of peers is dependent on complying with informal rather than formal rules and work rates.[21] Approval of peers, thus, might actually be linked to relatively low levels of effort and productivity as workers ban together to resist control by supervisors.

In some instances, rather than satisfaction comprising a factor leading to productivity, productivity generates satisfaction. Katz and Kahn link organizational conditions that foster self-expression with high productivity. Employees and volunteers who invest their self-esteem into their job will give their all.

The fourth type of organizational effect on motivation is particularly relevant for volunteers, as well as workers. Here levels of commitment and effort are high when individual employees or volunteers internalize the collective goals of the organization. Whereas in the third of Katz and Kahn's types, individuals invest themselves in their role in the organization, in the last type, individuals identify with the goals of the organization as a whole. The difference is in personally internalizing the goals of an organization providing care to preschool children in contrast to identifying one's self-esteem in the job of a nutritionist in the preschool program.

The types of incentives that Katz and Kahn describe are distributed within organizations in some fairly predictable patterns. Follett's work describes a perspective of managers that is profoundly different from that of workers in an organization, where the former are concerned about the organization and its goals and the latter relate primarily to the interpersonal relationships of co-workers in their immediate subgroup within the organization. These differences, which exist in all organizations, naturally cause conflict. The distance and disagreements between workers and managers leads to what some refer to as workplace sabotage. These are deliberate, hostile acts that range from "self-created down time" and lying, to snipping cables on computers.[22] Conflict, whether it results in violence or in lower productivity, can be addressed. Follett herself advocated ways of resolving conflict through cooperation and shared power.[23] Her point that places in the organizational hierarchy generate different perspectives is critical to an understanding of the kinds of incentives and disincentives that exist and how they relate to productivity.

Research indicates that differences in occupations indeed explain patterns of relationships between satisfaction and productivity. H. Roy Kaplan and Curt Tausky found in their review of studies completed during the 1960s and 1970s that the intrinsic value of work varied between occupational groups. Table 5.2 presents the findings.

The general pattern in Table 5.2 is that the more routine and low skilled the job, the more workers value their employment for instrumental (monetary) purposes. Incumbents of the more professional and managerial occupations, on the other hand, get more personal, intrinsic rewards from their work. This pattern is most dramatic when those surveyed are asked whether they would care about being promoted if they knew they would get steady increases in their salaries without being promoted. Of the middle managers, 71 percent reported they still wanted promotions. In contrast, 74 percent of the blue-collar workers surveyed said they would not care about promotions if they received steady increases anyway.

Kaplan and Tausky found studies with comparable data on job satisfaction for workers through middle management.[24] Recent research has demonstrated the importance

TABLE 5.2 ORIENTATIONS TO WORK AMONG WHITE- AND BLUE-COLLAR WORKERS
AND STUDENTS

Questions and Responses	Blue-Collar Workers	Technical Students	Middle Managers
Is the most important thing about getting a promotion			
Getting more pay	78%	67%	62%
Getting more respect from friends	22%	33%	38%
Which job would you choose if you could be sure of keeping either job			
Better than average pay as a truck driver	73%	77%	67%
Less than average pay as a bank clerk	27%	22%	32%
If you could be sure your income would go up steadily without getting a promotion, would you care about getting promoted?			
No	74%	60%	29%
Yes	26%	40%	71%
If by some chance you had enough money to live comfortably without working, would you work anyway?			
I would work anyway	21%	87%	89%
I would not work	79%	13%	11%

Sources: Blue-Collar Workers (National Sample of 274, Male): Curt Tausky, "Meanings of Work Among Blue Collar Men," *Pacific Sociological Review* 12 (Spring 1969): 51.
Vocational Students (1,379, Male): Bhopinder S. Bolaria, unpublished study of vocational-technical training students, University of Maine, Orono, 1970, cited in H. Roy Kaplan and Curt Tausky, "Humanism in Organizations: A Critical Appraisal," in Dean L. Yarwood, ed., *Public Administration, Politics and the People* (New York: Longman, 1987), 150–151.
Middle Managers (151 in 3 Firms): Curt Tausky, "Occupational Mobility Interests," *Canadian Review of Sociology and Anthropology,* 4 (November 1967): 246.

to senior professionals and managers of being able to make service contributions in their work. Satisfaction comes from accomplishments. Empowerment and discretion are key, even when there is risk of personal failure. More than monetary rewards, recognition by peers and managers is valued.[25]

Writings on organizational culture confirm the importance of occupations. Harrison M. Trice, in particular, has focused on subcultures within organizations based on occupations. These subcultures tend to provide for their members a definition of mission and organizational goals that is often distinct from those held by management. Likewise, occupations define expected levels of effort and work pace that are at odds with those managers desire.[26]

WORKING CONDITIONS

The attitudes and behaviors of employees and volunteers depend in part on the physical and social conditions within which they work. Systems analysis at the center of the scientific management movement included the effects of the design of work stations and the arrangement of assembly lines. The Hawthorne experiments Mayo and his associates conducted not only are responsible for identifying worker motivation as a factor in organizational productivity, but also for examining the effects of working conditions. In fact, the research began with a focus on working conditions. Lighting was, for example, changed in the plant and then the effects on workers measured after each change. Likewise, humidity, temperature, and hours of sleep were used as variables.

The initial series of lighting experiments did not indicate clear relationships between work environment and efficiency, but some anomalies led to a focus on motivation and efforts. Workers responded to changes in lighting, temperature, and the like with a temporary increase in energy and enthusiasm. After the initial spurt, work efforts returned to levels prior to the change. Researchers concluded that the changes per se prompted increases, albeit temporary, in employee morale. This phenomenon is known as the "Hawthorne effect."[27]

Subsequent research indicates that there are limits to the amount of productivity that come from improvements in working conditions. Frederick Herzberg describes working conditions as a dissatisfier or **hygienic factor,** rather than as a satisfier or **motivating factor.** Employees, in other words, will complain about working conditions, but once conditions are satisfactory, improvements will not become a source of high morale and motivate new levels of effort. If one were to express this in mathematical terms, working conditions can have a negative value or zero, but not a positive value as a factor of productivity. Herzberg's listing of hygienic and motivating factors is presented in Table 5.3.

Like some of the theories critiqued above, Herzberg's two-factor theory of motivation makes the assumption that all individuals approach work in the same way. Thus, some of the motivators such as achievement and challenging work are generally salient more for those in professional and managerial jobs than for those in routine, low-skilled ones. Also, some studies have suggested important modifications in how pay relates to motivation. It still works primarily as a dissatisfier, but in some circumstances can be used as a form of recognition, a motivating factor.[28] Research confirms other features of Herzberg's theory, including the important, but hygienic, effects of working conditions.[29]

Sexual and racial harassment in the workplace is a component of working conditions. Sexual harassment can take the form of demands for sexual favors in order to have job security or advancement or it can be seen as a generally hostile

TABLE 5.3   HERZBERG'S TWO-FACTOR THEORY

Hygiene Factors	Motivators
Job context	*Job content*
Policies and administration	Achievement
Supervision	Recognition
Working conditions	Challenging work
Interpersonal relations	Responsibility
Money, status, security	Growth and development

work environment.[30] Racial harassment is of the latter variety. Harassment because of race or gender or sexual orientation is fundamentally an issue of discrimination in that it creates a hostile setting for individuals because of their race or gender. It is included in the provisions of the 1964 Civil Rights Act outlawing discrimination in employment.

Sexual and racial harassment negatively affects productivity. At a minimum, both victims and perpetrators of harassment are distracted in time and emotional energy from their jobs. Some victims feel guilt and shame and assume that they are somehow to blame. Some suffer emotionally and/or physically because of the tension and have to seek treatment.[31]

The costs are, of course, to employers as well as individual employees. The U.S. Merit Systems Protection Board estimated the cost of sexual harassment to the federal government between 1978 and 1980 to have been $189 million; in the 1985 to 1987 period, the estimated cost was $267 million. Included in these calculations are the costs of

1. Replacing employees who left their positions because of sexual harassment
2. Compensating employees for sick leave for work missed to avoid sexual harassment and/or to secure treatment
3. Paying medical insurance claims for employees seeking professional help in dealing with the effects of harassment
4. Receiving less effort on the job from those involved in harassment.[32]

Studies of state governments have identified hostile working environments owing to harassment as the largest single cause of the higher quit rates for women and minority employees.[33] As in other working conditions, sexual and racial harassment is hygienic, not motivating. One can work toward ridding the workplace of gender and race-based harassment and eliminating the negative effects, but it is difficult to envision how there might be improvements beyond that point and thus further increases in productivity.

EVALUATION

How one determines whether or not productivity can be improved is based largely on the basic assumptions at the foundation of managerial approaches. TQM, for example, is sometimes known as Continuous Improvement because this approach postulates that an organization can always accomplish its mission in a more efficient and effective manner. In contrast, scientific management is based on the belief that it is possible to identify the best way of doing something. At an abstract, theoretical level one might argue with and reject both of these assumptions. Operationally, managers tend to act as if there is always room for improvement.

Another distinction is critical for personnel management. Deming, an aforementioned key author of TQM, insists that the focus of analysis for determining how to improve productivity has to be *process,* not *people.*[34] As previously mentioned, this challenges the common practice of evaluating the performance of individual employees as a way of ensuring high levels of productivity. Chapter 9 discusses performance appraisal in more detail. The point here is that there is a dispute about what managers should use as the unit of analysis and focus of their efforts to improve. The position most managers and this author take is that both process and employees are important. The ingredients of productivity that have been discussed thus far include both—job design relates to process and skill, and effort relates to employees and volunteers as individuals.

Regardless of what goes into productivity, measuring what agencies do can in itself be quite a challenge.[35] Ideally, managers could determine how well their organizations are accomplishing their missions, and evaluations of personnel management could include looking for ways of improving. Police departments, for example, could see whether their services make a community safer, environmental agencies whether health is better, and community service organizations whether families are more secure and self-sufficient.

It is not always easy to evaluate organizational performance. Not only are indicators such as crime rates, incidents of respiratory or other illnesses, and income levels imperfect measures, but the activities of individual public agencies and nonprofit organizations are not the only forces that are responsible for safety, health, and comfort. Reform efforts of the 1990s and early twenty-first century have included holding managers accountable for outcomes; there is a recognition that only some of the relevant determinants are under managerial control. One of those determinants is agency personnel. Thus, there is a reemphasis on the need for managers to evaluate how well they are utilizing their human resources. This means being certain to design jobs appropriately, fill the positions with employees and volunteers who have the right skills, motivate individuals to work energetically, and provide working conditions that enable them to work efficiently and effectively.

SUMMARY

Productivity is sometimes difficult to define and measure. Nonetheless, productivity is of obvious importance. Difficulties in measurement provide little excuse for failing to achieve high levels of productivity.

The key variables for productivity are job design, employee and volunteer skills, individual effort, and working conditions. This chapter has reviewed research and theories that explain each variable and how it relates to productivity. It is noted that productivity itself is both a dependent and an independent variable. That is, at least for some individuals, the accomplishment of projects, tasks, and objectives brings about a sense of satisfaction, which in turn prompts more effort to get more accomplished. It would be a mistake, however, to assume that everyone identifies their self-esteem and self-worth with their work. This is not to condemn those who find other aspects of their life more important but to recognize that realistic, effective approaches to human resource management must be aware of differences in how individuals relate to work.

It is also important to note that while the focus of personnel management is typically individuals, an important feature of work, especially in public and nonprofit agencies, is that it is done in groups. Theorists like Follett and Likert and proponents of such management approaches as TQM recognize the significance of groups in the work setting. Policies and procedures of personnel management sometimes are limited because they do not always include groups as actors. As we move to the remaining subjects of this book, we should not repeat this error.

DISCUSSION QUESTIONS

1. What are the ways in which workers can affect decisions made in their organizations? Be sure to include informal as well as formal ways.
2. Apply the basic ingredients of productivity to an organization with which you are familiar. Are there ways in which you think human resources might be used better?
3. Relate this chapter to the previous three chapters. Do you see efforts to eliminate patronage, respect the constitutional rights of employees, and establish a socially diverse workforce as compatible with what is required for productivity or as threats?

GLOSSARY

Human relations school Approach to management that emphasizes the need to have a happy, satisfied workforce in order to have high levels of productivity. Work environments and informal activities in the organization are used to increase worker satisfaction

Hygienic factor An influence on productivity that can have a negative effect when it is not fully present

Industrial sociology Academic field of research and learning based on the human relations school of management

Job design Assignment of duties and responsibilities to a particular position, based on tasks that need to be done and on flow or sequence of work

Motivating factor An influence on productivity that tends to increase outputs more for every additional amount that exists of the factor

Motivation theory Conceptual framework linking work effort with the reasons why individuals work and work hard

Participatory management Approach to management that assumes workers can and will assist in making their organization run better and thus should be involved in managerial decision making

Scientific management Approach to management that assumes there is a single best way of doing things and jobs are designed accordingly. This approach is associated with assembly line technology

Theory X Perspective that individuals dislike work and try to avoid it if possible, and thus need coercive, strict managerial control

Theory Y Perspective that individuals get enjoyment and satisfaction out of work and thus need managers who are supportive and provide only general direction

Total Quality Management (TQM) Approach to management that relies on customers for definitions of quality, on workers to provide information about how work is done and might be improved, and on managers for continuing to make the products/services and the work better

SOURCES

Campbell, J. R., & Campbell, R. J. eds. (1988). *Productivity in organizations*. San Francisco: Jossey-Bass.
Useful collection of essays that discuss various approaches to the subject of productivity in organizations, generally public, nonprofit, and private.

Deming, W. E. (1986). *Out of crisis*. Cambridge, MA: MIT–CAES Press.
The basic explanation of Total Quality Management, by its originator.

Gortner, Harold F., Nichols, Kenneth L., & Ball, Carolyn. (2007). *Organization Theory. A Public and nonprofit perspective* (3rd ed.) Belmont, CA: Wadsworth.
A thoughtful and thorough review of research and theories on organizational behavior, accountability, and productivity.

Maslow, A. H. (1954). *Motivation and personality*. New York: Harper.
One of the most frequently cited classic theories of motivation. Maslow specifies a hierarchy of needs that individuals seek to satisfy.

Mayo, E. (1939). *The human problem of industrial civilization*. Cambridge: Harvard University Press.
The study of the Hawthorne electric plant that initiated the human relations approach to management.

Taylor, F. W. (1919). *The principles of scientific management*. New York: Harper and Bros.
The seminal statement of scientific management, the precursor of contemporary industrial engineering.

NOTES

1. See, for example: Hugh Heclo, *A Government of Strangers;* Hugh Heclo, "Issue Networks in the Executive Establishment," in Anthony King, ed., *The New American Political System* (Washington, DC: American Enterprise Institute, 1978); Frank R. Baumgartner and Bryan D. Jones, *Agendas and Instability in American Politics* (Chicago: University of Chicago Press, 1993); Randall B. Ripley and Grace A. Franklin, *Congress, the Bureaucracy, and Public Policy*, 5th ed. (Pacific Grove, CA: Brooks-Cole, 1991); Douglas Yates, *Bureaucratic Democracy: The Search for Democracy and Efficiency in American Government* (Cambridge, MA: Harvard University Press, 1982); Arthur R. Tenner and Irving J. DeToro, *Total Quality Management: Three Steps to Continuous Improvement* (Reading, MA: Addison-Wesley, 1992); Richard M. Hodgetts, Fred Luthans, and Sang M. Lee, "New Paradigm Organizations: From Total Quality to Learning to World-Class," *Organizational Dynamics* (Winter 1994): 4–19.

2. Max Weber, *The Theory of Social and Economic Organization*, trans. A. M. Henderson and Talcott Parsons (New York: Oxford University Press, 1947), 329–340.

3. Frederick W. Taylor, *The Principles of Scientific Management* (New York: Harper and Bros., 1919).

4. Frederick W. Taylor, *Scientific Management* (New York: Harper and Bros., 1945), 59.

5. Yitzhak Fried and Gerald R. Ferris, "The Validity of the Job Characteristics Model: A Review and Meta-Analysis," *Personnel Psychology* 40 (March 1987): 287–322; Lisa R. Berlinger, William H. Glick, and Robert C. Rodgers, "Job Enrichment and Performance Improvement," in John R. Campbell and Richard J. Campbell, eds. *Productivity in Organizations* (San Francisco: Jossey-Bass, 1988); Ricky W. Griffin, "Effects of Work Redesign

on Employee Perceptions, Attitudes, and Behaviors: A Long-Term Investigation," *Academy of Management Journal* 34 (October 1991): 425–435.

6. F. J. Roethlisberger and W. J. Dickson, *Management and the Worker* (Cambridge: Harvard University Press, 1939); T. North Whitehead, *The Industrial Worker,* vols. 1 and 2 (Cambridge: Harvard University Press, 1939); G. A. Pennock, "Industrial Research at Hawthorne and Experimental Investigation of Rest Periods, Working Conditions, and Other Influences," *Personnel Journal* 9, no. 2 (February 1930): 296–309.

7. Abraham H. Maslow, *Motivation and Personality* (New York: Harper, 1954).

8. Relevant studies are discussed in M. A. Wahba and L. G. Bridwell, "Maslow Reconsidered: A Review of the Research on the Need Hierarchy Theory," *Organizational Behavior and Human Performance* 15 (1976): 212–240; Robert A. Ullrich, *A Theoretical Model of Human Behavior in Organizations* (Morristown, NJ: General Learning Corporation, 1972), 9–15. Also, see, Chiris Argyris, *Integrating the Individual and the Organization* (New York: Wiley, 1964), 79–92, where he argues that need-fulfillment and happiness are not necessarily related.

9. Douglas McGregor, *The Human Side of Enterprise* (New York: McGraw-Hill, 1960).

10. Carole L. Jurkiewicz and Roger G. Brown, "GenXers vs. Boomers vs. Matures," *Review of Public Personnel Administration* 18, no. 4 (Fall 1998): 18–37.

11. Katherine C. Naff and John Crum, "Working for America: Does Public Service Motivation Make a Difference?" *Review of Public Personnel Administration* 19, no. 4 (Fall 1999): 5–16.

12. Rensis Likert, *New Patterns of Management* (New York: McGraw-Hill, 1961).

13. Warren G. Bennis, *American Bureaucracy* (Chicago: Aldine Publishing, 1970).

14. R. Cole, *Japanese Blue Collar: The Changing Tradition* (Berkeley: University of California Press, 1971); R. Dore, *British Factory—Japanese Factory* (Berkeley: University of California Press, 1973).

15. W. E. Deming, *Out of the Crisis* (Cambridge: MIT—CAES Press, 1986).

16. William G. Ouchi and Alfred M. Jaeger, "Type Z Organization: Stability in the Midst of Mobility," in Dean L. Yarwood, ed. *Public Administration, Politics, and the People* (New York: Longman, 1986), 155–163.

17. Thomas Li-Ping Tang and Edie Aguilar Butler, "Attributions of Quality Circles' Problem-Solving Failure: Differences Among Management, Supporting Staff, and Quality Circle Members," *Public Personnel Management* 26, no. 2 (Summer 1997): 203–226.

18. Anna C. Goldoff and David C. Tatage, "Joint Productivity Committees: Lessons of Recent Initiatives," *Public Administration Review* 38 (January/February 1978): 184–186.

19. Daniel Katz and Robert L. Kahn, *The Social Psychology of Organizations* (New York: John Wiley & Sons, 1966).

20. Victor H. Vroom, *Work and Motivation* (New York: John Wiley & Sons, 1964).

21. Mary Parker Follett, *Creative Experience* (New York: Peter Smith, 1924); E. M. Fox, "Mary Parker Follett: The Enduring Contribution," *Public Administration Review* (November/December, 1968): 520–529.

22. Ron A. DiBattista, "Forecasting Sabotage Events in the Workplace," *Public Personnel Management* 25, no. 1 (Spring 1996): 41–52; Ron A. DiBattista, "Creating New Approaches to Recognize and Deter Sabotage," *Public Personnel Management* 20, no. 3 (Fall 1991): 347–352.

23. Henry Metcalf and Lyndall Urwick, *Dynamic Administration: The Collected Papers of Mary Parker Follett* (New York: John Wiley & Sons, 1941).

24. Frank Friedlander, "Importance of Work Versus Non-Work Among Socially and Occupationally Stratified Groups," *Journal of Applied Psychology* (December 1966): 437–441; J. C. Hunt and J. W. Hill, "The New Look in Motivation Theory and Organizational

Research," *Human Organization* (Summer 1969): 100–109; Department of Health, Education, and Welfare, *Work in America* (Cambridge, MA: MIT Press, 1973).

25. Kerry D. Carson, Paula Phillips Carson, C. William Roe, Betty J. Birkenmeier, and Joyce S. Phillips, "Four Commitment Profiles and their Relationships to Empowerment, Service Recovery, and Work Attitudes," *Public Personnel Management* 28, no. 1 (Spring 1999): 1–14; Jonathan P. West and Evan M. Berman, "Career Risk and Reward from Productivity," *Public Personnel Management* 28, no. 3 (Fall 1999): 453–472.

26. Harrison M. Trice and Janice M. Beyer, *The Cultures of Work Organizations* (Englewood Cliffs, NJ: Prentice-Hall, 1993); Harrison M. Trice, *Occupational Cultures in the Workplace* (Ithaca, NY: ILR Press, 1995).

27. Elton Mayo, *The Human Problem of Industrial Civilization* (New York: Macmillan, 1939); F. J. Roethlisberger and William J. Dickson, *Management and the Worker* (Cambridge, MA: Harvard University Press, 1939).

28. See, for example, Victor H. Vroom, *Work and Motivation* (New York: John Wiley & Sons, 1964); J. S. Adams, "Inequity in Social Exchange," in *Advances in Experimental Social Psychology*, L. Berkowitz, ed. (New York: Academic Press, 1965); W. Clay Hammer, "How to Ruin Motivation with Pay," *Compensation Review* 3 (Summer 1975); and Edward E. Lawler, III, "New Approaches to Pay: Innovations that Work," in *Perspectives on Personnel/Human Resource Management*, Herbert G. Henemann, III, and Donald P. Schwab, eds. (Homewood, IL: Richard D. Irwin, 1978); Thomas Li-Ping Tang and Jwa K. Kim, "The Meaning of Money Among Mental Health Workers: The Endorsement of Money Ethic as Related to Organizational Citizenship Behavior, Job Satisfaction, and Commitment," *Public Personnel Management* 28, no. 1 (Spring 1999): 15–26.

29. V. M. Bockman, "The Herzberg Controversy," *Personnel Psychology* 24, no. 2 (Summer 1971): 155–189; Benedict S. Grigaliunas and Frederick Herzberg, "Relevancy in the Test of Motivation-Hygiene Theory," *Journal of Applied Psychology* 55, no. 1 (February 1971): 73–79.

30. Dennis L. Dresang and Paul J. Stuiber, "Sexual Harassment: Challenges for the Future," in Carolyn Bann and Norma M. Riccucci, eds. *Public Personnel Management: Current Concerns—Future Challenges* (New York: Longman, 1991); Jane H. Bayes and Rita Mae Kelly, "Managing Sexual Harassment in Public Employment," in Steven W. Hays and Richard C. Kearney, eds. *Public Personnel Administration: Problems and Prospects*, 3rd ed. (Englewood Cliffs, NJ: Prentice-Hall, 1995).

31. Helene L. Gosselin, "Sexual Harassment on the Job: Psychological, Social and Economic Repercussions," *Canada's Mental Health* 32, no. 3 (September 1984): 21–24; David J. Miramontes, *How to Deal with Sexual Harassment* (San Diego: Network Communications, 1984); Catherine MacKinnon, *Sexual Harassment of Working Women: A Case of Sex Discrimination* (New Haven: Yale University Press, 1979).

32. U.S. Merit Systems Protection Board, *Sexual Harassment in the Federal Workplace: Is It a Problem?* (Washington, DC: Government Printing Office, 1981); U.S. Merit Systems Protection Board, *Sexual Harassment in the Federal Workplace: An Update* (Washington, DC: Government Printing Office, 1988).

33. Kris Bosworth, *Turnover among Women and Minorities in Wisconsin State Government* (Madison, WI: La Follette Institute of Public Affairs, 1988); Rita M. Kelly and P. Stambaugh, "Sexual Harassment in State Government," in M. E. Guy, ed. *Men and Women in the States* (Armonk, NY: M. E. Sharpe, 1992).

34. W. Edwards Deming, *Out of the Crisis* (Cambridge, MA: MIT–CAES Press, 1986).

35. D. Ammons, *Accountability for Performance: Measurement and Monitoring in Local Government* (Washington, DC: International City/County Management Association, 1995); Robert Denhardt, *The Pursuit of Significance* (Belmont, CA: Wadsworth, 1993).

Chapter 6

Organization for Personnel Management

How a jurisdiction organizes to conduct the activities of personnel management affects how well managers are able to balance productivity, diversity, and public values. Most large nonprofit organizations and government jurisdictions have a central body that is responsible for personnel management. That body, usually called a Human Resource Office or Personnel Office, might emphasize standardization and consistency or it may provide services and consultation in a decentralized system of management. In the former case and in smaller nonprofit and government bodies, line agency managers can expect to have more control over who gets hired and fired and how much they get compensated, but they will also, of course, have more work to do.

Organizational structures affect efficiency. Organization has to do with workflow. If some individual or agency has too much work to do, there will be delays in getting action and the quality of decisions may suffer. Organizations also have to do with power and appearance. Units are created or reorganized to convey the message that a particular problem is important. Separate, visible offices to monitor equal employment policies or to pursue cuts in the number of full-time positions or to provide employees with assistance send messages about priorities to managers, workers, and the public.

LEARNING OBJECTIVES OF THIS CHAPTER

- Have a conceptual framework for considering the relationships between agency tasks and organizational arrangements
- Understand the historical development of personnel management structures in government
- Know how personnel organizations have been designed to ensure accountability

ORGANIZATION THEORY

During the first part of the twentieth century, scholars and managers thought that there was a single best way of organizing to perform a task. Researchers devoted their energies to identifying that single best way. While they searched, a set of common-sense rules prevailed as guidelines reflecting the best wisdom and experi-ence.[1] Since the middle of this century, there has been a greater appreciation of the complexity of tasks, technologies, policies, and sociopolitical environments. A general approach referred to as contingency theory emerged to specify what types of organi-zations are appropriate for various situations.

James D. Thompson, a leading figure in the contingency approach to the study of organizations, drew from the work of Talcott Parsons and offered a way of concep-tualizing organizations that provides a useful framework for this chapter.[2] Thompson suggests that there are three distinct levels of responsibility and control in organiza-tions: technical, managerial, and institutional (see Figure 6.1).

The **technical core** is the activity necessary to deliver whatever services or produce whatever goods an organization is supposed to provide. The technical core of a shoe manufacturing company is the set of tasks and resources that go into cut-ting the leather, treating it, sewing it, and gluing it, so that shoes are made. For an agency issuing drivers' licenses, the technical dimension consists of administering tests about traffic laws, checking eyesight, conducting road tests, taking photos, and providing licenses to those who meet the necessary requirements.

The **managerial dimension** of organizations secures the resources that are needed for the technical tasks and controls and coordinates the technical activity. It is at the managerial level that decisions are made about the what, when, and how much of technical operations. A shoe manufacturer needs to make decisions about what kinds of shoes to make, when to have them ready, and in what quantity. Simi-larly, a manager of a licensing agency needs to decide what hours the office will be open, what tasks to assign to employees, and how to ensure an adequate inventory of forms and other supplies.

Finally, the **institutional responsibilities** are to maintain the kinds of relations with groups, individuals, and other organizations necessary for the agency to function, if not prosper. Marketing and public relations are institutional activities for a shoe company. For a drivers' licensing agency, public support and political accountability are the salient issues. This means courteous service and enforcement of standards designed to ensure highway safety.

As technologies change, organizational structures tend to change as well. Like-wise, different managerial and institutional settings tend to generate different

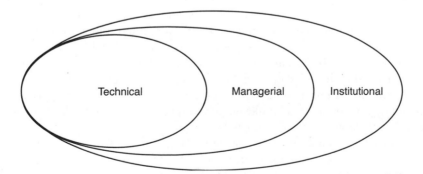

Technical   Managerial   Institutional

FIGURE 6.1   Organizational Dimensions.

organizational characteristics. Organizational structures, in other words, can be viewed as dependent variables, changing in response to other factors. Organizational structures act also as independent variables, affecting parts or the whole of the setting in which an organization operates. An organization that does not, for example, change with new technologies or different tasks that need to be accomplished may be ineffective or inefficient, or both. This general point can be illustrated through a brief review of the history of personnel organization in government.

HISTORY OF PERSONNEL ORGANIZATION IN GOVERNMENT

Size and complexity are two key determinants of organizational structures. Prior to the establishment of merit systems—and even today in small jurisdictions—personnel management was simply a part of general agency management. There was no separate, central agency. The technical tasks of personnel management were not demanding of special expertise, and the number of employees was small enough not to require considerable effort. Employees were hired, compensated, promoted, and fired by managers without any need to adhere to standard policies or to secure central approval. Personnel management, in other words, was located in the managerial dimension of agencies and did not require its own structure.

With the growth in government and public personnel policies, central offices emerged. The passage of the Pendleton Act of 1883 and its counterparts at the state and local level included the establishment of a central citizen watchdog agency to ensure compliance with merit system principles. These **civil service commissions** or **personnel boards** consisted of three to seven members who served for fixed, staggered terms that did not coincide with the terms either for legislators or the chief executive. No more than a bare majority was allowed from the same party, in order to ensure a substantially bipartisan composition.

The requirement for a competitive examination process to gain entry to government employment meant the emergence of professionals to develop and administer examinations. That plus payrolling constituted the first tasks in the technical core of personnel agencies. The staff of the first agencies usually reported to the civil service commissions/personnel boards. The director or manager of this staff was appointed by these boards and often served as executive secretary to the board or commission.

Governments grew and, more importantly, the scope and complexity of public personnel management increased. Classification systems were established to be certain that employees were being paid in a consistent manner. Government included new professional and technical skills and thereby placed new demands on the selection process. Employees enrolled in retirement and health insurance programs. Courts expanded their recognition of public employee rights. Unions and collective bargaining developed. Public employers adopted affirmative action policies.

The structure established at the inception of the merit system was no longer adequate. The technical core grew in size and specialization. Professionals who were expert in psychometrics, job analysis, compensation, and organizational psychology were needed. Civil service commissions could no longer manage this core. These boards typically consisted of citizens who usually met for no more than four to six hours once a month.

Many jurisdictions reorganized in order to create congruence between the tasks and the structures of personnel management. Except for smaller jurisdictions, governments increasingly abandoned the traditional civil service commission structure in the 1970s and 1980s. New central bureaus formed, with new managerial structures, new specialists, and new institutional linkages. Agency managers lost both the work and the responsibilities of personnel management and had to depend on central bureaus for information and for decisions.

An important feature of the Reinventing Government reforms of the 1990s was the re-emergence of agency managers as the primary source of personnel management. Central personnel offices have been downsized and in some cases eliminated, and their responsibilities delegated to agencies. Governments have contracted with private vendors to recruit job applicants, develop and administer tests, conduct training programs, and administer health insurance. While statutes still usually give central office responsibilities for compliance with antipatronage laws and for the negotiation of union contracts, their role is now more service than control oriented. Single pay systems and a common personnel policy framework provide consistency across agencies, but many of the day-to-day functions are increasingly in agency hands.

TECHNICAL CORE STRUCTURES OF PERSONNEL MANAGEMENT

Most of the central agencies in governments and in nonprofit organizations that have such agencies are structured around the following core tasks:

- Recruitment and selection, or staffing
- Classification
- Compensation
- Performance evaluation
- Employee training and development
- Collective bargaining

Appended to the central agency, but maintaining organizational distinctness, may be two other units: an affirmative action office and an appeals board. The latter is separate to serve the substantive and symbolic need to have a third and neutral party as the final source of determination in a dispute between an employee and a supervisor. Some affirmative action advocates point out the need to have affirmative action concerns integrated into all phases of personnel management, and thus a separate office, they argue, is counterproductive. Others contend that until there is a meaningful, comprehensive commitment to diversity, there is a need for a visible, full-time advocate and consultant for equal employment and affirmative action.[3]

Figure 6.2 presents an organization chart, with staffing levels, for a central personnel agency that might be used in a nonprofit organization or public jurisdiction of about 4,000 employees.[4] This chart is based on the position that there should be a separate affirmative action unit.

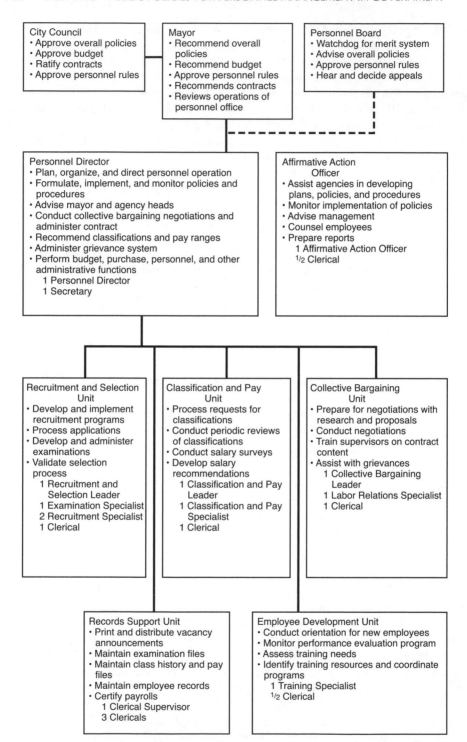

FIGURE 6.2   Organization of Central Personnel Agency for City Government of 4,000.

Source: Adapted from Bureau of Intergovernmental Personnel Programs, *Organizing the Personnel Function* (Washington, DC: Civil Service Commission, 1978), *15.*

AGENCY LINKAGES

Missing from the chart in Figure 6.2 is the organizational link between the central personnel agency and line agencies. That link can be operational instead of structural. That is, the link could be made through processes in which agency officials participate in position analyses, examination development, human resource planning, and the like, but the central personnel office has responsibility for these functions. In addition, agencies could be represented on the negotiating team for management in collective bargaining.

It is critical that agency needs are visible. A common pattern is where the rules and structures designed to provide for fairness and consistency can make the central personnel office become insensitive to the unique needs of various line agencies. A central unit trying to process the examinations, classification and reclassification requests, compensation, training programs, and so forth for a workforce of 30,000 to 50,000—the number of employees in most state and large city governments—can get bogged down and hopelessly behind. Backlogs at the center cause serious operational problems for agencies.

Delegation

One response to this problem has been for central personnel bureaus to delegate authority to agencies to conduct some of the key personnel management functions, with central agency assistance and general direction. Agency managers, for example, would develop their own entrance exams and promotional tests instead of using those designed and administered by the personnel bureau. The federal government took its first steps to delegate authority for personnel management to line agencies in 1938. President Franklin D. Roosevelt issued an executive order mandating that each federal agency establish a unit to be in charge of personnel management. This unit was then given authority to make classification decisions and to promote employees. This step was taken in response to a suggestion the Brownlow Commission made that examined management in the federal government and, inter alia, found that the Civil Service Commission was too rigid and control-oriented.

President Truman reiterated the need for delegation in 1948, in President Jimmy Carter's Civil Service Reform Act of 1978, and again in 1993 in the National Performance Review headed by Vice President Al Gore.[5] The Carter initiative strongly encouraged **delegation** in selection, classification, and performance evaluation for all positions except administrative law judges and jobs common to all or most agencies. The exceptions were designed primarily to maintain consistency and to allow for a more efficient selection process. Vice President Gore's task force, emphasized the general themes of the "reinventing government" movement,[6] and argued that customer and agency needs could best be met by having the central Office of Personnel Management "steer and not row" (i.e., provide general guidance and direction, and let agencies take care of the work and details).[7] This has been the thrust, also, of reforms in some state governments and large nonprofit organizations. Delegation has required that agency managers understand the tools and purposes of personnel management.

Delegation and Technology

Technologies can be a determinant of what should and should not be delegated. Many organizations are finding that with the use of computers, examination questions can be stored and retrieved from a central bank in a way that makes examination development most efficient if this task is not delegated to agencies. Similarly, scoring exams, certifying candidates, and inviting those certified for interviews—all tasks that had been delegated to agencies—can now be done quickly and accurately through a centralized, computerized system. The concern, in short, is getting the job done. Whether agencies or a central office is the best place for getting the job done depends heavily on the task and the technology.

Withdrawal of Delegation

What has been delegated can always be withdrawn. Delegating carries the danger that a task will not be done or someone will take advantage of their discretion and do something inappropriate.[8] A central personnel agency that has delegated authority to a parks department or to a regional field office to develop and administer its own examinations must be certain the parks department or field office has the capacity to do the work and does not engage in patronage or favoritism. If the department either cannot or does not handle the responsibility, then the central personnel agency can withdraw the authority it had delegated.

Communication Between Central Personnel Offices and Agencies

Where there is delegation, there is a need for structures to maintain communication and direction between line agencies and the central agency. These structures are obviously necessary if common standards and direction are to be meaningful at all. Messages need to get to the agency people who will be making personnel decisions, and information must reach the central office if it is to monitor line agency behavior for compliance with statutes and rules. In addition, if central agencies are to provide relevant services as well as necessary controls, then channels for line agency personnel staff to voice their concerns, problems, and suggestions are needed.

Two basic structural responses have been made to this need for linkage. One, which states like California and Wisconsin use, is an advisory group of personnel managers from various departments and agencies. This group meets on a regular basis to share concerns, make suggestions, and maintain communication with the central personnel agency. The central agency, in turn, uses an interagency group like this for reactions to changes being considered and to explain central policies and guidelines.

Another structural response is to establish a unit and/or identify positions within the central agency responsible for serving and monitoring the personnel management activities in specific line agencies. Figure 6.3, which presents the organizational structure of the federal Office of Personnel Management, includes this feature.

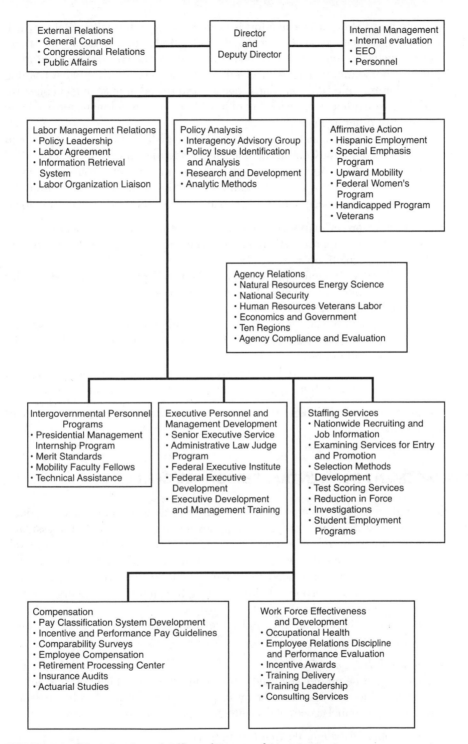

FIGURE 6.3   Organization of Office of Personnel Management.

In some jurisdictions a special effort is made to work with small agencies, which do not have the capacity to accept much, if any, delegated authority. Sometimes these agencies can be clustered in ways that take advantage of the strengths and interests of the agency personnel managers involved. Someone particularly good at training supervisors, for example, and someone especially interested in engaging in collective bargaining can provide the basis for a pool in which a personnel manager from one agency can assist other agencies.

Achieving the right balance between control and discretion, consistency and responsiveness, is not easy. Central and line agencies tend to coexist in rather hostile, adversarial relationships. Agencies compete with one another for resources. Individuals vie with one another for status. In addition, positions and roles differ within the network of personnel management. One scholar has described these roles as follows:

1. Supervisors are primarily oriented toward meeting work unit objectives. They are unlikely to support costly or cumbersome personnel procedures required by laws or regulations.
2. Centralized staff agency personnel are likely to support a single set of rules and regulations, and to advocate centralization of personnel functions in the name of efficiency and uniformity.
3. Agency personnel managers have loyalties divided between professional standards and service to supervisors. They are also subject to influence by employees and unions.
4. Regulatory employees are likely to favor increased oversight for their agency. Their values support the application of a common policy to individual cases.[9]

These differences pose challenges to efforts to work in ways that maximize the use of existing resources.

MANAGEMENT IN A CENTRAL PERSONNEL OFFICE

Much of what managers of a central personnel agency do is what any manager does. They secure the staff, office space, and supplies needed to complete the assigned tasks. Records are gathered and organized in a way that provides timely access. Evaluation and analysis are conducted in order to identify strengths and weaknesses and remedy problems before they become unmanageable or fatal to the organization. Managerial leadership is responsible for directing the energies of the organization and minimizing counterproductive conflict.

In addition to these generally applicable managerial duties, there are tasks specific to a central personnel agency. The following is a checklist of these tasks:

- *Develop Policies and Rules*
  These cannot be promulgated and enforced unilaterally, but legislators, chief executive officers, and others who must approve policy proposals rely very heavily on the personnel agency and its director for suggestions for improvement.

- *Prepare and Distribute Written Instructions*
  Laws and rules need to be translated and elaborated into rather detailed instructions for employees and managers.

- *Train Operating Staff*
Written communication is rarely sufficient. Training sessions must be held in order to ensure that those who on a daily basis must interpret and apply laws, rules, and guidelines know what is intended.

- *Make Certain Personnel Management Functions are Performed*
The reference here is to the core technical tasks of personnel management (i.e., selection, classification, compensation, development, employee assistance, and so forth).

- *Participate in Management Problem Solving*
As a fundamental part of agency and jurisdictional management, personnel managers contribute to the analysis of problems and proposals. The Total Quality Management (TQM) approach relies heavily on teams of employees to identify problems and to generate and evaluate potential solutions. Managers, however, retain the responsibility for deciding which solutions to adopt.[10]

- *Negotiate Contracts*
Where there is collective bargaining, no matter what the scope and no matter where responsibility for contract negotiation formally rests, personnel managers must participate in negotiations. Contracts also include private vendors of goods and services. Management must also negotiate the details of these contracts.

- *Process Appeals and Grievance*
The head of a central personnel agency often is the final source of appeal before the involvement of a neutral third party like an administrative law judge, arbitrator, personnel board, or appeals commission. This is both an administrative and a quasi-judicial role.

As part of getting missions accomplished and jobs done, managers mediate between the core technology components of an organization and salient actors and elements of the organization's environment. Sometimes they have the help of analysts, public relations specialists, and liaison personnel in other organizations. Whether those resources are available or not, heads of personnel agencies in government have always played a major and direct role in the linkages between their agencies and the political institutions and processes around them.

INSTITUTIONAL RELATIONS

The status and location of the central personnel agency in the organization generally have generated considerable debate and heat. Of all the aspects of personnel management organization, this is the one with the most symbolic importance. The rhetoric usually argues that placing personnel management close to the chief executive officer is essential for integrating human resource policies with the general mission and concerns of an organization, while the argument for separation and distance from the chief executive officer is that the professionalism and integrity of human resource management is compromised when CEOs and politicians meddle.

This is not, however, to say that there are no substantive issues. As pointed out at the beginning of this text, there is a need for a delicate balance between profession-alism and accountability. The structure of institutional relations is an important ingredient in establishing that balance.

Relationship to the Chief Executive Officer

Personnel management is not always a concern of chief executives, especially those elected to office. The reformers of the late 1800s and early 1900s were generally anx-ious to strengthen the offices of chief elected officials. Chief executives acquired new powers and, in particular, had new responsibilities for the formulation and adminis-tration of budgets. Personnel management was not, however, a part of this effort. Instead, as already pointed out, civil service commissions and personnel boards were established to isolate personnel management from political officials.

A major and visible departure from this traditional separation was made when President Roosevelt's Committee on Administrative Management made its report in 1937. That committee, dominated by individuals familiar with management patterns in the private sector, said:

> Personnel administration is an integral part of general administration; the specialized per-sonnel agency of highest rank should therefore be closely attached to the President's office. The principle of division of labor requires that personnel administration be given the undivided attention of professionally qualified persons; but the responsibility for developing adequate and constructive policies, standards and activities throughout the Executive Branch of the Government cannot be segregated from general administration and separately discharged without disadvantage both to the administration of the person-nel function and to general administration.[11]

Specifically, this committee recommended replacing the Civil Service Commis-sion with an advisory body, having that advisory body examine candidates for the head of a central personnel agency and certify three names to the president for appointment. The president would be allowed to dismiss the personnel head without consultation with the advisory unit. The Senate approved this proposal, but it failed to get enough support in the House. Until the 1978 Civil Service Reform Act, the chairperson of the U.S. Civil Service Commission did not serve at the president's pleasure and had an unworkable set of responsibilities.

The chair of the Civil Service Commission, and the commission itself, was in an awkward, self-contradictory position. It was a watchdog that was supposed to exercise surveillance over itself. The commission made policy, administered policy, and adjudi-cated disputes concerning its own behavior. There was, in essence, no watchdog and no third party. The vulnerabilities of this system became all too evident when, during the administration of President Richard M. Nixon, Fred Malek produced a manual to inform Nixon loyalists about how they could use and/or get around the system to appoint politically acceptable individuals to civil service positions.[12] The abuses that resulted became one of the articles of impeachment against President Nixon and helped create a receptive environment for the proposals incorporated in the 1978 Civil Service Reform Act.[13]

The federal reform act followed the general model suggested by the National Civil Service League—the same organization that played a major role in securing passage of the Pendleton Act—and the model used in large nonprofit organizations and also adopted by a number of state and local governments.[14] That model provides for a central personnel agency headed by someone who serves at the pleasure of the chief executive officer. Governments also established a full-time body to hear appeals and a civil service commission or personnel board to act in a watchdog and advisory capacity. In the case of the federal government, the personnel agency is the Office of Personnel Management. The appeals and watchdog function are combined in the Merit System Protection Board.

Civil service reform efforts in the 1970s and 1980s included provisions to make personnel management more integral to policy making and implementation generally and to have directors of the central personnel agency serve at the pleasure of the chief executive officers. This proposal generated considerable debate. The common pattern within legislative bodies was for the issue to become highly partisan, with the majority party (regardless of whether it was Republican or Democrat) favoring the change and the minority party charging that the proposal meant a return to spoils and patronage.[15]

The National Civil Service League, in presenting its proposal to remove the isolation of personnel management from chief elected officials and make civil service commissions only advisory doubted whether the initial intent of these commissions was ever fulfilled. The league argued:

> The claim that these commissions are insulating the system against pressures is often unfounded. Experience in many jurisdictions has shown that the deliberations of so-called independent commissions frequently reflect political expediency rather than the requirements of good public personnel administration.[16]

The International Personnel Management Association, on the other hand, saw continued virtue in having political independence for the personnel system and advocated that the personnel director be named by a civil service commission rather than by the chief executive.[17]

The patterns in state governments are mixed, although most adopted the basic model advocated by the National Civil Service League. Each of the 50 states has a full-time head of a central personnel agency, and the governor appoints most either directly or indirectly. In 21 states, the governor appoints the personnel director who serves at the governor's pleasure. In 15 states, a director of administration or director of finance appoints the directors, and the personnel agencies are located within those departments. In the remainder, directors are appointed by civil service commissions or personnel boards. Almost all of those appointed by civil service commissions are further isolated from the dynamics of politics by their term of office. They are classified civil servants with permanent tenure. In three states, personnel directors serve a fixed term (four or five years). Medium to large urban governments follow patterns similar to state governments.[18]

Civil Service Commissions/Personnel Boards in Government

Chief executives in government and civil service commissions or personnel boards are linked because mayors and governors, with the consent of legislative bodies, appoint members of these boards and commissions. The federal parallel is the Merit System Protection Board, which replaced the Civil Service Commission with the passage of the 1978 Civil Service Reform Act. This link is intentionally weak. Members serve for fixed terms that do not coincide with that of the chief executive, thus limiting the ability of the mayor, governor, or president to appoint or remove members. Moreover, chief executives are kept from appointing more than a bare majority from any one political party. A number of jurisdictions also specify that one member be a lawyer and another member have personnel management experience. There may be traditions that there be a certain balance of representation from women, minorities, labor, business, and the like. A major reason for these provisions is to establish distance between these commissions and chief executives and make the commissions independent from politics.

Although some state and local governments retain traditional civil service commissions with a relatively broad scope of authority, most have provided these bodies with a rather short list of tasks. Almost all act as watchdogs and advisory bodies. The watchdog function is usually performed when personnel boards serve as appeal bodies. The focus, then, however, tends to be on individual cases, rather than the system as a whole. Perceptive boards can treat individual cases as, potentially, symptoms of larger problems, but this is asking a lot from part-time, citizen bodies.

State and local personnel boards/civil service commissions are also usually involved in the promulgation of personnel rules. Like other administrative agencies, personnel departments issue rules that elaborate on laws passed and specify how a particular law is to be implemented. These rules must be based on a statute or ordinance, and they have the force of law. The typical procedure for promulgating new or revising existing rules is for proposals to be considered at a public hearing and then to be submitted to the personnel board for its approval. Once approved by the board or commission, the chief executive of the jurisdiction and/or legislative body must approve.

Finally, in some jurisdictions these boards and commissions have administrative roles. In one-half of the states and municipal governments, personnel boards must approve the classification of positions and the allocation of positions to salary ranges. This approval is a review and acceptance of the technical work of personnel staff. The process is, frankly, boring for everyone involved. Controversies are almost welcomed. Unless the personnel staff does an outrageously incompetent job, controversy is highly unlikely. Involvement in administration other than through compensation and classification actions is very rare. Only three states have civil service commissions that have extensive involvement in the administration of their central personnel agencies.

Labor Relations

Another issue is whether labor relations should be structurally separate from the rest of personnel management. The argument for separation states that negotiating and administering contracts are tasks distinct from more traditional personnel management and therefore should be separate. The counterargument is that there is a need for compatibility and integration between what is and is not bargained. Two-thirds of the states that engage in bargaining appear to have found the argument for integration convincing. In these states, the federal government and those nonprofit organizations that have unionized workforces, the director of personnel has responsibility for labor relations.

Budget Offices

During the 1960s, there was a general movement to merge agencies responsible for management functions and policies into a single department. This usually meant merging budgeting, personnel, and purchasing. The purpose was to strengthen the ability of chief executives to manage. Placing management functions all into a department of administration or management services would, it was hoped, ensure coordination and consistency and thereby increase both the chief executive's base of knowledge about management and increase the ability to provide common direction.[19] A line agency, for example, would be less able to play off a personnel department against a budget office. Agencies could not go to the personnel department with requests to reclassify jobs and then present an affirmative response as leverage to get increased funds from the budget office.

The logic of consolidating personnel and budgeting assumed equal footing for the two. Where budget and personnel are placed side-by-side, however, budget is likely to dominate the content of decisions. The experience of most jurisdictions has been a loss of weight given to the concerns of personnel management. Position analyses and classification decisions were heavily affected by what a budget office determined could be afforded, rather than by the duties and responsibilities assigned to the job. Appeals and grievances were settled based more on calculations about the costs of settlement and the costs of pursuing the appeal or grievance, rather than on the policies and precedents that might be established.

There must, of course, be coordination and joint action between budget and personnel offices. Agencies seeking to make an appointment must get authorization to spend the money, and they must get authorization to recruit, examine, and select for a particular position in a particular classification. Ideally, a job is defined according to assigned duties and responsibilities, then budget concerns determine whether the job can be filled and whether it should be filled on a full- or part-time basis.

Some chief executives are attracted to a structure that places budget and personnel in the same department because the department head can resolve conflict rather than it requiring the attention and energies of the chief executive. From the standpoint of most personnel directors, gubernatorial and mayoral involvement is preferable to resolution by an agency head whose primary concern is costs. Separate status and visibility generally provides a better opportunity for personnel management input than does membership in a merged department.

Purchasing Departments

Contracts for services have important implications for personnel policy. These contracts are, however, administered by purchasing departments, not personnel offices. In some cases, contracting out is specifically an attempt to avoid the regulations, compensation plans or union contracts of the organization. If governments or nonprofit organizations are contracting to run away from problems in personnel management, the problems will, of course, persist.

Some contracts include bad personnel policy. There may be exploitation of workers with low wages, no benefits, and/or no job security. Contracts may have no processes for dealing with grievances and/or for evaluating employee performance. Contracts may even be a way of providing patronage to campaign contributors and political supporters.[20]

Although personnel managers traditionally have not been involved in the writing or monitoring of contracts, the perspectives and expertise of personnel managers are needed.[21] It is especially important for personnel managers to participate in contracting out decisions when these contracts replace existing employees. That might ensure that contracting is neither adopting bad personnel practices nor avoiding problems that need to be resolved.

Legislative Bodies

Legislatures have not been major participants in personnel management processes in government. They do not, for example, play a role in personnel that is at all similar to the role played in budgeting. There are, however, the kinds of linkages between legislative bodies and personnel agencies that are common to most administrative agencies.

Except for a handful of states such as Michigan and California where the constitutions include statements of public personnel management policy, legislative bodies pass laws that establish the legal framework within which personnel management takes place. In most states, there are state personnel laws that apply to local governments, and the federal government has laws and regulations that apply to state and local jurisdictions. The major federal laws that apply are the Fair Labor Standards Act, equal employment opportunity laws, and merit system requirements attached to the receipt of certain federal funds. For the most part, school boards, county boards, city councils, and state legislatures are free to pass their own personnel policies. Many of these legislative bodies in the early twenty-first century have wrestled with whether to provide domestic partner benefits for employees of their respective governments—a microcosm of the general debate about support for civil unions and marriage between same-sex couples.

In addition to passing laws, legislative bodies are linked to public personnel management agencies through budgets, procedures for confirming the appointments of senior personnel people, and members of personnel boards, and ratifying collective bargaining agreements. Legislative bodies usually approve—even if through the process of not objecting—administrative rules promulgated by the personnel agency. Casework for constituents includes personnel matters, although there obviously are some inquiries and suggestions that legislators might make that would be regarded as inappropriate, if not illegal.

Small local governments and many of the nonprofit organizations are frequently structured in a way that keeps at least part of the governing body close to personnel management issues and practices. Some boards, for example, have personnel subcommittees that play an active role in selection, compensation, and disciplinary decisions. These committees, in some instances, are actually the appointing authorities and supervisors.

With the passage of the 1978 Civil Service Reform Act, Congress decided to take more seriously its responsibility to provide oversight over personnel management in the federal government. A provision of the act states that the **General Accountability Office (GAO),** an auditing and review arm of Congress, must submit annually a report that examines adherence to merit principles in the federal civil service system and the general operation of the Office of Personnel Management. In addition, Congress directed the GAO to report on the implementation by agencies of the policy to develop and use employee performance evaluation systems. In essence, there are now two watchdogs over the federal personnel system, the Merit System Protection Board and the General Accountability Office.

SUMMARY

Organizational structures do make a difference. They direct the flow of information, and they identify who has formal authority and responsibility. When the flow of information and the scope of authority do not match the tasks being done or the external environment of the organization, inefficiency and ineffectiveness are likely to result. Reorganizations are necessary to keep pace with events. Reorganizations are also needed to signal changes in policies and priorities. A new unit is often interpreted as intent to pursue or emphasize a new policy.

As public personnel management has grown in scope and complexity, so also have the organizational structures of personnel management in government. Larger nonprofit organizations and government jurisdictions have seen the emergence of specialized and separate agencies. The most recent developments have also recognized the need to provide more political accountability and a more central and coherent management role for personnel systems. Personnel directors and agencies have been moved closer to chief executives.

As overall personnel management responsibility has moved closer to elected executives, there has been a simultaneous movement to delegate increasing authority to line agency and field office managers for their own personnel. Generally this is a welcomed development that often substitutes the opportunity to meet specific agency needs for the frustrations of relying on central standards, rules, and procedures. Devolution of responsibility does, on the other hand, mean more work for agencies and a need for more personnel management expertise among agency managers.

DISCUSSION QUESTIONS

1. What are the implications of personnel management delegation for agency and field office managers?
2. Are part-time, citizen watchdog civil service commission/personnel boards worth keeping? If so, what should their role and their authority be?
3. Describe the relationship between the chief executive officer and the human resource management officer in a specific (your choice) organization or government. What are the formal authority and appointing relationships? How, if at all, are evaluations of personnel policies and practices made?
4. Do formal organizational structures matter? Are not informal ties what really count?

GLOSSARY

Civil service commission A bipartisan or nonpartisan body, often with part-time citizen members, with responsibility for serving as a watchdog to prevent patronage or other abuses. These commissions can hear disciplinary appeals and/or have direct supervisory roles

Delegation When a central office, like a personnel bureau, gives authority to agencies to perform functions and make decisions that otherwise would be handled by the central bureau

General Accountability Office (GAO) An organization that conducts performance audits and policy analyses for the United States Congress. It is a staff agency of Congress

Institutional responsibilities for an organization The establishment and maintenance of relationships between an agency and other groups and organizations that affect how effectively the agency will operate

Managerial dimension of an organization The actions needed to coordinate or direct the technical activity of an organization and to secure the resources needed for these tasks

Personnel board Another term for "civil service commission"

Technical core of an organization The activities essential to provide the services or produce the goods for which an organization is responsible

SOURCES

Cayer, N. J. (1995). Merit system reform in the states. In S. W. Hays, & R. C. Kearney, eds., *Public personnel administration: Problems and prospects* (3rd ed.). Englewood Cliffs, NJ: Prentice-Hall, pp. 291–305.
A summary analysis of civil service reforms, including those related to organizational issues, since the mid-1970s.

Kettl, D. F., Ingraham, P. W., Sanders, R. P., & Horner, C. (1996). *Civil service reform: Building a government that works.* Washington, DC: Brookings Institute.
A brief critique of both the federal civil service and the reform efforts of the National Performance Review.

National Performance Review (1993). In *From red tape to results: Creating a government that works better and costs less.* Washington, DC: National Performance Review.
Report of the task force on reinventing the federal government, chaired by Vice President Al Gore.

Thompson, J. D. (1967). *Organizations in action: Social science bases of administrative theory.* New York: McGraw-Hill.
Review of organizational theory literatures and classic presentation of the contingency approach to organizations.

NOTES

1. Herbert A. Simon, *Administrative Behavior,* 2nd ed. (New York: Macmillan, 1957).
2. James D. Thompson, *Organizations in Action: Social Science Bases of Administrative Theory* (New York: McGraw-Hill, 1967).
3. Lora Liss, "Affirmative Action Officers: Cops, Robbers, Puppets, Spies or Change Agents?" Paper presented to American Sociological Association, August 1975.

4. The basic framework for this figure can be found in U.S. Civil Service Commission, Bureau of Intergovernmental Personnel Programs, *Organizing the Personnel Function: A Guide for Local Government Managers* (Washington, DC: U.S. Civil Service Commission, April 1978), 15. In addition to some minor modifications of the federal suggestion, collective bargaining is added to the personnel functions of this hypothetical model.

5. National Performance Review, in *From Red Tape to Results: Creating a Government That Works Better and Costs Less* (Washington, DC: National Performance Review, 1993).

6. David Osborne and Ted Gaebler, *Reinventing Government: How the Entrepreneurial Spirit Is Transforming the Public Sector* (Reading, MA: Addison-Wesley, 1992).

7. The Office of Personnel Management was better at reducing its staff and mission than at defining a new direction and mission for itself. Donald F. Kettl, Patricia W. Ingraham, Ronald P. Sanders, and Constance Horner, *Civil Service Reform: Building a Government That Works* (Washington, DC: Brookings Institution, 1996), 63–65.

8. Dennis Daley, "Organization of the Personnel Function: The New Patronage and Decentralization," in Steven W. Hays and Richard C. Kearney, *Public Personnel Administration: Problems and Prospects*, 2nd ed. (Englewood Cliffs, NJ: Prentice-Hall, 1990), 20–28.

9. Donald E. Klinger, "Political Influences on the Design of State and Local Personnel Systems," *Review of Public Personnel Administration* 1, no. 3 (Summer 1981).

10. Steven Cohen and Ronald Brand, *Total Quality Management in Government* (San Francisco: Jossey-Bass, 1993), 76–150.

11. Floyd W. Reeves and Paul T. David, *Personnel Administration in the Federal Service: President's Committee on Administrative Management* (Washington, DC: Government Printing Office, 1937), 37.

12. White House Personnel Office, "The Malek Manual," in Frank J. Thompson, ed. *Classics of Public Personnel Policy*, 2nd ed. (Pacific Grove, CA: Brooks/Cole, 1991), 58–81.

13. U.S. House of Representatives, Post Office and Civil Service Committee, *Final Report on Violations and Abuses of Merit Principles in Federal Employment* (Committee Print 94–28), (Washington, DC: Government Printing Office, 1976).

14. Dennis L. Dresang, "Diffusion of Civil Service Reform: State and Federal Government," *Review of Public Personnel Administration* 2, no. 2 (Spring 1982): 35–49.

15. Dennis L. Dresang, "Public Personnel Reform: A Summary of State Activity," *Public Personnel Management* 7, no. 5 (September/October 1978): 287–294.

16. National Civil Service League, *A Model Public Personnel Administration Law* (Washington, DC: National Civil Service League, 1970), 5.

17. International Personnel Management Association, *Guidelines for Drafting a Public Personnel Administration Law* (Chicago: International Personnel Management Association, 1973).

18. Dresang, "Public Personnel Reform," 291.

19. Joe E. Nusbaum, "State Departments of Administration: Their Role and Trends of Development," *State Government* 35 (Spring 1962): 124–129.

20. Donald F. Kettl, "Privatization: Implications for the Public Work Force," in Carolyn Ban and Norma Riccucci, eds., *Public Personnel Management: Current Concerns—Future Challenges* (New York: Longman, 1991), 254–264.

21. Edward M. Meyers, "Regulation of Federal Contractors' Employment Patterns," *Public Administration Review* 49, no. 1 (January/February 1989): 52–60.

Chapter 7

Succession Planning

In 2011, the largest generation in American history will be gray. According to the U.S. Census Bureau, the number of people in the United States who will be celebrating their sixty-fifth birthday will jump to 3.3 million, an increase of 21 percent from the year before. The ranks of the retired will grow from one in eight in 2006 to one in five in 2030.

Already some employers, private and public, are hosting retirement parties for almost one-third of their employees. In the federal government, the number of people over 50 years old was 34 percent in 2005. More than one-third of the civilian workers in the federal government will be eligible for retirement in 2010.[1] The pattern is similar in state governments and large nonprofit organizations. Some occupations, especially in the managerial, transportation, environmental, and health fields, will have retirement rates near 50 percent.[2]

Obviously, the vacancies that emerge from these retirement rates create opportunities for individuals. Another way of responding to these demographic facts is to worry about how organizations are going to fill so many positions. The challenge is especially serious because retirements naturally mean the exodus of the most experienced, senior staff.

To varying degrees, organizations are preparing for the retirement of baby boomers.[3] The conscious efforts of assessing the effects of retirements and designing strategies for filling impending vacancies is known as **succession planning**. This process has been available to personnel managers for more than two decades. Initially, it was touted as a way of taking steps to get more women and minorities in middle and senior positions. But succession planning has been on the shelf, collecting dust, until now. Even with the obvious challenges of replacing baby boomers, serious succession efforts are increasing, but not common.

Succession planning follows the following basic steps:

1. Identify expected vacancies.
2. Determine critical positions and functions.
3. Identify current employees who might be developed to fill vacancies.
4. Provide training and mentorships to develop current employees with potential.
5. Develop strategy for recruiting employees with needed skills and abilities.
6. Evaluate results and determine what further measures are needed.

Succession planning begins with not only cataloging positions that will be open because of expected retirements, but also with assessing organizational needs. Given the number of baby boomers, it is almost inevitable that agencies and firms will have to consider not filling every vacancy and doing their work in a different way. Organizational assessments may suggest redesigning workflow. New technologies may be the answer.

The usual response to a vacancy is to treat it individually and to try to find a replacement who is someone like the recent incumbent. The focus is typically on a position. Clearly, individual positions and individual employees are the building blocks of organizations. The point is that succession planning invites considering the whole when dealing with the individual parts. Position analyses are critical to developing an inventory of the skills and abilities that are being lost when incumbents leave. The assessment of current employees and job candidates is essential for knowing what pool of talents and experiences an organization has and what it needs.

The full range of personnel management concerns and policies should be included in succession planning, and the scope of personnel functions should go beyond hiring. To analyze the workforce in terms of skills, retirements, and turnover without also determining the status of diversity in the workforce is to separate a fundamental policy objective from personnel planning. A focus on new hiring and layoffs may neglect consideration of career development for current employees or the possibilities that come from restructuring jobs. Increasing reliance on part-time, older workers or employees with responsibilities for caring for family members may generate a need for redefining how and when work is done. Turnover might be a function of low salaries or poor morale. In short, when done properly, succession planning can provide a framework for evaluating and improving the functions of personnel management.

LEARNING OBJECTIVES OF THIS CHAPTER

- Understand how general patterns of decision making apply to the arena of human resource management
- Appreciate the contribution of succession planning
- Learn a model and set of techniques that might be used for succession planning
- Apply the model to a hypothetical organization

INCREMENTALISM AND PERSONNEL MANAGEMENT

For the most part, personnel management follows the incremental pattern of decision making associated with budgeting and policy making generally.[4] Incremental decision making is a limited search for alternative solutions to a problem, a search that generally stops when a satisfactory but not necessarily optimal solution is found. The result of this pattern most frequently is a small change or adjustment to the status quo rather than an attempt at a more comprehensive or radical solution. In part, **incrementalism** is a consequence of the limits of information, time, and wisdom.[5] Managers simply cannot be expected to identify all possible alternatives

and weigh all the costs and benefits. In part, incrementalism emerges from our inclination to minimize risks and avoid uncertainty.[6] We prefer the known to the
unknown, even if by not being bold and adventuresome, we only satisfy rather than
maximize our goals.

In managing people, incrementalism means accepting current positions and
structures as the framework within which one must work. If any changes are to be
made, they are modest adjustments in the current base. For the most part, personnel
activities do, in fact, concentrate on hiring replacements and on making modest
adjustments in response to specific problems. Alterations in the duties or responsibilities assigned to a position might be made when the position is vacated and then
refilled. Increases or decreases in the number of positions allocated to an agency
usually occur as part of a budget exercise. Managers who must cut the size of their
staff cope by not filling whatever vacancy happens to exist rather than analyzing how
they might creatively redeploy existing personnel. Managers alter training programs,
work schedules, and reporting relationships in order to address a specific issue or
satisfy a request from a particular individual. In short, there is more continuity than
change. What change occurs is usually modest.

Ad hoc, piecemeal decisions can have significant consequences for larger goals
and issues. The strictness of law enforcement becomes a function of the number of
police officers. Providing assistance to those in need depends on how many social
workers are hired. A shift from providing after school activities for young people to
running a program to divert boys from joining gangs is best explained by a new hire
that successively won a lucrative contract recently awarded by a government agency.
In other words, questions about mission and direction can be answered explicitly and
integrated into human resource planning or implicitly through decisions made on the
basis of incremental staffing decisions.

Although routines are essential for efficiency and although as individuals we
prefer to avoid uncertainties and major decisions, there is the need and the capacity
for careful and rational decision making. Social psychologists tell us that, within the
obvious limits of available information and analytical abilities, we can identify and
weigh objectives and then calculate how best to achieve those objectives. They warn
us, however, that because our inclinations are not to make decisions rationally, we are
well advised to adopt a set of procedures to discipline ourselves.[7] This is the perspective to apply to succession planning specifically and human resource planning generally. The procedures themselves do not prescribe any particular outcome. They are
designed to guide managers to act carefully and systematically and to break out of
the natural inclination to decide incrementally.

USE OF HUMAN RESOURCE PLANNING

The practice of identifying and forecasting personnel needs and devising strategies
for meeting those needs is recent in personnel management activity. A survey of
private-sector organizations reveals that whereas in the mid-1960s there were only
a few fragmented attempts at human resource planning, by 1975, 86 percent of the
firms responding compiled human resource plans and by 1990 almost all large

organizations had plans.[8] In the public sector, there has been far less involvement.[9] To encourage more jurisdictions to plan ahead, the federal government published a manual with simple computer programs, providing a step-by-step procedure for calculating retention rates and then combining an organization's retention rate with general actuarial data to determine replacement needs.[10] The federal government itself took major steps to assess its needs as it approached the beginning of the twenty-first century. The Office of Personnel Management commissioned a study by the Hudson Institute and participated in a major study launched privately by the National Commission on the Public Service, known as the Volcker Commission.[11] While these efforts were all at the level of the jurisdiction as a whole, the benefits and the processes of human resource planning also apply to individual agencies.

Planning and Diversity

Since the mid-1970s, almost all organizations and jurisdictions have complied with standards set by the Equal Employment Opportunity Commission (EEOC) by formulating **affirmative action plans**.[12] These plans identify the proportion of women and minority-group members in the various units and at the various levels of an organization, compare these percentages with the percentage of available and qualified affirmative action candidates in the general working population, and then set goals and formulate strategies to correct imbalances. In other words, affirmative action plans are succession plans with a strategic emphasis on diversity goals.

Most personnel textbooks that discuss affirmative action and human resource planning keep the two separate. The approach used here, however, integrates the two. A merger of affirmative action and succession planning provides managers the opportunity to pursue simultaneously agency missions, productivity, employee satisfaction, and diversity. Demographic analyses point to the need to anticipate more diverse workforces.[13] The diversity includes a higher proportion of nonwhites and women, more inclusion of workers with disabilities, and an increase in part-time employment of older people. As Robert T. Golembiewski argues, organizations must make important changes in their rules, structures, and cultures to respond effectively to a different profile of employees.[14]

Planning and Downsizing

Political and financial pressures sometimes require agency managers to reduce their staff. The most common response has been incremental. Agency managers prefer cuts through **attrition**. As employees retire or resign, the positions they vacate are left open or removed from the roster.[15] Another untargeted, incremental approach has been to provide incentives for employees to retire early. To implement the cutback targets set by the Al Gore task force to reinvent government, the federal government used a program to give $25,000 payments to employees who resigned or retired early. While this could be used somewhat selectively, the program essentially was limited to the pool of employees near retirement. The strategy in early retirement programs is to shift costs from the payroll to pension plans and then to replace retirees with new, lower-paid employees or to eliminate the position(s). The problem, of course, is that resignations and retirements occur randomly, and agency managers may find some of these vacancies damaging.[16]

A planned **downsizing** allows for smart proactive decision making rather than just coping and reacting. Agency heads, perhaps working with a task force, can determine how best to continue with fewer people. That might require redefining the agency mission, restructuring work and positions, and acquiring or developing new skills. To implement such a plan, a manager may want to take advantage of some anticipated retirements, but there may also be a need to terminate the employment of some workers through a **reduction in force (RIF)** or **layoff**.

Reductions in force are typically complicated and require even more planning. Union contracts and public personnel rules usually provide employees with bumping rights that allow an individual faced with a nondisciplinary termination to take a position away from a less senior person. Thus, a manager who is considering downsizing through layoffs needs to consider the potential effects of bumping. One effect may be to have employees in jobs to which they have a right but not necessarily an interest or ability. In addition, the process almost inevitably lowers morale. In other words, while the intent behind downsizing may be to lower costs and increase productivity, the process inherently threatens key ingredients of productivity—competence and motivation—discussed in Chapter 5. Succession planning needs to extend beyond people and positions and also to cover training, counseling, and incentives.

APPROACHES TOWARD SUCCESSION PLANNING

A common method of formulating plans for the personnel needs of an organization is to begin by defining the organization's goals and then translating those goals into human resource requirements.[17] This top-down approach has the strength of logic behind it. Objectives should determine needs. Nonetheless, the beauty of logic is not always matched by the ease of implementation. For some organizations, mission statements and objectives are vague or contradictory, the outcome of political compromise or very general goals. Objectives are sometimes difficult to translate into personnel needs.[18]

Another approach to human resource planning might be referred to as bottom-up. This perspective emphasizes information on current employees. Organizations that are downsizing may use a bottom-up approach. A jurisdiction whose prime concern is public sector labor costs will tend to use a planning process that begins with the salaries of employees and then anticipates the effects on organizational output and organizational goals under different strategies for reducing labor costs. Also, organizations that take a best athlete approach use a bottom-up perspective. These organizations get the best people and let them determine precisely what the objectives are or should be. This approach is more likely to be taken by a nonprofit organization or a state or local government unit that depends heavily on getting federal government grants.

Clearly, it is essential to combine both the top-down and bottom-up approaches. Despite the difficulties sometimes involved in identifying missions and organizational goals and then calculating what human resources are required, such an attempt must be made.[19] At the same time, labor costs, diversity, competencies, and other workforce traits are of vital concern. In some situations they may be the primary concern. The approach used here, incorporated in the model presented below, uses the lessons of earlier chapters and includes the multiple goals and multiple purposes of personnel management.

A MODEL FOR SUCCESSION PLANNING

Succession planning can be sophisticated and comprehensive or it can be relatively simple. In part, this depends on the size, complexity, and resources of a government or nonprofit agency. Initially establishing a system of planning and collecting the necessary information generally requires more effort than subsequent exercises. The planning that takes place after one constructs the procedures and gathers the data is a matter of refinement to get more precision or accuracy and/or of concentration on select issues or problems. There is, in other words, a kind of incrementalism in the planning process itself.

Figure 7.1 presents a general outline for a succession planning process. It serves primarily as a checklist for proceeding in an orderly and systematic fashion. Following checklists such as this helps us discipline ourselves lest we get seduced by a shortcut or an apparently satisfactory solution and thus risk neglecting an option that is better than satisfactory.

There are four major phases to human resource planning:

1. Determining organizational objectives
2. Analyzing critical variables
3. Selecting strategies
4. Evaluating results

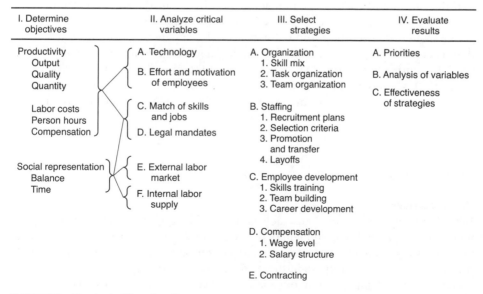

I. Determine objectives	II. Analyze critical variables	III. Select strategies	IV. Evaluate results
Productivity Output Quality Quantity	A. Technology B. Effort and motivation of employees	A. Organization 1. Skill mix 2. Task organization 3. Team organization	A. Priorities B. Analysis of variables C. Effectiveness of strategies
Labor costs Person hours Compensation	C. Match of skills and jobs D. Legal mandates	B. Staffing 1. Recruitment plans 2. Selection criteria 3. Promotion and transfer 4. Layoffs	
Social representation Balance Time	E. External labor market F. Internal labor supply	C. Employee development 1. Skills training 2. Team building 3. Career development	
		D. Compensation 1. Wage level 2. Salary structure	
		E. Contracting	

FIGURE 7.1   Strategic Planning Process.

The distinctions between phases are analytical and meant to portray a logical thinking process. In fact, of course, we often anticipate the implications of one phase or one decision on another, and so the actual sequence is rarely neat and orderly.

To explain the planning process in a less dry and abstract manner, consider an example of a state agency responsible for administering a student loan program. The name of this fictitious agency is the College Aid Board (CAB). The agency's legislative mandate is to provide low-interest (4 percent) loans to needy and able individuals who want to attend one of the state's eight colleges or two universities. As a condition of receiving the loan, an individual must be a full-time student. There are no restrictions about graduate or undergraduate student status or about how many years one may receive a loan. There are, however, limits on how much one may receive—no more than $5,000 per year and no more than $20,000 total per individual. CAB receives a fixed sum every year for administrative expenses and the agency is authorized to provide loans totaling $50 million annually. The initial capital was raised through a special bond.

The head (executive director) of CAB is appointed by the governor and confirmed by the state senate for fixed five-year terms. This arrangement is to provide a balance between accountability on the one hand and safeguards against using the loans as patronage on the other. The staff has civil service status and consists of an executive assistant, a personnel manager, an information officer, personal secretary to the executive director, five accountants, 17 loan examiners (to determine the eligibility of loan applicants), five loan officers (to select recipients), ten loan collectors (to oversee repayment), and 16 clerical support persons. The loan officers are organized on a team basis and rank slightly higher than examiners or collectors. Figure 7.2 presents an organization chart and Table 7.1 provides personnel management information for the staff of the CAB.

For purposes of this exercise, suppose that the state population figures show that the number of college-age individuals will be about the same for the next ten years. The state's economy is diversified and stable, and there is no reason to anticipate a higher or lower proportion of high school graduates continuing on to college than is currently the case. Leaders in the legislature have indicated they will link spending authorization for CAB in proportion to the number of students receiving loans. Fifty-six percent of the staff—including all of those in senior positions—will, it is estimated, retire within the next three years. The task is to develop a human resource plan to cover the next five-year period.

Determining Objectives

Productivity
In the situation that has been presented, clearly a major objective that must guide planning is a response to the retirement of over half the senior staff. There are no changes in policy, such as the elimination of need as a criterion or extension of the program to private schools, to incorporate in the plan. In other words, staff adjustments are to occur while maintaining current organizational goals and a quality of service at least at the current level. The primary work outputs of CAB are the number of applications

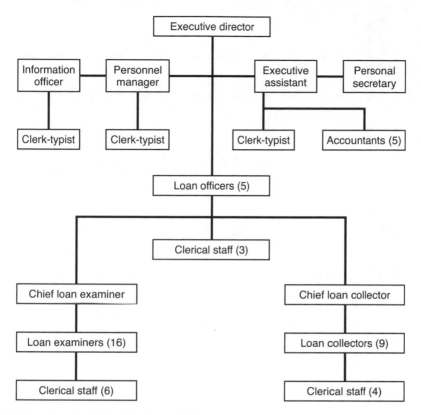

FIGURE 7.2   Organization of College Aid Board.

processed and the number of loans made. The amounts of the loans do not have a significant effect on workload: It takes as much time and effort to process a $500 loan as it does a $5,000 loan. Virtually all students in the program borrow near the maximum allowed, so it is also the number rather than the amount of loans that are important for securing repayments.

Currently, CAB is making 12,000 loans annually. There were 30,000 students who applied for loans, and of these, 23,000 were deemed eligible. Given the projections of student population trends, we can expect this to be a continuing pattern.

To calculate the implications of the losses to retirement on the organization's need for staff, it is necessary to compute the number of person hours currently used to process applications and to analyze the implications on each step of the process, because CAB is functionally organized. Currently, application processing requires 47,840 person hours (40-hour week × 52 weeks a year, including paid vacation and holidays x 23, the number of employees in the loan examination department). The average effort to process a loan application, in other words, is 0.63 person hours (47,840 ÷ 30,000, the number of applications). This should be disaggregated to more useful information, that is, by occupational grouping. It takes 1.17 person hours for the loan examiners and 0.42 person hours for clerical workers. One could pursue the question of whether or not these are productive rates or whether one might reduce the person hours consumed by

TABLE 7.1 COLLEGE AID BOARD STAFF

Name	Position	Age	Sex	Ethnic Identity	Handicap	Current Salary $ per Year	Years with CAB	Years at Current Position	Education or Certificate	Performance Evaluation (on 10 point scale) Current	Potential
Harold White	Director	63	M	White	None	$88,500	7	7	BA	9	9
Jane Smith	Personnel manager	64	F	White	None	$74,200	2	2	MPA	8	9
John Brown	Information officer	63	M	White	None	$64,900	21	4	BA	9	9
Susan Lang	Personal secretary	37	F	White	None	$37,900	17	17	High school	9	9
Patrick Tracy	Accountant	62	M	White	None	$63,700	29	29	CPA	9	9
Dennis Anders	Accountant	60	M	White	None	$61,800	27	27	CPA	8	8
Sam Long	Accountant	64	M	White	Polio	$61,500	23	23	CPA	7	8
James Whitehead	Accountant	40	M	African American	None	$42,900	13	13	CPA	8	9
Cynthia Downs	Accountant	29	F	White	None	$35,200	1	1	CPA	8	8
John Macky	Loan officer	64	M	White	None	$56,400	28	20	BA	8	9
Dan Shoreman	Loan officer	64	M	White	None	$54,600	26	19	BA	7	7
Jesse Stone	Loan officer	45	M	White	None	$45,900	20	14	BA	8	8
Steven Edwards	Loan officer	37	M	White	None	$37,600	6	6	MBA	9	9
Paul Green	Loan officer	62	M	African American	None	$50,400	23	13	MPA	8	9
Joel Garber	Chief loan examiner	63	M	White	None	$54,500	29	16	BA	9	9
Richard Doyle	Loan examiner	63	M	White	None	$49,900	34	28	BA	7	8
Norman White	Loan examiner	62	M	White	None	$49,900	34	28	BA	8	8
Ken Short	Loan examiner	56	M	White	None	$46,200	22	15	BA	8	9
Maria Gonzalez	Loan examiner	59	F	Hispanic	None	$47,800	28	25	BA	9	9

TABLE 7.1 (CONTINUED)

Name	Position	Age	Sex	Ethnic Identity	Handicap	Current Salary $ per Year	Years with CAB	Years at Current Position	Education or Certificate	Performance Evaluation (on 10 point scale) Current	Potential
Peter Rose	Loan examiner	51	M	White	None	$46,800	22	17	BA	6	8
Jonathan Good	Loan examiner	62	M	White	None	$51,700	27	27	BA	7	7
Al Piper	Loan examiner	58	M	White	None	$50,200	26	26	MPA	7	8
Martin Salter	Loan examiner	32	M	African American	None	$39,400	9	9	BA	6	8
Hal Winters	Loan examiner	62	M	White	None	$50,200	26	16	MBA	7	9
Patricia Lane	Loan examiner	63	F	White	None	$49,900	34	24	MPA	9	9
Mark Dikeman	Loan examiner	37	M	White	None	$36,400	15	12	MPA	7	8
James Johnson	Loan examiner	62	M	African American	None	$49,500	35	25	BA	7	7
Terrence Potter	Loan examiner	33	M	White	None	$37,800	1	1	MBA	7	9
Carlos Sanchez	Loan examiner	64	M	Hispanic	None	$48,500	32	22	MPA	8	8
Judy Jones	Loan examiner	29	F	African American	None	$38,500	2	2	MPA	8	9
Gary Updike	Loan examiner	29	M	White	Left arm missing	$38,500	2	2	MPA	8	8
Lee Timber	Chief loan collector	62	M	White	None	$55,300	38	25	BA	9	9
Richard Shore	Loan collector	62	M	White	None	$51,900	29	22	BA	7	7
Michael Van Dike	Loan collector	63	M	White	None	$50,500	20	12	BA	7	7
Chris Manner	Loan collector	64	M	White	None	$55,900	29	25	BA	8	9
Harold Peters	Loan collector	64	M	White	None	$49,800	24	24	BA	7	8
Thomas O'Leary	Loan collector	62	M	White	None	$49,000	19	19	MPA	7	9
John Miller	Loan collector	62	M	White	None	$52,200	27	25	BA	8	8
Jeffrey Duncan	Loan collector	57	M	White	MD	$41,700	19	15	BA	8	8
Mary Kanter	Loan collector	25	F	White	None	$38,500	2	2	MBA	8	9
Thomas Swift	Loan collector	24	M	African American	None	$38,500	2	2	MPA	7	9

TABLE 7.1 (CONTINUED)

Name	Position	Age	Sex	Ethnic Identity	Handicap	Current Salary $ per Year	Years with CAB	Years at Current Position	Education or Certificate	Performance Evaluation (on 10 point scale)	
										Current	Potential
Jennifer Patrick	Clerk-typist	62	F	White	None	$39,000	31	25	High school	9	9
Deborah DeVries	Clerk-typist	60	F	White	None	$39,000	27	20	High school	8	9
Barbara Rockman	Clerk-typist	55	F	White	None	$38,600	26	20	High school	9	9
Teresa King	Clerk-typist	49	F	African American	None	$38,500	26	19	High school	7	8
Virginia Terra	Clerk-typist	41	F	White	None	$38,000	19	10	High school	8	8
Brenda Black	Clerk-typist	34	F	African American	None	$36,000	5	2	High school	9	9
Nancy Arawn	Clerk-typist	33	F	White	None	$36,800	6	1	BA	6	8
Maria Castro	Clerk-typist	33	F	Hispanic	Epilepsy	$35,000	3.5	3.5	High school	6	6
Lisa Mellon	Clerk-typist	31	F	White	None	$35,300	4	4	BA	6	8
Susan Hart	Clerk-typist	30	F	African American	None	$33,000	0.5	0.5	High school	7	7
James Klover	Clerk-typist	29	M	White	None	$33,800	1	1	BA	5	8
Mary White	Clerk-typist	29	F	African American	None	$34,000	2	2	High school	7	7
Patricia Cruz	Clerk-typist	25	F	Hispanic	None	$33,800	1	1	High school	7	7
Anna Ballard	Clerk-typist	24	F	White	Blind	$33,800	1	1	BA	9	9
Rachel Ruiz	Clerk-typist	21	F	Hispanic	None	$33,000	0.5	0.5	High school	6	8
Ruth Browning	Clerk-typist	21	F	White	None	$33,000	0.5	0.5	High school	5	7

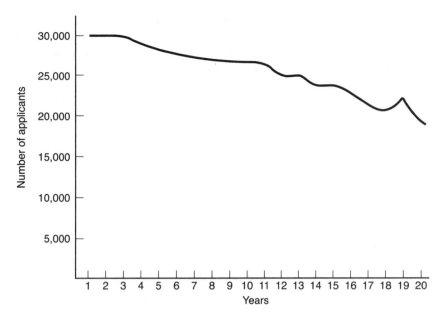

FIGURE 7.3 **Projected Decline in Student Loan Applications.**

the process. For our purposes, let us assume that these are good rates. The standards of 1.17 person hours for loan examiners and 0.42 for clericals then can be used in determining staffing needs. A full-time employee works 2,080 hours per year. If the number of applications or loans were to change—either increase or decrease—one could calculate the effects on the need for full-time or part-time staff, given the above calculations.

Management of the agency must be treated separately from other functional areas. Care has to be taken to provide for sufficient management of the functions of the agency, regardless of workload. The management of CAB is already at minimal strength and, if CAB is to exist at all, it would seem to be a mistake to reduce managerial staff.

In sum, the determination of objectives includes a definition of the agency's general mission and a calculation of the personnel needed to accomplish that mission. A major concern in calculating what human resources are needed is productivity. This calculation involves disaggregating the staff by occupational category and determining the person hours (and thus the number of full- and part-time employees) to do the needed tasks. Whether one begins with service goals and determines what human resources are needed or one starts with a definition of staff limits and calculates what kinds of agency goals are possible, personnel planning necessarily involves the best possible match between what needs to be done and the resources available to do it.

Retirements
Succession planning is always needed, but especially when there is considerable turnover. In the case of our hypothetical CAB, the challenge is to plan for staff losses

due to retirement. Besides the sheer number (23 of the 41 employees) that will retire in the next three years, assuming that these individuals will retire at the age of 65, the expected turnover will be concentrated both in the higher levels of the agency and in the accountant category. The challenges will be to bring in a new management team and to find and hire qualified accountants. As noted above, the exodus of baby boomers is a general phenomenon in the United States, not something that will be confined to CAB. This, of course, makes the tasks of adjustment all that more difficult. One cannot, for example, assume there will be a sufficient supply of accountants with a CPA available for meeting needs through new hires. Also, there may not be enough accountants so that the agency might count on outsourcing this work.

Diversity

Productivity is not the only concern as we proceed. As pointed out in Chapter 4, the definition of who should be represented in the workforce has changed over time, but the concern for having employees of diverse backgrounds has been constant.

Assume for purposes of this example that the commitment of the jurisdiction is for the most comprehensive and challenging diversity goals. The objective is to have a social profile in each job classification that reflects that of society. We can go one step further and define this as a five-year objective. Table 7.2 compares diversity goals to the current social background traits of the CAB staff.

Clearly, the major diversity challenge confronting this hypothetical agency is to remedy an imbalance between the sexes—an imbalance that is not going to change with the projected pattern of retirements. Males are overrepresented to a considerable extent in every job category except clerical, where females are overrepresented. Representation of minorities and people with disabilities poses less of a problem here. One might reasonably expect an additional Latino among the ranks of accountants, loan officers, or loan collectors, but otherwise the current workforce generally represents the state's population.

Moving to an objective is rarely a simple matter. The next phase in the planning exercise is to consider the variables that enable us to be more precise and accurate about our staffing needs.

Analyzing Critical Variables

Technology

Technology is directly related to productivity. On the one hand, technology provides guidelines for defining jobs and structuring an organization. How a task is completed is obviously critical for the needed skills. To construct a road, one needs engineers to plan and supervise, equipment operators to move earth and to lay the construction material, laborers to supplement machinery work and to complete some of the tasks that require precision, and so forth. The construction of our fictitious CAB was relatively simple. We followed the steps that are integral to the technology of loan management.[20]

Another way in which technology affects productivity and human resource planning is through change. A general tendency in technological changes is to reduce the need for human labor. This means existing tasks can be accomplished with lower

TABLE 7.2 COLLEGE AID BOARD SOCIAL REPRESENTATION PROFILE AND OBJECTIVES

	Current (%)	Objectives (%)
Accountants		
Male	80	50
Female	20	50
White	80	85
African American	20	10
Hispanic	0	5
Handicapped	20	10
Loan Officers		
Male	100	50
Female	0	50
White	80	85
African American	20	10
Hispanic	0	5
Handicapped	0	10
Loan Examiners		
Male	82	50
Female	18	50
White	70	85
African American	18	10
Hispanic	12	5
Handicapped	6	10
	(N = 17)	
Loan Collectors		
Male	90	50
Female	10	50
White	90	85
African American	10	10
Hispanic	0	5
Handicapped	10	10
	(N = 10)	
Clerks		
Male	6	50
Female	94	50
White	66	85
African American	25	10
Hispanic	19	5
Handicapped	13	10
	(N = 16)	

labor costs and efforts. In addition, technological changes can improve accuracy, speed, and quality, so those objectives that had not been feasible become possible. Although organizations can become obsolete because of technological changes, it is more common to have an interaction between new objectives and new technologies that results in different—and sometimes fewer—employees.[21]

One strategy for succession planning for the CAB is to rely more heavily on computer technology to get agency work completed. It may be, for example, that the need for CPAs might be reduced by adopting new software and then training and networking CAB employees so that transactions could be recorded, traced and analyzed correctly. Another option, which might be pursued with new uses of computer technology, would be to restructure workflow. One could envision, for example, an approach that was based more on cases than on specialization of labor. Instead of having distinct positions for loan officers, loan examiners, and loan collectors, employees might have cases and follow individuals from the time they apply for a loan, through when they receive it, and pay it back. The current pool of clerical workers might be transformed into paraprofessionals that support case workers, not only in record keeping, but also in communicating with CAB customers.

Match Between Skills and Jobs

Securing a match between the skills and interests of individual employees and the needs of the organization can contribute toward both productivity and diversity. Organizations sometimes are slow to take advantage of new technologies and are reluctant to try new ways of defining jobs and tasks because they lack staff with the skills to adopt the changes.

Ideally, managers should have an information system that includes an inventory of the various skills and interests of employees.[22] These skills and interests should go beyond those used or required for current jobs and current technologies. With a more complete inventory in hand, one can then respond more readily when there are changes in mission, technology, or organization.

Human resource planning generally and succession planning specifically requires such an inventory. The best way to develop the data base that describes current internal human resources is to involve the employees, through interviews and discussions. An individual employee needs to provide information about his or her own career and job interests. Relevant skills might be tucked away in avocations and hobbies that are not standard entries in personnel files.

It should be noted that despite the clear need for succession planning by organizations, few are fully engaged.[23] Individual employees, therefore, are well advised to be assertive rather than passive in taking advantage of the opportunities presented by the baby boomer retirements. Individual career planning, which will be covered more in Chapter 11, ideally is integrated into organizational succession planning. When the latter is incomplete or is simply not happening, then individual career planning is essential for employees.[24]

Effort and Motivation of Employees

An important step in succession planning is to assess whether or not there are motivational problems that adversely affect individual or collective output. What is important in this assessment is an identification of the reasons for poor motivation, if indeed there is such a problem.

As pointed out in Chapter 5, individuals identify with their work in different ways. While it may be difficult to gather good data on employee orientations toward work, it would be foolish in light of what we have learned about motivation to plan strategies that assume everyone is the same. Professionals tend to place self-esteem in their job and it will be important for them to achieve and to see positive results from their work. Mentoring programs and other efforts to enable young professionals to assume more responsibility are likely to be effective. Support staff is less likely to identify with the mission of the organization and be more concerned about work environment issues. For these individuals training programs to make them both competent and comfortable with technological innovations that affect them will be important.

Legal Mandates

Succession planning, like other aspects of personnel management, must be consistent with provisions of the law. For public agencies, laws might specify both objectives and ways in which those objectives might be attained. The definition of who is eligible for a student loan and what the limits of the loans are were established for the CAB in the law that created that agency. Civil service laws and EEOC rules specify the selection procedures that must be used. Most jurisdictions are bound by law to follow some kind of seniority system for staff layoffs. Succession plans can lead to recommendations for changes in the law, but until those changes are adopted, goals and strategies must fall within the existing legal framework.

External Labor Market

The nature of employment outside an agency has important influences on both productivity and diversity within the agency. Productivity is affected by labor costs. Governments and nonprofit organizations must try to compete with other employers and so they must compensate their employees at or near market rates. If those rates are too high, then an agency must be prepared to pay dearly for the staff it needs or it must alter its output goals accordingly.

With an eye toward the external labor market, few organizations are willing to commit themselves to short-term diversity goals of reflecting the composition of society generally. If, for example, only 10 percent of the accountants in society are women, then the CAB will have to hire more than its share to achieve its goal of 50 percent female accountants. The kind of competition in which the CAB would have to engage to reach the 50 percent goal would contribute to dynamics that are ideal from the standpoint of redressing imbalances in society. There would be clear messages and incentives to women to become accountants. However, CAB's short-term gains will become some other employer's losses. It could become legally and practically difficult to expect every employer to have at least a mixed, if not a balanced, workforce. Thus, while an agency might aspire to being a leader in diversity, a plan must be reasonable within a broader social context.

Internal Labor Supply

Succession planning places a heavy emphasis on the analysis of the internal labor supply. These analyses attempt to determine turnover and then to identify the replacement needs of the organization. To make best use of current employees,

provide for career development, and forecast vacancies due to retirements, resignations, and the like, several inquiries must be made:

1. As mentioned earlier, there should be an inventory of the skills and interests
   of current employees.
2. The ages and retirement plans of employees can be used to calculate anticipated vacancies because of retirements.
3. Past career patterns should provide fairly reliable estimates on vacancies that
   might be expected because of death, disability, resignations, and dismissals.
4. Information from employee-training programs indicate what kinds of skills
   are being developed within the current workforce.

This is, of course, a demand for considerable data. For all but the smallest
employers, this argues for a sophisticated personnel management information system
using computerized data processing. The data on current employees will in most
cases be more reliable and complete than data used in other analyses. This will
frequently work in favor of current employees, a tendency that serves the more
general goal of providing careers and not just jobs in government.

After careful consideration of the critical variables, managers will have a more
precise idea of what vacancies are likely to occur and how those vacancies relate to
the productivity and diversity objectives of the agency. In addition, there will be
enough information generated to make reasonable judgments about what strategies
to pursue. The various strategies listed in the model raise issues to which entire
chapters are devoted in this text. What is appropriate here is not a reiteration of that
material but rather a discussion that relates the first two phases of succession planning to the selection of strategies. For this, we again make use of the information
presented on our hypothetical CAB.

Selecting Strategies

Organization

A review of an organization's objectives and resources may reveal that the agency
should be restructured. A unit organized according to the technology of its tasks or
mission, like the CAB, is likely to reorganize with changes in technology. A decision
to adopt automatic data processing, for example, may be accompanied by a decision
to reduce clerical staff and to centralize bookkeeping and word processing. Moving
to a case-oriented approach to work, instead of the current specialization of tasks,
would also prompt reorganization. As organizations increase and decrease in size,
they tend to need, respectively, more and less hierarchy. Another example of when
reorganization is used as a strategy is when in so doing the agency can achieve a
better match between the skills of the current workforce and the needs of the
organization. A skills and interests inventory of current employees and Total Quality
Management (TQM) analyses by teams of employees can be very useful in suggesting ways of restructuring position assignments.

A reorganization is sometimes primarily a political symbol, a message from top
officials to a certain clientele that efforts are being made to meet their needs.[25] Within

the bureaucracy, reorganizations are invariably viewed as threats by some and opportunities by others. Managers should anticipate where opposition and support are likely to come from and then decide whether to continue a reorganization plan or modify it.

Staffing

In the narrow sense of the term, succession planning produces a document that itemizes how many retirements there are likely to be, what kinds of personnel the organization will need, and what must be done to train current employees and to hire needed staff. Used more comprehensively, succession planning regards staffing as one of a number of approaches to meeting organizational objectives. Changing technology, as already discussed, is another approach.

The first step, after the organizational needs are known, is to determine which vacant positions might be filled by current employees. Laws, administrative rules, or collective bargaining agreements sometimes mandate giving current employees first consideration. In some instances, in fact, current employees must be promoted or transferred, not just considered for the vacancies. The second step in staffing is to recruit new employees for the vacancies that remain after utilizing current employees. For some organizations, of course, we are including volunteers as well as employees.

Employee Development

Some programs for employee development flow from staffing plans and decisions. In all probability, the movement of employees within an agency requires training and mentoring programs. Likewise, new employees need some training and orientation.

If the technology used by the organization is going to change—such as a decision by CAB to adopt computer technology—then plans need to be made to prepare current and beginning employees. Public agencies must frequently respond to new and different legal mandates. Employees need to be informed about the provisions of these mandates and how they affect their respective jobs. Sometimes when planners examine the morale, motivation, and work culture of employees, they find a need for the kind of training program that helps employees understand what the objectives of the organization are and how each employee can or does contribute toward attaining those objectives.

There are three general types of employee development strategies that can be generated by succession planning. One is linked to the career development of existing employees. This strategy is often specific to the needs of employees moving from one job to another. A second strategy is to focus on skills training and is based on an inventory of the skill and knowledge levels of current employees compared to the skill requirements that the organization has or will have. Finally, there may be a need for organizational development and team building. This strategy is sometimes appropriate for addressing motivational problems. Trainers and training programs are frequently criticized because they are not relevant to organizational and/or employee needs. Proper succession planning should help meet this concern.

Compensation

The levels at which an agency's employees are compensated are a response to a variety of factors. Some of these factors, like the dynamics of collective bargaining where that applies, are outside the scope of succession planning. Compensation policies can, on the other hand, be regarded as strategies for meeting needs identified in the succession planning exercise. The Hudson Institute and Volcker Commission reports on the federal government identified as problems the relatively low wages of the federal government and the need for salary differences to respond to the costs of living in various parts of the country.[26] The Winter Commission on the revitalization of state and local public services made a similar point.[27]

Low wages and/or inadequate provisions for recognizing especially meritorious performance can cause poor motivation and productivity. A comparison of salaries within the agency and in other organizations or jurisdictions can prompt concern about retention or recruitment of good employees. Internal salary comparisons can reveal inequities or discriminatory patterns. Political mandates and cost control measures can limit the kinds of compensation strategies that managers can consider.

Compensation, more than other dimensions of personnel management, is usually tied to schemes and policies that go beyond the boundaries of a specific agency. The information generated in succession planning is important to the establishment and application of those policies, but it is not as determinate as in an area such as staffing. This is important both in devising compensation strategies and considering the relationship between compensation and other ways of meeting personnel needs.

Contracting

Contracting has been and will be a strategy for meeting human resource needs. A time when contracting is appropriate is when an organization needs a particular service or expertise for only a specific and relatively short period of time. If the CAB decides to use computer technology in its operation, it might be wasteful to hire permanent employees to develop and install the system. It makes more sense to contract for that job with a firm and include in the contract a requirement that CAB employees be trained to operate the system. Likewise, a relatively small organization such as CAB that would have only periodic and minimal maintenance work on its equipment might contract for that service rather than hire a full- or part-time employee to do the work.

Sometimes cost-benefit calculations, rather than concerns about temporary workload or specific projects, lead to contracting as a strategy. Some organizations have contracted with private firms to provide services, like garbage collection, or to do work, like building maintenance, because the private firm will do it for a lower cost than the agency or jurisdiction can do it.

Evaluate Results

The final step in the succession planning process is the evaluation of results. This evaluation is simplified if the preceding steps, especially the first one of identifying objectives, are followed carefully. Evaluation requires standards against which what has happened can be measured. Without these standards, it is virtually impossible to recognize success and failure. At the same time, once a succession planning process is established, the evaluation of results is to a large degree the first step in planning for the period beyond.

Evaluation begins with a comparison of original objectives and final accomplishments. In the case of the hypothetical CAB, for example, one would want to know whether the productivity and diversity goals were achieved. For the latter, this means constructing a social representation profile of employees and matching it against the goals presented in Table 7.2. For the former, one would determine whether student loan applications, checks, and repayments were occurring without any delays or declines when compared to current rates. In addition, it would be useful to calculate the workload per employee with the new staff and compare the results with current workload ratios. These comparisons, quite apart from judging whether changes in technology, organization, and staffing were successful, might generate a reconsideration of objectives.

An evaluation that ends with matching results and objectives is incomplete. Invariably, questions arise about why success was or was not achieved. This leads to an examination of the analyses and strategies used. One might conclude that better data are needed or that the cause-effect relationships that were used are invalid. Perhaps the analyses were not faulty, but the choice of strategies overlooked important forces. Few planning efforts are without fault. The purpose of evaluation is to identify and then to improve the limitations of previous efforts.

SUMMARY

Planning, whether in personnel or in some other policy or management area, is frequently neglected because of the costs in time and money. Ironically, the result may be more costs and more waste than if a planning effort had been made. Taking the time to assess where one is, anticipate the future, and devise strategies for meeting current and future needs is not going to solve all problems or ensure an effective response to change. One is, however, more likely to be prepared and avoid serious mistakes. Moreover, planning is in many ways doing more carefully and systematically what one does in any case. Decisions have to be made about organization, staffing, training, compensation, and contracting. In the absence of planning, they are likely to be made in a disjointed manner and are likely to be based on incomplete information and guesses.

DISCUSSION QUESTIONS

1. If you were an agency manager about to launch a succession planning process, whom would you invite to participate in this process, and why?
2. What, if any, differences are there likely to be in succession planning for an agency that is expanding its staff as compared with an agency that is downsizing?
3. What might you do to take advantage of the opportunities that will occur because of baby boomer retirements? Will your strategy change if the organization for which you are working does not engage in succession planning?
4. Are there some circumstances in which the costs of time and energy to do human resource planning are just not worth it?

GLOSSARY

Affirmative action plans A specific type of planning that attempts to achieve diversity and social representation throughout an organization

Attrition The process of reducing staff by not replacing employees who retire or resign

Downsizing Efforts taken to reduce the number of employees in an agency

Incrementalism A pattern of decision making in which the search for alternative solutions to a problem is limited and the process stops as soon as a satisfactory, but not necessarily optimal, solution is identified. Incremental changes are modest adjustments from the status quo

Layoff The termination of employment for an individual for nondisciplinary reasons, such as reorganization or downsizing

Reduction in force (RIF) A layoff that occurs in order to downsize the staff in an agency (sometimes RIF is used as a verb)

Succession planning Process of anticipating retirements and other types of departures and then designing ways of ensuring an adequate pool of talent to continue the work of the agency

SOURCES

Ban, C. (1995). *How do public managers manage? Bureaucratic constraints, organizational culture, and the potential for reform.* San Francisco: Jossey-Bass.
A good general discussion of public management that places human resource planning in the context of the public sector.

Rothwell, William J. (2002). *Succession planning: Ensuring leadership continuity and building talent from within* (2nd ed.). New York: American Management Association.
An in-depth discussion of the need for succession planning and the steps that organizations—public and private—should take.

Schuler, R. S. (1992). Strategic human resource management: Linking the people with the strategic needs of the business. *Organizational Dynamics* 21:18–23.
A theoretical statement describing the role of human resource planning.

NOTES

1. Office of Personnel Management, www.opm.gov/hr/employ/products/succession/succ_plan_text
2. www.stateline.org/live; Blue Wooldridge, Barbara Clark Maddox, and Yan Zheng, "Changing Demographics of the Work Force," *Review of Public Personnel Administration* 15, no. 3 (Summer 1995): 60–72.
3. Jonathan P. West and Evan M. Berman, "Managerial Responses to Aging Municipal Workforce," *Review of Public Personnel Administration* 16, no. 3 (Summer 1996): 38–58.
4. D. Braybrook and C. E. Lindbloom, *A Strategy of Decision* (New York: Free Press, 1963); A. O. Hirschman and C. E. Lindbloom, "Economic Development, Research and Development, Policy Making: Some Converging Views," *Behavioral Sciences* 7 (1962): 211–222; H. A. Simon, *Administrative Behavior: A Study of Decision-making Processes in Administrative Organization,* 3rd ed. (New York: Free Press, 1976).

5. C. E. Lindbloom, "The Science of Muddling Through," *Public Administration Review* 19, no. 2 (March/April 1959): 79–99; Aaron Wildavsky, *The Politics of the Budgetary Process,* 3rd ed. (Boston: Little, Brown, 1980).

6. Irving L. Janis and Leon Mann, *Decision Making: A Psychological Analysis of Conflict, Choice, and Commitment* (New York: Free Press, 1977); J. D. Steinbruner, *The Cybernetic Theory of Decisions* (Princeton: Princeton University Press, 1974).

7. Janis and Mann, *Decision Making.*

8. A. R. Janger, *The Personnel Function: Changing Objectives and Organization,* Conference Board Report No. 712 (New York: Conference Board, 1977). See also, John Bryson, *Strategic Planning for Public and Nonprofit Organizations* (San Francisco: Jossey-Bass, 1995).

9. James L. Perry and Debra J. Mesch, "Strategic Human Resource Management," in Carolyn Ban and Norma M. Riccucci, eds., *Public Personnel Management: Current Concerns— Future Challenges,* 2nd ed. (New York: Longman, 1997), 21–34.

10. U.S. Civil Service Commission, *Planning Your Staffing Needs: A Handbook for Personnel Workers* (Washington, DC: U.S. Civil Service Commission, 1977).

11. William B. Johnston, *Civil Service 2000* (Washington, DC: Office of Personnel Management, 1989); National Commission on Public Service, *Leadership for America* (Lexington, MA: Lexington Books, 1989).

12. Equal Employment Opportunity Commission, *Affirmative Action and Equal Employment* (Washington, DC: Government Printing Office, 1974); W. B. Chew and R. L. Justice, "EEO Modeling for Large, Complex Organizations," *Human Resource Planning* 2 (1979): 57–70.

13. W. Johnson and R. Packer, *Workforce 2000: Work and Workers for the 21st Century* (Indianapolis: Hudson Institute, 1987); R. Kleeman, *The Changing Workforce: Demographic Issues Facing the Federal Government* (Washington, DC: General Accounting Office, 1992); Stephen Hays and Richard Kearney, "State Personnel Directors and the Dilemmas of Workforce 2000," *Public Administration Review* 52, no. 4 (1992): 380–388.

14. Robert T. Golembiewski, *Managing Diversity in Organizations* (Tuscaloosa: University of Alabama Press, 1995).

15. Betty D. Robinson and Marvin Druker, "A Contextual Model for Public-Sector Downsizing," *Sociological Practice Review* 13 (1992): 73–82.

16. Carolyn Ban, "The Challenges of Cutback Management," in Ban and Riccucci, *Public Personnel Management: Current Concerns—Future Challenges,* 269–280.

17. James P. Begin, *Strategic Employment Policy: An Organizational Systems Perspective* (Englewood Cliffs, NJ: Prentice-Hall, 1001), Patrick M. Wright and Cary C. McMahan, "Theoretical Perspectives for Strategic Human Resource Management," *Journal of Management* 18 (1992): 295–320; Cynthia A. Lengnick-Hall and Mark L. Lengnick-Hall, *Interactive Human Resource Management and Strategic Planning* (Westport, CT: Quorum Books, 1990).

18. Dale R. Collins, "Human Resource Assessment—The Link to Mission," *Public Personnel Management* 26, no. 1 (Spring 1997): 1–6.

19. Donald Klingner, "Developing a Strategic Human Resource Management Capability in Public Agencies," *Public Personnel Management* 22, no. 4 (Winter 1993): 565–578.

20. For a presentation of organization theory based on the technology of tasks, see J. D. Thompson, *Organizations in Action* (New York: McGraw-Hill, 1967).

21. James L. Perry and Kenneth L. Kraemer, "The Implications of Changing Technology," in Frank Thompson, ed., *Revitalizing the State and Local Public Service: Strengthening Performance, Accountability, and Citizen Confidence* (San Francisco: Jossey-Bass, 1993), 225–245.

22. Perry and Mesch, 28–29.

23. William J. Rothwell, *Effective Succession Planning*, 2nd ed. (New York: American Management Association, 2001), 31–40.

24. An approach to individual career planning can be found in Dennis L. Dresang and Mark Huddleston, *Public Administration Workbook*, 5th ed. (New York: Longman, 2008).

25. Harold Seidman, *Politics, Position, and Power: The Dynamics of Federal Organization*, 3rd ed. (New York: Oxford University Press, 1980); Murray Edelman, *The Symbolic Uses of Politics* (Urbana: University of Illinois Press, 1964); I. M. Destler, *Presidents, Bureaucrats, and Foreign Policy: The Politics of Organizational Reform* (Princeton: Princeton University Press, 1974).

26. W. Johnson and R. Packer, *Workforce 2000: Work and Workers for the 21st Century* (Indianapolis: Hudson Institute, 1987); National Commission on Public Service, *Leadership for America* (Lexington, MA: Lexington Books, 1989).

27. Frank J. Thompson, ed., *Revitalizing State and Local Public Service* (San Francisco: Jossey-Bass, 1993).

Chapter 8

Position Analysis
and Job Evaluation

"But that is not in my job description!"

One of the most irritating and frustrating responses a manager hears from an employee is a complaint that an assignment does not fit some predetermined definition of his or her duties and responsibilities. The complaint is heard as passive aggression, as a sign of conflict between a manager and an employee. Sometimes, frankly, the complaint is legitimate. Employees are asked to do work for which they are not being paid. At other times, however, the fault is with a human resource management system that is rigid and invites employees to think too narrowly about their jobs and the challenges and changes their agency faces.

The way in which an organization defines jobs is of fundamental importance to employees and to the tasks of personnel management. Positions are the basic building blocks of an organization and a link between an organization's mission and its employees. This applies to public, private, and nonprofit organizations alike. The duties and responsibilities attached to various positions determine what kinds of people should be hired, what career structures and training opportunities are needed, what compensation is appropriate, and what standards for job performance should be required. A key to the effective use of volunteers is a clear description of the tasks that they need to perform. Volunteers want to know what they can and should do to help the organization and they, like paid employees, need job descriptions.

Organizational positions are, in short, the basic unit of analysis for human resource management. Although some positions are unique, most can be clustered with similar ones. Schemes that group similar positions aim at simplifying other personnel management work and at compensating employees equitably. Plans that analyze jobs and classify them according to similarities provide a framework for almost all of personnel management activity.

An organization is distinct from a group because it has a division of labor that is relatively structured and constant. In his classic statement on bureaucracy, the German sociologist Max Weber used the concept of "office" to indicate that the various clusters of activities that constituted a job in an organization remained the same, regardless of the incumbent.[1] People might come and go, but the duties and responsibilities of an office remained the same.

A fundamental responsibility of a manager is to assign duties and responsibilities to each position in his or her agency. Managers need to determine how work will be done and who will do what. The techniques and processes of position analysis are designed to make these determinations in a systematic, consistent, and orderly manner. Job evaluations, on the other hand, apply a set of criteria to rank jobs within an organization according to what they contribute to the goals and activities of the organization.

Managers will make personnel decisions, with or without systematic analysis. The difference is in the quality of the decision. Organizational missions and strategies provide the general context and direction. Position analysis and job evaluation provide the specifics upon which discrete, detailed action can be taken.

Position analysis and work design began with the emergence of the scientific management school at the turn of the twentieth century. The basic approach of this school, as pointed out in Chapter 5, was to determine the single most efficient and effective way of completing a task and then to define jobs accordingly. The initial focus of Frederick Taylor, Frank and Lillian Gilbreth, and others was on body motions. Although their successors broadened the scope of their work, attention remained focused almost exclusively on manufacturing industries in the private sector where assembly-line technologies were predominant. In the public sector, this approach was and is most appropriate for tasks like operating a garbage truck, processing income tax returns, plowing snow, and the like. Analytical and managerial jobs and work that cannot or should not be routinized do not lend themselves well to Taylor's techniques. Time and motion studies that emphasize the most efficient use of body movement and energy are only one type of work analysis. Other approaches focus on the sequence of work, legal mandates for policy implementation, and the varying amounts of complexity and discretion required by the tasks that need to be accomplished.

The conceptual foundation for position analysis derived from Frederick Taylor's scientific management theory is no longer as applicable as it initially was. Organization theorists no longer subscribe to the assumption that one can determine a single best way of doing things, and public agencies generally do not utilize assembly-line technologies.[2] Total Quality Management (TQM) and Continuous Improvement, in fact, assume that no matter how well an agency is doing, it can still do better.

Despite the abandonment of some of the assumptions of scientific management, positions and position analysis remain key to personnel actions such as recruitment, selection, and employee development. Positions and position classifications remain fundamental to the design of compensation systems.[3] Internal fairness is a major principle of compensation. This means that employees in the same kinds of positions should receive the same pay, except perhaps for differences based on seniority or productivity. Position analyses, combined with position classification and job evaluation, provide the information necessary to establish and maintain a fair, sound compensation system.

Position analysis and **job evaluation**, in other words, are essential analytical tasks in human resource management. Managers are well served if these analyses are sensitive to the needs of their respective agencies and to the varying nature of work within each agency. Managers are likely to find themselves victimized by standards and rules that assume either that all jobs are static and routine or that they are all dynamic and general in nature. The information in this chapter will enable managers to participate more effectively in the analyses and definition of work in their agencies.

LEARNING OBJECTIVES OF THIS CHAPTER

- Know how to analyze positions
- Be able to write position descriptions
- Know how position classifications are developed and used
- Understand how to compare and evaluate jobs

APPROACHES TO POSITION ANALYSIS

A position analysis is basically a study of the duties and responsibilities assigned to a job and the technology or technologies that must be utilized in order to contribute to the work of the organization. It cannot be emphasized too strongly that the focus of analysis here is on the job and not on an employee.[4] Managers will either do position analyses themselves or work with a consultant or personnel specialist in a central personnel office who will do the analyses.

Managers and personnel specialists can choose among several well developed approaches toward position analysis. Personnel offices in some organizations have put together hybrids of their own. The most commonly used approach is an adaptation of the Job Analysis Schedule of the federal Department of Labor. That approach will be discussed last and presented in some detail. First some of the other widely known approaches will be explained.

Position analysis questionnaire   E. J. McCormick designed this approach. He identified 194 questions to solicit information about the kinds of data workers use in their job, the kinds of mental processes used, and the outputs they produce. The answers are coded in a standard scheme that rates each of the items according to the extent of use, the importance to the job, the amount of time, the possibility of occurrence, and the applicability. The position analysis questionnaire is used primarily for compensation and selection purposes. It does not provide information useful for employee development or for setting performance standards.[5]

Task inventory procedure   In this approach employees and their supervisors list the tasks performed in each job in the agency. Unlike the position analysis questionnaire, there is no standard, single questionnaire or listing. Tasks are recorded in a standard format on a questionnaire so that employees and supervisors can indicate how important each task is and how much time is spent on each task.[6] Once task inventory questionnaires are designed, it is relatively easy to collect and analyze data on the job category being analyzed. The information collected is particularly useful for designing training and orientation programs. This approach, however, does not allow for comparisons and evaluations across jobs in order to determine equitable compensation.[7] Other limitations of this approach are that it is time-consuming and the quality of information can vary widely between employees.

Critical incident technique   This approach emphasizes the link between job behaviors and effective performance. A panel of experts identifies examples of specific work experiences that are responsible for either desired or undesired outcomes. Analysts then use these illustrations to identify the job behaviors that should be associated with each job or category of jobs.[8] Critical incident technique provides useful information for training programs and for performance evaluation. This approach, however, does not provide the kind of information about duties and responsibilities that is needed for classifying similar jobs, for hiring new employees, or for designing equitable compensation.

Ability requirements scales   E. A. Fleishman and his associates developed a measure using 52 different abilities needed on jobs. Job experts use a 7-point scale to rate how important each of these abilities is to a given position.[9] This approach is particularly relevant for examination and selection processes. It could also be used to classify jobs and, if an employer so chooses, to establish compensation.

Functional job analysis   The most common approach to job analysis focuses on the duties and responsibilities assigned to a position. The assumption here is that all jobs involve working with data, people, and things, thus providing some ground for comparisons. In addition, it is assumed that jobs have structure and boundaries that can be defined, thus allowing them to be a basic unit for analysis. This approach is sometimes referred to as a whole job analysis, with an emphasis on the concept that jobs can be defined distinct from their incumbents and that agencies value jobs according to the differences in their functions, duties, and responsibilities.[10] These job analyses provide a basis for a wide scope of personnel transactions, including selection, compensation, performance evaluation, and employee development. The methods of collecting and analyzing data, as later described, is not as quantitative as other approaches, but there are standards and procedures for being systematic. The narratives developed by this approach can be used in conducting job evaluations and other analyses that do involve some quantitative calculations.

CONDUCTING A FUNCTIONAL JOB ANALYSIS

While organizations vary to some extent in precisely how they use functional job analysis, the following general description is widely applicable and includes governmental, private, and nonprofit sectors.

Job Factors

As in other objects of study, jobs can be analyzed according to common factors or dimensions. Although approaches used by employers, consultants, and scholars vary in some details, they focus on essentially the same **job factors**.[11] The federal government and about one-third of the state governments, for example, analyze jobs according to

1. Knowledge required
2. Supervisory responsibility

3. Discretion
4. Complexity
5. Effects of action
6. Consequence of error
7. Personal contacts
8. Physical demands
9. Work environment

Some consulting firms use systems that consolidate this list into four to six factors, but then use subfactors. A number of consultants and jurisdictions use a factor called responsibility, for example, which includes supervisory responsibility, discretion, effects of action, and consequence of error (numbers 2, 3, 5, and 6 in the list above).

The factors, whatever the system used, direct the analysis to describe each position and/or category of positions in a common and comprehensive way. It would be similar to directing someone to describe fruit according to shape, color, water content, weight, and nutritional value.

Each factor has scales or levels that further describe jobs. All positions involve some kind of physical effort; for example, some are rather sedentary and require minimal energy whereas others consist of almost constant lifting, pulling, climbing, and the like.

Not all factors have the same number of levels. The key is to have the number of levels needed to make meaningful distinctions. The knowledge required factor typically has around ten levels, which includes various combinations of formal degree education and technical training with what one learns through experience on the job. Analysts find, on the other hand, that they need only four or five levels to describe physical effort, as illustrated in Table 8.1.

Note that in this particular guide, no examples of work within the organization are given for level 5, the highest level. It is nonetheless included, both because these analytic systems are designed for jobs generally rather than for specific organizations and because an analyst may discover unexpectedly one or more positions that do fit the highest level.

Job Information

The first task in position analysis, given the factors and the kinds of level definitions and guides found in Table 8.1, is to collect information about specific positions and/or categories of positions and then locate them at a level on each factor. The factor system itself, of course, provides guidance for the kind of information that is needed. One must determine the kind of physical effort required in a position, the number of people supervised, and whether the authority exists to hire and fire, the consequences of making an error, and so forth. Usually a questionnaire, such as the one provided in the exercise included in this chapter, is used to gather systematically the needed information. Questionnaires are completed by incumbents and then verified and supplemented by interviews with supervisors. Sometimes the analyst actually observes the work.

While three-fourths of all medium- to large-scale public, nonprofit, and private employers in the United States use some form of factor approach to position analysis,[12]

TABLE 8.1	PHYSICAL EFFORT JOB FACTOR	
Level	Definition	Guide
1	Work requires ordinary physical effort to sit, stand, walk, bend, reach, or carry light items.	Work is primarily sedentary in office environment. There may be some intermittent walking or standing; lifting light tools, supplies; e.g., lifting of audio-visual equipment or boxes; operating switchboard or keyboard.
2	Work requires frequent periods of physical activity requiring more than ordinary strength, stamina, agility, or dexterity.	Work requires physical effort such as sitting continuously in a restricted position for extended periods; prolonged operation of machines, tools, equipment, or vehicles requiring a moderate level of dexterity, agility, or stamina; frequent lifting of objects around 20 pounds; or work requiring close, continual attention to functional detail; e.g., standing for prolonged periods using copy machines, sorting mail, collating materials, and performing assays in the laboratory; long periods of sitting when operating computers.
3	Work requires regular periods of physical effort such as carrying loads up and down stairs, or over rough, uneven, or rocky surfaces; pushing, pulling heavy loads; bending or stooping in confined areas; prolonged or intensive operation of machines, tools requiring high levels of dexterity or stamina.	Work requires regular physical effort such as lifting 40-pound bags into a truck; pushing large laundry or mail containers; prolonged periods of typing on a word processor at high speeds; continuously walking and standing while assisting physicians with patients; carrying a 30-pound pack through a wooded area.
4	Work requires either frequent and prolonged periods of effort such as described at level 3 or recurring lifting of people or objects weighing about 80 pounds; episodes of intense physical effort requiring exertion of maximum strength.	Work requires strenuous physical effort for a sustained period of time such as operation of a jackhammer; loading bags of cement; fighting structural or forest fires; or episodic but intense activities like grappling or fighting with adults, extricating injured people from wrecked vehicles; occasional lifting of more than 100 pounds.
5	Work requires frequent and prolonged periods of physical effort such as described at level 4 or regular periods of effort like lifting of people or objects more than 100 pounds.	

Source: Adapted from *Wisconsin Quantitative Evaluation System,* Wisconsin Task Force on Comparable Worth (Madison, WI: State Department of Employment Relations, 1986), 222–224.

the traditional approach that most organizations still use is narrative, open-ended descriptions for collecting and recording information about specific jobs. This is often referred to as a whole-job approach. In virtually all instances, these narratives include statements about the duties and responsibilities of the position, the tasks that must be completed, and the knowledge and skills needed to do the job. Implicitly, of course, these statements address some common job factors. But the narratives are inherently not completed in comparable, systematic fashion. The uneven character of the information they provide becomes a serious problem as an agency becomes larger and more complex.[13]

Whether using a factor- or a whole-job approach, usually the best source of information about the characteristics of a position is an incumbent employee in the position. Supervisors are not always fully aware of all that their employees are doing and all of the conditions in which they are working. However, it is essential to secure job information from a variety of sources for the following three reasons:

1. Employees realize that an analysis of their position can have implications for the pay they are receiving. This may prompt them to inflate the complexity, discretion, and so forth of their job.
2. Some employees may understate the characteristics of their position. They may not want to take the time necessary to provide complete descriptions; they may be cynical about the implications of a position analysis; and/or they simply may not have the ability to articulate what their job is like.
3. Supervisors may, from the perspective of the organization, define the position differently from an employee either because they are not satisfied with the scope of work being done by a current incumbent or because a pending change in mission or technology will require a change in the characteristics of the position.

Time and resources may not allow for as thorough an information-gathering process as is ideal, but the importance of reliable information requires at least some checks through supervisor interviews and job observation. Checks can be made on a random basis or when the analyst suspects that what is available is incomplete or inflated.

POSITION DESCRIPTION

A common use of the information collected through position analysis is the development or revision of position descriptions. A **position description** is a narrative statement that summarizes the nature of a specific job. Many government jurisdictions require through law or administrative rule that there be a position description for every job or every class of jobs. Regardless of the legal requirements, virtually every medium to large-scale organization has position descriptions.

Frequently, these documents do little other than fill file folders and collect dust. In many cases, they are now available on the Internet. Position descriptions are intended to be a ready source of reference for job applicants, employees, volunteers, supervisors, personnel managers, budget analysts, and agency managers. By reading a position description, job applicants are supposed to get a good idea of what working in that position would be like. Employees should use the position description as a set of guidelines for their work performance. Personnel specialists should be able to use position descriptions when recruiting, developing examinations, designing training programs, and the like. Supervisors, managers, and budget analysts should be able to use these same documents as aids in completing evaluations and in making management decisions. There are six basic elements in a position description.

Title

This is a brief description of the job, for example, Receptionist, Prison Guard, Budget Analyst, or Agency Personnel Manager.

Work Activities and Procedures

This section is the core of the position description and is usually a rather detailed and thorough itemization of tasks, duties, and responsibilities assigned to the position. In addition to explaining what the tasks are and, if applicable, what sequence must be followed, this statement includes a description of the materials and equipment that must be used, the types of interpersonal interactions that occur, and the kind of supervision given and/or received.

Work Location

Indicates the city and perhaps facility where the employee will work. If there is a system of rotation among localities or if there is substantial travel involved, this is noted.

Social Environment

An effort is made to describe the kind of interpersonal conditions in which the employee will work. This includes information about the number of co-workers, the range of occupational identities, contact with the public, and whether there are recreational facilities or social clubs associated with work.

Conditions of Employment

Some local and state governments require their employees (or sometimes their applicants for employment) to meet a residency requirement. In order to work for some public employers, one must subscribe to a specific code of ethics, declare personal financial interests, or abide by rules governing other employment or economic activities. Religious organizations might specify a preference or a requirement that employees have a particular religious affiliation. All of these conditions can be explained in the position description.

Career Opportunities

The position description should outline promotional opportunities and can include what options there are for lateral movement to related career paths and what kinds of training programs are available. If the jurisdiction has a general policy of filling all vacancies through open competition or of restricting the selection process initially to current, interested employees, this, too, might be explained.

Position descriptions should be written so that employees, applicants for employment, and supervisors can read and use them. Jargon often makes the descriptions inaccessible and defeats at least part of their usefulness.[14]

As noted at the outset of this chapter, agency managers can find position descriptions more of a hindrance than a help. Resistant employees can use outdated or inaccurate position descriptions to erect a wall defending a narrow range of responsibilities. The written words of a position description often fail to invite the initiative and creativity that an agency manager may seek in employees.

These limitations of position descriptions argue for the importance of accuracy and currency. On the other hand, it must be acknowledged that position descriptions can serve as useful checks on an arbitrary or disorganized manager.

POSITION CLASSIFICATION

Taxonomy is as fundamental a part of personnel management as it is basic to other fields of study and operation. Biologists classify species, political scientists categorize types of governments and ideologies, and personnel specialists place individual positions into broader groupings. Although each position might have traits unique to it, it is possible to cluster jobs according to similar duties and responsibilities and talk of police officers, auditors, radiologists, attorneys, and the like. The U.S. Department of Labor publishes a *Dictionary of Occupational Titles* that offers a classification of jobs, with titles and brief descriptions of positions throughout society. Each organization typically has its own more specific scheme of **position classification**.

There are a number of reasons why one might want to group or classify positions. One advantage, for example, would be to have candidates for similar jobs go through one examination and selection process. There might be a desire to provide for the easy movement of employees from one position to a similar one.

When layoffs are necessary, it would be reasonable to target those with the least seniority in given classifications. Trainers might want jobs grouped according to areas of expertise and training needs. Those responsible for devising and maintaining compensation schemes might want positions classified according to level of complexity or responsibility or physical demands. Like having one position analysis that serves a variety of purposes, it is useful to have a classification system that agency managers can use for a wide array of functions.

The major concern when classification systems were first initiated was paying similar wages to employees who did essentially the same work. At the time, this was not primarily a commitment to the principle of fairness. The issue was efficiency and economy, and this translated into standardization.[15]

Chicago was the first major jurisdiction to adopt a position classification system. The city relied on the work of E. O. Griffenhagen, a consultant who worked with Commonwealth Edison Company. Private firms used position classification systems just for manual labor and clerical jobs. When Chicago established its system in 1905 to 1910, it included almost all of its positions, as did public jurisdictions that followed.

The U.S. Congress established a Joint Commission on Reclassification of Salaries that reported in 1920. The commission's study noted the wide range of salaries paid to federal employees doing the same work not only between agencies but within the same agency. Managers within the federal government sometimes competed with one another for a valued employee, offering higher salaries even though the job tasks remained the same. Despite the plea for uniformity in titles and pay, nothing was done. Two years later the federal Bureau of Efficiency arrived at similar findings. Using both reports as a basis, Congress passed the Classification Act of 1923. The act created the Personnel Classification Board and mandated that it group positions into classes based on similar duties and responsibilities and then provide for equal compensation for equal work.

Subsequent to the passage of this act, the Personnel Classification Board was abolished and its responsibilities were assigned to the Civil Service Commission. The Classification Act of 1949 replaced that of 1923, although it continued the same principles. A feature of the 1949 legislation was to distinguish between the maintenance of the general system, which was the responsibility of the Civil Service Commission, and the classification of individual positions, which was placed in the hands of departments and agencies and then subjected to postaudits by the Civil Service Commission.

During 1970, Congress passed two laws that are important to position classification in government. The Intergovernmental Personnel Act included a provision that required state and local governments getting grants under this act to develop classification and equitable pay systems. The other legislation, the Job Evaluation Policy Act, called on the Civil Service Commission to complete a study of position classification and report its findings to Congress. This two-year study led to the development and introduction of the ability requirements scale method described earlier in this chapter. That system became a model adopted widely throughout the public sector.

Classification Series

A feature common to position classification systems is that groups are made according to occupational categories. Occupational categorization is, however, just one step. The next task is to be precise about levels of difficulty, types of expertise, kinds of responsibilities, and the like. The result is the development of a **classification series** in which positions are grouped according to level of expertise and/or responsibility. Each level is given a number. Accountant 1, for example, is a new hire who is still on probation. Accountant 2 is an apprentice learning the variety of accounting problems that might occur and mastering the details of relevant policies and procedures. Accountant 3 is the objective level, where employees have enough knowledge and experience to be left on their own. Help is only needed in unusual situations. Accountant 4 is an expert who is able to handle virtually any situation. A very complex operation might even have an Accountant 5 to innovate and develop new procedures when needed. Occupations and organizations vary in the number of levels that are necessary; some have only one level whereas others may have as many as seven.

Classification Specifications

A key part of position classifications is a written statement of **classification specifications**, fondly referred to as class specs. These are as important to position classification as specifications are to a procurement process. They provide rules and guidelines for those who must classify specific positions and, like a position description, convey to employees what is expected of them.

The identification and use of benchmark positions can be useful in developing classification specifications. A **benchmark position** is one that is considered typical or standard within a class or class series. Such a position can provide the basis for drafting an initial statement and then testing its applicability to both similar and dissimilar positions.

The basic elements of a classification specification are as follows:

1. Title.   This is a brief description that identifies the basic nature of the work and separates the classification from others.

2. Nature of work.   This description includes the kinds of actions and assignments that can be expected, the procedures to be followed, and the amount of supervision received.

3. Examples of work.   To a large extent, this section elaborates on the preceding item. Included here are representative samples of duties and responsibilities.

4. Knowledge, skills, and abilities.   This section relates to the selection criteria and process, so it is often written with the cooperation of those responsible for selection. Note that knowledge, skills, and abilities are distinct from aptitudes and personality traits.

5. Licenses and certificates.   Where there are requirements for a driver's license, admission to the bar, Certified Public Accountant status, and the like, they are stated here. If a jurisdiction would like to include desirable accomplishments (such as years of experience or certain college courses or degrees) in a classification specification, it is important to make the distinction clear between desirable and required.

Figure 8.1 presents an example of classification specifications for a receptionist. In many jurisdictions, classifications—with their written specifications—are established

---

Title: Receptionist
Nature of Work: The primary responsibility is to respond to
    individuals seeking information and assistance from the
    agency and to enable them to communicate with the
    appropriate official within the agency. Work also
    includes general office duties, such as word processing,
    filing, and scheduling.
Examples of Work: Answer phones and personal inquiries;
    verbally convey basic information about the agency;
    schedule appointments and meetings; operate word
    processing equipment; file electronic and hard copy;
    general office work; related duties as required.
Knowledge, Skills, and Abilities: Ability to operate multi-
    office telephone system; good interpersonal skills;
    knowledge of office practices and procedures; ability to
    type at net speed of fifty words per minute; knowledge
    of agency mission and organization; ability to operate
    word processing equipment.
Licenses and Certificates: None required.

FIGURE 8.1   Classification Specifications for Receptionist.

through an administrative rule process. This might make change cumbersome and, despite the disadvantages, prompt agency managers to cope with specifications that are not current.

MAINTAINING A CLASSIFICATION SYSTEM

No system is self-implementing. Even if one captures in a classification specification an accurate description of a job, technologies change, agencies alter missions, managerial styles differ, and employees develop.

Delegation

One way of keeping a classification system current and relevant is for the central personnel office to delegate authority for classifying individual positions to agency managers.[16] The role of a central personnel unit would then be to provide a general classification scheme that would ensure equity and comparability across agency boundaries and to monitor agency actions through audits and training programs. Under this arrangement, agency managers would not only make many of the day-to-day classification decisions, but would also be encouraged to suggest when additions, deletions, and revisions to the classification system were needed.

Delegation can, of course, only be done when agencies have the capacity to perform the tasks. Small jurisdictions may not need to have delegation. In large jurisdictions, several small agencies might pool resources for classification activities.

Surveys

Once a classification system has been established, personnel transactions usually involve individual positions and changes affecting those positions. Inevitably, however, there is a need for periodically surveying an entire classification or group of classifications either in response to change or in an effort to be certain that the classifications are current.[17] In the early 1980s, for example, many employers conducted **classification surveys** of clerical positions. A prime reason was the increased use of word processing technologies and the increased complexity of clerical jobs. Positions that had been designed with file cabinets and manual typewriters in mind were becoming curious antiques.

Classification surveys invariably raise expectations about increases in pay and anxieties about the consolidation and elimination of positions. Agency managers are well advised to communicate carefully about the need for and the purposes of a survey. Employee involvement is essential both to secure needed job information and to reduce anxieties.

Reclassification

Employees can grow in their jobs. Technically, the focus in position classification and **reclassification** should be on jobs, not employees. However, it is difficult to disentangle the two when an employee develops, takes on more responsibilities and, de facto, changes the job itself. In most cases, managers regard this as positive and in any case must recognize the evolution of jobs in order to maintain the integrity of the classification system.

Almost all organizations provide for change and growth by allowing reclassifications of specific positions and the employees in those positions. Some jurisdictions require employees seeking reclassification to pass a noncompetitive examination in order to advance to another classification. Other employers base reclassifications on the way a job has evolved and require evidence, from the employee and supervisor, that the employee has actually been doing work that is different from that described in the position descriptions and classification specifications.

Grade Creep

In part because reclassifications are frequently regarded as a way of getting a promotion and a salary increase, there can be collusion between employees and supervisors. This is especially likely when jobs do not lead to any obvious advancement opportunity within the organization. It is also more prevalent where agencies have a budget-driven limit on the number of employees they can have.

The federal government during the 1970s was a prime example. For political reasons, agency managers were not allowed to increase their number of positions or employees. Politicians did not want to be accused of allowing an expansion of government. Yet, agencies were allocated more salary money than they could spend, given their limits on the number of employees. A way of spending the money and of pleasing employees was to reclassify positions, even when this was not fully justified on the basis of what employees were doing. This often had a lasting effect in that the positions remained overclassified even after employees left them. Thus, **grade creep** or classification inflation occurred. Classification surveys can be used to correct this.

Appeals

Given the implications of classifications for compensation and advancement and the games that employees and their supervisors are sometimes tempted to play, one might expect those in charge of making reclassification decisions to be suspicious and to reject some requests. One might also anticipate the possibility of mistakes.

In the interest of fairness, there are usually opportunities for employees to appeal classification decisions that affect them. The first appeal is to the official who made the decision or to that official's immediate superior, and further appeal is to an individual or a body that is genuinely a third party.

ALTERNATIVES TO POSITION CLASSIFICATION

There are serious problems with the principles and practices of position classification. Grade creep has been mentioned as one of the major games employees and supervisors play to get around what they regard as some of the limitations of position control and position classification. The whole general approach and concept of position analysis and position classification is based on scientific management and assembly-line technology, which have been somewhat discredited. Position descriptions and classification specifications can become limits on what employees will do rather than narratives of what in fact they are doing. Are there any alternatives?

Rank-in-Person

A type of classification system that is common to many professions is **rank-in-person**. College professors, teachers, physicians, and attorneys, for example, do basically the same job tasks at the beginning and at the end of their careers. They teach courses, practice medicine, and litigate cases. Advancement in their careers and increases in their compensation are based not so much on doing something different or more complicated, but rather in meeting professionally established criteria for performing well. Professors must publish research and teach effectively, physicians must heal people, and lawyers must win cases. As they achieve these objectives and accumulate the experience to make it more probable that they will achieve, they rise in their respective professions.

There are examples of rank-in-person systems already in the public sector. Most teachers and many college professors are, for example, public employees. The Foreign Service and the military are also examples of rank-in-person systems. Individual Foreign Service officers and military personnel rise in rank and retain their ranks, barring some disciplinary action, regardless of their precise job assignment at any one point in time. Given the fact that there are so many professionals in the public service, it is somewhat surprising that there continues to be so much reliance on position classification and so little on rank-in-person.[18]

Broad Classifications

The British system of classification is to group positions into several broad categories— clerical, scientific, technical, executive, and administrative—and to allow for relatively easy movement, by employees and managers, from position to position within those categories. In contrast, U.S. public jurisdictions typically have only one position in almost one-half of their classifications and less than ten in almost three-fourths of the classifications. Lateral movement is quite obviously limited with narrowly defined classifications. Broad classifications remove, for employees and managers, many of the barriers to employees' mobility and interchange.

Narrower classifications, on the other hand, tend to provide employees with more security. It is more difficult for managers to reassign tasks if that means establishing new or revised classifications. Efforts to move to broader classifications have been successful in achieving the ends of managers and employees alike.[19] An approach that has been adopted increasingly since the early 1990s, but is still used by only a few employers is **broadbanding**.[20] This involves collapsing a number of related classifications into a broader, common salary range. Since classifications are essentially kept intact and the effects are on how these classifications relate to compensation, broadbanding will be discussed in more detail in Chapter 14.

The *Dictionary of Occupational Titles* and most position classification systems include a gender bias. Jobs traditionally filled by men tend to be more narrowly defined than jobs filled by women. Engineers, for example, are distinguished by their specialty, that is, electrical, chemical, civil, and the like. Rather than having a classification of crafts workers, we have plumbers, electricians, carpenters, and locksmiths. On the other hand, the terms nurse and clerical include jobs that have visible and important specialties. Because classifications are so important to personnel management, the gender bias in class structures can have serious implications. The narrow classifications for jobs traditionally filled by men provide more security and have pay responsive to external markets. The broader classifications for female-dominated jobs, on the other hand, allow for more internal mobility and rely on internal pay rates.

Collective Bargaining and Classifications

Some employers—primarily state and local governments—have allowed collective bargaining on the relationship between position classification and compensation. In these situations, management retains the right to determine agency missions and to assign duties and responsibilities to positions. However, the process of then determining how much each position classification will be paid is one that is negotiated. Similarly, the maintenance of the system can be negotiated. Reclassifications and reclassification appeals can be covered under the contract. In some instances bargaining may place a limit to the number of reclassification requests that can be made—either tied to money available for increases in salaries or to position responsibilities at the time the contract is signed. Where the major or sole operational purpose of the classification system is for compensation administration, there is a strong push for including classification issues in the scope of bargaining. Indeed, there may be anomalies when one bargains for pay scales and then management unilaterally allocates positions to classifications and assigns classifications to pay scales.

In part, bargaining on the assignment of salary ranges to position classifications is a way of placing a value on jobs. Within an organization, union and management negotiate the ranking of jobs, as represented by where they are placed on the salary schedule. A more common approach is to use a job evaluation system based on position analyses.

JOB EVALUATION

In an organization, jobs, like people, are to be valued.[21] Compensation is attached to positions. Organizational hierarchy is built on the value of position. Values will be set. The question is whether they will be bargained, be set in an intuitive, implicit way, or be established in a conscious, systematic manner.

Values attached to positions include supervisory responsibility, complexity, hazardous duties, and the like. Promotions, transfers, layoffs, and other personnel movements occur within a framework that at least to some extent reflects what an organization values.

How to Evaluate Jobs

Like many other aspects of human resource management, job evaluation can be done intuitively. Small organizations, in particular, evaluate and rank their jobs in an informal, intuitive way. They are likely to follow traditional norms of ranking the relatively few managerial positions at the top, followed by professional, then supervisory, crafts, and clerical/maintenance. Medium- to large-scale employers, however, rely on intuition at the risk of being inconsistent and ineffective.[22]

Position analyses that use a factor system—such as that described earlier in this chapter—provide a sound base for systematic job evaluation. One can conduct job evaluations of positions, classifications, or classification series. When a classification is the unit of analysis, the common approach is to identify a benchmark position to represent the whole classification. When the classification series is the unit of analysis, then a benchmark position in the objective level of the series can be used.

Traditionally, individual analysts from a central personnel office conducted job evaluations. A pattern that has become increasingly common since the early 1980s is to have a team of people, including both employees and managers, evaluate jobs. Although it is more efficient to use individual analysts rather than teams, the latter generates more credibility and acceptance for the results of the evaluation and can minimize the biases of individual raters. Individuals are sometimes predisposed to regard certain professions or trades highly or to inflate the complexities and responsibilities of managerial jobs or to disregard work traditionally done by women. Representative groups can provide a check on these biases.

Ideally, who evaluates a job should not have any effect on the specific factor levels assigned to the job.[23] In fact, most contemporary job evaluation systems are not vulnerable to subjective or speculative judgments by raters. The following are basic steps taken to minimize bias or subjectivity:

1. Use complete and accurate job information.
2. Use a job evaluation system that is inclusive and clear in its descriptions of the various factors and factor levels.
3. Train the evaluators so that they understand the job evaluation process and are alert to potential sources of bias.
4. Remove the job title from the information provided to raters so that they focus on specific details for each factor rather than make an initial overall judgment.
5. Have individuals in the team use a secret ballot to assign factor levels to the job being evaluated, thereby gaining the benefits of group discussion about the job but avoiding pressure.
6. Review factor level assignments by individuals within the team and eliminate the highest and lowest scores to minimize the effects of raters who, for whatever reason, rate outside the norm.
7. Check the reliability of the process by having different teams evaluate a common sample of jobs. If different evaluators reviewing the same jobs do not agree at least 85 percent of the time, then an inquiry must be made to determine the source or sources of subjectivity.

Values and subjectivity should play no role in assigning a job to a high, medium, or low rating of physical demands, supervisory responsibility, or other job factor. However, the relative importance of each factor is a value judgment appropriately made by each employer. A state government might, for example, weight knowledge required, discretion, and consequence of error at 10, supervisory responsibility, complexity, effects of action, and personal contacts at 6, and physical demands and work environment at 3. A nonprofit organization that provides services more directly than a state government might place higher weights on personal contacts and physical demands and less on knowledge required and effects of action. The weights reflect the needs and values of the specific employer.

It is important to use the same weights for all jobs in the same organization. Job evaluation systems that have distinct weights for each category of jobs lose sight of the fundamental point that the weights are the values of the employer, not what is valued by a particular occupation. Also, separate weights for different types of jobs may incorporate societal biases, rather than employer needs and values.[24]

To evaluate a job, analysts first use the quantitative position analysis system to assign the job to the appropriate level for each factor. Then the weight for each factor is multiplied times the level to calculate the factor score. The total job evaluation point is the sum of all the factor scores. Table 8.2 illustrates this for three positions in a hypothetical government.

What one has at the end of this process is a ranking of all jobs within an organization according to how an employer values complexity, physical effort, consequence of errors, and other job factors.[25] It is important to note that the ranking is employer-specific, not society wide. One employer can, of course, borrow the system and rankings of another, thereby avoiding the time and expense of designing or adapting a unique system. Any such borrowing does not alter the basic fact that job evaluation takes

TABLE 8.2   ILLUSTRATION OF JOB EVALUATION SCORING

Job	Factor	FACTOR Level	x	FACTOR Weight =	FACTOR Score
Accountant	Knowledge required	6 (of 10)	10	60	
	Discretion	3 (of 6)	10	30	
	Consequence of error	4 (of 5)	20	80	
	Physical effort	1 (of 5)	5	5	
				Total Points	175
Librarian	Knowledge required	7 (of 10)	10	70	
	Discretion	4 (of 6)	10	40	
	Consequence of error	3 (of 5)	20	60	
	Physical effort	1 (of 5)	5	5	
				Total Points	175
Janitor	Knowledge required	2 (of 10)	10	20	
	Discretion	1 (of 6)	10	10	
	Consequence of error	1 (of 5)	20	20	
	Physical effort	4 (of 5)	5	20	
				Total Points	70

place within, not between, organizations. As already discussed, the purpose of evaluating and ranking jobs is to establish fairness and equity within an organization.

Job Evaluation and Comparable Worth/Pay Equity

Quantitative job evaluations like those just described can help eliminate the effects of decisions to fill some jobs, such as nurses, librarians, secretaries, and child care workers, primarily with women and to set the compensation levels low. **Comparable worth**, or **pay equity**, refers to the policy and practice of setting compensation in accordance with the value of a job to an employer absent any consideration for whether the job is typically filled by men or by women. Quantitative job evaluations rank jobs within an agency or organization according to factor level points and the weights of factors, not gender.[26]

One influence on the value of positions is societal or market, which is external to the organization. The focus of this chapter is on the internal market within the organization.

An internal evaluation or market system is needed because virtually every employer has some jobs for which they are either the only employer or the major employer in a community. In these situations, the most appropriate source for setting values is within, rather than outside, the organization. In structuring the organization and setting compensation, all jobs can be evaluated and ranked. Then pay can be set for those jobs where there are legitimate market comparisons and the remaining jobs can be paid in accordance to how they rank when compared to the market-oriented jobs.

Compensation is discussed more completely in Chapter 13. Here we dealt with the issue of how to evaluate and rank jobs within the organization in order to identify internal equity that can be used as one of the guideposts for setting pay. Since the external market is generally suspect regarding pay for female-dominated jobs, the internal equity guideposts are especially important for employers following comparable worth or pay equity policies.[27]

SUMMARY

Personnel management consists of matching people and positions. In order to proceed with the tasks of personnel management, then, it is necessary to understand people, on the one hand, and positions, on the other. This chapter has been about positions and how they might be analyzed, described, classified, evaluated, and ranked on a systematic basis.

The need for treating positions in a careful manner, using a common yardstick and consistent set of values, is to recognize that some positions can be grouped together because of basic similarities. These groupings provide for efficiency and equity. Efficiency is served because there is no need to establish separate selection processes, training programs, pay scales, and the like for every position, when some of them share common traits. Equity and fairness are served because employees doing the same or comparable work can have the same rewards and opportunities.

Obviously, individual employees are unique and they will make their job somewhat unique. Positions should, and usually do, allow for the uniqueness that comes from individual incumbents and the changing circumstances in which the duties and responsibilities of a position are performed. Managers face the challenge of balancing the need for uniqueness with the need for efficiency and fairness. Put another way, it is important to avoid placing rigid constraints on supervisors and employees with positions described too narrowly and to keep from exploiting employees with vague, open-ended positions. Unfortunately, there is no magic formula. Instead, we must rely on vigilance, good professional judgment, and, at times, the checks of an appeal process.

DISCUSSION QUESTIONS

1. Why is it important to focus on positions as distinct from the people who are in positions? How is information on positions used in personnel management?
2. What are the advantages and disadvantages of defining position classification narrowly? Do agency managers and employees value narrow classifications differently?
3. Why are classification surveys and appeals important? What are the obstacles to maintaining integrity in position classification?
4. What are the ways in which position classification and job evaluation contribute to a compensation system that is equitable?

Position Analysis Exercise

This exercise is to give students an opportunity for hands-on experience in position analysis. This exercise will also enable the student to generate data that can be used in completing other exercises in this text. To complete the exercise, it is necessary to select a position in a governmental agency or nonprofit organization. The form provided below should be used to record the information.

PREPARATION

Before beginning the analysis, you should familiarize yourself with both the agency and the general occupation that you are studying. You should know what the organization does, how it is structured, and what changes management might be planning. Occupational information can be obtained directly from associations, and from professional references and the U.S. Department of Labor's *Dictionary of Occupational Titles.*

METHODOLOGY

This description of a position is based on what incumbents actually do. It is necessary to have a behavioral base. It is equally important to avoid getting locked into the status quo. It is essential to secure the manager's or supervisor's definition of the job and its requirements as well as the incumbent's.

To gather the required information, the student should interview one or more incumbents of the position and the relevant supervisor(s) of the position under analysis.

In addition, the student might observe someone performing in the position if that position involves physical activity. Existing class specifications, job descriptions, and similar documents should be reviewed. Information from each interview, observation, and document review can be recorded on copies of the position analysis form in Figure 8.2 but in any case must be summarized on the form.

POSITION ANALYSIS FORM

(1)   *Title of position:*

(2)   *Name of agency:*

(3)   *Brief description of agency mission(s):*

(4)   *Summary of duties and responsibilities of position.*
     (Relate to (a) agency mission, (b) data, (c) people, and (d) things.)

(5)   *Description of tasks:*

	Task	Percentage of time (specify if daily, weekly, monthly, or annual)	Importance of task to agency mission(s)		
			Essential	Important	Supportive
1.					
2.					
3.					
4.					
5.					

(6)   *Relation to other jobs*
     (a) Transfers:

     (b) Promotions:

         From:

         To:

     (c)   Supervision received:

     (d)   Supervision given:

                    (Form continues on following pages.)

(7)   *Skills required for machines, equipment, and work aids:*

Skill	Need immediately	Can acquire through postentry training

(8)   *Knowledge and abilities for task accomplishments:*

Knowledge and ability	Need immediately	Can acquire on the job

(9)   *Worker traits:*
   (a) Aptitudes

   (b) Temperaments

   (c) Interests

   (d) Physical

   (e) Licenses and certificates required

   (f) Vocational or educational preparation required

   (g) Experience(s) required

(10)   *Traits, skills, knowledge, and ability necessary for career advancements:*

   1. _____

   2. _____

   3. _____

(11)   *Social representation of work force in this position classification.*
   (Complete after position is classified if this is a new position.)
   (a) Men   _____

      Women _____

      Total   _____

(b) White   _____
     African-Amercian   _____
     Spanish surname   _____
     Native American   _____
     Other   _____
     Total   _____
(c) Handicapped   _____

(12) *General comments*:

(13) *Basis of analysis*:
      (a) Interviews:

      (b) Documents:

      (c) Literature reviewed:

      (d) Other:

(14) *Analyst*:

(15) *Reviewed by*:
      (a) Agency personnel:

      (b) Personnel Office Supervisor:

FIGURE 8.2   Position Analysis Form.

COMPLETING THE POSITION ANALYSIS FORM

Most of the form is self-explanatory, but the following comments might prove useful.
Item Four. This should be a narrative summary. The summary description should include how the duties and responsibilities of the position relate to the mission of the agency, what kind of data the incumbent must work with, and what is done with that data, how the incumbent relates to other people, and what kinds of equipment and work aids the incumbent will use. Not every position, of course, will have all of these dimensions.
Item Five. A task is a distinct, identifiable work activity that constitutes one of the logical and necessary steps in the performance of a job, such as addresses envelopes, answers telephone, directs visitors to appropriate office. Each task should be listed.

Depending on the position, estimate the percentage of time spent on each task on a daily, weekly, monthly, or yearly basis. A routine job can, for example, be analyzed on a daily or weekly basis, whereas a budget analyst position should be analyzed on an annual basis. Be certain to use the same basis (daily, weekly, etc.) for all of the tasks.

Check whether each task is essential, important, or supportive to the accomplishment of the agency mission. Essential means the agency would fail if this task were not performed. Important refers to a contribution that determines how well or how efficiently the mission would be accomplished. Supportive includes those activities necessary for the institutional well being of the agency, but which have only indirect effects on agency missions.

Item Six. Specify the positions from which and to which an incumbent in this position might transfer. The descriptions of supervision should include the number of people supervised and an indication of whether there is close supervision or independent work.

Items Seven and Eight. It is important to note whether or not the knowledge, skills, and abilities are required as soon as one begins work or whether they can be acquired after one is appointed.

In some position analyses, the information in Items 7 and 8 is provided separately for each of the tasks listed in Item 5. This frequently requires considerable repetition. This form is meant to be more efficient, but it does require the analyst to make reference to position tasks.

Item Nine. Complete in narrative form.

Item Ten. Relate this to the information in Item 6(b).

Item Eleven. Use numbers, not percentages, in presenting a profile of the current workforce.

Item Thirteen. Specify who was interviewed and what documents and literature were reviewed. If possible, attach copies of documents.

Item Fifteen. Do not complete; not necessary for purposes of this class exercise.

GLOSSARY

Ability requirements scales An approach to position analysis that measures fifty-two different abilities used on jobs and scores these abilities on the basis of how important they are to the job

Benchmark position A typical or standard job within a classification or classification series that can be used as a point of comparison within and between position classifications

Broadbanding The establishment of a salary range with a wide gap between the minimum and maximum and then the assignment of a relatively large number of position classifications to that range

Classification series Levels within a position classification that indicate increasing difficulty and responsibility

Classification specifications Formal, summary statement of the work and the requirements associated with a position classification

Classification survey A study of an existing position classification to see if specific positions are properly assigned and to determine whether any adjustments should be made in the classification itself

Comparable worth A policy consciously to eliminate the practice of depressing the wages of jobs traditionally filled by women and instead setting compensation in accordance with job factors

Critical incident technique An approach to position analysis that identifies the job behaviors that prompted specific outcomes, some desired and some undesired

Functional job analysis The most common approach to position analysis. The focus is on the duties and responsibilities assigned to a specific job, regardless of the characteristics of the incumbent

Grade creep A situation in which over time positions have been assigned to a classification that is higher than justified by actual duties and responsibilities

Job evaluation The process of analyzing jobs in order to rank them within an organization according to various job characteristics and the relative importance of those characteristics to the functioning of the organization

Job factors A common set of dimensions, ranging from four to ten depending on the system, used to analyze in each position within an organization

Pay equity Another term for comparable worth

Position analysis The process of studying the characteristics of a specific job. There are different approaches to the analysis of positions

Position analysis questionnaire An approach to position analysis that relies on a specific instrument with 194 questions and a code for scoring answers

Position classification A category of positions with substantially similar duties and responsibilities

Position description A narrative, usually following a standard format in an organization, that summarizes the nature of a job and what it requires

Rank-in-person An alternative to position classification, in which individuals are categorized according to their qualifications and accomplishments rather than their duties and responsibilities

Reclassification Movement of a position to a different classification because the actual work done by the incumbent has changed over time

Task inventory procedure An approach to position analysis that is based on an inventory of job tasks provided by an employee and his or her supervisor

SOURCES

Bemis, S. F., Belensky, A. H., & Soder, D. A. (1983). *Job analysis: An effective management tool.* Washington, DC: Bureau of National Affairs.
A discussion of job analysis and detailed instructions on how to use several different approaches.

Harvey, R. J. (1991). Job analysis. In M. D. Dunnette, & L. M. Hough, eds., *Handbook of industrial and organizational psychology* (Vol. II). Palo Alto, CA: Consulting Psychologists Press. *Review of concepts, history, and scholarship of job analysis.*

National Academy of Public Administration. (1991). *Modernizing federal classification: An opportunity for excellence.* Washington, DC: National Academy of Public Administration. *Report of a task force of scholars and officials that reviews the nature of the position classification system used in the federal government and makes recommendations.*

Treiman, D. J., & Hartmann, H. I. (1981). *Women, work and wages: Equal pay for jobs of equal value.* Washington, DC: National Academy Press. *Examination of the causes and characteristics of gender-based wage inequities and an explanation of point-factor job evaluation.*

NOTES

1. Max Weber, *The Theory of Social and Economic Organization,* trans. A. M. Henderson and Talcott Parsons (London: Oxford University Press, 1947), 329–340.

2. Nicos P. Mouzelis, *Organization and Bureaucracy: An Analysis of Modern Theories* (Chicago: Aldine, 1968), 79–96; Charles Perrow, *Complex Organizations: A Critical Essay* (Glenview, IL: Scott, Foresman, 1972), 61–96; Michael M. Harmon and Richard T. Mayer, *Organizational Theory for Public Administration* (Boston: Little, Brown, 1986), 67–118.

3. Robert J. Harvey, "Job Analysis," in Marvin D. Dunnette and Leaetta M. Hough, eds., *Handbook of Industrial and Organizational Psychology,* Vol. II (Palo Alto, CA: Consulting Psychologists Press, 1991), 71–163; National Academy of Public Administration, *Modernizing Federal Classification: An Opportunity for Excellence* (Washington, DC: National Academy of Public Administration, 1991); Carolyn Ban, "The Navy Demonstration Project: An 'Experiment in Experimentation,'" in Carolyn Ban and Norma M. Riccucci, eds., *Public Personnel Management: Current Concerns—Future Challenges* (New York: Longman, 1991), 31–41.

4. Samuel B. Green, John G. Veres, and Wiley R. Boyles, "Racial Differences on Job Analysis Questionnaires: An Empirical Study," *Public Personnel Management* 20, no. 2 (Summer 1991): 135–144.

5. E. J. McCormick, P. R. Jeanneret, and R. C. Mecham, "A Study of Job Characteristics and Job Dimensions as Based on the Position Analysis Questionnaire (PAQ)," *Journal of Applied Psychology* 56 (1972): 347–368; E. J. McCormick, R. C. Mecham, and P. R. Jeanneret, *Position Analysis Questionnaire (PAQ) Technical Manual* (Logan, UT: PAQ Services, Inc., 1977).

6. Juan I. Sanchez and Edward L. Levine, "Determining Important Tasks Within Jobs: A Policy Capturing Approach," *Journal of Applied Psychology* 74, no. 2 (March 1989): 336–342; Juan Sanchez and Scott L. Fraser, "On the Choice of Scales for Task Analysis," *Journal of Applied Psychology* 77, no. 4 (November 1993): 545–553.

7. James P. Clifford, "Manage Work Better to Better Manage Human Resources: A Comparative Study of Two Approaches to Job Analysis," *Public Personnel Management* 25, no. 1 (Spring 1996): 89–102.

8. J. C. Flanagan, "The Critical Incidents Technique," *Psychological Bulletin* 51 (1954): 327–358.

9. F. A. Fleishman, *Manual for the Ability Requirements Scale* (Palo Alto, CA: Consulting Psychologists Press, 1991); E. A. Fleishman and M. E. Reilly, *Human Abilities: Their Definition, Measurement, and Job Task Requirements* (Palo Alto, CA: Consulting Psychologists Press, 1991).

10. U.S. Department of Labor, Employment and Training Administration, *The Revised Handbook for Analyzing Jobs* (Washington, DC: Government Printing Office, 1991).

11. Harold Suskin, "The Factor Ranking System," in Harold Suskin, ed., *Job Evaluation and Pay Administration in the Public Sector* (Chicago: International Personnel Management Association, 1977), 136–138; Stephen F. Bemis, Ann Holt Belensky, and Dee Ann Soder, *Job Analysis: An Effective Management Tool* (Washington, DC: Bureau of National Affairs, 1983); Jai B. Ghorpade, *Job Analysis: A Handbook for Human Resource Directors* (Englewood Cliffs, NJ: Prentice-Hall, 1988).

12. Comptroller General of the United States, *Options for Conducting a Pay Equity Study of Federal Pay and Classification Systems* (Washington, DC: General Accounting Office, 1985), 26.

13. Donald J. Treiman, *Job Evaluation: An Analytic Review* (Washington, DC: National Academy of Sciences, 1979).

14. Philip C. Grant, "What Use Is a Job Description," *Personnel Journal* 67, no. 2 (February 1988): 45–53; C. Berenson and H. D. Ruhnke, "Job Descriptions—A New Handle on an Old Tool," *Personnel Journal* 49, no. 11 (November 1970): 954–983.

15. William Howard Taft, *Economy and Efficiency in the Government Services,* H. Doc. 458 (Washington, DC: Government Printing Office, 1912).

16. Larry M. Lane, "The Office of Personnel Management: Values, Policies, and Consequences," in Patricia W. Ingraham and David H. Rosenbloom, eds., *The Promise and Paradox of Civil Service Reform* (Pittsburgh: University of Pittsburgh Press, 1992); John F. Fisher, Harold H. Leich, and Robert E. Reynolds, *Decentralizing Position Classification* (Chicago: International Personnel Management Association, 1964).

17. Gilbert A. Schulkind, "Monitoring Position Classification—Practical Problems and Possible Solutions," *Public Personnel Management* 4, no. 1 (January/February 1975): 32–37.

18. Donald F. Kettl, Patricia W. Ingraham, Ronald P. Sanders, and Constance Horner, *Civil Service Reform: Building a Government that Works* (Washington, DC: Brookings Institution, 1996).

19. Ban, "The Navy Demonstration Project."

20. Sally Coleman Selden, Pat Ingraham, and Willow Jacobson, "Human Resource Practices in State Governments: Findings from a National Survey." Paper presented to the American Society for Public Administration, Orlando, FL, April 10–14, 1999.

21. Alfred J. Candrilli and Roald D. Armagast, "The Case for Effective Point-Factor Job Evaluation, Viewpoint 2," *Personnel* 64 (April 1987): 33–36.

22. Robert R. Fredlund, "Valuing Work: Complications—Contradictions—Compensation," *Public Personnel Management* 12, no. 4 (Winter 1983): 461–468.

23. Jonathan Tompkins, "Sources of Measurement Error and Gender Bias in Job Evaluation," *Review of Public Personnel Administration* 9, no. 1 (Fall 1988): 1–16.

24. Kermit R. Davis, Jr., and William I. Sauser, Jr., "A Comparison of Factor Weighting Methods in Job Evaluation: Implications for Compensation Systems," *Public Personnel Management* 22 (Spring 1993): 91–106; Donald J. Treiman and Heidi I. Hartmann, *Women, Work and Wages: Equal Pay for Jobs of Equal Value* (Washington, DC: National Academy Press, 1981).

25. Kermit R. Davis, Jr., and William I. Sauser, Jr., "A Comparison of Factor Weighting Methods in Job Evaluation: Implications for Compensation Systems," *Purbli Personnel Management* 22, no. 1 (1993), 48–69.

26. Treiman and Hartmann, *Women, Work and Wages.*

27. Davis and Sauser, "A Comparison of Factor Weighting Methods," 91–106.

Chapter 9

Performance Evaluation

Managers, inevitably and incessantly, evaluate their employees. Likewise, co-workers, legislators, and customers constantly judge the work of an employee. Reputations develop. Managers decide who to assign a given task, who to send to a training program, and who to promote to another position. In large part, these decisions are based on conclusions about the quality of work completed by individual employees. Performance evaluation is integral to day-to-day administrative decisions and to long-range plans for reorganization and change.

On the other hand, managers neglect performance evaluation in many ways. The neglect relates to the care with which employees are judged. Informal, casual evaluations are almost inherently subjective. If some measures are not taken to be consistent and objective, conclusions are vulnerable to being wrong and unfair.

Moreover, the traditional focus on individual workers may be misleading. Employees increasingly work primarily in groups. Perhaps teams rather than individuals would be the more appropriate unit of analysis for performance evaluation. Chapter 8 discussed how and why positions are analyzed; this chapter is about the people in those positions.

LEARNING OBJECTIVES OF THIS CHAPTER

- Understand why managers evaluate employee performance
- Know some of the major problems of determining how well a job is being done
- Be able to recognize and critique various methods of performance evaluation
- Apply a particular approach to performance evaluation
- Understand the issues involved in the assessment of teams rather than—or in addition to—individuals
- Understand the implications of who does the evaluating
- Know what employees can do if they think errors have been made in their evaluations

THE USE OF PERFORMANCE EVALUATIONS

It may seem obvious that managers evaluate employees. Almost anyone with work experience will, nonetheless, observe that it is equally obvious that performance is rarely, if ever, seriously or systematically evaluated. This paradox was an issue during personnel management reform efforts of the 1970s and again in the 1990s.[1] A major concern of these reforms was to increase productivity. In governments there also was political pressure to reduce the number of government employees, while at the same time increasing productivity. An approach common to the Reinventing Government movement was to hold agency managers responsible for performance outcomes and then force these managers to evaluate, diagnose, and improve the performance of their staff.[2]

The evaluation of employees and their performance, of course, occurs naturally and constantly. Almost as a matter of course, we judge each other's work and attitudes, and we rank people along some scale of best to worst. What does not occur naturally and frequently is a conscious and systematic evaluation and the communication of these conclusions to those being evaluated.

Individuals as the Unit of Analysis

The use of systematic methods of appraising individual employee performance began in the public sector. The federal government developed forms in the 1850s to use in rating employees according to personal traits and work habits. When New York City established its civil service system in 1883, it also adopted a procedure for employee evaluation. School districts began using forms for evaluating teachers in 1896. In contrast, the private sector did not use individual performance evaluation seriously until just prior to World War II.

The federal Civil Service Reform Act of 1978 included a provision mandating performance evaluations of employees:

Each agency shall develop one or more performance appraisal systems, which

1. provide for periodic appraisals of the job performance of employees
2. encourage employee participation in establishing performance objectives
3. use the results of performance appraisal as a basis for training, rewarding, reassigning, promoting, demoting, retaining, and separating employees.[3]

Reform legislation at the state and local levels during the 1970s also included language mandating or encouraging performance appraisals.[4] Specific provisions varied, but the basic intent was to affirm the importance of appraising the performance of employees.

The attention paid to performance evaluation systems can properly be regarded both as a hope and an indictment. The hope is for a personnel management function that can have considerable payoff to employees, agency managers, and the people being served by governments and nonprofits. The indictment is of the ways in which existing systems have or have not operated.

A major reason for the ineffectiveness of employee evaluations is the lack of a response to those who have asked, "So what?" If supervisors, managers, and employees are not convinced that a performance evaluation will be put to some use, they are not likely to treat performance appraisal exercises seriously.[5] It is not pleasant to face an individual and point out where he or she has failed. Most managers prefer to avoid unpleasant confrontations and either exaggerate the positive aspects of an employee's performance or fail to conduct the appraisal at all. In fact, performance evaluations frequently have been divorced from the rest of personnel management, thereby inviting employees and supervisors alike to treat the evaluation process frivolously.

Ironically, the potential uses of sound performance evaluations are so numerous and important that there should never be a problem responding to the "So what?" query. The possible, and desirable, uses that follow include rewards and sanctions that clearly affect both individuals and organizations.

1. Human resource planning.   Planning should be based in part on an understanding of the strengths and weaknesses of the existing workforce.

2. Examination validation.   The validation of selection tests depends, in part, on data indicating how well current employees are performing.

3. Probation and promotion.   The best way to assess someone for passing probationary status or for being considered for a promotion is to evaluate his or her current work performance.

4. Merit pay increases.   Although pay does not always provide an incentive for more and better work, where compensation depends in part on job performance, evaluations are necessary.

5. Employee development.   Where weaknesses are identified and where there are performance patterns indicating potential that is not fully utilized, performance evaluations can lead to career counseling and training programs geared to the needs of an individual employee.

6. Demotions and dismissals.   Negative actions typically are taken in extreme cases where poor performance or the violation of laws or work rules is visible and obvious. In such a situation, performance evaluations are useful to document the failures and negligence.

7. Layoffs.   Seniority is the most frequently used criteria for deciding who should be laid off when reorganization and/or financial difficulties occur. In some cases—including the layoffs of federal government employees immediately after World War II—performance evaluations were among the determinants of who got laid off.

Agency managers sometimes use **performance management** with individuals on their staff. This involves the following four basic steps:

1. Set goals.   The initial step is to define clear goals for each individual employee.

2. Measure performance.   It is essential to measure often and allow for correction.

3. Provide feedback.   Employees need information and coaching in order to contribute effectively and consistently.

4. Reinforce positive behaviors.   To encourage employees, managers need to recognize and reward the work behaviors they value.

It should be pointed out that serious volunteers also appreciate the direction and the feedback that are integral to performance management.

This is a general approach toward personnel management that invites a variety of specific techniques for completing these steps. A key component is the use of performance evaluation in an integrated and strategic way to get employees to accomplish agency goals.

The multiple use of performance evaluations appears to make more sense on paper than in reality.[6] Supervisors perceive a role conflict when they, on the one hand, reward or sanction an employee and, on the other hand, threaten the employee.[7] Conceptually, these are not conflicting roles. Indeed, they can be approached in a complementary way. Before employees are dismissed, for example, they should be told what the problems are and given an opportunity—through training programs, counseling, and the like—to rectify the situation.

Performance evaluations should be able to generate both rewards and sanctions. Nonetheless, the sticks seem to overshadow the carrots. Employees and their supervisors almost inevitably view performance evaluation as required primarily to build a case for disciplinary action. When an individual is having his or her performance evaluated seriously, the natural assumption is that there is a problem.

Team Approach as Unit of Analysis

Advocates of Total Quality Management (TQM) argue that employee performance evaluation is not only awkward and uncomfortable for those involved, it is also simply wrong.[8] According to this approach, employees do and should work in small groups and so the focus of managerial evaluations should be on teams, not on individual positions or employees. If there is a problem with productivity, it is in the system of work, not the personnel. Quality depends on customer feedback and worker cooperation in responding to customers. Individual performance evaluation needs to be abandoned, because it focuses on the wrong unit and because it fosters competition rather than cooperation among employees.[9]

While the customer focus and the role of systems and groups are very valuable contributions of the TQM approach, the conceptual incompatibility of employee performance appraisal has not led to its demise. A 1990 survey of private sector organizations that have TQM as their central management philosophy revealed that very few of them actually discarded performance evaluation.[10] Managers must decide when individual employees should be retained, encouraged, developed, or disciplined.

The experiences of organizations that emphasize team management, in other words, suggest the integration of individual performance evaluations, rather than abandoning them.[11] Annual, pro forma evaluations serve no useful purpose and may indeed impede the group dynamics important to TQM. On the other hand, the identification of employees who have potential for further development or who need special attention can occur within the Quality Management context. The interaction and feedback of work teams seem more constructive and natural than the ritualistic, annual evaluations that are traditional in most organizations.

The lessons of research on employee motivation also suggest the value of multiple approaches to performance evaluation. Individuals, as stated in Chapter 5, approach work in different ways. Professionals who invest personal self-esteem in their work are eager to be productive and to be recognized by their peers. Evaluation occurs within their professional setting—when projects are completed, cases are won, patients are healed, and families are helped—rather than through arbitrary annual dates and criteria on a standard form. Employees, on the other hand, who are not as personally invested in their jobs, relate more to the guidance provided by supervisors, co-workers, and organizational routines. For them it is important that expectations are clear and evaluations are fair. In short, it is important in our discussion of performance evaluation to avoid the assumption that one size, or approach, fits all.

PROBLEMS OF MEASUREMENT

The reluctance of employers and managers to use performance evaluations mean-ingfully might reasonably be based on their doubts about whether employee perfor-mance can be measured. There are some occupations that readily lend themselves to measurement. One can, for example, calculate the speed and accuracy with which an employee enters data or processes forms. It is, however, more difficult to gauge the quantity or quality of what budget analysts, environmental engineers, social workers, or managers do. Generally, work that requires analysis and judgment defies easy measurement. Many of the professional and paraprofessional positions in govern-ment are included in this category. You know an outstanding social worker when you see one, but it is hard to describe or measure the performance precisely. Even if one focuses on measurable results of an organization, for example, the reduction in the number of families on welfare, it is not always clear how to trace that to the contribu-tions of individuals on the staff.

One way of considering performance is to gauge the contribution that an employee makes to the achievement of organizational goals. If a budget office, for example, attempts to cut overall expenditures by 5 percent while still retaining the current level of services, and a budget analyst responsible for transportation policy matters identifies at least 5 percent of expenditures that can be cut within a deadline, then a positive evaluation of that budget analyst's performance is appropriate. This results-oriented approach is very attractive. It is also, however, difficult to apply to some public agencies. Public policies enacted by legislative bodies and approved by chief executives are frequently the result of hard bargaining and compromise. Some nonprofits pursue objectives that represent similar negotiations between members of their boards. These policies can be stated in vague ways, rather than as clear mes-sages to employees, volunteers, and the people being served. For example, trans-portation agencies encourage the use of mass transit in order to conserve energy and yet also facilitate safe and comfortable automobile travel by constructing and main-taining an extensive network of roads and highways. Organizations that provide care for the poor and disadvantaged can appear to be like Dr. Jekyll and Mr. Hyde. While at times they act compassionately to serve the needy, at other times they act sternly in an effort to eliminate waste, cheating, and abuse. What is the balance supposed to be between mass transit and automobile travel or between care for the poor and safe-guarding against cheating?

Employees cannot always be certain about the standards that will be used in judging their performance. The use of customer feedback and team participation in production analysis can resolve many of the evaluation issues in these agencies. Still, some decisions about individual employees will have to be made. It is therefore better to think about the criteria and systems for evaluation, rather than allow the evaluation to occur in a loose or even misguided manner.

TYPES OF PERFORMANCE EVALUATION

Through the 1950s, the title of this chapter would have been Employee Evaluation, rather than Performance Evaluation. The approach presented would have emphasized personality traits and work habits instead of job behavior and work performance.

Trait Rating

Some organizations still evaluate employees according to traits and characteristics such as grooming, friendly disposition, honesty, and initiative. While these may be traits that are generally desired in people and, especially, in those people with whom one works, there are two major problems with evaluating employees and volunteers according to a list of traits. First, the terms used lend themselves to different interpretations. Grooming for some means clean-shaven men, for others neatly trimmed beards and mustaches, and for others simply that whatever hair is on the head is washed and brushed. For some, honesty is almost synonymous with being religious, whereas for others the concern is with whether office supplies ever find their way home.

In addition, **trait rating** systems are frequently unrelated to job performance. Traits are at best indirectly relevant. If courtesy is a job behavior desired for someone examining applicants for drivers' licenses, then that should be stated directly, rather than citing a trait such as friendly disposition and assuming that someone with such a personality will naturally treat applicants courteously. In some instances, traits may imply behavior contrary to that required in a job. There is, for example, very little room for creativity and initiative for drivers' license examiners.

Forced-Choice Rating

Under a **forced-choice rating** system, supervisors are given a list of descriptive terms or phrases, such as completes work on time or work frequently includes minor inaccuracies. Supervisors then must choose from those phrases to describe their employees. The major purpose of constraining supervisors to a set list of descriptors is to encourage consistency and objectivity. This is also a way of communicating to supervisors the kinds of behavior patterns they should look for and to employees the kinds of behavior for which they will be rewarded or sanctioned. The limitation is in the list itself: It has a beginning and an end. Behaviors not anticipated when the list was constructed are difficult to include in an evaluation.

This limitation urges care and caution in constructing the list of forced-choice options. One way of exercising care is to involve the employees. One of the provisions of the 1978 Civil Service Reform Act is employee participation in performance evaluation. Employees can bring the understanding and perspective that comes from action at the ground level. Moreover, employee participation can have the effect of reducing the negative, judgmental character of a performance evaluation system and emphasizing its utility as a way of communicating goals and problems. Employee—and volunteer—participation can also increase the acceptance of the evaluation system once it is installed.[12]

The exercise in this chapter uses a performance evaluation involving forced-choice ratings and includes employee participation, through the behaviorally anchored rating scales (BARS). Following passage of the 1978 Civil Service Reform Act, federal agencies began implementing BARS. In part, this system was used because of successful experiences in other public jurisdictions, nonprofit organizations, and the private sector.

Essay

Evaluating employees by writing an essay about their work can be the sole form of evaluation or a component of another technique. An increasingly common system of performance appraisal uses both a forced-choice rating and an essay. The essay is valued as a way of compensating for the restrictions inherent in a forced-choice system. Indeed, the virtue of the essay—it is open-ended and unstructured—is also its vulnerability—the content need not be comparable in scope from one evaluation to another. A lack of structure provides for spontaneity, but it also allows the unimaginative or reluctant evaluator to complete an appraisal that says little and is therefore useless. Again, given the structure of forced-choice rating and the lack of structure of essays, a system that combines these two approaches can be attractive.

Goal Achievement

Some managers use a contractual approach. They begin with an understanding, often formalized in writing to their employees, about what will be accomplished during a given period of time and what will happen if the agreed goals are or are not achieved. The most widely known technique that uses this approach is **management by objectives** (MBO).[13]

The MBO technique begins with a very simple premise: Employees and volunteers cannot work to accomplish the goals of their organization if they are not clear about what those objectives are and what they as individuals need to do to contribute toward the achievement of those goals.[14] The first step in the MBO process is, therefore, the establishment and articulation of goals, both for the agency as a whole and for individual employees and volunteers. The original, orthodox MBO system uses a participatory process for setting goals. Individual employees offer suggestions for what their objectives should be for the next year; these suggestions are aggregated by supervisors and forwarded to the next level up in the organization; this process is repeated until top management receives the suggestions and can consider which ones most closely match management's perceptions of the needs of the organization as a whole; and then the selection of objectives is communicated back down to the employees. That communication specifies what rewards will be provided for achieving established objectives. Once goals are established, employees are given freedom to achieve their respective objectives. Performance appraisal occurs through periodic (usually monthly, quarterly, or semiannual) sessions in which progress is reported, problems are raised, and, if necessary, modifications are made in the objectives or the timetable.

A common alteration made in this ideal version of the MBO process is to set goals at the senior management level and limit the involvement of employees. Because of the role and responsibility of legislative bodies in policy making, government agencies frequently follow this pattern. Another change made by public employers is in the rewards promised for the attainment of MBOs. Frequently there is not enough flexibility in the compensation system to link salary increases to the MBO process. If there is flexibility, it may only apply to senior managers. Where this is the case, some jurisdictions use the MBO goal-setting/performance evaluation system just for senior management, assuming that managers will use whatever authority and skills they have to get their agencies to achieve the objectives that were agreed on between senior managers and the mayor, governor, school board, or other authority.

Another alteration of the MBO model is to establish the contract with a team or group of employees, rather than with individuals. Rewards go to all members of the group if the agreed-upon goals are achieved. Customers can define quality, and managers, employees, and—where applicable—volunteers translate these into specific team goals.

Some MBO systems have evolved into results-oriented approaches, with objectives that lend themselves to fairly precise measurement. Tennessee's state government, for example, set an objective that no telephone in a state office would go unanswered for more than three rings. A school system pursued an objective of maintaining a bulletin board near the central office featuring the personal life and background of one of the teachers. These objectives satisfy the criterion of being attainable, and they were the kind of objectives that left little doubt about whether they were attained. These are not, however, objectives central to the mission of state governments or school systems. Objectives need to be more specific than improve the quality of health care or provide clean and safe recreational facilities. Too much specificity may, however, lead to mundane and irrelevant goals. Also, results-based evaluations are not directly useful for employee development. If measured achievements are below desired levels, further inquiry is required to determine what improvements should be made.

Ranking

An approach toward performance evaluation that can be used when only a limited number of employees can be given a merit pay increase, a training opportunity, or promotional consideration is to rank rather than rate the employees. **Rating** is done on an absolute scale and conceivably a number of employees might receive the same rating. In **ranking**, employees are ordered relatively from best to worst. Although ties are possible, ranking emphasizes making distinctions between employees.

Ranking is sometimes difficult. Employees may have different occupational identities or their strengths and weaknesses may not be comparable. There are occasions, however, when a choice must be made. One example is when only a small number of employees can receive a merit pay increase. Deciding on promotions, when they do not require different skills or new supervisory responsibilities, is another example. Whereas ranking employees is necessary for making certain decisions, it is not conducive to communicating to individual employees what their specific strengths and weaknesses are. Consequently, many jurisdictions use ranking in addition to, not instead of, some other rating- or goal-oriented performance evaluation system.

In rare instances, it is obvious how employees are ordered from best to worst. Where this is not self-evident, however, there are methods that assist the process. One is to start at the extremes and work toward the middle, that is, to identify the best, then the worst, then the second best, then the second worst, then the third best, and so forth. It is usually easier to identify the extremes than to make distinctions among those in the middle, and often the merit awards, promotional nominees, and the like can be arrived at without making a precise ordering of those in the middle.

Ranking employees, it should be noted, is more directly contradictory to the principles of Quality Management than any of the other forms of performance evaluation. To order employees as a way of parceling out some kind of reward or prize is clearly to foster a competitive environment. The dynamic is the opposite of the cooperative relationship among employees that the thinking behind TQM advocates. Moreover, to rank employees conveys the message that individuals are responsible for quality, rather than systems or a general agency's responsiveness to customers.

Mixed Approaches

Mixtures and combinations of approaches to performance evaluation occur and are appropriate. Some municipalities have established a system that combines management by objectives with behaviorally anchored rating scales. The list of job dimensions on the rating scales for most positions is so long that the only feasible way of operating is by selecting some of the dimensions on the list. That selection can be done through a management by objectives process.[15] The virtue of this is, of course, to integrate a focus on employee behaviors with a focus on agency objectives.

THE EVALUATORS

"Stated broadly, the rater is more important than the rating technique, and the larger the number of component raters employed, the greater the resulting validity."[16] This was the conclusion of a quasi-experimental study of personnel evaluation systems used in the U.S. Army. The assumption made in the discussion thus far has been that managers rate their employees. If one looks at common practice, this assumption is warranted. If, on the other hand, one looks at the research just cited, this is not what is prescribed.

Although managers and supervisors typically evaluate their employees, there are many examples where others assess performance. Students at most colleges and universities evaluate their courses and instructors. Adaptations of the Quality Management include identifying who the customers of an agency are and asking customers to help define quality service and evaluate performance. Professionals frequently appraise one another's work, in formal and informal ways. Employee self-evaluations can be valuable in the design of training and development programs.[17] All of these sources provide important feedback, but they have not replaced agency managers as key evaluators. Some employers use a formal approach to performance evaluation known as 360-degree appraisals, in which managers receive information simultaneously collected from customers, subordinates, peers, volunteers, and employees themselves. This acknowledges and values the different perspectives on employee and team performance.[18] Regardless of who else is involved, managers have the responsibility to make personnel decisions and therefore are the common participants in the process.

Research findings and experience indicate there are higher levels of validity when groups of co-workers evaluate individual members. Groups provide evaluations with high validity ratings because groups offset the judgmental errors that individuals tend to make. Groups also bring a broad scope of perspectives and provide a check on individual biases, thus placing more weight on the performance itself.[19] Group evaluations can provide very useful information to managers. Peer evaluations are especially appropriate for professionals and others who invest self-esteem in their work and who have jobs that cannot be defined precisely. Managers responsible for making decisions on employee opportunities, sanctions, and rewards, of course, rely on more than the group evaluations. And research shows that most employees regard the evaluation of their managers as the most important one.[20]

There are five common judgmental errors that individuals make when they evaluate individual performances. They are as follows:

1. Halo effect.   Once an individual has done well, there is a tendency to generalize this to a positive image in a broad sense and to expect excellence in the future. Negative information about that individual is likely to be discounted as an exception, rather than as representative evidence.

2. Constant error.   When a teacher acquires a reputation as a tough grader or an easy grader, in essence, this means that the teacher is constantly in error. Likewise, there are managers who evaluate their employees according to standards that are above or below the norm. These evaluations are often adjusted by others, in that they treat the employee as having been judged too harshly or too generously because of who evaluated them.

3. Recency error.   When evaluations are completed once a year, the evaluators tend to remember the most recent performance and not weigh equally the pattern of performance throughout the year.

4. Central tendency error.   A central tendency error occurs when an evaluator treats all employees the same. Some of the ranking techniques are designed as guides for those who have a difficult time making distinctions between their employees.

5. Personal bias.   Stereotypes and prejudices abound in our society and make their way into individual judgments about other people. If supervisors believe there is substance behind ethnic images, fear the consequences of disabilities that they do not fully understand, or hold to traditional distinctions between the sexes, then evaluations are likely to reflect those views and fears.

It is, of course, important to counter personal biases and other individual judgment errors. Employers are liable when promotions, transfers, and disciplinary actions are based on discriminatory appraisals.[21] It is especially important to be able to justify the termination of individuals over 40 years old who have sound performance evaluation data.[22]

Performance evaluation systems that are job-related and can be applied in a consistent manner provide checks on the personal biases of evaluators. Training and sensitizing evaluators can also help reduce errors.[23] Many times errors are unintentional. Regardless of intent, judgmental errors obviously detract from the value of the evaluations.

APPEALS

Given the probability of at least some errors being made occasionally in performance evaluations, one would expect that employees would have the right to appeal or to rebut their ratings and evaluations. Given the chilling effect of appeals and grievances on supervisors and managers, one would expect that employees would not be allowed to contest their performance evaluations. There obviously is a tension here. This is a classic example of an argument for fairness on one side and a plea to let managers manage on the other. There is no obvious resolution, and what is allowed varies from one organization to another. Some employees work for agencies that have given them full appeal rights, some jurisdictions provide an opportunity to respond and register disagreement but not to appeal, and other public employers do not allow either appeals or rebuttals. Most collective bargaining contracts include clauses allowing appeals.

Demands for the opportunity to reply to a performance evaluation and to remove objectionable and unsubstantiated remarks rise from a concern about the rewards and penalties that might flow from performance evaluations. An employee may suspect that he or she is becoming a victim of a **constructive discharge**, which is a dismissal based on a record of negative performance evaluations that are not based on facts or evidence. A constructive discharge is when someone is set up. Obviously, such an employee will want to challenge the negative performance evaluations. Likewise, someone who believes that negative evaluations are disqualifying them from getting merit increases, promotional consideration, or some other reward is likely to want to scrutinize and alter those evaluations.

William H. Holley, Jr., completed a study of arbitration cases involving performance evaluations.[24] He pointed out that arbitrators' decisions do not create binding precedents, but the pattern of decisions does provide guidelines for agency managers. Holley identified the following guidelines that have emerged from arbitration cases involving public employees:

1. Where there is collective bargaining, the design and alteration of performance evaluation systems must be completed in consultation with the union(s).
2. Employees must be informed of the criteria against which they will be judged.

3. Standards of performance that employees are expected to meet must in fact be attainable.
4. Supervisors must communicate the results of their evaluation to employees.
5. Employees have the right to inspect and review their own performance evaluation records.
6. Employees have the right to respond to adverse or negative comments included in their performance evaluations.
7. A procedural violation does not entitle the employee lodging the grievance any relief, unless that employee would otherwise have been promoted or rewarded.

These are guidelines that embody common sense, fair play, and good management practices. If performance evaluations are going to be meaningful and be the basis for personnel management decisions, then it is only reasonable that employees realize they have a stake in the quality of the performance evaluation process. Their rights should be guarded. The guidelines Holley identified are impressive because employee rights are recognized, while at the same time there appears to be an appreciation for the needs of agency managers.

It is hard for even the best and the most confident employees not to feel somewhat anxious and threatened by performance evaluations. For some, ego and self-esteem are at stake. Evaluations can have an important impact on an employee's career, and employees must have confidence in the evaluation system, the person doing the evaluation, and the way in which the results of the evaluation will be used. This is asking a great deal. Nonetheless, there is evidence that employees recognize the importance of performance evaluations and support the use of evaluation systems.[25] That support can be built on by seeking employee participation in the design and implementation of performance evaluation systems. The exercises at the end of this chapter are types of performance evaluation that rely heavily on employee participation.

PERFORMANCE INTERVIEW

Managers are both judges and coaches. These are contradictory roles. A judge acts dispassionately and may determine harsh consequences, whereas a coach is empathetic and tries to develop potential. Nonetheless, managers need to communicate the results of performance evaluations to their employees and/or teams, and they need to solicit a response from those being evaluated.[26] As mentioned above, evaluations are a source of tension and anxiety.

The challenge to managers is in most cases to assuage fears, to counter skepticism, and to solve problems. A traditional pattern of interaction during the appraisal interview is for the manager to explain the results and prescribe any necessary changes, then seek confirmation from the employee that he or she understands what the manager said. A more effective and accepted interview process is to have an open dialogue about evaluation results.[27] Ideally, the manager and the employee, volunteer, or team discuss and agree on strategies for improvement. The appraisal process should not only review past performances, but also set clear and attainable objectives for the future.

SUMMARY

With or without a performance evaluation system, employees and volunteers will be evaluated. Systematic and careful evaluation are preferred over casual and impressionistic assessments. Since the 1964 Civil Rights Act, the emphasis has been to adopt evaluation systems that are more job-related and less personality- or trait-related. Nonetheless, many employees and supervisors remain skeptical about the value and fairness of performance evaluations. Adherents of the Quality Management philosophy consider the appraisal of individual performances as a diversion from the real concerns about productivity. No one regards performance evaluation as a pleasant experience. Everyone, even employers using TQM, however, regards performance evaluation as necessary.

The question, then, is not so much whether to evaluate behavior, but how and why. The suggestions made here are that ritualistic, annual evaluations be replaced with ones specific to decisions about individual employment and development actions and that agency managers use different approaches based on patterns of how employees and volunteers relate to their positions. It is unlikely that a single system or technique will meet the various needs that any manager has for performance evaluation. In general, employees with jobs that are routine and relatively precisely defined can have their performance evaluated in standard, detailed ways. Professionals, on the other hand, might place more emphasis on narrative forms and peer evaluation. The exercises included in this chapter, along with narratives, are best used in accordance with the kinds of positions being evaluated and in some cases one will want to use more than one approach—perhaps a hybrid.

DISCUSSION QUESTIONS

1. Should the performance of groups or individuals be evaluated? If both, then how would you relate the two?
2. How do volunteers relate to performance appraisal?
3. What would you do to reduce the stress and tension in performance evaluations, or is there inherent conflict in this process?
4. Who should conduct performance evaluations? Are evaluations equally useful for rewards, disciplinary actions, and employee development regardless of who conducts the assessments?
5. Should employee performance evaluations be approached differently depending on whether a job is professional or more routine and low-skilled? If so, how?
6. To encourage serious and extensive use of performance evaluations, should employees have only limited rights to appeal their evaluations? If so, what would those limits be?

Performance Evaluation Exercises

Performance evaluations, like other personnel management functions, must be job-related. The two most job-related approaches toward performance evaluation focus on either behaviors or results.

1. JOB BEHAVIORS

One of the most widely used approaches to performance evaluation is known as behaviorally anchored rating scales (BARS). The BARS approach has a relatively low rate of rater error and is relatively effective in fostering communication between employees and supervisors about job performance.[28]

A BARS evaluation is based on statements (behavioral anchors) about job behavior and worker activity that is under the control of the employee being rated. These statements are attached to scales in order to rate performance as good, fair, or poor.

The development of a BARS system relies on a panel (or panels) of incumbents, supervisors, clients, and others familiar with the job. For this exercise, using such a panel is not necessary or practical. Act as if you are the panel and generate and rank statements in accordance with the following steps.

Step One. List, in no particular order, some statements about behavior in the job you have analyzed in the position analysis exercise. If, for example, one had analyzed the position of police officer, a list might include the following statements:

Position: Police Officer

Job Behaviors:

1. Attends and participates in neighborhood events
2. Files complete reports in a timely manner
3. Violates department rules designed to protect due process rights when making an arrest
4. Occasionally makes errors when completing reports
5. Offers ideas and suggestions as well as responds to others in team meetings
6. Attends neighborhood events but occasionally arrives late
7. Rarely attends team meetings

Step Two. Assign each behavioral anchor statement to a job dimension (defined as tasks on page 1 of the Position Analysis Form on page 165). Revise or discard ambiguous ones and, where necessary, add more anchor statements. Again, the following illustrates the example of a police officer:

Job Dimension	Job Behaviors
Law enforcement	2, 3, and 4
Community relations	1 and 6
Quality team management	5 and 7

Step Three. Give each behavioral anchor (or statement generated in step 1) a value of 1 to 7. This must be done within each job dimension. Values assigned to the example of the police officer are as follows:

Law Enforcement

7. Arrests suspects in manner that minimizes disruption in immediate environment, complies with all regulations providing due process protections, and files complete report immediately
6. Arrests suspects in manner that minimizes disruption in immediate environment, complies with all regulations providing due process protections, and files complete report within 48-hour period

5. Arrests suspects with little disruption in most instances, complies with all regulations providing due process protections, and files complete report within 48-hour period

4. Arrests suspects with little disruption in most instances, complies with all regulations providing due process protections, and occasionally files a report that needs further clarification

3. Occasionally requires additional guidance or assistance in making arrests, complies with all regulations providing due process protections, and files a report that almost always needs further clarification

2. Almost always requires guidance or assistance in making arrests, occasionally fails to comply with a regulation providing due process protections, and files a report that almost always needs further clarification

1. Almost always requires guidance or assistance in making arrests, usually fails to comply with regulations providing due process protections, and files a report with mistakes and with items that need further clarification

Community Relations

7. Initiates and helps organize neighborhood events designed to build good community relations and knows virtually all the residents in the community

6. Initiates and helps organize neighborhood events and knows long-term residents in the community

5. Helps organize neighborhood events and knows long-term residents in the community

4. Attends and participates in neighborhood events and knows most long-term residents in the community

3. Attends most neighborhood events and knows most leaders in the community

2. Attends most neighborhood events but often arrives late and knows some community leaders

1. Rarely makes it to neighborhood events and knows few of the community leaders

Quality Team Management

7. Always attends quality team meetings, usually suggests agenda items, and offers useful ideas in response to others

6. Always attends team meetings, occasionally suggests agenda items, and offers useful ideas in response to others

5. Always attends team meetings and offers useful ideas in response to the suggestions of others

4. Usually attends team meetings and frequently offers useful ideas in response to the suggestions of others

3. Usually attends team meetings and occasionally offers useful ideas in response to others

2. Rarely attends team meetings

1. Rarely attends team meetings, is not constructive, and may even be disruptive when participating

Step Four. Weight the job dimensions in accordance with the position analysis. The top possible performance rating should be the same for all positions in the jurisdiction. Usually 100 is the maximum number of position points possible.

In this illustration, if there were only the three dimensions used above, the weight assigned to law enforcement might be 7, thus the maximum score for this dimension would be 49 (i.e., 7×7). Community relations might have a weight of 4 for a maximum score of 28, and quality team management would then have a weight of 3.3 for the remaining 23 points.

2. JOB RESULTS

The focus in a results-based approach shifts from behaviors to what is actually accomplished. In a sense, this approach asserts that what matters is not what kinds of behaviors employees engage in, but rather what results they achieve. How one does a job is not as important as that the job gets done. The assumption here, of course, is that one can measure what gets done. Since this is not always possible, behavior and results-based approaches can be and are used by the same organization.

The most widely used performance evaluation approach based on results is management by objectives (MBO). This exercise explains how to design an MBO-style, results-oriented performance evaluation system.

Step One. Identify the key dimensions of the job, based on what you have done in the position analysis exercise.

Step Two. Generate one or more measurable performance goals for each of the major job dimensions, and write the goals in the appropriate spaces on the form below. The goals should be directly related to the job dimension and must be measurable in objective, quantifiable terms. For the job of administrative assistant, for instance, with its job dimensions of word processing, photocopying, and telephone answering, we would generate such goals as type final drafts of technical reports at an average rate of one page every four minutes or provide average turnaround of less than one hour on top-priority photocopy requests.

Step Three. Discuss the goals with the job incumbent (ideally the one you interviewed for the position analysis). The performance level expected should be *reasonable* from the perspective of both the individual and the organization. Make modifications as necessary.

Step Four. In the form below, set weights for the performance goals, reflecting their relative importance to the organization.

Results-Based Evaluation Worksheet

Incumbent:_____

Job Title: _____

		PERFORMANCE EVALUATION			
Performance Goal	Goal Weight (%)	Superlative	Successful	Marginal	Not Acceptable

GLOSSARY

Central tendency error The influence on evaluations when the evaluator does not make distinctions between performances

Constant error The influence on evaluations when the evaluator is generally more harsh or generous than the norm

Constructive discharge Dismissal of an employee based on a record of negative performance evaluations that were consciously conducted with the purpose of justifying the termination and which were not substantiated by facts or evidence

Forced-choice rating An evaluation system that provides evaluators with a predetermined set of descriptors that must be used in completing the evaluation

Halo effect The positive influence that a good reputation can have on an evaluation

Management by objectives (MBO) A type of performance management that uses contracts to specify annual goals for individual employees and the rewards to be granted if goals are reached

Performance management An explicit plan in which each employee has well defined goals, performance evaluations, and rewards or sanctions based on the achievement of the goals

Personal bias The influence on an evaluation of any stereotype or prejudice held by the evaluator

Ranking Performance evaluation that compares employees to one another and then orders individuals from best to worst

Rating Performance evaluation that uses an absolute scale and judges the performance of each employee according to that scale

Recency error The influence that the most current events or performances have on an evaluation

Trait rating Evaluation of employees according to individual characteristics, such as grooming, honesty, initiative, and friendliness

SOURCES

Cardy, B., & Dubbins, G. (1993). The changing face of performance appraisal: Customer evaluations and 360-degree appraisals. *Human resource division news* 16, no. 1 (Spring): 17–18. *Report on the incorporation of customer evaluations into the assessment of employee performance assessments.*

Glaser, M. (1993). Reconciliation of TQM and traditional performance improvement tools. *Public productivity and management review* 16, no. 4 (Summer): 97–119. *Discussion of the issues in performance evaluation raised by TQM.*

Morrissey, O. L. (1993). *Performance appraisals in the public sector: Key to effective supervision.* Reading, MA: Addison-Wesley. *A general review of research and issues involving performance evaluation in government agencies.*

Shaw, B. (1990). Employee appraisals, discrimination cases, and objective evidence. *Business Horizons* (September/October): 61–65. *Discussion of legal issues that are present in performance evaluations.*

NOTES

1. James L. Perry, "The Merit Pay Reforms," and Carolyn Ban, "Research and Demonstrations Under CSRA: Is Innovation Possible?" in Patricia W. Ingraham and David H. Rosenbloom, eds., *The Promise and Paradox of Civil Service Reform* (Pittsburgh: University of

Pittsburgh Press, 1992); Robert W. Bellone, "Performance Appraisal: A Policy Implementation Analysis," *Review of Public Personnel Administration* 2, no. 2 (Spring 1982): 69; A. Saltzstein, "The Fate of Performance Appraisal: Another Death in the Bureaucracy?" *Review of Public Personnel Administration* 3, no. 3 (Summer 1983): 129–132.

2. National Performance Review, *From Red Tape to Results: Creating a Government that Works Better and Costs Less* (Washington, DC: Government Printing Office, 1993).

3. U.S. Congress, Civil Service Reform Act of 1978 and Reorganization Plan No. 2 of 1978, Public Law 95–454, Sec. 203.

4. Dennis L. Dresang, "Public Personnel Reform: A Summary of State Government Activity," *Public Personnel Management* 7, no. 5 (September/October 1978): 287–294. See also symposium edited by Nicholas P. Lovrich, Jr., "Performance Appraisal Reforms in the Public Sector: The Promise and Pitfalls of Employee Evaluation," *Review of Public Personnel Administration* 3, no. 3 (Summer 1983): 1–132.

5. Gerald T. Gabris and Douglas M. Ihrke, "Improving Employee Acceptance Toward Performance Appraisal and Merit Pay Systems: The Role of Leadership Credibility," *Review of Public Personnel Administration* 20, no. 1 (Winter 2000): 41–53.

6. Danny L. Balfour, "Impact of Agency Investment in the Implementation of Performance Appraisal," *Public Personnel Management* 21, no. 1 (Spring 1992): 1–16.

7. Herbert H. Meyer, Emanuel Kay, and John R. P. French, Jr., "Split Roles in Performance Appraisal," *Harvard Business Review* 43, no. 1 (January/February 1965): 123–129.

8. James S. Bowman, "At last, An Alternative to Performance Appraisal: Total Quality Management," *Public Administration Review* 54, no. 3 (July/August 1994): 129–136.

9. W. E. Deming, "Letter to the Editor," *Business Week*, April 15, 1991; W. E. Deming, *Out of the Crisis* (Cambridge, MA: MIT–CAES Press, 1986); Peter R. Scholtes, "Total Quality or Performance: Choose One," *National Productivity Review* (Summer 1993): 25–43.

10. E. K. Johnson, *Total Quality Management and Performance Appraisal: To Be or Not to Be* (Washington, DC: Office of Personnel Management, 1990).

11. Mark Glaser, "Reconciliation of TQM and Traditional Performance Improvement Tools," *Public Productivity and Management Review* 16, no. 4 (Summer 1993): 97–119.

12. Gary E. Roberts, "Linkages Between Performance Appraisal System Effectiveness and Rater and Ratee Acceptance," *Review of Public Personnel Administration* 12, no. 3 (May-August 1992): 19–41; Nicholas P. Lovrich, Jr., and Ronald H. Hopkins, et al., "Participative Performance Appraisal Effects upon Job Satisfaction, Agency Climate, and Work Values: Results of a Quasi-Experimental Study in Six State Agencies," *Review of Public Personnel Administration* 1, no. 3 (Summer 1981): 51–74; and B. S. Steel, "Participative Performance Appraisal in Washington," *Public Personnel Management* 14, no. 3 (Summer 1985): 153–169.

13. Robert Rodgers and John E. Hunter, "Impact of Management by Objectives on Organizational Productivity," *Journal of Applied Psychology* 76, no. 4 (Fall 1991): 322–336.

14. Peter Drucker, *The Practice of Management* (New York: Harper & Row, 1954); "Public Sector MBO" [special feature], *Public Personnel Management* 5, no. 2 (March/April 1976): 83–102; J. S. Wickens, "Management by Objectives: An Appraisal," *Journal of Management Studies* 5 (1968): 365–370; J. M. Ivancevich, "Changes in Performance in a Management by Objectives Program," *Administrative Science Quarterly* 19 (1974): 563–574.

15. Peter Allan and Stephen Rosenberg, "The Development of a Task-Oriented Approach to Performance Evaluation in the City of New York," *Public Personnel Management* 7, no. 6 (January/February 1978): 26–32.

16. A. G. Bayroff, Helen R. Haggerty, and E. A. Rundquist, "Validity of Ratings as Related to Rating Techniques and Conditions," *Personnel Psychology* 7, no. 1 (Spring 1974): 112. See also N. K. Napier and G. P. Latham, "Outcome Expectancies of People Who Conduct Performance Appraisals," *Personnel Psychology* 39, no. 1 (Winter 1986): 827–837.

17. Donald J. Campbell and Cynthia Lee, "Self-Appraisal in Performance Evaluation: Development versus Education," *Academy of Management Review* 13, no. 4 (Fall 1988): 302–314.

18. Bob Cardy and Greg Dubbins, "The Changing Face of Performance Appraisal: Customer Evaluations and 360-Degree Appraisals," *Human Resource Division News* 16, no. 1 (Spring 1993): 17–18.

19. Craig Eric Schneier, "Multiple Rater Groups and Performance Evaluation," *Public Personnel Management* 6, no. 1 (January/February 1977): 13–20; A. S. DeNisi and J. L. Mitchell, "An Analysis of Peer Ratings as Predictors and Criterion Measures and a Proposed New Application," *Academy of Management Review* 3 (April 1978): 369–374.

20. Linda deLeon and Ann J. Ewen, "Multi-Source Performance Appraisals: Employee Perceptions of Fairness," *Review of Public Personnel Administration* 17, no. 1 (Winter 1997): 22–36.

21. Bill Shaw, "Employee Appraisals, Discrimination Cases, and Objective Evidence," *Business Horizons* (September/October, 1990): 61–65.

22. Christopher S. Miller, Joan Kaspen, and Michael H. Schuster, "The Impact of Performance Appraisal Methods on Age Discrimination in Employment Act Cases," *Personnel Psychology* 43, no. 4 (Fall 1990): 555–578.

23. Gary E. Roberts, "Perspectives on Enduring and Emerging Issues in Performance Appraisal," *Public Personnel Management* 27, no. 3 (Fall 1998): 301–320; Roy W. Ralston and Rollie O. Waters, "The Impact of Behavioral Traits on Performance Appraisal," *Public Personnel Management* 25, no. 4 (Winter 1996): 409–422; Clinton O. Longenecker and Nick Nykodym, "Public Sector Performance Appraisal Effectiveness: A Case Study," *Public Personnel Management* 25, no. 2 (Summer 1996): 151–164.

24. William H. Holley, Jr., "Performance Appraisal in Public Sector Arbitration," *Public Personnel Management* 7, no. 6 (January/February 1978): 1–5; See also W. H. Holley, Jr., and H. S. Field, "Performance Appraisal and the Law," *Labor Law Journal* 7 (July 1975): 523–530.

25. Nicholas P. Lovrich, Jr., Paul L. Shaffer, Ronald H. Hopkins, and Donald A. Yale, "Do Public Servants Welcome or Fear Merit Evaluation of Their Performance?" *Public Administration Review* 40, no. 3 (May/June 1980): 214–222; O. L. Morrissey, *Performance Appraisals in the Public Sector: Key to Effective Supervision* (Reading, MA: Addison-Wesley, 1903).

26. Joan L. Pearce and Lyman W. Porter, "Employee Responses to Formal Performance Appraisal Feedback," *Journal of Applied Psychology* 71, no. 3 (Summer 1986): 211–218.

27. James R. Larson, "The Dynamic Interplay Between Employees' Feedback-Seeking Strategies and Supervisors' Delivery of Performance Feedback," *Academy of Management Review* 18, no. 4 (Fall 1989): 408–422.

28. S. Zedeck, N. Imparato, M. Krausz, and T. Oleno, "Development of Behaviorally Anchored Rating Scales as a Function of Organizational Level," *Journal of Applied Psychology* 59 (1974): 249–252; D. Schwab, H. Heneman and T. DeCotiis, "Behaviorally Anchored Rating Scales: A Review of the Literature," *Personnel Psychology* 28, no. 4 (1975): 549–562; Y. Fried and G. R. Ferns, "The Validity of the Job Characteristics Model: A Review and Meta-Analysis," *Personnel Psychology* 40, no. 2 (Summer 1987): 287–322.

Chapter 10

Selecting Employees

Intuition inevitably has a major influence on hiring. And intuition can provide an excellent basis for selecting a new employee—if one has the *right* intuition. There are managers who take the same kind of pride in sensing who would make a good employee as someone purchasing a used car takes in judging a good vehicle. In both situations a prediction is being made about future performance. In both cases, however, it is often necessary to go beyond the immediately apparent information and make guesses on more subtle data. When hiring employees and purchasing used cars, error rates are very high and mistakes are frequently costly.

The judgments of managers can include biases that exclude some individuals for personal traits not related to potential or actual job performance. These judgments are also likely to be based on generalizations and assumptions about cause and effect that may have little empirical support. If one has had a very effective budget analyst who was a graduate of a well known, private liberal arts college, applicants for similar positions who are graduates of the same type of college are likely to be regarded very highly. Likewise, many would be very reluctant to hire an ex-offender, if they had a previous employee who was an ex-offender and had been arrested shortly after being trained and oriented for a job.

Examinations, based on position analyses and psychological research, should counter possible biases of appointing authorities and provide them with a list of candidates ranked according to their ability to do the job. The civil service requirement that applicants for employment must compete with each other in an examination limits intuition.

Although techniques for screening and ranking job candidates are increasingly sophisticated, the capacity for securing the most competent people for employment is still severely limited. It is very difficult to identify and measure the characteristics that make an individual a productive employee. Moreover, both individuals and the technology of jobs change over time. Even if one could measure job-related skills at the time of application, it would not be possible to anticipate all the changes that might occur during the period of a normal career.

One must, in other words, proceed with caution and humility. Even with the latest in technology and the best of efforts, mistakes will occur. Despite the obvious limitations, human judgment and intuition still play important roles. The hope is to reduce the number and the severity of errors and to place the primary emphasis on job-related competencies, rather than moods, impressions, and biases. Personnel selection cannot be regarded as a science, but we cannot afford to let it be an art. It is, and should be, more like a craft that combines both art and science.

LEARNING OBJECTIVES OF THIS CHAPTER

- Know the ways in which employers can and do screen applicants for jobs
- Understand the policy objectives of the selection process
- Be able to write a job vacancy announcement and construct an employment examination
- Know how to have an effective interview for a job
- Understand the role of probation in selection

THE SELECTION PROCESS: AN OVERVIEW

Steps 1 through 3 are to prepare for the identification and evaluation of candidates. The remaining steps solicit and screen candidates. These steps might be considered as a series of sieves, as illustrated in Figure 10.1, in which the number of candidates increasingly declines until finally one is offered the job. The criteria and process used at each step are of critical importance. Someone who might excel in the competition at a later step may never have a chance to do so if screened out in an earlier one. The steps described are fairly standard from one employer to another. Government selection processes are codified in law or rules, and managers can participate in some steps, but they can do little to alter the process. Some nonprofit organizations also have written rules and policies that guide the selection of new employees.

Recruitment	Application	Examination(s)	Certification and Veterans' Preference Points	Interview	Offer	Probation
External						
Internal						
External						

FIGURE 10.1   Steps in the Selection Process.

Step 1. Complete Human Resource Planning and Position Analysis

The selection process should begin with the planning and analysis described in Chapters 7 and 8. Ideally, no vacant position would be filled until and unless management has reviewed whether or not that position serves the short- and long-term needs of the agency and until the position has been analyzed in a thorough and systematic way. The urge to fill a vacancy as soon as possible frequently takes for granted the need for the position and also assumes that the nature of the position will remain the same. Positions in which there is high turnover or where the work is relatively standard and routine can safely be filled without systematic evaluations of agency needs, technological changes, and the like. On the other hand, many highly skilled and senior-level jobs should be filled only after review of agency needs.

A selection process that does not begin with succession planning or some other form of human resource planning and a job analysis runs the risk of identifying inappropriate candidates and perhaps of being challenged legally. Under civil service rules and laws, if there is a change in the description or the requirements of a job in the midst of a selection process for a position, the whole process must be declared void and begun again. For example, one jurisdiction that was searching for an agency manager decided that it was narrowing the pool of possible candidates too much by stating that candidates must have *experience* administering programs. It was decided that candidates could demonstrate they had the *ability* to administer a program, either through pointing to experience or by arguing for the relevancy of other work and training. This decision was not made until job candidates had already taken examinations and interviews were being scheduled for the top scorers. One of the candidates objected to the change and threatened a lawsuit. The jurisdiction knew it was vulnerable: It had to void nine months of work and start over, wasting more than $85,000 that had been spent on the process up to that point.

Step 2. Identify Necessary Knowledge, Skills, and Abilities

From the position analysis, it should be clear what attributes an individual should have in order to fulfill the assigned duties and responsibilities. With this step, one is laying a foundation for the recruitment plan and the examinations that will help to secure the most desirable candidate. In general, managers have the best chance of making quality hires if the applicant pool is large and has a broad array of candidates.

Step 3. Develop Indicators of Required Knowledge, Skills, and Abilities

Every aspect of the selection process serves as a screening and testing mechanism. The content of a job vacancy announcement or recruitment advertisement prompts potential applicants to consider whether they are eligible and whether the job is attractive. Application blanks solicit information that helps to sort the candidates. Examinations, obviously, are intended to distinguish candidates from one another. Once the job and the kind of person needed to do the job have been defined, indicators of the knowledge, skills, and abilities required must be developed. These might include performance on a verbal skills test, experience in a particular occupation, completion of a given training program, and evaluations by former employers. Whatever indicators are developed must then be integrated into one or more of the succeeding steps in the selection process.

Step 4. Devise a Recruitment Plan

Managers cannot appoint people who do not apply. A goal of having a competent and diverse workforce will never be attained if there are only members of a single gender or race in the applicant pool or if a source of highly qualified individuals is not reached. Governments, in particular, are often passive in communicating position openings. Formal announcements are not widely or aggressively distributed. The primary means of communication is response to inquiries. **Recruitment** can be internal and restricted to current employees, or it can be external and invite applications from anyone that might be interested and qualified.

Step 5. Screen Applicants for Minimum Qualifications

Indicators developed in Step 3 are applied to the information provided in application forms or résumés. If some applicants do not have the minimum qualifications required, there is no sense in having them take the examination or proceeding any further in the selection process.

Step 6. Construct and Administer Examination(s)

Civil service examinations are commonly regarded as synonymous with the public sector selection process. Since the passage of the Pendleton Act, the emphasis has been on examinations rather than patronage for entry into government jobs. Since the passage of the 1904 Civil Rights Act, the emphasis has been on making these examinations job-related. Likewise, that law mandates that private employers and nonprofit organizations use job-related employment examinations. A considerable segment of this chapter is devoted to a discussion of the legal, psychometric, and policy dimensions of tests for employment. To avoid patronage, favoritism, or discrimination, managers do not administer or score exams, although managers may and should help determine the content and purpose of the test. Examination administration is properly the responsibility of a central personnel office or some neutral body.

Step 7. Apply Laws and Rules for Certification and Veterans' Preference Points, or Develop a Short List

A public policy that uniquely affects government hiring is to advantage military veterans by adding points to examination scores—usually 5 points for a veteran and 10 points for a disabled veteran. Government employers are constrained in another way. Public employers use a mechanism called **certification** to eliminate patronage and favoritism in the selection process: Managers must choose from among the top threeto five scorers on employment examinations. Nonprofit organizations and other employers have considerable flexibility in deciding how many people to put on their short list of top candidates.

There have been numerous variations among government employers in the number of candidates certified for appointment and in how veterans' preference points are applied, but the basic concepts and processes remain the same. Recent modifications have been made because of a recognition that certifying a small number of names implicitly assumes much greater validity and precision in examinations than most personnel professionals believe exist and because of a recognition that veterans' preference points have an adverse impact on women and nonveterans with disabilities.

Step 8. Make a Selection

This step is, of course, the one toward which the entire process has been building. Because of the time and effort that frequently go into the other steps, it is with some relief that both candidate and manager reach this stage. Commonly, appointing authorities will interview the top candidates, check references, and then make a choice. Technically, interviews and reference checks are not always required. Nonetheless, most managers want to meet with the finalists and add their own judgment to the evaluations made in the examinations. It is at this critical point that intuition plays a role.

Step 9. Evaluate Performance During Probationary Period

Probation is an examination. Unfortunately, managers commonly regard the previous step, make a selection, as the final step in the selection process. The final step, in fact, is when a manager advances the new appointee from probationary to permanent status. In many ways, the probationary period of employment is the best and most valid test of all. Here managers are not dealing with indicators, examinations, or interviews. They are dealing with actual performance on the job. Managers have an opportunity to catch an error in judgment or a fault in the examination process. Moreover, managers can dismiss the employee without the appeals and the requirements for proof of just cause that come with dismissals once the employee has permanent status. Few managers take full advantage of the probationary period, and many later regret that they let this opportunity slip by.

RECRUITMENT

Governments and nonprofit organizations, as mentioned earlier, typically spend little time and money advertising their position vacancies. Recruitment is passive; information is provided in response to inquiries. The assumption is usually that only those seeking employment are among the potential pool of applicants. This assumption contrasts sharply with the aggressive posture many private-sector employers take. They are anxious to get the best talent available; they try to entice top managers, professionals, and technicians away from their current employers, as well as to attract new graduates and others without jobs. The most notable exception to the generally low-key, passive approach of public agencies has been the military. Billboards, websites, television ads, radio spots, and field staff are all part of the arsenal of military recruiters.

One reason some employers have been complacent about recruiting job applicants is simply that there have been more qualified people seeking employment than there have been positions. This has not always been the case. In a 1989 report to the federal Office of Personnel Management, the Hudson Institute warned of pending shortages in key occupations.[1] The highly respected Volcker Commission also reported in 1989 and voiced a concern about attracting and retaining the most talented individuals.[2] Indeed, a major feature of the national economy at the turn of the twenty-first century was a labor shortage, and, as pointed out in the discussion of succession planning, the retirements of baby boomers is going to create vacancies.

Recruitment efforts should be based on human resource plans and position analyses.[3] It seems obvious that before one can reach potential applicants or even respond to questions, it is essential to know what the job is like, what the manager is looking for, and which groups, if any, are underrepresented. One of the first questions that needs to be posed, for example, is whether to restrict consideration of applicants to current employees in the agency. A succession planning analysis may show that by filling a vacancy internally, career development can be appropriately provided for current employees. Large agencies and jurisdictions have the choice of restricting applications to employees in a specific unit or to all employees, regardless of the unit for which they work. To save costs and to provide career mobility opportunities to current employees, some organizations always consider whether they can get a qualified individual by restricting their search to their existing workforce.

There is, of course, a possible cost to **internal recruitment**. Restricting the applicant pool may mean that the best available person will not be hired or that no progress will be made toward achieving a diverse workforce. By casting the widest possible net, one can be more certain of reaching these goals.

It may very well be that a current employee is the best available person for a job. If so, employees should be able to demonstrate their superiority in an open, competitive process. Incumbent employees, because of their familiarity with the agency and its functions, frequently have an edge over other applicants. In other words, using a widely based, aggressive recruitment strategy is not necessarily inimical to providing career advancement opportunities to current employees. The apparent advantage of restricting recruitment (lower costs and favoring residents and/or existing employees) may be short-term at best.

Communicating position vacancies to potential applicants, like other communication processes, requires attention to both the media and the message. The most effective and the most expensive means of communication is the face-to-face meeting between a recruiter and potential applicant. This may be the only effective way of getting senior managers and professionals who already have jobs to consider a move to a similar position in an agency. Likewise, aggressive, face-to-face recruiting may be required to break through the suspicions and hostilities of some minority groups and get them to apply for jobs. Resources are limited, and one reaches fewer people per dollar spent by sending individual recruiters, so most jurisdictions use this approach selectively, if at all. Whether or not a formal recruiter is used, informal personal networks will carry messages about job opportunities and candidates. Although by their nature these networks are unsystematic and imperfect, they are, in fact, relied on very heavily.

Another relatively effective approach is advertising in newspapers and in professional journals and newsletters.[4] Newspapers are a traditional place where individuals seeking jobs or job changes have sought information. Almost all of the major newspapers in the United States are now online and are easily accessible. Public agencies, like other employers, also post job notices on websites. The federal Office of Personnel Management has contracted with a firm that relies heavily on the Internet to advertise job opportunities. Addresses of some of the most widely used sites are included in the appendix to this book.

The journals, newsletters, and websites of professional associations obviously reach fewer individuals, but the message is directed at the most relevant and interested audience. Many professional associations include opportunities for prospective employers and employees to meet at conferences, which can provide opportunities for jurisdictions to recruit.

Executive search firms work to match employee needs with the right individuals. These firms, sometimes referred to as head hunters, aggressively pursue people who have already established successful records and try to persuade them to consider leaving their current employers. Search firms are useful for identifying good candidates for highly technical or very senior management positions.[5] This recruitment approach is compatible with civil service laws if it is used along with an open posting of the vacancy and if all candidates go through the same examination process. Although the latter requirement sometimes makes public employers unattractive to potential applicants, it is a necessary step to avoid the substance or appearance of favoritism or patronage.

Other recruitment approaches include radio and television advertisements, posters for bulletin boards, and bulletins or brochures that are published periodically listing available jobs. Whereas these approaches are the most frequently used, they are also the least effective. These are passive efforts that rely heavily on the initiative of potentially interested individuals.

JOB ANNOUNCEMENTS

Regardless of what channels and methods are used in communicating a job vacancy, a written job announcement must be prepared. Civil service rules and laws usually require that a job opening be advertised for a minimum period of time (often 30 days) before a position can be filled. Beyond the formal requirement, a written statement is a useful reference both for recruiters and potential applicants.

Based on a **job announcement**, individuals develop a perception about both the position and the employer. A major function of job announcements is self-selection by potential applicants. Ideally, the information in a job announcement would encourage applications from those with the proper interests and qualifications, while at the same time prompting those who are not suited to the position to screen themselves out. An announcement that is accurate is important for conveying the right information about the nature of the job and the kinds of skills and backgrounds required. An announcement with the right style will communicate effectively and attract attention. Jargon and cumbersome language can cause misunderstandings and simply turn away potential applicants.

A job announcement includes the following:

- **Title.**   The title is a descriptive, working title of the position, not necessarily a formal classification title.
- **Salary.**   In most cases, the entry here will be the salary range attached to the position. If the salary is negotiable or if it depends on experience, this is stated.
- **Job description.**   Key duties and responsibilities, including what, if any, supervisory responsibilities are explained. This statement is probably the most important part of the job announcement for attracting the attention of those who should apply and for discouraging those without the appropriate interests and skills.
- **Location.**   For many positions, it is important to indicate not only where the incumbent would work but also how much traveling is necessary.
- **Education, certification, and experience requirements.**   Included here are minimal requirements, desired traits, and what, if any, substitutes will be allowed for education and/or experience. It is common, for example, to count additional experience as equivalent to certain types of education, and vice versa.
- **Examination process.**   Applicants should know what types of examinations they will have to take, when these will be scheduled, and how many examinations there will be.
- **Equal opportunity employment.**   There are standard phrases that are often used to reiterate a jurisdiction's commitment to equal opportunity employment and to diversity.
- **Administrative information.**   Those who wish to apply for the position need to know: (1) the deadline for making application; (2) the information required as part of making application or where application forms can be obtained; and (3) the address and/or fax number to use to send applications and inquiries.

Job announcements can include information on the jurisdiction or the community for which a successful candidate would be working. This is provided primarily to attract candidates. Likewise, if unusual or special fringe benefits are available, these might be included. If there are flexible hours that one might arrange or if the employer is amenable to job sharing for the position, this might be included in the job announcement. Some organizations also note whether the position is covered under a collective-bargaining agreement.

Style is as important as content in constructing a job announcement. Generally, the style of writing common to newspapers is most effective in reaching broad audiences. Sentences should be simple and vocabulary fairly elementary. Even when placing vacancy listings in professional journals and newspapers, one should avoid jargon.

Finally, extra care should be taken to avoid spelling, grammatical, and typographical mistakes. Sometimes these mistakes convey misinformation. Certainly they convey a sloppy, unattractive image of the employer.

APPLICATION FORMS

The most frequently used selection technique, in both the public and private sectors, is a review of **biodata**, the personal information about a candidate's background, interests, education, and experience.[6] Biodata can be provided in the form of responses to questions on an application form or culled from a curriculum vita or résumé written by the candidate. The evaluation of this information is used either for screening candidates prior to the administration of other tests and selection mechanisms or as an examination itself.[7] If this is the sole test, a system is usually designed for scoring the information provided by candidates in order to rank them.

Despite the common usage of application forms and curricula vitae, job applicants typically pay little attention to relating their preparation and achievements to the job that is being filled. Most candidates prepare a single vita that they submit for all the jobs they are seeking. Extraneous information is not uncommon. Ironically, although almost all application forms have been purged of questions soliciting information that might be used in a discriminatory way, some individuals volunteer their marital status, health, age, and even race.

Employers use application forms to solicit information about job candidates in a systematic way, which allows for better comparative analyses. Typically, these forms ask for name, address, Social Security number, and other information that can be used in establishing a file and administering the rest of the selection process. Educational background and job history are included. Applicants are usually asked to list several individuals who might be used as references. Many application forms inquire about military service. If justified by the nature of the job, there may be questions about personal bankruptcy or criminal record. (Increasingly credit and criminal records are available on websites for employers to consult if they seek this information.) See Figure 10.2 for a sample application form.

For economical reasons, personnel offices that use application forms usually have a standard form for all jobs. However, just as a standard curriculum vita can provide some irrelevant information and ignore what is most important, a standard application can be incomplete. Managers can supplement a standard form with a questionnaire that solicits information directly relevant to the position being filled.

Although state and local governments can no longer be sued by employees under the Americans with Disabilities Act, procedures that had been developed prior to the ruling in *University of Alabama* v. *Garrett* are still useful for those jurisdictions who choose not to discriminate. And, of course, nonprofit organizations are still prohibited from discriminating against those with disabilities. Questions asking about disabilities that are not job-related should not be included on the application form. Assistance in simply filling out the form should be available, if needed. The intent, of course, is that individuals be screened in and out of the selection process based on whether they can do the job despite a disability.[8]

If the evaluation of biodata is the only basis for screening and ranking the candidates, it is essential to secure the same kinds of information from all applicants. In these instances, special efforts must be made to construct supplemental questionnaires to the standard application form or to design an application form specifically for the vacant position. In addition, a scoring system must be devised. Points need to be assigned to certain information or to candidates' certain achievements. The scoring system should, in addition, weight information and achievements according to job requirements.[9]

To administer a scoring system requires more careful evaluations than simply screening applicants on the basis of minimal eligibility requirements. The most reliable method of scoring is to use a panel that has been informed about the job traits being sought and that has experience in reviewing curricula vitae and job application forms.[10] Reliability, as is explained in more detail later, is assured when candidates receive approximately the same score either when rated by a different, but similar,

---

APPLICATION FOR EMPLOYMENT OR PROMOTION

CIVIL SERVICE TITLE OF POSITION
FOR WHICH YOU ARE APPLYING

Name (First, Middle, Last)	Former Last Name if Used on Previous Applications or Previous Employment	

Complete Present Mailing Address	Residence Telephone No.	Permanent Address if Different from Mailing Address
No. & Street _____ Apt. # ___		
City _____ County ___	Business Telephone No.	
State & Zip	Social Security Number / Age / Birthdate (Month/ Day/Year)	

IF YOU ARE A VETERAN, DISCHARGED UNDER HONORABLE CONDITIONS FROM THE ACTIVE FEDERAL MILITARY SERVICE OF THE UNITED STATES ARMED FORCES, YOU MAY BE ELIGIBLE FOR VETERANS PREFERENCE POINTS, (NOTE: ACTIVE DUTY FOR TRAINING PURPOSES AS A MEMBER OF THE NATIONAL GUARD OR OTHER RESERVE COMPONENT IS NOT CREDITABLE FOR VETERANS PREFERENCE POINTS.) PLEASE ENTER EXACT DATES IN SPACES PROVIDED. DATE OF ENTRY ON ACTIVE DUTY _____
(Mo,Day,Year)

DATE OF DISCHARGE _____   IF YOU SERVED OUTSIDE THE CONTINENTAL UNITED STATES, INDICATE WHERE:
(Mo, Day,Year)

_____   AND INCLUSIVE DATES OF OVERSEAS SERVICE: _____   TO _____
(Country or Theater of Operations)   (Mo,Day,Year)   (Mo,Day,Year)

SERVICE-CONNECTED DISABILITY INFORMATION: Do you have a service-connected disability, incurred during the service dates indicated above, and recognized by the Veterans Administration?   YES ___ NO ___   (You may be requested to furnish documentation of above entries.)

WHAT TYPE OF EMPLOYMENT ARE YOU SEEKING: (CHECK ONLY THOSE TYPES YOU WILL ACCEPT)
___   PERMANENT (FULL TIME)   ___   TEMPORARY (LESS THAN 6 MONTHS)   ___   SUMMER ONLY

___   PART TIME (LESS THAN 40 HR./WK.)   ___   SEASONAL (YEARLY RUSH PERIODS OF VARYING LENGTH)

WHEN WILL YOU BE AVAILABLE FOR EMPLOYMENT (CHECK ONE OF THE FOLLOWING.)
___ NOW   ___ BEGINNING _____   ___ UPON ___ WEEKS NOTICE FROM MY PRESENT EMPLOYER

EDUCATION AND TRAINING

Circle the Highest Grade or Year Completed in School 1 2 3 4 5 6 7 8 9 10 11 12	Name and Location of High School	Graduated Yes No	Month and Year Diploma was Granted

Training Beyond High School, College or University, Nursing, Business College, or other Schools You Have Attended, Under Credits Earned, Indicate Number of Hours and Q for Quarter Hours and S for Semester Hours.	Circle the Number of Years in College or University 1 2 3 4 5 6 7 8		

Name and Location	Dates Attended		Credits Earned	Major Field	Degree Conferred and Year
	From	To			

(Form continues on following pages.)

FIGURE 10.2   Sample Job Application Form.

panel or when rated by the same panel at a different time. In other words, the scoring is not arbitrary or whimsical.

The federal Office of Personnel Management touched off a storm of controversy in the late 1980s when it proposed certifying college graduates with a minimum 3.0 grade point average (on a 4.0 scale) for appointment to entry-level professional positions. The advantages would have been a simple mechanism that would provide a speedy process and maximum discretion to appointing authorities in federal agencies. A grade point average, however, is not a common yardstick

---

WORK EXPERIENCE--Provide a Complete Description of All Qualifying Experience

This Information May be Used to Determine if Your Application is Accepted. Be Specific. Part or All of Your Grade or Rating May be Based on This Information. Start With Your Present or Most Recent Job. Include Service in the Armed Forces and Any Self-employment. For Part Time Work, Show the Average Number of Hours Worked per Month. Indicate Any Change in Job Title Under the Same Employer as a Separate Position. If You Have Volunteer Experience Relevant to the Position for Which You Are Applying, Please Use a Separate Sheet to Identify the Volunteer Organization, Your Position and Responsibilities, the Number of Hours per Month Worked and the Total Period of Your Participation.

Present or Most Recent Employer	Kind of Business	Location (City and State)
Your Title	Reasons for Leaving or Considering Leaving	Name and Address of Reference
Your Duties		Total Time Employed ___ Full Time / If Part time # of ___ Part Time / hours/month
		From (Mo.&Yr.) — To (Mo.&Yr.)
		Monthly Salary / Beginning — Ending or Present

Employer	Kind of Business	Location (City and State)
Your Title	Reasons for Leaving	Name and Address of Reference
Your Duties		Total Time Employed ___ Full Time / If Part time # of ___ Part Time / hours/month
		From (Mo.&Yr.) — To (Mo.&Yr.)
		Monthly Salary / Beginning — Ending

Employer	Kind of Business	Location (City and State)
Your Title	Reasons for Leaving	Name and Address of Reference
Your Duties		Total Time Employed ___ Full Time / If Part time # of ___ Part Time / hours/month
		From (Mo.&Yr.) — To (Mo.&Yr.)
		Monthly Salary / Beginning — Ending

If Necessary, Attach Additional Sheets Using the Above Format to Provide Employment Data Describing Qualifying Experience.

May We Conduct a Personal Background Check Including Contact of Your References Names Above and Review Other Records as May Be Required for Some Positions?   ___ Yes   ___ No.   If No, Please Explain.

FIGURE 10.2   Sample Job Application Form.   (*Continued*)

SPECIAL SKILLS AND QUALIFICATIONS

Served Formal Apprenticeship?   ___ Yes   ___ No

What Trade   _____

How Long   _____

When   _____

Where   _____

Current License or Registration as a Member of Some Trade or Profession

Office Work
The Following Information Must be Provided if You are Applying for Positions Requiring Typing or Shorthand Ability.

Number of Words per Minute, Typing   _____

Shorthand   _____

Experience in Transcribing Mechanically Recorded Material?   ___ Yes   ___ No

When _____

List Office Machines Other than Typewriter which You Can Operate Skillfully.

List memberships in Professional or Technical Associations

FOR RESEARCH AND REPORT TO THE EQUAL OPPORTUNITY COMMISSION, PLEASE MARK THE APPROPRIATE AREA.

ETHNIC GROUP

___   Black – (Not of Hispanic Origin) All Persons Having Origins in Any of the Black Racial Groups of Africa.

___   Asian or Pacific Islanders–All Persons Having Origins in Any of the Original Peoples of the Far East, Southeast Asia, the Indian Subcontinent, or the Pacific Islands. This Area Includes, For Example, China, Japan, Korea, the Philippine Islands, and Samoa.

___   American Indian or Alaskan Native – All Persons Having Origins in Any of the Original Peoples of North America and Who Maintain Cultural Identification Through Tribal Association or Community Recognition.

___   Hispanic – All Persons of Mexican, Puerto Rican, Cuban, Central or South American, or Other Spanish Culture or Origin, Regardless of Race.

___   White – (Not of Hispanic Origin) All Persons Having Origins in Any of the Original Peoples of Europe, North Africa or the Middle East.

SEX

Female

Male

___

___

I UNDERSTAND THAT ALL THE INFORMATION ON THIS APPLICATION IS TRUE AND COMPLETE TO THE BEST OF MY KNOWLEDGE, AND THAT ANY FALSE OR MISSING JOB RELATED INFORMATION MAY DISQUALIFY ME FOR THIS POSITION.

SIGNATURE _____   DATE _____

FIGURE 10.2   **Sample Job Application Form.**

when earned at different colleges, at different times, and in different majors. In addition, appointing authorities would have so much discretion that favoritism and patronage might creep into the selection process. The Office of Personnel Management did not implement the proposal. Instead, it developed examinations known as Administrative Careers with America for entry-level professional and administrative jobs, and it uses sophisticated, job-related methods of scoring biodata for filling higher (GS 11–12) positions.

Another concern is whether application forms and personal background statements provide accurate information. Some studies have found that 20 to 50 percent of job applications and résumés contain information that is not true.[11] There are four areas in which there are frequent discrepancies between applicant responses and the records of previous employers:

1. Previous position held
2. Duration of employment
3. Previous salary earned
4. Reason for leaving[12]

The largest discrepancies occurred among statements of the duration of previous employment and the previous salary earned. In both categories, slightly more than 50 percent of the applicants overestimated the information they provided. One-fourth of the applicants gave reasons for leaving their previous employer that disagreed with the records of those employers. Not surprisingly, applicants cited a factor such as low pay, whereas employers recorded something like a violation of work rules. Almost 15 percent of the applicants listed someone as a previous employer who had no record or recollection that the individual actually had ever worked for them.

In short, it appears that a substantial number of people will exaggerate their work record in order to secure a job and to get a higher salary. The findings of the research cited here are consistent with studies conducted on the accuracy of information job applicants provide during interviews.[13] It is very costly to verify all information contained on application forms. At a minimum, however, some caution and attention to suspicious answers seems warranted.

MINIMUM QUALIFICATIONS

A major use of information secured through job applications and/or curricula vitae is the screening of applicants on the basis of whether they meet minimum qualifications. Ideally, individuals would learn what the minimum qualifications are from the job announcement and then only apply if they meet those qualifications. One of the tasks in the selection process is to screen applicants to be sure that they meet minimum qualifications. Those who do not meet these requirements and therefore will not be considered any further are, of course, so informed. By notifying these individuals, one allows them an opportunity to correct misinformation or to supply missing data. The most common qualifications that determine eligibility are discussed in the sections that follow.

Residency Requirements

Some state and local governments have adopted a policy of requiring those who work for them to be resident citizens of the state or community. Some jurisdictions have gone one step further and require that one be a resident in order to apply for a job. At least in principle, this policy runs counter to the concern for hiring the most qualified and, in some communities, for diversifying the workforce. Individuals concerned about the limitations that such a policy places on their freedom of choosing where to live and where to work have challenged residency laws in court. The Supreme Court has ruled, however, that public jurisdictions may impose **residency requirements** without infringing on constitutional rights.[14]

The policy reasons for residency requirements are varied. The rationale used in arguments before the Supreme Court has been that residing in the community conveyed a unique understanding of the community and its problems, thereby enabling employees to serve better. For some jurisdictions residency requirements are like veterans' preference points—a commitment to provide job opportunities first to one group, then to others. A more negative perspective is a residency requirement that has the effect of excluding members of some groups. Ironically, a number of communities that whites had controlled and now have a majority or plurality of African-American or Chicano residents have retained residency requirements that originally were adopted to exclude minorities.

Often when there are contradictory public policies, procedures and guidelines exist for determining which policy should prevail. Most jurisdictions are very reluctant to grant exceptions to requirements that current employees reside within the city, county, or state boundaries. On the other hand, mechanisms for reaching beyond the limits of a residency requirement on the selection process are virtually standard. Statutes or ordinances authorize the chief executive or the director of personnel to determine whether a shortage of qualified personnel or a shortage of qualified minority group members resides within the jurisdiction. If they determine that there is a shortage, then they may approve the acceptance of applications from nonresidents.

Education and Experience Requirements

Minimal education and experience requirements are supposed to be based on the duties and responsibilities of the job. In most cases, the requirement that an applicant have a certain degree and a specified number of years of experience in order to be regarded as eligible is arbitrarily established and serves more as an administrative convenience than as a legitimate screening mechanism. How, for example, does one determine that two years of experience in a specific field is necessary? Is one-and-a-half years not enough? Perhaps one year is satisfactory? And what if the experience was bad? Likewise, is a master's degree necessary? What about someone who has done postgraduate work but has not quite completed the degree? What about someone coming out of a strong, relevant undergraduate program? Which specialties qualify?

Employers are increasingly aware of the vulnerability to legal challenge of arbitrary education and experience requirements. They also recognize that these requirements may be counterproductive to the goal of achieving a highly competent, diversified workforce.[15] Even at their best, education and experience requirements tend to measure quantity rather than quality. To screen applicants on the basis of whether they have a college degree or whether they have experience in a certain field is not to evaluate them on how challenging their course work was, what their level of performance was, or what they learned from the education and work experiences. Unlike residency requirements or veterans' preference points, there is no public policy other than a concern for competence that lies behind education and experience requirements. Thus, they must be job-related.

One approach is to allow years of experience and years of education to be substituted one for the other. Another approach is to include the phrase "or equivalent" to the statement about minimum education and experience requirements.

Still another approach is to assume that there simply will be no training and experience requirements unless there is a demonstrable need for them. A demonstrable need would be a statutory or professional need for certification. A law degree, for example, may be required in order to represent someone in court. A physician must meet state requirements for a license. For most positions, of course, there are no demands for these kinds of credentials. In these instances, one might state that experience and/or training in a particular field is needed or desired without specifying a specific number of years of experience or education. More reliance would be placed on examinations to screen and rank candidates. That, as pointed out previously, could include scoring biodata supplied on a résumé or job application but not excluding applicants who did not meet some arbitrary standard.

Age, Disability, and Other Personal Traits

There are, as pointed out in Chapter 4, legal prohibitions against defining eligibility in a way that excludes members of certain groups. Nonetheless, if a job has demands that require certain traits and skills, the appropriate requirements may be specified to screen into the selection process only those candidates who have the required traits. These traits are referred to as **bona fide occupational qualifications (BFOQ)**. Jobs that, for example, require manual dexterity are clearly inappropriate for individuals with certain types of disabilities. Some positions in correctional institutions have legitimate gender requirements. Prison chaplains, obviously, must have a certain religious identity. Religious nonprofit organizations may, as pointed out in Chapter 4, restrict employment to those of their respective creed, even when job duties are not related to religious beliefs or practices.

The purpose of minimum qualifications is, of course, to determine which of the applicants are eligible, not to identify which are the most preferred. Examinations move the selection process from a stage where there is a list of eligibles to one where candidates are ranked according to some indicator that purports to predict who is likely to perform the best on the job.

EXAMINATIONS

The legal mandates of the 1964 Civil Rights Act, as supported by the *Griggs* v. *Duke Power* (1971) case, can be viewed as requiring compliance with a basic principle of personnel management: Applicants for a position should be selected primarily on the basis of how well they can do the job. The legal and professional mandates are for job-related examinations. To be useful, employment examinations must discern the different abilities of the various applicants and rank them according to how well they are likely to do in the job. At a minimum, these tests must help screen out the incompetent and those who are inappropriate for the tasks associated with the position.

The Americans with Disabilities Act reinforces the importance of focusing on testing for abilities that are job-related. Employers should be certain what kinds of abilities a job demands and design examinations accordingly. Depending on the disabilities of specific applicants for a job, it may be necessary to devise alternative but comparable examinations so that the relevant abilities are measured, without influence from irrelevant disabilities. It would be psychometrically better if all applicants could be tested with the same format and instrument, but a format that accommodates certain disabilities may be prohibitively expensive to administer to all applicants.

For some positions several different types of tests, each designed to measure a needed skill or knowledge, are used. Multiple testing can be structured so that all candidates take all examinations and then the scores are combined for a total or composite score. Alternatively, the examinations can be arranged in a series and candidates must achieve a certain score or ranking at one stage in order to be able to take the test at the next stage. This approach is taken:

- When the skills or abilities are cumulative. For example, if one cannot do simple mathematical computations, then one cannot do calculus.
- When the array of skills and abilities are such that one is more important for the job than another. For example, if a secretary cannot type, then there is no need to evaluate how that person might serve as a receptionist.
- When some examinations are very costly to administer. For example, if an oral examining board needs to examine candidates for a senior management position, they should meet with the top ten, or less, and not with everyone who applies.

Whether the examination is a single exercise or a series of exercises, the same concerns about quality and **validity** apply.

The development of examinations begins with the required knowledge, skills, and abilities as identified in position analyses. This information should indicate what needs to be measured and how heavily each knowledge, skill, and ability should be weighed in the scoring system. Before devising ways of measuring knowledge, skills, and abilities, there are several questions that should be asked.[16] The questions are illustrated here with regard to hiring a driver's license examiner.

1. What proportion of the applicant population is likely to have a sufficient level of the required knowledge, skill, or ability to perform adequately? The smaller the proportion, the greater the need to test for that knowledge, skill, or ability. If, for example, a transportation department manager were hiring someone to determine whether someone should be given a driver's license and the position would require reading answers on applications and examination, reading might be identified as a necessary ability. If one anticipated that virtually everyone who would apply for such a position would be able to read at a level sufficient to do the job, a reading test would not be necessary.

2. Will more of a required knowledge, skill, or ability lead to a better job performance? If the answer to this is affirmative, then there should be a test to determine which of the applicants have the highest level of the knowledge, skill, or ability in question. A manager may want driver's license examiners that are as service- and customer-oriented as possible. This puts a value on interpersonal relations, especially since it is likely some applicants for getting a license are likely to become frustrated and hostile. A test based on hypothetical situations could be used to rank candidates on how they would handle the situations. Beyond a minimal level, on the other hand, the ability to read more quickly or even with more comprehension is not likely to have any effect on job performance. Again, a reading test does not seem necessary.

3. If a knowledge, skill, or ability is not tested, could serious consequences result? If the answer to this is yes, then an examination is necessary. A driver's licensing examiner who is unable to operate the equipment that measures the vision of applicants or who cannot distinguish essential driving skills from the nervous behaviors of an inexperienced driver during a road test could be responsible for allowing unsafe drivers on the highway.

4. Is a knowledge, skill, or ability needed as soon as one begins work, or can it be learned on the job? A manager might reasonably determine that a detailed understanding of state driving and safety rules and a knowledge of the process for administering the exams can be acquired during the probationary period after someone is on the job. If so, this knowledge does not need to be tested as part of ranking job candidates.

5. Is a knowledge, skill, or ability needed for advancement in the job or career stream? Career advancement may depend on an employee's ability to improve the driver's license examining process. If this is the case, candidates could be tested on the concepts of tests and test measurement. Early indications about the potential contributions that individuals might make are useful not only in making selection decisions but in planning and training functions.

Once decisions have been made about which types of knowledge, skills, and abilities require tests, then the challenge is to find or develop ways of measuring these characteristics. This can be a creative, innovative process.

TYPES OF EXAMINATIONS

Few examinations directly measure performances that are required in a job. Typically, it is prohibitively expensive and/or impractical to have job applicants actually administer a road test, compile a budget, plan a program, complete a position analysis, arrest a speeding driver, fight a forest fire, repair a snowplow, serve a family in need, or do other tasks that are part of the job for which they are being considered. Instead, examinations attempt to measure the traits, knowledge, skills, and abilities that are thought to be necessary to do well in a particular job. It is necessary, in other words, to infer from the examination how an individual will perform in a position. The evidence is indirect.

Examinations that have been used in personnel selection can be categorized according to what they try to measure. The following sections address these categories.

General Intelligence

Psychologists and educators have tried for years to develop examinations that measure the intelligence of an individual. The most commonly known examination provides an intelligence quotient, or IQ, rating. Applicants for higher education programs take the Scholastic Aptitude Test (SAT), American College Test (ACT), Graduate Record Examination (GRE), or some other standard test that has been designed to indicate intellectual capabilities.

Although these tests have traditionally been part of selection processes, they have been given less frequently since the 1964 Civil Rights Act and the *Griggs* v. *Duke Power* ruling. The verbal and symbolic components that are so important to conceptual thinking and therefore so essential to these examinations are also integral to the cultural identity of individuals. As vividly pointed out in the musical *My Fair Lady,* accents and the various ways in which a common language is used are closely associated with societal differences.

Cultural differences between ethnic, regional, and class groups in the United States manifest themselves in language and in other symbols. To illustrate this, a ninth-grade English class in Winston-Salem, North Carolina, tested the verbal skills of employees of a major publishing company. The employees earned a D grade when they failed to define turf as black shoes (instead of the street), G.Q. as nice rags (instead of food, cat litter, or pig shoes), and chill pill as to be cool (instead of a fat lady, a pork chop, or Batman's shoes). Despite considerable efforts, standard intelligence examinations are still not free from cultural influences.[17]

Aptitude Tests

Like intelligence tests, aptitude tests are standardized instruments that attempt to measure certain traits of individuals. Aptitude tests are based on linkages between various skills and interests on the one hand and different kinds of occupations on the other. A preference for working with things rather than people and an ability to work with tools would seem to indicate that one would be more appropriate as a carpenter than as a social worker.

Aptitude tests have the major limitation that they work with broad and general categories.[18] The focus in hiring is on specific positions in specific agencies.

Personality Traits

Psychologists use a number of standardized tests, including the Minnesota Multiphasic Personality Inventory, the Edwards Personality Preference Scale, and the Strong Vocational Aptitude Test, to construct a personality profile of individuals. These instruments are used to determine an individual's level of self-confidence, depression, aggression, and similar characteristics.

Again, as with other standardized tests, there might be questions about general categories and about the linkages to the particular positions being filled. The other issue that emerges here is whether there are legitimate grounds for selecting individuals because of their personality. The distinction that must be made—and sometimes is difficult to make—is between what is needed to perform effectively on the job and what is a personal preference of the supervisor or appointing authority.

Written Performance

Because of the wide array of occupations and responsibilities in the public sector, these examinations vary considerably. Accountants will be given accounting problems, highway engineers may be asked to complete calculations similar to those required on the job, and clerks will be told to alphabetize some terms or names. There is an obvious advantage to a written performance examination because it can be tailored for specific positions and therefore yield the maximum amount of relevant data on each candidate.

Oral Examinations

For some professional and managerial jobs, an oral question-and-answer session is appropriate. Oral examinations can be structured or unstructured. Under a structured format, questions are prepared ahead of time. All candidates are asked the same questions. No follow-up or clarifying questions are permitted, and the panel administering the examination is instructed not to give any feedback to the candidates during the examination. Unstructured examinations allow for more spontaneity and for more probing. Certain areas are to be covered with each candidate, but the way in which questions are phrased is left up to panel members, and the time spent on each area may vary from one candidate to the other. The most obvious trade-off between structured and unstructured oral examinations is the greater measure of comparability associated with the former and the potential for learning more about each individual candidate with the latter. Various mixes of the two types of oral examinations are possible.

Sometimes oral examinations are clearly the most appropriate type of test for the position being filled. Nonetheless, they are expensive and they risk being influenced by the personal biases of the examiners. Because of the expense of bringing panel members together with candidates, oral examinations are usually administered to relatively few applicants. Other examinations and screening mechanisms are used to identify the top five to ten candidates, who are then invited to the oral examinations. The face-to-face encounter provides not only more but different information from that available from other examinations. This runs the risk of examiners confusing the impressions they acquire because of the physical appearance or the mannerisms of the candidates with the evaluations they make based on more job-related criteria.

Work Performance

This category overlaps, to some extent, with the previous two. On work performance tests, candidates are asked to complete some of the tasks assigned to the position for which they are applying. Applicants for a clerical job can do an exercise in filing. Accountants can solve financial calculation problems. Social workers can respond to hypothetical cases. The major advantage of work performance examinations is, of course, that they are directly related to position responsibilities. They should be used wherever they are appropriate and whenever possible.[19]

Assessment Centers

An **assessment center** is a technique that uses multiple approaches to test for the variety of knowledge, skills, and abilities that are needed in a position. Assessment centers were established in the private sector to identify managerial talent. They have been used less frequently by governments and nonprofits, but there, too, the use has focused primarily on managerial positions. Typically, assessment centers include simulations of stressful decision-making situations, small-group exercises that test leadership skills, in-basket exercises that require the establishment of priorities and delegation of work, assignments designed to examine communication skills, and the like. Assessment centers have been used both to select managers and to identify training needs for incumbent managers.[20]

Although assessment centers are expensive, employers and participants generally have a very positive reaction to assessment centers. Those who go through the program report that, although the experience was demanding and exhausting, it was fair and seemed relevant. Employers are pleased with the resulting appointments, although employer satisfaction is based more on impressions than systematic evaluations.[21]

Random Selection

There are some jobs where the skill level is low enough that almost anyone with good work habits could do what is required. Examinations in these instances cannot provide meaningful distinctions between candidates. For example, routine work cleaning buildings does not lend itself easily to preemployment examination. Perhaps the fairest way to employ individuals for this kind of position is to assign numbers to all applicants and then randomly select from the pool of numbers. Those selected could then be interviewed by the appointing authority for factors like good work attitudes, work habits, and probable compatibility with co-workers.

Medical Examinations

The Equal Employment Opportunity Commission (EEOC) has promulgated rules under the Americans with Disabilities Act prohibiting preemployment medical inquiries and examinations. Employers may, however, make job offers contingent on passing a medical examination. The examinations or inquiries may go beyond job-related considerations, but if an individual is rejected, it may only be for something job-related.[22]

EXAMINATION VALIDITY AND RELIABILITY

It is no easy task to construct a test based solely on job-related criteria, that weighs knowledge, skills, and abilities according to their importance in the job, identifies which individuals have the best preparation and the best potential, and complies with cost and time constraints. The challenge is particularly awesome when dealing with governmental and nonprofit organizations, where there is such a wide variety of specialties and occupations and where there are so many professions and paraprofessions that defy precise measurement.

There are two major concerns that need to be addressed:

1. An examination must be reliable, that is, it should yield consistent and trustworthy results. A reliable test will score an individual's performance the same regardless of when it is taken or who administers it. Vague questions will often make a test unreliable. Likewise, unstructured, oral examinations are inherently unreliable.
2. Examinations must also be valid, that is, measure what they are intended to measure. An IQ test may be reliable and provide consistent results for a given individual, but it may tell us very little about how well prepared a person is to be a police officer, firefighter, or social worker.

Reliability

There are three major ways of determining **reliability**, i.e., whether a test is trustworthy and will yield consistent results. Perhaps the most obvious way is called test-retest. Under this procedure, the same test would be administered to the same people at two different times. The two administrations should be fairly close together in order to minimize the effects of experience or maturation. If candidates rank in approximately the same order and score approximately the same both times they take the test, then the test is reliable.

To avoid the problems that might occur by using the same questions two times, the alternate forms method has been developed. Here one compiles a pool of questions or examination items designed to measure the same thing. When constructing the examination, testers put together two tests, each one from a different random sampling of the pool of questions. If individuals score approximately the same on both examinations, then the examinations are regarded as reliable.

Finally, the split-half method tests for reliability by dividing questions measuring the same knowledge, skill, or ability into odd- and even-numbered items. Scores on the two sets are subjected to correlational analysis. If individual scores on both halves of the examination are about the same, then the test is considered reliable.

Validity

The American Psychological Association's Division of Industrial-Organizational Psychology has issued a statement on types and strategies of examination validation that is commonly accepted.[23] There are several ways of determining validity, some of which are impractical in government and others that are very appropriate.

Data-Based Models

Predictive criterion-related model   The ideal method of developing and validating an examination is the least practical. The predictive criterion-related model uses an experimental research design to validate an examination. A test is developed to measure the various knowledges, skills, and abilities identified as necessary through the position analysis. Then, half of the applicant pool is given the test and half is not. Individuals are then hired randomly from the applicant pool, without regard for whether or not they took the examination and without regard for the scores achieved on the examination. After those hired have been on the job for a period of time, their performances are rated. By correlating performance ratings with whether an examination had been taken and what score, if any, was earned, one then knows the validity of the examination. Figure 10.3 presents the steps of the predictive criterion-related validation model.

The legal requirements of the merit system in which individuals are hired on the basis of how well they do on an examination presents a major and obvious obstacle to

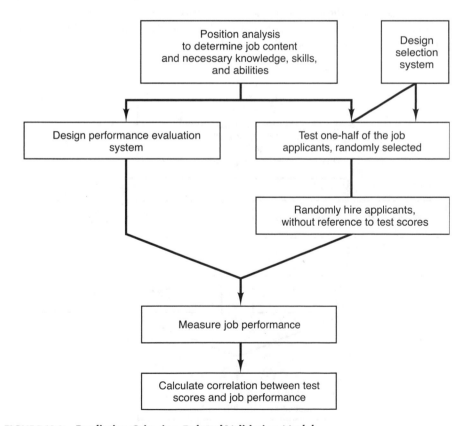

FIGURE 10.3   **Predictive Criterion-Related Validation Model.**

the use of this validation model. Agency managers, even if it were legal, are not going to hire individuals randomly in order to conduct experiments.

Moreover, for many positions, performance cannot be rated precisely enough to yield data useful for this kind of analysis. Finally, few job categories have enough positions to allow for this kind of experimental design or meaningful statistical analysis.

Although the predictive criterion-related model is not practical, it is a useful reference for what one might like to approximate. It also helps to keep in proper perspective what other approaches might hope to attain. As becomes clear in the discussion to follow, other approaches have serious limitations. These need to be acknowledged both in terms of the confidence placed in them and in the resources allocated to them.

Concurrent criterion-related model   A way of coping with a requirement that those hired must be high achievers on an employment examination is to see if there is a correlation between precisely how well an employee does on the examination and how well that employee does on the job. This is the strategy of the concurrent criterion-related model. The starting point is, again, the position analysis. With a sound understanding of the job, the examination and a performance evaluation system are developed simultaneously. After those hired have been on the job for a period of time, their performance is evaluated. Examination scores and performance ratings are then compared. If those with high scores are those with the best ratings, and vice versa, then the examination is regarded as valid. Figure 10.4 outlines the steps of the concurrent criterion-related model.

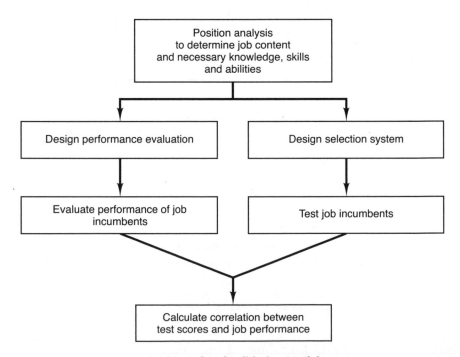

FIGURE 10.4   Concurrent Criterion-Related Validation Model.

This approach is more practical than the predictive criterion-related model, but there are some important limitations. This model, too, assumes performance can be rated and the ratings can be precise enough to provide scores that can be used in correlational analyses. Also, concurrent criterion-related validation is dependent on more positions in a given job category than is common in most public jurisdictions. Another limitation distinguishes it from the predictive model, that is, there are no controls for what individuals learn simply by being on the job. The random selection component of the predictive model is important primarily because it does control for job experience and focuses more heavily on the effects of the examination.

Logical Models

Content models Content validity is the most frequently used type of validation. In this approach an examination is reviewed to confirm that it actually measures some aspects of the job itself and/or something very similar to the job. An assessment center has content validation if the various exercises require the same kinds of knowledge, skills, and abilities that the job requires. Content validity requires a position analysis and an examination that consciously tries to test the knowledge, skills, and abilities identified as necessary by the position analysis. Content validation also requires a scoring system that weights the various characteristics being tested in accordance with the weight established in the position analysis.

In a review of the use of content validation since the passage of the 1964 Civil Rights Act and the involvement of the courts in setting standards for personnel selection, Stephen Wollack noted the emergence of the following criteria:

1. The test itself must be sound, that is, require candidates to perform tasks that seem reasonable.
2. The job analysis must be adequate, that is, cover all aspects of the job.
3. There must be a demonstrable relationship between the test and the job analysis.
4. The test must be used appropriately, that is, scores must distinguish between the most and least competent candidates, and multiple tests or test items must be used for measuring multiple traits.[24]

Construct validity models Construct validity is established when one can show that a particular trait, such as intelligence, creativity, empathy, or industriousness, has been measured and is job-related. The difficulty both of measuring traits and of demonstrating that they are job-related has discouraged the use of IQ, personality, and other examinations that require this kind of validity. Intuition and judgment may indicate that a social worker should have empathy, but it is difficult to prove that this is necessary and it is almost impossible to measure.

DETERMINING PASSING SCORES

A passing score on an examination would be based on a determination of the minimal level of knowledge, skills, and abilities needed to do a minimally satisfactory job. Our ability to measure job performance and to measure knowledge, skills, and abilities is too imperfect to apply this standard most of the time. Instead, passing scores are usually determined by administrative and professional judgment. The factors that most frequently play a role in this judgment are

- The number of available candidates—the larger the number, the higher the score for passing
- The number of positions being filled from the same examination—the larger the number, the lower the score for passing
- The labor market situation—the more competitive the market for certain skills, the lower the score for passing
- Confidence in the examination itself as a screening mechanism—the higher the validity and reliability, the higher the score for passing
- The estimated acceptance rate of employment offers that will be made—the higher the acceptance rate, the higher the score for passing

Of these factors, the fourth (confidence in the examination) should be the most important. This factor expresses a concern for the quality of the individual who might be appointed. If the examination is valid and reliable, then the scores that candidates earn are meaningful and should be treated seriously. If the examination is likely to lead to an error, then scores should be regarded cautiously. In such a situation, more reliance will have to be placed on the intuition and judgment of the appointing authority.

Although confidence in the examination should rank highest when considering where to set the score for a passing grade, concerns about the labor market and the estimated acceptance rate frequently dominate. Managers are sometimes so eager to fill a position that the question of who fills it is less important than that it is filled.[25]

Merit system laws include a requirement that someone other than the appointing authority administer the examinations and score the performances. Typically, a central personnel office, agency personnel specialist, or a panel of experts that the personnel staff gathers score examinations. The purpose of isolating managers from the scoring process is to help make selection fair and objective in substance and appearance.

VETERANS' PREFERENCE POINTS

A public policy that has been incorporated in the selection of governmental personnel since the beginning of this country is the preferential hiring of military veterans. Most countries have such a policy. In part, the rationale is simply to include this as one of the benefits available to those who have served in the military. In part, the intent is to provide a transition from military to civilian life. Nonprofit organizations typically do not have a veterans' preference policy.

The specific ways in which the general policy of providing an employment benefit to veterans is translated into practice vary from one jurisdiction to another. A major issue is how to determine who qualifies as a veteran. Some jurisdictions simply defer to the federal government—whoever qualifies for federal veterans' benefits qualifies for state and local civil service preference. Other jurisdictions specify whether or not one must have served in combat or in wartime, whether the children, parents, or spouses of veterans also qualify, and whether there is a time period after discharge beyond which this benefit no longer applies. Veterans' preference, dependent on the jurisdiction, may be available only for entry into a civil service system, for entry and one promotion, for entry and unlimited promotions, or for entry, promotions, and protection against layoffs.

Jurisdictions also vary in how they apply the benefit. The states of Massachusetts and Iowa, for example, have laws that provide an absolute preference for veterans who are among the top ten scorers on examinations for city (but not state) employment. Absolute preference means that managers have no choice. They must offer the job to a certified veteran if one applies and is qualified. Most other jurisdictions add points to the examination scores of veterans. It is common to give veterans five additional points and to give them ten points if they are disabled. In other words, if a veteran scored 85 on the examination, that individual's total score would be 90, or 95 if disabled.

Preference to veterans comes at a cost to women, minorities, and people with nonservice-related disabilities. In fact and in principle, there is a conflict between the public policy goals of diversity and veterans' preference. There have been limits on the number of women allowed into the various armed services, thus limiting the opportunities for women to become eligible for **veterans' preference points**. These limits were lifted in the 1960s. But, during the administration of President Ronald Reagan, the military reimposed a number of limits on women in the military. No more than 1,000 women volunteers were accepted between 1983 and 1988, basic training was no longer coed, and 23 jobs—such as carpenter, mason, electrician, and engineer—were restricted to men. Although minority representation in the military is larger than their percentage of the general population, almost half of the discharges of minorities have been in categories that disqualify them for veterans' benefits—including preference points on civil service exams. There have always been regulations that prevent people with disabilities from enlisting.

Despite commitments and strong laws supporting affirmative action, courts, including the Supreme Court, have upheld veterans' preference points. The Supreme Court, in fact, has upheld the Massachusetts law providing absolute preference.[26] The courts understand the contradictions in policies supporting affirmative action and veterans' preference, and they understand that veterans' preference has an adverse effect on the employment of minorities and, especially, women and people with disabilities. Nonetheless, they have ruled that the U.S. Constitution has not been violated and conflicting public policies must be resolved by legislative action.

CERTIFICATION

Once candidates have their examination scores—with or without veterans' preference points—then a number or percentage of those with the highest scores are certified for appointment. Agency managers must select from the certified list. Although certification preceded the establishment of merit systems, this is now regarded as key to a fair and open selection system.[26] As in administering and scoring examinations, the objective is to keep the appointing authority from fixing the process to favor any particular individual. If a third party—usually the same individuals who score the examination—provides a list of individuals from which the agency managers must select to fill the vacant position, then it will be difficult to fix the process to favor a specific person or group.

The civil service reform efforts of the mid- and late 1970s invariably included a consideration of how many names to certify for appointment. The certification step itself was not questioned. Reformers agreed that change was needed, but there was no consensus on the nature of that change. The result is that we now have an almost infinite variety of practices.

The traditional practice is referred to as the rule of three. That is, the top three candidates are certified for appointment. Given the current appreciation about the imperfection of examinations and the difficulties of measuring precisely the type of knowledge, skills, and abilities that are needed in public sector jobs, a concern has emerged that three is simply too small a number. There have been several approaches to change.

1. Selecting, albeit on an arbitrary basis, some number larger than three—five, seven, and ten are most common
2. Using a percentage of the candidates eligible (meeting minimal qualifications)
3. Combining the previous two approaches, for example, using a percentage but also specifying a minimum and/or maximum number that can be certified
4. Applying a categorical approach, that is, grouping candidates into something like satisfactory, good, and excellent categories and then certifying everyone who falls in the excellent group
5. Basing the number of those certified on the level of confidence in the examination

The civil service system in Michigan uses this last approach. If the validity and the reliability ratings of the test are high, as it might be in a performance test such as using a keyboard, then a small number can be certified. If the validity and reliability ratings are low, as might be true for a middle-management position, then a longer list is certified to the manager. The Michigan system has the clear advantage of being based on something other than an arbitrary cutoff point.

Certification and Affirmative Action

There is a convergence between the concerns of promoters of a more competent public workforce and advocates of affirmative action on the need for abandoning the traditional rule of three for certification. Both favor certifying more names. Those concerned about competence point to the imprecision of examinations. Those concerned about social balances likewise point to the imprecision of examinations and past problems of biases in examinations. There is the assumption that by certifying more names there will be a greater chance that diverse candidates will be included. This does not, of course, guarantee that managers will hire women, minorities, or people with disabilities, but at least it provides them with the opportunity to make that choice.

As mentioned, veterans' preference points, when combined with certification procedures, have an adverse impact on women, minorities, and people with disabilities. With the exception of just a few jurisdictions, names are certified after total scores, including the addition of veterans' preference points, are computed. Examination scores tend to cluster with only a few points separating the top candidates. The five or ten veterans' preference points, therefore, have a considerable impact on the final rankings and on those certified for appointment. In other words, veterans whose examination scores are within five (or ten if the veteran is disabled) points of the score of a nonveteran, bump that nonveteran from the certified list and, thus, from consideration for appointment. The example in Table 10.1 illustrates this situation. In the situation presented, which is not unusual, let us assume the nonveterans are women and let us assume that the rules of certification for this jurisdiction are to certify the candidates with the top five total scores. Although three women, candidates A, B, and E, were among the top five according to the examination scores, none of them would be certified. Instead, the certified list would assure the appointment of a veteran, candidates C, D, F, G, and J.

To avoid the possibility of veterans bumping nonveterans with top examination scores from the certified list, in 1977 the states of Wisconsin and North Dakota initiated a new and simple modification of the application of veterans' preference points and certification rules. Certification in these jurisdictions occurs in two steps.

First, candidates are certified on the basis of their examination scores only. Then, additional names are certified of individuals who, with the combination of examination scores and veterans' preference points, earn total scores at least equal to the lowest score of someone certified on the basis of examination performance only. In other words, candidates A, B, C, D, and E in the illustration presented in Table 10.1 would be certified under a rule of five on the basis of their examination scores. Candidates C and D did not need their veterans' preference points to secure certification. In addition, candidates F, G, I, and J would be certified because with their examination scores and veterans' preference points they had a total score of at least 95, the lowest score of those certified on the basis of the examination only. The manager in this case could choose from a list of nine candidates.

Another modification that has been made is to compile a separate, additional list of affirmative action candidates. Typically, these candidates have to earn at least a passing grade on the examination or rank among the top third or fourth of the eligible

TABLE 10.1   IMPACT OF VETERANS' PREFERENCE POINTS

Candidate	Examination Score	Veterans' Points	Total Points
A	98	0	98
B	97	0	97
C	97	5	102
D	96	5	101
E	95	0	95
F	94	5	99
G	94	10	104
H	93	0	93
I	90	5	95
J	90	10	100

candidates taking the examination. As in the Wisconsin and North Dakota system for using veterans' preference points, the certification of a separate list of affirmative action candidates occurs after candidates are certified on the basis of examination scores or examination scores and veterans' preference points. To present managers with an opportunity to diversify their workforce, it is necessary to provide them with more names than they might otherwise have. Giving managers only a select list of women, minorities, or disabled candidates, however, violates the rights of other job applicants.

INTERVIEWS AND SELECTION

In governments where certification is used, managers are free to select anyone on the certified list on almost any basis. Discrimination on the basis of race, color, sex, and disability is, of course, prohibited. Although it is common for managers to interview those who have been certified before making a choice, most civil service laws do not require it. What is required is that all certified candidates receive equal treatment: If one candidate is interviewed, then all must be.

When a short list is developed without certification and veterans preference rules, managers typically have discretion on how to proceed with the names on the short list. The usual practice is to interview the top several candidates.

Interviews are almost inherently unsystematic.[28] They place heavy reliance on subjective judgment and impressions.[29] Courts have recognized this in considering charges of bias. Managers are not liable for exercising this kind of judgment, but they are for asking questions that are not job-related and from which one might reasonably infer discriminatory intent. In *Weiner* v. *County of Oakland* (1976), for example, the Supreme Court decided that questions such as the following substantiated a claim of sex bias:

"Did Mrs. Weiner's husband approve of her working?

Would her family suffer if she were not home to prepare dinner?

Could she work with young, aggressive men?"

This evidence and a pattern of hiring men and not women who were on the certified list were enough to bring a ruling against Oakland County.

Interviews are useful for evaluating interpersonal skills, and they can be made more systematic by using a checklist of questions to ask and subjects to cover.[30] Few managers have had training in interviewing techniques and approaches. It is impractical for an agency manager to get this training if he or she does not make appointments very often. In this situation it would be useful, however, for the manager to get an orientation from a personnel manager and have guidelines on how to focus on job-related issues. The fundamental question that managers should ask and those being interviewed should answer is: "Why do you want this job?"

Managers also should be mindful of the importance of the interview in the decision of the applicant to accept or reject a job offer, if one is made. Interviews are more than an opportunity for the employer to evaluate the candidate: Candidates also make evaluations.[31] The top few candidates—those on the short list—probably look attractive to other employers, too. They may get more than one job offer. It would be very disappointing for a manager to lose a top candidate to another employer because the interview was not a dialogue and did not present an opportunity to sell the job to the candidate.

In part because interviews are such a common feature of selection processes, researchers have focused considerable attention on this subject. In a review of much of this research, Neal Schmitt provides a useful summary of major findings. Among the patterns and lessons he identifies, the following are particularly important:

- Early impressions are critical. Interviewers tend to reach a final decision within four minutes after the interview begins.
- Unfavorable responses and impressions have a greater impact on how an interviewee is rated than do favorable responses.
- Visual cues or "body language" have more of an effect than verbal cues.
- Interviewers can and do use job information to minimize the use of irrelevant questions and answers.
- Interviewers tend to rate those with attitudes and traits similar to their own more favorably than interviewees who are different.
- Structured interviews are more reliable than those conducted without lists or guidelines.[32]

A study completed by Michael Willihnganz and Lawrence S. Meyers found that the time of day when interviews occurred and the sequence in which candidates are interviewed have no effect on performance or on ratings.[33]

These lessons are important for candidates as well as managers. Someone being interviewed typically has the same frustrations about subjectivity as the person conducting the interview.

The impact of sex-role stereotypes on an interviewer can present dilemmas for women. If they act feminine, they may not get nontraditional jobs, and if they act assertive and confident, they may be rejected as pushy or phony.[34] When women are asked illegal questions about marital status, children, and the like, they can state their legal rights, but by doing so may lose any chance of getting a job offer. One suggestion for dealing with this common problem is to avoid answering the question directly and instead to answer the implied question with reassurance about a serious commitment to the job and the schedule that is required.[35]

The selection of which candidate should be offered the job may depend on a check of references. A candid assessment by a current or former employer can be very useful information for a prospective employer. Unfortunately, these assessments are usually neither candid nor useful. Usually one lists references who are only going to say positive things, and most people are, in fact, reluctant to be negative when responding to a reference check. Some organizations have a policy that the only information that will be provided in response to a reference check is confirmation that an individual did work there and perhaps the dates of employment. Nonetheless, reference checks are common and occasionally do yield important warnings or confirmation of either positive or negative impressions gleaned from an interview.[36]

Interviews and references are inherently the most invalid part of the selection process. Probation is the most valid.

PROBATIONARY PERIOD

The last and the best stage of the selection process is the probationary period. Almost all positions that convey tenure or an indefinite period of employment require that employees serve a probationary period before they get long-term job security. Positions that are filled on a contract basis for a fixed term or on an at-will basis usually do not have probationary periods. (Chapter 13 discusses job security and dismissal policies.)

What better way to tell if someone can do a job than to have him or her actually doing the job? An evaluation of performance during the probationary period is direct evidence of how suited a person is for a job. There is no need to make the kinds of inferences that are involved in basing selection on examination scores or previous education and experience.

The only inference is that the pattern of behavior seen during probation is what one can expect for the indefinite future. It is, in other words, conceivable that someone would work energetically and enthusiastically during the probationary period in order to get a job and then work below that level after he or she had permanent or indefinite status. Aside from this situation, the probationary period allows an agency manager to see how an individual fulfills assigned duties and responsibilities before making a long-term commitment to that individual.

Traditionally, probationary periods have been for six months. The length of probationary periods in most organizations now varies with the type of job. A relatively routine job that requires a low level of skill may not require even a six-month probationary period: It may be possible to judge whether an individual can do the job in a matter of several weeks. On the other hand, professional and managerial jobs that include a variety of responsibilities may require two or more years of probation. Some tasks in these positions are important but are not done frequently, and thus a longer period of probation is needed. Some evaluations are difficult to make and require rather lengthy periods of observation.

Some jobs have a seasonal dimension. It would, for example, be a mistake to have a forest ranger or a game warden serve a probationary period from November to May and not be able to judge what the employee can do during the peak summer months. Likewise, budget analysts have very different workloads and responsibilities throughout the various times of the budgetary year. These positions require at least a one-year probationary period.

Employees in some positions begin their employment with an intensive training period. This is typical for police officers and firefighters. Some entry-level management positions begin with an internship and training program. These training periods are part of the probationary period. Usually, probation lasts for the entire training period and the first six months to two years on the job. A condition of passing probation, in other words, is successfully completing the training program.

From a manager's perspective, probationary periods are advantageous because employees have very limited appeal rights if they are terminated. Beyond the general prohibition against discrimination, the only limitations on managers are procedural. The federal government, for example, requires that employees on probation who are going to be terminated receive written notice and be allowed the opportunity to make a written reply. These employees are not, however, entitled to make a verbal response, and they do not have any appeal rights based on the substance of the reasons for their termination. Managers do not have to prove their case, as is necessary when an employee is dismissed after achieving permanent status.

One would expect a much higher rate of dismissal during probation than occurs. In almost all public jurisdictions, 80 to 90 percent of the employees pass probation and receive permanent status. It is highly improbable that the selection process has been that effective in identifying the best job candidates.

There are several reasons why managers do not take full advantage of the probationary period. First, most individuals do not regard probation as part of the selection process. In the minds of most, the selection process ends with the letter offering a job. Perhaps if probation were treated just like an examination, there would be more meaning to passing and failing. In addition, it is costly to terminate an employee and start over again with someone else on a certified list or start all over again with the entire selection process. The temptation is strong to stick with a potentially satisfactory employee rather than seek someone better. Furthermore, it is difficult to confront people face-to-face and inform them that their work is not satisfactory and they are dismissed. From this standpoint, the costs of dismissing someone during probation are not significantly different from dismissing a permanent employee.

SUMMARY

The selection process typically commands a major proportion of personnel management resources. Employers assume, not unreasonably, that productivity and efficiency can be accomplished by hiring good people. A mark of good managers is the quality of people that they employ. Although considerable efforts have been made to be thoroughly systematic and scientific in screening and selecting people for employment, the individual judgment and impressions of the appointing authorities have played and will continue to play a major role.

The contributions of personnel management to this process are to ensure an applicant pool that includes competent individuals and members of all societal groups, to design and administer examinations that are job-related and distinguish between the best and the worst candidates, and to help managers use interview techniques and selection criteria that are legal and effective in securing a competent, socially balanced workforce. Selection processes and instruments draw from the internal policies of the organization, the mandates of the law, and the findings of relevant psychological research.

The state of the art is far beyond the standard written examinations that traditionally were used and that tested little other than language skills. The need for further development and refinement, on the other hand, begs for further and rather substantial work. Regardless of how sound and precise the selection processes might become, managers will continue to play a critical role. They still will—and should—have the major influence on the definition of the jobs to be filled and the final word on which of the top candidates should receive the job offer.

DISCUSSION QUESTIONS

1. How would you respond to a proposal that a single agency, rather than unit managers, do the hiring for all positions in an organization?
2. Why are public employers prevented from offering a job on the spot to someone whom an agency manager or recruiter finds would fit a vacant position?
3. How do steps taken to prevent discrimination in the selection process on the basis of race, gender, or disability enhance or compromise efforts to hire the best qualified people?
4. What should a manager do to prepare to interview a job applicant? How should a job applicant prepare?

Job Announcement Exercise

Prepare a job announcement for the position you analyzed in the previous chapter. Critique actual job announcements for similar positions in somewhat comparable organizations. You can find these announcements in newspapers or on the websites in the appendix. Be certain in your own job announcement to provide information on all nine items discussed in this chapter.

CONSTRUCTING AN EXAMINATION EXERCISE

Step One. Outline the kind(s) of testing you would conduct to identify the best candidates for the position you analyzed for the position analysis exercise. In your outline, specify what types of knowledge, skills, and abilities the various components of the examination are designed to measure and provide one or two sample questions or test items to illustrate the nature of the exam.

Step Two. Design a scoring system for your examination. Where appropriate, devise a method of weighting scores on the various components of the examination to correspond with the relative importance of different dimensions of the position you are filling.

Step Three. Based on the discussion in this chapter on the different types of validity, determine which type is most appropriate for the position.

INTERVIEW EXERCISE

Work with a classmate and practice conducting a job interview and being interviewed.

1. Give your classmate a copy of the job announcement you completed for this chapter.
2. Assume that your classmate is on the short list or the certified list. Interview your classmate for the job. Limit the interview, including any time you allow for him or her to ask questions, to 15 minutes.
3. Swap roles with your classmate and use the job announcement that he or she completed.

4. Critique one another, both as interviewer and as interviewee. Consider the following questions:

   • Was the discussion job-related?
   • Were the questions within the bounds permitted by law?
   • Did the interviewer sell the job as well as test the applicant?
   • Did the interviewee ask good questions?
   • Was there anything the interviewee could have done to improve the impression he or she made in those critical first few minutes of the interview?

GLOSSARY

Assessment center A type of examination (not a place or institution) that involves simulations and hands-on exercises

Biodata Personal information about an individual's background, experience, education, and interests

Bona fide occupational qualification (BFOQ) Job-related requirements that an individual must be of a certain gender, racial, religious, or other group that is protected from discrimination

Certification A formal step in the selection process for civil service positions in which a set number or percentage of applicants who earned the highest scores on examinations, with veterans' preference points if applicable, are listed as eligible to be appointed

Executive search firm An agency that is hired to identify and recruit applicants for a particular vacancy

Internal recruitment A selection process limited to current employees in the organization

Job announcement An advertisement for applicants for one or more vacant positions

Probation The last phase of the selection process in which a person serves in the position for which they have applied for a set period

Recruitment The steps taken to get people to apply for a job

Reliability A determination of objectivity or whether a test measures the same thing on a continual or repeated basis

Residency requirements Stipulations that in order to hold or in some cases to apply for a job one must live in a certain jurisdiction

Validity A determination of whether a test is actually measuring what it intends to measure

Veterans' preference points Points that are added to examination scores of eligible veterans who apply for civil service positions

SOURCES

Ban, Carolyn (2006). Hiring in the federal government: Political and technological sources of reform. In Norma M. Riccucci, ed., *Public personnel management: Current concerns, future challenges* (4th ed.). New York: Longman, 2006.
A broad review and assessment of hiring policies and practices in the federal government.

Medley, H. A. (1978). *Sweaty palms: The neglected art of being interviewed.* Belmont, CA: Wadsworth.
Discussion of the job interview from the applicant's perspective.

National Commission on Testing and Public Policy. (1990). *From Gatekeeper to gateway: Transforming testing in America.* Chestnut Hill, MA: Boston College, 1990.
Report of a task force that reviews changes that have taken place in employment examinations, especially since the passage of the 1964 Civil Rights Act, and makes recommendations.

Schmitt, F., & Hunter, J. (1998)). The validity and utility of selection methods in personnel psychology: Practical and theoretical implications of 85 years of research findings, *Psychological Bulletin* 124, 2: 62–274.
A summary and discussion of psychological research related to the selection of employees.

Schmitt, N. & Borman, W. C., eds. (1993). *Personnel Selection in Organizations.* San Francisco: Jossey-Bass.
A collection of essays, some with a concern for psychometrics, on various aspects of the selection process.

Smart, B. D. (1983). *Selection interviewing: A management psychologist's recommended approach.* New York: John Wiley & Sons.
Discusses the job interview from the manager's perspective.

NOTES

1. William B. Johnston, *Civil Service* 2000 (Washington, DC: Office of Personnel Management, 1989).
2. National Commission on the Public Service, *Leadership for America* (Lexington, MA: Lexington Books, 1989).
3. Robert L. Armacost and Rohne L. Jauernig, "Planning and Managing a Major Recruiting Project," *Public Personnel Management* 20, no. 2 (Summer 1991): 115–126.
4. Amy B. Kaplan, Michael G. Aamodt, and Doreen Wilk, "The Relationship Between Advertisement Variables and Applicant Responses to Newspaper Recruitment Advertisements," *Journal of Business and Psychology* 5 (1991): 383–395.
5. Clyde J. Scott, "Employing a Private Employment Firm," *Personnel Journal* 68, no. 9 (September 1989): 78–83; Jean P. Kirnan, John A. Farley, and Kurt F. Geisinger, "The Relationship Between Recruiting Source, Applicant Quality, and Hire Performance: An Analysis by Sex, Ethnicity, and Age," Personnel Psychology 42 (1989): 293–308.
6. J. E. Hunter and R. F. Hunter, "Validity and Utility of Alternative Predictors of Job Performance," *Psychological Bulletin* (Spring 1984): 72–98.
7. Craig Russell, Joyce Mattson, Steven E. Devlin, and David Atwater, "Predictive Validity of Biodata Items Generated from Retrospective Life Experience Essays," *Journal of Applied Psychology* (October 1990): 569–580.
8. J. Edward Kellough and Robert C. Gamble, "The Americans with Disabilities Act: Implications for Public Personnel Management," in Stephen W. Hays and Richard C. Kearney, eds., *Public Personnel Administration: Problems and Prospects*, 3rd ed. (Englewood Cliffs, NJ: Prentice-Hall, 1995), 247–257; J. G. Frierson, Employer's Guide to the Americans with Disabilities Act (Washington, DC: Bureau of National Affairs, 1992).
9. R. A. Ash, J. C. Johnson, E. L. Levine, and M. A. McDaniel, "Job Applicant Training and Work Experience Evaluation in Personnel Selection," *Research in Personnel and Human Resource Management* 7 (1989): 183–226; F. A. Mael and A. C. Hirsch, "Rainforest Empiricism and Quasi-Rationality: Two Approaches to Objective Biodata," *Personnel Psychology* (Winter 1993): 719–738.

10. Hannah R. Rothstein, Frank L. Schmidt, Frank W. Erwin, William A. Owens, and C. Paul Sparks, "Biographical Data in Employment Selection: Can Validities Be Made Generalizable?" Journal of Applied Psychology 75 (1990): 175–184.

11. Irwin L. Goldstein, "The Application Blank: How Honest Are the Responses?" Journal of Applied Psychology 55, no. 5 (1971): 491–492. See also, Debra D. Burrington, "A Review of State Government Employment Application Forms for Suspect Inquiries," Public Personnel Management 11 (Spring 1982): 56; Alan L. Colquitt, "Recruiters Beware: Lying is Common Among Applicants," HR Focus (October 1992): 5.

12. Irwin L. Goldstein, "The Application Blank: How Honest Are the Responses?" Journal of Applied Psychology (October 1971): 491–492.

13. Thomas E. Becker and Alan L. Colquitt, "Potential Versus Actual Faking of a Biodata Form: An Analysis Along Several Dimensions of Item Type," Personnel Psychology 45 (1992): 389–408.

14. *McCarthy v. Philadelphia Civil Service Commission* 424 U.S. 645 (1976); Shapiro v. Thompson 406 U.S. 137 (1969); *Detroit Police Officers Association v. City of Detroit* 416 U.S. 134 (1974); *Memorial Hospital v. Maricopa County* 414 U.S. 632 (1974).

15. Rodney B. Warrenfeltz, "An Achievement Based Approach to Evaluating Engineering Technicians," Public Personnel Management 18, no. 3 (1989): 243–262.

16. National Commission on Testing and Public Policy, *From Gatekeeper to Gateway: Transforming Testing in America* (Chestnut Hill, MA: Boston College, 1990); David Lewin, "Cautions in Using Job Analysis Data for Test Planning," *Public Personnel Management 5*, no. 4 (July/August 1976): 255–257.

17. Margaret E. Griffin, "Personnel Research on Testing, Selection, and Performance Appraisal," *Public Personnel Management* 18 (Summer 1989): 127–137; Richard D. Arvey, *Fairness in Selecting Employees* (Reading, MA: Addison-Wesley, 1979), 85–110; V. E. Boehm, "Negro-White Differences in Validity of Employment and Training Selection Procedures: Summary of Research Evidence," *Journal of Applied Psychology* 56, no. 1 (1972): 33–39.

18. Robert P. Tett, Douglas N. Jackson, and Mitchell Rothstein, "Personality Measures as Predictors of Job Performance: A Meta-Analytic Review," *Personnel Psychology* 44 (1992): 703–742; Edwin E. Ohiselli, "The Validity of Aptitude Tests in Personnel Selection," *Personnel Psychology* 26 (1972): 461–477.

19. James E. Campion, "Work Sampling for Personnel Selection," *Journal of Applied Psychology* 56, no. 1 (1972): 40–44.

20. W. C. Byham, "The Assessment Center as an Aid in Management Development," *Training and Development Journal* 25, no. 12 (1971): 10–12; Douglas W. Bray and Donald L. Grant, "The Assessment Center in the Measurement of Potential for Business Management," *Psychological Monographs: General and Applied* 80 (1966).

21. Allen I. Kraut, "New Frontiers for Assessment Centers," *Personnel* 53, no. 4 (July/August 1975): 30–36.

22. U.S. Equal Employment Opportunity Commission, *A Technical Assistance Manual on the Employment Provisions (Title I) of the Americans with Disabilities Act* (Washington, DC: Government Printing Office, 1992).

23. Division of Industrial-Organizational Psychology, American Psychological Association, *Principles for the Validation and Use of Personnel Selection Procedures* (Washington, DC: American Psychological Association, 1975); David E. Terpstra and Elizabeth J. Rozell, "The Relationship of Staffing Practices to Organizational Level Measures of Performance," *Personnel Psychology* 46 (1993): 27–48; Paul R. Sackett and Richard D. Arvey, "Selection in Small N Settings," in Neal Schmitt and Walter C. Borman, eds., *Personnel Selection in Organizations* (San Francisco: Jossey-Bass, 1993), 418–447.

24. Stephen Wollack, "Content Validity: Its Legal and Psychometric Basis," *Public Personnel Management* 5, no. 6 (November/December 1976): 397–408. See also Jeffrey J. McHenry,

Leaetta M. Hough, Jody L. Toquam, Mary A. Hanson, and Steven Ashworth, "Project A Validity Results: The Relationship Between Predictor and Criterion Domains," *Personnel Psychology* 43 (1990): 703–742.

25. Frank A. Malinowski, "Test Passing Points in State and Municipal Agencies," *Public Personnel Management* 9, no. 4 (July/August 1980): 274–277; Wayne F. Cascio, Ralph L. Alexander, and Gerald V. Barrett, "Setting Cutoff Scores: Legal, Psychometric, and Professional Issues and Guidelines," *Personnel Psychology* 41 (Spring 1988): 1–24; Richard E. Biddle, "How to Set Cutoff Scores for Knowledge Tests Used in Promotion, Training, Certification, and Licensing," *Public Personnel Management* 22 (Spring 1993): 63–79.

26. *Fenney* v. *Massachusetts* 327 U.S. 465 (1978).

27. Paul P. Van Riper, *History of the United States Civil Service* (Evanstan, IL: Row, Peterson, 1958), 104, 162–165, 422–424.

28. Richard Arvey and James Campion, "The Employment Interview: A Summary and Review of Recent Research," *Personnel Psychology* (Summer 1992): 281–322.

29. Steven J. Cesaere, "Subjective Judgment and the Selection Interview: A Methodological Review," *Public Personnel Management* 25, no. 3 (Fall 1996): 291–306.

30. M. A. Campion and J. P. Hudson, Jr., "Structured Interviewing: A Note on Incremental Validity and Alternative Question Types," *Journal of Applied Psychology* 79 (1984): 998–1002; Michael A. Campion, Elliott D. Pusell, and Barbara K. Brown, "Structured Interviewing: Raising the Psychometric Properties of the Employment Interview," *Personnel Psychology* 41 (1988): 25–42, Christopher Daniel and Sergio Valencia, "Structured Interviewing Simplified," *Public Personnel Management* 20, no. 2 (Summer 1991): 126–134.

31. Robert Gifford, Cheuk Fan Ng, and Margaret Wilkinson, "Nonverbal Cues in the Employment Interview: Links between Applicant Qualities and Interviewer Judgments," *Journal of Applied Psychology* (November 1985): 729–736.

32. Neal Schmitt, "Social and Situational Determinants of Interview Decisions: Implications for the Employment Interview," *Personnel Psychology* 29, no. 3 (May/June 1976): 79–101; Robert L. Dipboye, *Selection Interviews: Process Perspectives* (Cincinnati: South-Western Publishing Co., 1992); Bradford D. Smart, *Selection Interviewing: A Management Psychologist's Recommended Approach* (New York: John Wiley & Sons, 1983); Thung-Rung Lin, Gregory H. Dobbins, and Jiing-Lih Farh, "A Field Study of Race and Age Similarity Effects on Interview Ratings in Conventional and Situational Interviews," *Journal of Applied Psychology* 77 (1992): 363–371.

33. Michael A. Willihnganz and Lawrence S. Meyers, "Effects of Time of Day on Interview Performance," *Public Personnel Management* 22, no. 4 (Winter 1993): 545–550.

34. Madeline E. Helman and Melanie Stopeck, "Attractiveness and Corporate Success: Different Casual Attributions for Males and Females," *Journal of Applied Psychology* (May 1985): 379–388.

35. H. Anthony Medley, *Sweaty Palms: The Neglected Art of Being Interviewed* (Belmont, CA: Wadsworth, 1978), 170–172.

36. Michael G. Asmodt, Devon A. Bryan, and Alan J. Whitcomb, "Predicting Performance with Letters of Recommendation," *Public Personnel Management* 22, no. 1 (Spring 1993), 81–90.

Chapter 11

Employee Training and Development

Managers commonly regard training as both a cure-all and a waste. Whenever an agency encounters a problem, proposals for solutions invariably include training programs. Poor supervision in an organization? Train the supervisors. Broken machinery causing downtime and delays? Train the operators and mechanics. Conflict and poor morale among employees? Implement interpersonal relations training. Problems with legislators or board members? Train them.

Yet, one of the most vulnerable items in an agency's budget is the allocation for training programs. Perhaps too much is expected of training, and when all expectations are not met, a credibility problem emerges. Perhaps programs are not planned and executed well. The linkage between training needs and the agenda of courses, seminars, and conferences may not be clear.

In fact, trainers chastise one another for being irrelevant. One author, M. Gene Newport, characterized common—but faulty—approaches to training programs as the following:

1. Smorgasbord. Offer a broad array in the hope that almost everyone will find something that might be useful

2. Bandwagon. Offer courses and seminars that are being offered in other organizations

3. Crisis. Offer courses that respond to an immediate and obvious need

4. Excursion. Offer courses that do not seem to head in any particular direction but seem interesting[1]

Another way of describing this situation is with the image of a salesperson, who tries to convince potential customers that they have a need that could be met—even if the individuals have not perceived the need before. The common dynamic is of a vendor or the training staff in an agency developing what they regard as an exciting and valuable set of sessions and then trying to convince everyone else to share their excitement.[2] Training and employee development, like other personnel management functions, must be integrated into the real needs of agencies and of employees.

LEARNING OBJECTIVES OF THIS CHAPTER

- Understand the training and development of employees from two perspectives: the manager and the employee
- Know ways of assessing the training needs of an agency
- Know how to design, execute, and evaluate training programs according to agency needs
- Understand the career patterns of public employees and the opportunities that exist within organizations

SYSTEMATIC APPROACH TO TRAINING

There is an emerging consensus among trainers about the steps to take in providing employee development programs.[3] They are:

1. Needs assessment
2. Curriculum development
3. Training execution
4. Program evaluation

Although the process is logical and the steps may be self-evident, each step raises a number of issues and demands some discussion.

Needs Assessment

Employee training and development should begin with a **needs assessment**. This step is based on the fundamental principle that it is what the agency needs and the employees need, rather than what a particular training officer or consulting firm has to offer or is interested in, that should determine the array of training programs and opportunities. Needs flow from work design, technological developments, succession planning, position analyses, and performance evaluations.

Training needs are identified at the confluence of the direction in which the agency is moving, the changes in technology that are occurring, and the career paths employees are or could be pursuing. Succession planning identifies what kinds of general knowledge and specific technological courses are most appropriate. The College Aid Board—the hypothetical agency described in the illustration used in Chapter 7—might decide to use computer technology for recordkeeping, accounting, and word processing. If so, and if the data available through performance evaluations and succession plans indicate there are existing employees who might be trained to use the new technology, then a clear training need has been identified.

Likewise, planning can provide the information necessary to let managers know where an organization's workforce is socially imbalanced. Position analyses and performance evaluations reveal, similarly, what knowledge and skills employees need to perform their current jobs more satisfactorily. Both managers and employees may benefit more from training poor performers than from disciplining them.

Training programs cannot fill all agency needs. Evidence of poor supervision may reflect more on how supervisors are selected than on what kind of training supervisors need. Downtime because equipment constantly needs repair could be the consequence of purchasing inappropriate equipment rather than a need for skill training for operators and mechanics. When police officers cannot accomplish all the patrol, community relations, and administrative work assigned to them, the problem may be workload rather than lack of skills; the solution may be restructuring task assignments rather than training. The kind of analysis and problem solving central to Quality Management would be useful in these cases to determine whether training might contribute to quality improvement.

Four basic questions help determine whether training is appropriate:

1. Is the problem one of lack of skills, knowledge, or ability? If the answer is yes, then training could be a remedy.
2. Do the employees have the preparation and the intelligence and/or skills required for the training program? If not, then little would be accomplished through participation in the program.
3. Will the organization be receptive to the skills or approaches that participants can bring back from a training program? There is a well known and documented case where training had only negative effects because newly trained employees could not apply what they had learned. Not only was the training wasted, but also the frustration of the employees led to severe tension.[4]
4. Is the perceived problem better resolved through a transfer of personnel, through reorganization or other approaches?

This checklist may reinforce the initial impulse to prescribe training or suggest a strategy other than developing current or newly hired employees.

Although training programs may not meet all of the needs that are evident for an organization or an individual, training does fill some needs. Some of these needs are not obvious. An important spin-off of conferences, seminars, and workshops is the informal networks that develop among participants. These informal networks frequently provide more ideas and contacts than are offered in the formal program. These ties, moreover, act as ongoing communication mechanisms that help individuals understand their organization and anticipate changes. It is hard to exaggerate the importance of these ties. Women and minorities, as they move into middle- and senior-management positions, have learned to appreciate the usefulness of these networks. They value training sessions as one way of replacing or supplementing the "old boy networks."[5]

Moreover, employees often value training programs as rewards. Although training often serves the purpose of enabling an employee to remedy a problem or address a limitation, seminars, conferences, courses, and the like can be a way for managers to recognize good performance. Training as a reward is most clear when the employee is being groomed for a promotion or new responsibility. Even in cases where promotion is not an issue, the opportunity to attend a training program is valued. The distinction, the break from regular responsibilities, and the advantages gained from increased knowledge and from the informal ties are coveted by employees. In a study that examined employee attitudes toward training and educational opportunities, respondents ranked this behind insurance and retirement programs as the most valued benefit.[6]

Clearly, nonobvious benefits and side effects cannot dictate an agenda of training programs. Their importance should not, however, be forgotten or underestimated. But, to provide relevant and useful training to avoid a smorgasbord, a bandwagon approach, crisis responses, excursions, or other fragmented programming, it is essential to assess agency needs.

The ranking of various training depends primarily on managerial concerns.[7] Reorganizations, changes in management techniques and styles, and the adoption of new technologies all typically have training components. Although agencies can benefit from a systematic planning process that identifies and ranks training needs, very few organizations, public, nonprofit or private, spend the time and money to do so. More typically, needs are visible as responses to specific events and developments.

Curriculum Development

The tasks of curriculum development flow in an almost obvious and natural way from needs assessment. If a collective bargaining agreement has just been ratified and supervisors and employees need to know the details of the contract, then a training session should be designed to convey this information. If a new software program is being introduced, then employees need a series of sessions on how to use the software. New employees need an orientation. The content of that orientation depends on the nature of the organization and the rules and policies governing employee benefits and work behavior.

An appreciation of the ways in which individuals learn has led to a wide variety of formats and approaches in employee training. Traditional classroom approaches, with textbooks, lectures, and discussions, are generally used only when conceptual learning is emphasized.[8] A widely used approach toward supervisory training has modules, each based on a common problem facing supervisors and each emphasizing participation by trainees in working through solutions. One widely used approach to supervisory training pointedly advertises itself as including no coverage of theories.[9] Although that might be carrying a point too far, trainers have benefited from some important principles emerging from research on learning. Stating objectives clearly, using positive reinforcement, building on motivation and interest, and learning by doing are among the most important principles.

Types of training programs include those conducted on the job and those held away from the work setting. **On-the-job programs** utilize the demands and resources of daily work and a designated mentor or supervisor-instructor to train an employee. These programs include the kind of instruction and orientation a supervisor or lead worker would be expected to provide to a new employee. Another type of on-the-job training is an **internship**, in which an individual is placed in a temporary position in a department or office in order to observe and learn how an organization is functioning and what specific people are doing. Interns are placed under the direction of a specific employee, who helps explain operations, answers questions, and assigns a task or array of tasks designed to acquaint the intern with the agency. Similarly, permanent employees rotate jobs or participate in inter- or intra-agency personnel exchanges (temporary ones) as a way of broadening their perspectives and bringing to agencies new ideas and new expertise.

Some training programs take employees away from their workplaces. An example is the classroom or formal course, whether given by the employee's agency or accomplished through a tuition reimbursement program. Some of these programs apply the learning by doing principle, which incorporates role playing and simulations. There are short one- to four-day courses that include discussions, lectures, films, and some hands-on learning experience.

Given the variety of training needs and learning approaches there is little likelihood that a single in-house training officer or even a staff in a training office would have the background and skills to provide all the necessary programs. Because of this, most governments and nonprofits rely heavily on consultants to provide the training programs that they need.

Training Execution

One of the first tasks of administering a training program is to select the participants, that is, the faculty and students. Agency managers can identify participants through the needs assessment. Given the importance of training opportunities to employees, individuals are generally concerned that the process of selecting participants be fair. Employees have their own communication networks, which, in the absence of other information, are likely to carry rumors and tales of favoritism and conspiracy. In response, some managers treat selection for training, especially if it might lead to promotion, as a competitive process, much like hiring.

Adages identify the importance of teachers to the quality of instruction. These general adages apply to employee training programs. The search for the best faculty may, however, be constrained. Financial constraints can limit options. Schedules may conflict. Vendors have their own approaches, which may not be perfectly matched with the unique needs of a specific agency. Within all these constraints, the search for the appropriate instructors can follow a number of different paths. Sources of ideas and evaluations of vendors include professional associations, universities, governmental associations (like the National Governors' Association, the Council of State Governments, and the National League of Municipalities) and other agencies that have had similar needs. Probably the most common way of tapping these resources and soliciting recommendations is through the informal networks among managers and executive directors.

Program Evaluation

The most common approach to the evaluation of training programs is the least useful. Almost all training programs include a questionnaire that is administered at the end of the program and asks participants to rank, rate, and/or critique various components of the program. This instrument gauges the reaction of participants to the program. It allows trainers to change courses and workshops so that they will elicit less criticism and more praise. That is of some value, but it begs the question, "What impact has the program had on employees?" Although it is more pleasant and satisfying to have praise than condemnation for the programs one designs and administers, it is very difficult to infer from these reactions if the organizational and individual needs have been met.

To pursue the evaluation of training beyond the issue of how participants react to the program, one might make distinctions between (1) what was learned, (2) what changes in job behavior resulted, and (3) what happened to agency performance, that is, impacts on costs, outputs, and goal accomplishment.[10] Each of these dimensions requires a different methodological approach. To determine what learning occurred, a before-and-after test can be administered. In this test, participants are examined to determine how much they know about the subject of the program before the program begins. Then, after the program they are tested again. Comparing the test scores measures how much learning resulted from the program. If the testing includes a control group—a group that does not participate in the training program—then one can be even more confident about how much learning is due to the training program, rather than experience, maturation, or some other factor.[11]

Evaluating how training affects job behavior is more difficult. A key to assessing behavioral changes, of course, is performance evaluation. If a sound performance evaluation system is not used or if raters using the system are not reliable, then it will not be possible to make a meaningful judgment on work behavior changes. Even with one of the most effective systems, like the behaviorally anchored rating scales (BARS) or the results-based system used in Chapter 9, judgment is involved. With these possibly obvious caveats, the evaluation of job behavior changes can be made by using a control group that did not participate in the training program and by evaluating performance before and after the training.[12] The changes that occurred in the behavior of those who received the training should be compared to the changes in the group that did not receive training.

When conducting these evaluations, it is important to allow enough time after the training program is complete for changes to be implemented. The posttraining performance evaluation should not be made until at least three months after the training program is over. Ideally, posttraining evaluations are made at successive periods in order to gauge the effects of training over time.

The most difficult dimension to evaluate—effects on the agency—is the most informative. So many variables go into the efficiency and effectiveness of an organization that it is difficult to isolate and measure the impact of a training program on the agency as a whole. Usually, for example, one cannot use a control group to identify the unique effects of a training program on an agency. Exceptions are confined to instances where an agency has several similarly structured units that do the same thing. This would be possible in an organization like the U.S. Post Office, for example, where units handling similar volumes and types of mail can be compared. Most agencies, however, do not have multiple, comparable units.

In most instances, one would have to rely on a pre- and posttraining measurement of the aspect of an agency where change is desired and then make inferences about whether training was the critical factor causing whatever change occurred. Reasonable measurements and inferences will be possible only where the desired changes are well defined and rather precise in scope.[13] Changes internal to an agency are generally easier to trace than changes involving groups or clientele in society. It would, for example, be more feasible to measure the impact of training if the concern were safety and avoiding a particular type of accident than it would be for improving the quality of care for the elderly or reducing the rate of a particular crime. For the latter cases, the focus has to be on changing the behavior of individual social workers and police officers and hoping that the result will be better care and fewer crimes committed.

The purpose of evaluations is not, of course, just to satisfy a manager's curiosity. The purpose is to remedy errors and make improvements. The feedback that evaluation provides is especially important when inferences, trial-and-error approaches, and intuition have to play a role in decision making. With the feedback, adjustments can be made. Without it, initial impulses and experiments become permanent.

Mentoring

Mentors can be used to provide on-the-job training. The old boys network is essentially a mentor program that has been in existence informally since the dawn of organizations. Those who have been with the organization for some time establish a relationship with new employees to orient them to the folkways of the agency with the goal of helping the newcomer succeed. The new employee is given advice, introduced to key people, and given opportunities through work assignments and group projects that will contribute to advancement. The old boys network is invaluable, but it also has two flaws: It assumes that continuity in the way the organization has been run is desired for the future and it is gender-specific.

Increasingly organizations are consciously and formally using mentorship programs as a way of developing employees. In part, this is to extend the benefits of mentoring to women.[14] Formal **mentor** programs now include the assignment of mentors to men and to women.

A problem with explicitly organized mentor programs is that there is sometimes confusion about the role of a mentor. Mentors, as mentioned above, have traditionally provided information, contacts, and opportunities to help an employee advance. A mentor can also, however, be someone who is a confidant and a supporter. This role emphasizes empathy rather than information. The mentor is more valued for the personal than the professional relationship. Both types of mentors may be valuable, but where the role is not clearly defined, there can be inconsistency and frustration.

Another issue that has arisen with formal mentor programs is the assignment of who will mentor whom. The match may not be a good one. Being an effective mentor takes time and energy. If someone is being told to serve as a mentor, but does not have the interest or the energy to do a good job, it is likely that the person being mentored will feel cheated and the assigned mentor may be resentful. To compensate for the inherent problems in formal mentor programs, managers need to take care in making assignments and in providing guidance and perhaps training to clarify what the objectives of the program are.

VOLUNTEERS

While it is natural to think of training and developing employees, it is critical to recognize the importance of the same for volunteers—the mainstay for many nonprofit organizations. Like for employees, training for volunteers should flow from organizational needs and should consider the skills and backgrounds of volunteers.

When an organization relies on volunteers for relatively routine, low-skilled work, such as serving meals to the homeless or getting a mailing out to members or potential donors, it is critical to define precise, assembly-line type tasks and to train volunteers so they understand what they should be doing. Especially given the turnover and the comings and goings of volunteers, this training is essential to avoid chaos and redundancy. Here task-oriented training is important for everyone, regardless of their backgrounds. Highly educated, professional people volunteer to help organizations they support. They, like everyone else, need to be told what to do to make their efforts valuable.

Board members and volunteers in executive and analytical positions also need training. Almost inevitably there is a need for an orientation to the organization's mission and current challenges. There may be a need for software training or some education about legal requirements or grant provisions. Here the individual's background is relevant. Some will need more training and orientation than others. It is essential to recognize the value not only to the organization to have everyone trained and informed, but also to the individual volunteers who are eager to contribute to the organization's success.

CAREER DEVELOPMENT

The primary concern thus far has been agencies. Career development, in contrast, emphasizes the needs and interests of individuals. In succession planning and job analysis, employees are resources that satisfy organizational needs. In career development, organizations are resources that can be used to satisfy individual needs. Performance evaluation can provide information for and a link between both organizations and individuals.

Actual Career Patterns

Governments generally do not provide career counseling and career development programs for their employees. Individual employees must generally shoulder responsibility for their own career planning. Moreover, governments and nonprofits generally are open systems in that people who are not currently employees can fill positions at all levels. At best, some agencies give preference to current employees. Even when preference is given, current employees may have to compete in the same process with outside applicants when they want to move to higher positions. Notable exceptions to this area are the Foreign Service, the military, and most paramilitary organizations, including police and fire departments. In these organizations, except for the very top position, those promoted from lower ranks fill middle- and senior-level positions.

The government bashing that reached fever pitch in the 1980s raised concern among some public officials about the effects this bashing might have on the retention of valued government employees. The Volcker Commission addressed this issue for the federal government and the Winter Commission for state and local governments. In general, the findings of these and other studies documented an understandably depressed feeling about all the government bashing, but nonetheless a high level of satisfaction with the kind of work and problem solving done in government jobs to counter any overall inclination to leave the public sector.

The federal government documented a general pattern, known as a glass ceiling, in the 1990s in which women and minorities advanced in their careers at lower rates than white men.[15] This was particularly evident among professionals and managers. As pointed out in Chapter 4, there are structural problems in how career tracks are defined in professions where women are predominant, providing fewer promotional opportunities. Other barriers were lack of access to training programs and a lack of mentoring. In addition, the federal government, like other public, nonprofit, and private employers, has had a difficult time creating a work environment free of sexual and racial harassment and this has led to higher quit rates for women and minorities.[16]

Typically an employee experiences upward mobility for the first five years in an organization and then plateaus.[17] The initial pattern of advancement establishes an expectation that turns to frustration when the rate of advancement does not continue.[18] This phenomenon is common to governments and nonprofits alike. Frequently size is an issue. There simply are not enough employees and levels of hierarchy in a local or state government agency or a particular nonprofit organization to provide for continued upward mobility for long-term employees.

It is possible in government to pursue a career in a single agency and eventually be appointed to head that agency. Elected chief executives make many of these appointments, however, so there is no sure path to the top. Studies of senior officials in state and local governments indicate that about 40 percent have served in two or more agencies within their current jurisdiction. Also, about one-third have worked for at least two different jurisdictions. Movement between jurisdictions includes different levels, that is, federal, state, and local.[19] As pointed out during the discussion of succession planning, the decades of 2010–2030 are going to be characterized by unprecedented opportunities for mobility as baby boomers retire from the workforce.

Reclassification

The most common way for government employees to advance in their careers is through reclassification. Compensation concerns often prompt the reclassification of positions. As an individual reaches the top of the pay range assigned to the position classification in which he or she is currently employed (compensation schemes are explained in more detail in Chapter 13), the employee seeks to have his or her position reclassified to a category in which there is a higher pay range.

A budget analyst, for example, may be in a Budget Analyst 2 classification and seek to move to a Budget Analyst 3 classification. In order to make such a move, it is necessary to argue that there have been changes in assigned tasks such that the Budget Analyst 2 is actually performing the work described in specifications for Budget

Analyst 3. If the Budget Analyst 2 has been doing a good job, it is not unreasonable to expect that, in fact, the supervisor has asked this employee to do increasingly more difficult and complex work. Often, the supervisor supports an employee's request for reclassification. This support may be prompted by a genuine job growth. It is also possible that a supervisor is simply trying to help an employee get more pay even though the job has not changed. This is, as described in Chapter 8, called grade creep. Used correctly, however, reclassification provides for some employee mobility.

Career Planning

As pointed out in Chapter 5, not everyone is concerned about having a career in which his or her responsibilities and challenges increase and in which the individual develops and grows. For some, work and jobs are simply not that important. Some do not have their self-esteem invested in how they earn a living. For them, work setting and adequate compensation are the central concerns. Others, primarily those in professions and paraprofessional work, do seek personal growth and development in their jobs. Careers are central to their lives and their identity.

This chapter includes instruments that can be used by individuals in planning their careers. Ideally, they would be used with advice and assistance from managers and from those involved in succession planning, but this is not a requirement.

Since the mid-1970s, public jurisdictions and public employees have taken important steps to provide for meaningful careers and career advancement in government. A feature of the federal 1978 Civil Service Reform Act was to establish programs for individuals in middle-management positions in the federal government to prepare for and become senior executives. In the late 1970s and early 1980s, state and local governments removed some of the structural barriers to career advancement of current employees. These barriers included heavy reliance on seniority for promotions, veterans' preference points applied to promotions, narrowly defined position classifications with inflated training and experience requirements, and rigid work rules that discouraged employee enrollment in various educational programs.[20]

The federal government moved quickly to implement the 1978 Civil Service Reform Act provision for the development of senior executives. Prior to the act, agencies had only memoranda from the Office of Management and Budget and the former Civil Service Commission encouraging the initiation of programs to develop senior managers. There was little positive response to these memoranda. After the act, however, 54 agencies immediately outlined programs and more than 600 candidates were selected from the ranks of middle management. Agencies varied some of the features of their programs. The length varied from six months to two years, and the array of approaches included formal training courses, briefing sessions, developmental work assignments, internships with mentors, shadow assignments, and the like. All programs emphasized managerial skills and all programs included individual development plans for each participant.[21]

The National Academy of Public Administration issued a report in 1992 advocating for **succession planning** and stressing the critical role of training and mentoring.[22] The Connecticut Department of Corrections has earned citations for its succession planning, a program known as Learning Journey. The Connecticut approach combines performance reviews, selection interviews, training, and apprenticeships.[23] Several federal agencies have taken advantage of the flexibility available in the Senior Executive Service and are engaged in succession planning.

Diversity goals have prompted some employers to pursue career development programs not only for senior management positions but also throughout the organization. The U.S. Supreme Court in *U.S. Steelworkers* v. *Weber* (1979) gave its approval to programs designed specifically to prepare employees who were members of protected classes to move into other jobs, as long as entry into those jobs was not restricted to graduates of these special upward mobility programs.[24]

Employee development uses a variety of strategies. One method has already been referred to—upgrading skills to qualify for and/or compete for positions. The programs used to develop senior managers are a prime example. In these programs, individuals learn management approaches, engage in mock decision-making exercises, and receive instruction in the prescriptions and prohibitions contained in relevant laws and collective-bargaining agreements. Other employee development strategies are used to train a payroll clerk to become a paraprofessional in the accounting field and a drivers' license examiner to become a planner for highway safety programs.

Another strategy to use in achieving mobility is to **cross** from one job category or career ladder where opportunities for advancement are limited to another with more potential for upward movement.[25] Another circumstance in which crossing to another career ladder may be advisable is when the size of a particular office is too small or the work is too elementary to provide many advancement opportunities. A switch to another location or an office where there is more work or more complex work may allow for mobility.

A third strategy for pursuing career advancement is through the use of **bridge positions**. These positions are specifically created to allow employees to move from one threshold to another within a career ladder. A temporary, trainee position at a paraprofessional level, for example, might be created to help those payroll clerks who wish to become accountants. Those organizations that have bridge positions usually require competition for appointment. Then, after successfully performing in the bridge position, the employee, without further competition, secures the permanent position.

Employees engaging in career planning are, naturally, concerned about whether there will be positions available if they participate in a training program and/or switch from one career ladder to another. Making changes involves disruptions and costs. There is a fear that these disruptions and costs will gain nothing. Although employees make changes with their own interests and abilities in mind, they also are concerned about projections for vacant positions. Agencies with conscious succession planning programs help employees who are planning career advancement by conveying information about job opportunities.

Managers who work with their employees in career counseling and development also have a concern. Employers recognize a risk in investing in an employee's growth and development only to see that employee leave to work for someone else. A policy issue that agency managers face is whether to limit their support for personal development to the jobs that their employees are currently performing or to allow for and support development that is related to careers, rather than jobs.

Accommodation of Disabilities

Careers rarely follow a steady path of progression. Most people experience plateaus and occasionally some setbacks, sometimes because of forces at work and sometimes because of other events in their lives. When an employee experiences a chronic health problem that affects his or her work, agency managers might make accommodations. As is the case when hiring employees, managers need to balance their own work requirements with what a disabled person, perhaps with some modifications in work schedule, location, or duties, can do. If accommodation cannot be made in the job that the employee had been doing when he or she became disabled, then a manager may be able to offer the employee some other, more suitable position in the agency. Organizations can problem solve and enable a person with a disability to continue to work while maintaining productivity.

Under some collective bargaining agreements and agency policies, the scope of accommodation is stronger than is mandated under the Americans with Disabilities Act. Managers, in these situations, offer an employee with a long-term medical condition a job within the agency that the employee can handle. There is no requirement to create or to reconfigure jobs to accommodate disabilities, but managers may, of course, go beyond what is required and design new positions that would fit a disabled employee's abilities.

Family and Medical Leave

Sometimes employees have a temporary need to care for themselves or family members. Under the federal Family and Medical Leave Act of 1993, employers are required to grant leave requests for the health needs of employees and their families. President Bill Clinton issued a memorandum on April 12, 1997, instructing managers of federal agencies to expand the provisions of the Family and Medical Leave Act to include participating in an employee's child's school activities and accompanying children and elderly relatives to medical appointments. Some state laws and collective bargaining agreements are, in various ways, more generous than the provisions required by federal law. California, for example, requires that family and medical leave be granted with compensation, whereas the federal law does not mandate compensation—only that the job continue to be available. Where there are differences between state and federal laws, the federal act stipulates that the more generous policy applies.

The federal law mandates that employees may take up to six weeks of leave without pay per year for the birth or adoption of a child and for family and personal medical needs. This leave can be taken on a part-time and/or intermittent basis. Employees are supposed to provide notice except, of course, in emergencies. If an employee has paid sick leave, vacation time, or a similar benefit available, he or she may use it for the mandated family and medical leave. If no such benefit exists, the leave might be without pay—an employer could, of course, offer pay.

Agency managers must allow employees to exercise their rights under the Family and Medical Leave Act and any applicable state or local laws or collective bargaining agreements. The **reasonable accommodation** test that balances employee and employer needs does not apply here, in part because the needs are presumed to be temporary and the benefits limited. The challenge to managers is to find ways of coping with the absences. Managers and employees may have to acknowledge that in some cases the level of productivity will decline somewhat.[26]

Layoffs

Until the 1980s, career patterns in the public sector generally did not include the possibility of **layoffs**. Only rarely was a program terminated or a public facility closed—perhaps to be located elsewhere—and employees laid off from their jobs. With budget reductions and the demand for reducing the size of government, however, layoffs and the prospects of layoffs touched many agencies and individuals. Layoffs are temporary, nondisciplinary dismissals of employees. Layoffs occur because of fiscal difficulties or the cessation or reduction of programmatic activities. Reorganizations also can prompt layoffs.

Some private sector economic activities are cyclical or highly dependent on the health of the economy, and layoffs are not uncommon. Employees and employers in these activities (coal mining, construction, steel mills, and the like) do not look forward to layoffs, but they have developed support systems and lifestyles that anticipate that possibility. Layoffs in nonprofit organizations usually occur because a particular grant or contract has expired and both work and funding reduced accordingly. The need for reductions in governments catch many by surprise. Some jurisdictions do not have rules or guidelines for determining which employees should or must be laid off. Setting these rules, or even using rules that are in the books but had never been tested, generated conspiracy theories and considerable hardship. Individuals interpreted layoffs as personal rejections. Agency managers faced tearful, depressed people.

A common rule for determining who is to be laid off is last hired, first fired. (The slogan rhymes, but it errs in labeling a layoff as a firing.) Position classification in government complicates the application of the simple seniority rule captured in the slogan. Employees who have their position eliminated in a downsizing or reorganization typically have **bumping rights** that allow them to replace less-senior individuals within equivalent or lower classifications, but not those in classifications not regarded as equivalent or comparable. Some jurisdictions limit bumping to within the agency that is downsizing or reorganizing, while others allow bumping within a classification across agencies. Usually one may bump to any classification in which an employee previously had a position in his or her career. Some personnel rules and collective bargaining agreements limit the potentially endless domino effect by allowing only up to a set number (usually three or five) of bumps any time a position is eliminated. In short, the layoff process can be complicated and affect a number of employees. A single layoff can also cause anxiety and uncertainty throughout an agency—or even several agencies.

One response of all organizations facing layoffs is to encourage employees who are nearing retirement to retire early. Rules are changed to provide eligibility for full retirement benefits for those opting to end their career earlier than planned. This, of course, requires additional expenditures and thus is not the most attractive option. Another common reaction of agencies is to curtail hiring people from outside the ranks of existing employees and, wherever possible, to transfer employees about to be laid off into vacant positions.

Those who seek government employment are sometimes regarded as individuals who want careers with security. A survey of private and public sector employees did not, however, indicate that government and private sector employees feel significantly different about their job security. In response to the statement, "I feel I have good job security," 66.4 percent of public sector employees and 68.8 percent of private sector employees responded affirmatively.[27] This survey was conducted, interestingly, in 1978, prior to the experience of layoffs in the public sector.

Reductions in the size of government have the effect of making employee development all the more critical. Both employees and managers can gain by anticipating changes. General training programs and individual career planning can help make changes opportunities rather than threats.

SUMMARY

Training is not a panacea. Training is, however, an integral part of public personnel management. There were two units of analysis and concern in this chapter: organizations and individuals. Diagnoses of organizational units and individual employees can generate training agendas. Through relevant training programs, organizations are better able to achieve their goals and individual employees are better able to pursue their careers. If, on the other hand, training reflects what trainers think is interesting, then training programs run the risk of operating in isolation, of losing credibility, and of being regarded as expendable.

Needs assessments are essential to design effective programs; trainers must be aware of the advantages and disadvantages of various techniques and approaches to learning. To determine training effectiveness requires systematic inquiry and judgmental inferences. One of the most important evaluation questions is the most difficult to answer, that is, the effects on work behavior and organizational accomplishments.

Career development for individual employees is closely linked to training activities. Enabling and encouraging individual employees to set and achieve personal career goals should be consistent with improving an organization.

DISCUSSION QUESTIONS

1. How would you determine whether a glass ceiling existed in an organization? What would indicate the possible existence of barriers? If barriers seemed to exist, how would you determine whether in fact they did exist?
2. Compare the options available to an agency manager who had an employee that acquired a long-term disability and an agency manager with an employee that faced a short-term

family or medical emergency. What problems must the manager solve and what alternative approaches may and may not be used?

3. How could you tell whether a particular training program was effective? Does your answer depend on whether the program is developing a skill, providing information, or introducing managerial approaches?

4. What are the advantages of succession planning? Are there any concerns that the idea of succession planning raises?

Career Planning Exercise

This exercise is designed to help individuals (employees or students) think systematically and develop career plans. Obviously one cannot control all the variables that affect our lives. However, one can pursue dreams realistically and strategically. The objective of a career plan is not to secure a particular position in a particular organization. Rather, it is to position oneself to be able to take full advantage of opportunities to get a certain kind of position in a certain type of organization. To plan, it is best to think of something specific. But in implementing the plan, it is best to think in terms of positioning oneself.

INSTRUCTIONS

Step One.   Answer the questions on the Career Objectives form. These questions include important information about your career objectives and your personal concerns.

The answer to Question 7 can be found in a job analysis and job description (like the one you completed in Chapter 8) and in job recruitment announcements (like in Chapter 10). List the competencies required in the Position Requirements and Personal Competencies form.

Step Two.   Complete the Position Requirements and Personal Competencies form, which assesses the extent to which you have the competencies required for the kind of positions you would like to fill and invites you to specify how you will get those competencies that you need but do not have now.

Step Three.   Complete the General Success Factors form, which lists skills and abilities that have been found generally to contribute to success in professional and managerial positions. Indicate which of these factors are relevant to your career objectives, and then specify how you will increase your preparedness in areas where you need further development. Examples of how to increase some skills and abilities include taking certain courses, getting training, gaining experiences, and volunteering for tasks and responsibilities. Be as specific as possible.

CAREER OBJECTIVE

1. Title and brief description of desired position:
2. Agency or type of organization:
3. Desired community location (geographic area or type of community):
4. Type of career opportunities that need to be available for partner or spouse, if any:
5. Time frame(s) in which desired positions are likely to become vacant (time available to get prepared):
6. Changes—in mission, technology, and organizational structure—likely by the time the desired positions become vacant:
7. Skills abilities, and other competencies required (or potentially required) for the desired positions:

POSITION REQUIREMENTS AND PERSONAL COMPETENCIES

	Personal Competencies			
		Need		
Position Requirements	Have	How to acquire	When	Cost

GENERAL SUCCESS FACTORS

			Personal Abilities	
Success Factor	Required in career objective	Have	Need to Improve	Plan for Improvement
Managing projects				
Organizing				
Planning				
Supervising staff				
Budgeting				
Making decisions				
Communicating				
Evaluating programs				
Innovating				
Influencing others				
Representing organization				

GLOSSARY

Bridge position A job specifically designed to allow employees to move from one threshold (like paraprofessional to professional) to another within a particular occupational category

Bumping rights The ability that an employee who has been laid off or who has lost a position for some other nondisciplinary reason has to take another position away from another employee

Crossing Moving laterally from one position classification to another, somewhat similar position in order to take advantage of more career advancement opportunities available in the latter classification

Internship A training program, usually with a set duration, in which an individual learns a set of skills and approaches with some combination of on-the-job training, formal sessions, mentorship, and job rotation. Some internships are a prelude to the assumption of positions in the organization that are included in the on-the-job training and job rotations

Layoff Termination of employment because of budgetary reasons and/or reorganization, rather than because of disciplinary reasons. Employees who are laid off can be rehired without going through the selection process if their positions (or equivalent positions) become available once again

Mentor An experienced employee who is given responsibility to train and orient a new employee and to help him or her advance successfully

Needs assessment The identification of the training and development programs that would be useful to an organization and its employees

On-the-job training An approach to training that relies heavily on the job itself. Employees are given job responsibilities and instructed at the work site as they perform the job tasks

Reasonable accommodation Responsibility of an employer to change the duties, location, hours, or other feature of a job so that a person with a particular disability or religion can do the work. The employer does not have to sacrifice productivity in order to accommodate the needs of a particular person

Succession planning Conscious efforts to anticipate which positions will have to be filled in the near future and to develop particular employees to fill these vacancies

SOURCES

Goldstein, I. L. (1993). *Training in organizations.* Pacific Grove, CA: Brooks/Cole.
An overview of training issues, as applied to public and private organizations.

Kraiger, K., Ford, J. K., & Salas, E. (1993). Applications of cognitive, skill-based, and affective theories of learning outcomes to new methods of training evaluation. *Journal of Applied Psychology*: 311–328.
Description and discussion of different approaches to the evaluation of training programs, with attention to advantages and limitations.

U.S. Office of Personnel Management. (1992). *Report of task force on executive and management development.* Washington, DC: Government Printing Office.
Description and discussion of training and development programs for senior executives in the federal government.

Van Wart, M., Cayer, N. J., & Cook, S. (1993). *Handbook of training and development for the public sector.* San Francisco: Jossey-Bass.
A series of essays that discuss ways of designing and evaluating training programs.

NOTES

1. M. Van Wart, N. Joseph Cayer, and S. Cook, *Handbook of Training and Development for the Public Sector* (San Francisco: Jossey-Bass, 1993); J. West and E. Berman, "Human Resource Strategies in Local Government: A Survey of Progress and Future Directions," *American Review of Public Administration* 23, no. 1 (1993): 279–297; M. Gene Newport, "A Review of Fundamentals," *Training and Development Journal* 22 (October 1968): 17–21.

2. George R. Gray, McKenzie E. Hall, Marianne Miller, and Charles Shasky, "Training Practices in State Government Agencies," *Public Personnel Management* 26, no. 2 (Summer 1997): 187–202.

3. Irwin L. Goldstein, *Training in Organizations*, 3rd ed. (Pacific Grove, CA: Brooks/Cole, 1993); John E. Butler, Gerald R. Ferris, and Nancy K. Napier, *Strategy and Human Resources Management* (Cincinnati: South-Western Publishing Co., 1991); Albert A. Vicere, "The Strategic Leadership Imperative for Executive Development," *Human Resource Planning* 15 (1992): 15–46.

4. Beryl A. Radin, "Leadership Training for Women in the Public Service," Report to Office of Personnel Management, October 1978.

5. *Ibid.*

6. Helen W. Daley and Donald D. Sylvia, "A Quasi-Experimental Evaluation of Tuition Reimbursement in Municipal Government," *Review of Public Personnel Administration* 1, no. 2 (Spring 1981): 13–23.

7. James K. Conant, "The Manager's View of Management Education and Training," *Review of Public Personnel Administration* 16, no. 3 (Summer 1996): 23–37.

8. Kurt Kraiger, J. Kevin Ford, and Eduardo Salas, "Applications of Cognitive, Skill-Based, and Affective Theories of Learning Outcomes to New Methods of Training Evaluation," *Journal of Applied Psychology* 78 (1993): 311–328; Craig Eric Schneier, "Training and Development Programs: What Learning Theory and Research Have to Offer," *Personnel Journal* 50, no. 4 (April 1974).

9. William Byham and James Robinson, "Interaction Modelings: A New Concept in Supervisory Training," *Training and Development Journal* 30 (February 1976): 28–37.

10. Donald L. Kirkpatrick, "Evaluation of Training," in Robert L. Craig, *Training and Development Handbook*, 2nd ed. (New York: McGraw-Hill, 1976).

11. Ronald R. Sims and Serbrenia J. Sims, "Improving Training in the Public Sector," *Public Personnel Management* 20, no. 1 (Spring 1991): 71–82.

12. *Ibid.*

13. Susan C. Paddock, "Benchmarks in Management Training," *Public Personnel Management* 26, no. 4 (Winter 1997): 441–460; Ronald Sims, "Evaluating Public Sector Training Programs," Public Personnel Management 22, no. 7 (Winter 1993): 591–616.

14. Ralph Ocon, Issues on Gender and Diversity in Management (Lanham, MY: University Press of America, 2006); Norma M. Riccucci, *Managing Diversity in Public Sector Workforces* (Boulder, CO: Westview Press, 2002).

15. U.S. Merit Systems Protection Board, A Question of Equity: Women and the Glass Ceiling in the Federal Government (Washington, DC: MSPB, 1992).

16. J. Edward Kellough and Will Osuna, "Cross-Agency Comparisons of Quit Rates in the Federal Service: Another Look at the Evidence," *Review of Public Personnel Administration* 15, no. 4 (Fall 1995): 58–68.

17. James K. Conant and Dennis L. Dresang, "Retaining and Recruiting Career Professionals," in Frank J. Thompson, ed., *Revitalizing State and Local Public Service: Strengthening Performance, Accountability, and Citizen Confidence* (San Francisco: Jossey-Bass, 1993); D. Harkins, Z. Leibowitz, and S. Forrer, "How the IRS Finds and Keeps Good Employees," *Training and Development* 47, no. 4 (1992): 76–79.

18. Jonathan P. West and Evan M. Berman, "Strategic Human Resource and Career Development Planning," in Steven W. Hays and Richard C. Kearney, eds., *Public Personnel Administration: Problems and Prospects*, 3rd ed. (Englewood Cliffs, NJ: Prentice-Hall, 1995), 79; Wisconsin Employment Relations Study Commission, *Wisconsin Civil Service* (Madison, WI: Department of Administration, 1977).

19. Deil S. Wright, Mary Wagner, and Richard McAnaw, "State Administrators: Their Changing Characteristics," *State Government* 50 (1977): 152–159; Laurie S. Frankel and Carol A. Pigeion, "Municipal Managers and Chief Administrative Officers: A Statistical Profile," *Urban Data Service Report* 7, no. 5 (February 1975): 1–17.

20. Dennis L. Dresang, "Public Personnel Reform: A Summary of State Government Activity," *Public Personnel Management* 7, no. 5 (September/October 1978): 287–295.

21. Loretta Flanders and Rudi Klauss, "Developing Future Executives: An Assessment of Federal Efforts in an Era of Reform," *Review of Public Personnel Administration* 2, no. 2 (Spring 1982): 119–133.

22. National Academy of Public Administration, *Paths to Leadership* (Washington, DC: NAPA, 1992).

23. West and Berman, 79–80.

24. James P. Guthrie and Catherine E. Schwoerer, "Older Dogs and New Tricks: Career Stage and Self-Assessed Need for Training," *Public Personnel Management* 25, no. 1 (Spring 1996): 59–72.

25. U.S. Merit Systems Protection Board, *Why Are Employees Leaving the Federal Government? An Analysis of an Exit Survey* (Washington, DC: Government Printing Office, 1990); U.S. Merit Systems Protection Board, *Balancing Work Responsibilities and Family Needs* (Washington, DC: Government Printing Office, 1991); U.S. Office of Personnel Management, *Report of Task Force on Executive and Management Development* (Washington, DC: Government Printing Office, 1990); Norma M. Riccucci, "Apprenticeship Training in the Public Sector: Its Use and Operation for Meeting Skilled Craft Needs," *Public Personnel Management* 20 (1991): 181–193.

26. Soonhee Kim, "Administering Family Leave Benefits and New Challenges for Public Personnel Management: The New York State Experience," *Review of Public Personnel Administration* 18, no. 3 (Summer 1998): 42–57.

27. National Center for Productivity and Quality of Working Life, *Employee Attitudes and Productivity Differences Between the Public and Private Sector* (Washington, DC: Government Printing Office, 1978), 29.

Chapter 12

Health and Safety

Although the common image of employment in government and in nonprofit organizations is of a desk job in a safe and even pleasant setting, there is a growing realization that there are some serious health and safety issues that need to be addressed.[1] In part, the concern is in response to dramatic acts of violence. The attacks on the Pentagon and the World Trade Center towers on September 11, 2001, certainly have raised awareness of the possibility of terrorist incidents. Violence is nothing new to the United States generally or to public sector targets specifically. Examples include the bombing of the federal office building in Oklahoma City in 1995, the Unabomber, the bombing on the campus of the University of Wisconsin-Madison in 1970, the various antigovernment militia groups in rural areas, and others who randomly target public employees and public buildings have generated serious concern. The randomness of these attacks means that everyone in the public sector is equally at risk. Fortunately these attacks are rare and so the risk is not high. Nonetheless, managers and employees are worried, and security and investigative agencies are on the alert.

Equally dramatic and more frequent acts of violence are committed not by hate groups and terrorists but by fellow employees, volunteers, and by customers. On July 19, 1995, for example, a City of Los Angeles employee who was angry over a negative performance evaluation brought a 9-mm semiautomatic pistol to work and at midday opened fire, shooting four supervisors who were ending their coffee break.[2]

The image of the public employee holding only a desk job is, of course, somewhat misinformed. Public employees include police officers, firefighters, and prison guards, whose work inherently involves the risk of physical harm. Nurses and other health care professionals work with patients and inmates who are sometimes out of control and aggressive and who can have contagious illnesses. Courtrooms are scenes where violence can take place. On March 24, 1998, two students opened fire on their school playground in Jonesboro, Arkansas, killing a teacher and four classmates. In 1999, schools from Colorado to Georgia and Connecticut to California experienced a rash of highly publicized incidents of violence and disruption. These incidents are dramatic reminders that schools, too, are vulnerable to acts of violence.

Sometimes women and minority employees are victimized by sexual and racial harassment. The harassment can involve physical violence, including rape and assault. Sometimes supervisors and/or co-workers create a hostile and stressful work environment through abusive remarks, visual displays, and degrading jokes.

In addition to concerns about violence and hostility in the workplace, there are other issues of health and safety. While public employers typically have not had to

240

address the problems of safety guards on machinery and hazardous chemical waste or noise pollution common to factory workers, offices have their own health concerns. Employees can suffer carpal tunnel syndrome from extensive work on computer keyboards. Chairs that are not ergonomically sound can cause back injuries. Ventilation systems can pollute air in office buildings. And, of course, there are employees, such as nurses, painters, and equipment operators, who work daily with hazardous substances.

Like other personnel management responsibilities, workplace health and safety issues are matters both of public policy and of productivity. Managers must comply with laws and regulations designed to ensure health and safety in the workplace.[3] In addition, managers have an important interest in ensuring that their employees are healthy and productive.

As pointed out in Chapter 5, poor working conditions can detract from productivity although good conditions tend not to contribute to creative problem solving and effective agency performance the way that skills, technology, and employee motivation can. Working conditions are more of a negative than a positive factor in the productivity equation. This is, of course, not to say that working conditions are not important. We value health and safety, per se, in addition to their effects on productivity. High turnover, absenteeism, and tardiness are costly and can be minimized with pleasant surroundings and personal and family support programs. Creativity and energy are not easily measured, but they are not likely to flourish in settings where the focus is on hostile relationships and signs of management disengagement.

LEARNING OBJECTIVES OF THIS CHAPTER

- Know the nature of violence in work settings
- Distinguish between types of sexual harassment and know the implications for managers
- Understand how to respond to employees with AIDS
- Understand how personal circumstances outside the workplace might affect the well-being and productivity of employees
- Know about employee assistance programs and wellness programs

VIOLENCE

Fatalities and Injuries

In 1992, the federal Centers for Disease Control and Prevention (CDC) issued a report on workplace violence and labeled homicides at work as an epidemic.[4] The National Institute for Occupational Safety and Health reported in 1997 that homicide was second only to motor vehicle accidents as the cause of fatalities in the workplace.[5] Murder is the leading cause of death in the workplace for women. For men, homicide ranks second to automobile accidents. Table 12.1 presents a breakdown by level of government. Comparable statistics do not exist for nonprofit organizations.

TABLE 12.1   FATAL WORK INJURIES RESULTING FROM TRANSPORTATION INCIDENTS AND
HOMICIDES, 1992–1994

	Total (Number)	Transportation (Percent)	Homicide (Percent)
Federal Government			
U.S. Postal Service	36	77.3	22.7
Justice, Public Safety	893	58.7	41.3
National Security	627	97.6	2.4
Other	643	96.8	3.2
State Government			
Justice, Public Safety	199	77.8	22.2
Construction	42	100.0	0.0
Education	61	88.6	12.4
Other	269	93.9	6.1
Local Government			
Justice, Public Safety	1,588	60.2	39.8
Construction	146	100.0	0.0
Education	102	59.4	40.6
Other	672	94.1	5.9

Source: Bureau of Labor Statistics, Department of Labor, *Fatal Workplace Injuries in 1994: A Collection of Data and Analysis* (Washington DC: Government Printing Office, 1996).

Male public employees killed on the job are usually in transportation or a protective service occupation, such as police officer, firefighter, or prison guard. Female victims of homicide in the workplace are usually in administrative support or service positions.[6] Between 1983 and 1993, the U.S. Postal Service suffered ten separate episodes of murder by current or former employees, in which 29 postal workers were killed and 16 wounded. The term **postie** emerged to refer to a disgruntled and unstable employee who was violent toward co-workers. Going postal means going beserk.[7]

Since 1987, the federal Department of Justice has kept statistics of violence and theft in the workplace. It reports that almost one million employees each year are victims of rape, murder, and assault and that more than two million are victims of theft. While public employees make up approximately 18 percent of the total U.S. workforce, they constitute 30 percent of the victims of violence. On male victims, strangers commit 58 percent of the assaults. In contrast, co-workers, supervisors, and others whom they knew victimized 60 percent of the female victims.[8] This suggests that managers need to take steps to minimize the risks of violence both from within the public workforce and from those without, who are the ones being served, apprehended, or supervised. Sexual harassment as a distinct form of violence is discussed separately below.

The CDC provides a set of recommendations to employers and managers who have workers at risk of being robbed and assaulted by criminals external to their own workforce. These include installing good lighting and surveillance cameras and scheduling and limiting access to the facilities. To deal with potential violence employees perpetrate, managers need to be vigilant to symptoms of stress and anger among workers and establish conflict resolution and employee assistance programs (to be discussed). In addition to taking preventive measures, agencies should establish emergency management plans.[9] Managers should make use of specialists and resources to help employees deal with grief in the aftermath of traumas that do occur.[10]

California took the lead among state governments in recognizing and responding to workplace violence. In part, this was at the urging of a recommendation to take preventive measures that the federal Department of Labor made in a 1995 report to all states. The model set by California includes explicit policies prohibiting violence, a list of examples of prohibited conduct, and procedures for reporting and investigating incidents.[11] Local governments, too, are increasingly developing policies and procedures to address workplace violence.[12]

Sexual and Racial Harassment

Despite educational programs, rule promulgation, and disciplinary actions, sexual and racial harassment continues to plague workplaces. The federal Merit Systems Protection Board completed surveys in 1980, 1987, and 1994 and found virtually no change in the reports by federal employees of the incidence of sexual harassment. In both 1980 and 1987, 42 percent of the women and 14 percent of the men in the studies indicated they had been victims of sexual harassment. In 1994, 44 percent of the women and 19 percent of the men surveyed reported they experienced sexual harassment.[13] There has been a marked increase in the extent to which federal employees are aware of what sexual harassment is. As Table 12.2 indicates, the increases in the proportion of women, and especially men, who understand sexual harassment are generally in the 20 percent range when comparing 1980 and 1995. There appears to be some improvement in the federal government. Only 5 percent of the respondents to the 2005 survey conducted by the Merit System Review Board indicated they had been sexually harassed in the previous two years.[14]

A study of local governments in 1999 showed an increase in understanding of what sexual harassment is, but nonetheless a continuance of the problem.[15] One concern that continues is the lack of awareness among employees about what to do if they are harassed.[16]

Sexual harassment was formally identified as a prohibited and discriminatory employment practice in 1980, when the Equal Employment Opportunity Commission (EEOC) published rules on this subject. A provision of the 1991 Civil Rights Act prohibits racial harassment. As with the Civil Rights Act of 1964, these regulations cover all employers with 15 or more employees.

The behaviors listed in Table 12.2 can be categorized into two types of sexual harassment: **quid pro quo** and **hostile working environment**. Each type is distinct, substantively and legally.

Quid pro quo Quid pro quo harassment is when employment or an employment benefit is dependent on the provision of sexual favors. A manager or supervisor who solicits sexual favors through granting promotions, transfers, or continued employment is using his or her power in the work setting to coerce sex. In the landmark case, *Meritor Savings Bank* v. *Vinson* (1986), the plaintiff, Michelle Vinson, agreed to have

TABLE 12.2 UNDERSTANDING OF SEXUAL HARASSMENT AMONG MEN AND WOMEN IN THE FEDERAL GOVERNMENT

Type of Uninvited Behavior by a Supervisor	Percentage of Women Who Consider It Harassment		
	1980	1987	1994
Pressure for sexual favors	91	99	99
Deliberate touching, cornering	91	95	98
Suggestive letters, calls, materials	93	90	94
Pressure for dates	77	87	91
Suggestive looks, gestures	72	81	91
Sexual teasing, jokes, remarks	62	72	83
Percentage of Men Who Consider It Harassment			
	1980	1987	1994
Pressure for sexual favors	84	95	97
Deliberate touching, cornering	83	89	93
Suggestive letters, calls, materials	87	76	87
Pressure for dates	76	81	86
Suggestive looks, gestures	59	68	76
Sexual teasing, jokes, remarks	53	58	73
Type of Uninvited Behavior by a Co-worker	Percentage of Women Who Consider It Harassment*		
	1980	1987	1994
Pressure for sexual favors	81	98	98
Deliberate touching, cornering	84	92	96
Letters, calls, other materials	87	84	92
Pressure for dates	65	76	85
Suggestive looks, gestures	64	76	88
Sexual teasing, jokes, remarks	54	64	77
Percentage of Men Who Consider It Harassment			
	1980	1987	1994
Pressure for sexual favors	65	90	93
Deliberate touching, cornering	69	82	89
Letters, calls, other materials	76	67	81
Pressure for dates	59	66	76
Suggestive looks, gestures	47	60	70
Sexual teasing, jokes, remarks	42	47	64

*Based on the percentage of respondents who indicated that they "definitely" or "probably" would consider the identified behavior sexual harassment.

Source: U.S. Merit Systems Protection Board, Sexual Harassment in the Federal Workplace: Trends, Progress, Continuing Challenges (Washington, DC: Government Printing Office, 1996), 7.

sex with her supervisor out of fear of losing her job. In addition, Vinson was subjected to numerous instances of harassment while at work, including fondling and indecent exposure. The U.S. Supreme Court ruled that the fact that Vinson did have sex with her supervisor did not detract from the coercive nature of the relationship.

In 1998, the Court issued several rulings clarifying issues of employer liability in sexual harassment. According to *Faragher* v. *City of Boca Rotan* (1998), employers are liable if a supervisor engages in quid pro quo harassment, even if managers in the agency make efforts to inform supervisors and employees that such behavior is prohibited. On the other hand, if the hostile working environment forms of sexual harassment occur despite efforts of an employer to prevent it, there is no liability.[17] Also, in *Oncale* v. *Sundowner Offshore Services* (1998), the Court ruled that the laws on sexual harassment apply to individuals of the same sex as well as to parties of the opposite sex.

Hostile Work Environment   The creation of a hostile working environment for minorities and for women is another form of harassment and discriminatory treatment. Examples are when supervisors, co-workers, and/or customers use derisive remarks, jokes, visual displays, taunting, leering, and other behaviors to make an employee feel uncomfortable or degraded because of his or her race and/or sex. Key to the determination of whether a behavior is harassment is when it is repeated and unwanted. It is not, for example, harassment to ask a co-worker for a date. It is harassment, however, to continue to press for a date after the co-worker has made it clear that he or she is not interested. The intent of the policy is to prohibit coercion, not romance.

The reasonable person standard, from the victim's perspective, was applied in *Ellison* v. *Brady* (1991). Here the Court held that the definition of what was hostile should be derived from concerns and sensitivities that the victim might reasonably have. This case involved sexual harassment, but the principle applies as well to racial harassment. What may be a good-hearted joke or an inconsequential remark to some may be regarded as an insult to another. What is important here is both that there be deference to the perspective of the individual who is offended and that the victim make clear to others that he or she objects.[18]

Harris v. *Forklift Systems* (1993) further clarified some of the issues in hostile work environment harassment. The setting was a construction company, traditionally regarded as an organization where jobs are filled by men and where the culture is crude and macho. The owner of the company continually made sexual remarks (for example, "You are a dumb-ass woman" and "Let's go to the Holiday Inn to negotiate your raise") to Harris, a female employee. She complained and secured a promise that he would stop. When he nonetheless continued, she quit and filed a sexual harassment suit. The Court ruled in favor of Harris and in so doing consciously applied the reasonable person standard. In addition, the Court determined that Harris could sue even though she did not provide evidence of damage to her psychological or economic well-being.

While victims of sexual or racial harassment may seek legal redress, most do not. Fewer than 6 percent of those who experience harassment pursue a formal complaint. The more common reactions are to try to cope, to handle the situation informally, or simply to quit. Research indicates that the single most effective way for victims of harassment to get supervisors or coworkers to stop is to inform them firmly that their behavior is objectionable.[19]

While the confrontation of harassers appears to work fairly well, agency managers need to remember that employees do not shoulder the responsibility of ending harassment. Applicable EEOC rules place the responsibility for establishing a work environment free of sexual and racial harassment on management. The courts have, in contrast to quid pro quo cases, considered employer liability on work environment on a case-by-case basis. Generally, if managers do all that can reasonably be expected and harassment occurs nonetheless, then they will not be held liable.

What are managers expected to do?

- Have a written policy that prohibits racial and sexual harassment
- Provide a process where complaints can be made either through a supervisor or, if the direct supervisor or manager is guilty of the harassment, to a third party
- Distribute and publicize the policy and the process for handling complaints so all employees and supervisory staff will know it
- Dispose of complaints fairly and expeditiously
- Resolve problems in ways that do not further penalize the victim with transfers or reassignments that he or she does not want[20]

Consensual relations Genuinely romantic relationships can, of course, develop between an employee and his or her supervisor and between co-workers. Consensual relations within an agency raise several important issues, however.[21] Romantic relationships sometimes deteriorate. It is not unusual for a partner in a romantic relationship gone sour to act out his or her frustration and anger through hostility in the workplace. That could be especially troublesome if he or she had supervisory power over the other individual. Another potential issue created by romantic relations between people who work together is the substance or appearance of favoritism. Again, this can be a serious concern if one employee has supervisory authority over the other.

It does not seem fair or realistic to prohibit consensual, romantic relationships within an agency. Managers can, however, anticipate potential problems by requiring disclosure and by making arrangements so that neither party has supervisory responsibility or authority over the other. The power differential can become either harassment or favoritism, and neither is acceptable.

SAFETY

A critical safety concern is obviously the prevention of the kinds of violence discussed above. Agencies have followed the advice provided by the CDC to minimize the likelihood of physical attacks on employees. Policies and procedures that are well publicized to prevent sexual and racial harassment are important and are legally required.

Safety also applies to accidents and to hazards that occur in the workplace. Private sector and nonprofit employers must comply with the regulations promulgated by the Occupational Safety and Health Administration (OSHA) to ensure safe working environments. Public sector employers are not covered under these federal rules, although 23 states have voluntarily opted to commit their state and local governments to these standards. Such OSHA regulations range from safety guards on machines to floors and stairs that are not slippery, and from measures to ensure indoor air quality to designs to make office furniture and equipment safe.

Some have criticized and ridiculed OSHA for some of the regulations that go into minute detail or that anticipate improbable scenarios. From the mid-1970s to the mid-1980s, the staff at OSHA pursued a no-risk policy that intended to eliminate any possibility of a workplace injury or illness. That indeed led to imagining the unlikely and to requiring measures that were very expensive and cumbersome. In response to criticisms, OSHA changed its standards from no risk to safety. Whether or not an agency is formally committed to meeting OSHA standards, the regulations certainly provide guidance for managers.

It is commonplace in many private organizations, especially factory settings, to have worker safety committees.[22] Managers rely on these committees both to identify safety concerns and to design strategies for avoiding accidents and illnesses. All organizations could easily benefit from this model and could easily add the issue of safety to the agendas of quality teams or other already existing staff groups.

Smoking

Research findings that secondary smoke as well as smoking itself are health risks[23] have led employers to ban smoking in the workplace or to confine smoking to specific areas. Increasingly, jurisdictions are passing laws and ordinances limiting where one may smoke as a way of promoting public health, not just employee health. As of the summer of 2007, 19 states have enacted bans on smoking in all public places.[24] Some also see cost savings in limiting smoking because of the cleaning and maintenance required for smoke pollution.[25]

A dilemma for some employers is the need to respond to the assertion of rights by both smokers and nonsmokers. There have been cases in which nonsmokers have successfully sued for unemployment compensation when they have refused to work in a setting with secondary smoke. On the other hand, Virginia and Delaware prohibit public sector employers from discriminating against smokers, and 18 other states have similar laws applied to protect employers.[26] The general lesson to managers, regardless of the specifics of local laws, seems to be to design a policy and designate locations in a way that balances an individual's right to smoke when he or she is not working with the need to provide other employees and the public with an environment that is free of smoke.

HIV/AIDS

HIV/AIDS is a *perceived*, but not an actual, workplace safety issue, except for those directly providing relevant health care. Despite efforts to educate people about HIV/AIDS, employees continue to misunderstand how it is transmitted.[27] Understandably, people fear getting HIV/AIDS. Unfortunately, there is some confusion of HIV/AIDS with contagious diseases that are airborne or are easily caught when touching something that an individual with the disease has touched.

The challenge to managers is to remind and to reassure employees that transmission of HIV/AIDS does not occur through casual contact, but instead requires transmission through blood or semen, most commonly through sharing needles to give injections of drugs or through sexual activity. Clearly, employees in health care need to take precautions, but most other workplaces and personal interactions do not pose risks.

Managers are prohibited from taking personnel actions against persons who do have HIV/AIDS just because they have the disease. HIV/AIDS is a protected disability under the Americans with Disabilities Act of 1990. Thus, managers are obliged to make reasonable accommodations—as discussed in Chapter 11—for people with HIV/AIDS who are able to continue working.[28] Agencies may not dismiss or transfer someone with HIV/AIDS because of the fears of other employees. The appropriate response to these anxieties is to provide education and reassurance.[29]

Employees who do have HIV/AIDS are likely to go through an initial stage of depression and/or anger, which may be manifest at work in lower productivity and perhaps irritability. Treatment can require frequent visits to a doctor. Managers can accommodate staff members going through this by allowing flexible work hours, the opportunity for more than the usual number of breaks, and other schedule adjustments.[30] The fear and bigotry associated with HIV/AIDS challenge managers to ensure supportive work environments.

PERSONAL CARE

Employee Assistance Programs

Employee assistance programs (EAPs) provide counseling, treatment, and other services to help individuals who are in trouble. The scope of problems extending beyond job stress includes personal and family issues, such as grieving, marital difficulties, financial worries, and the like.[31] Without exception, these programs include help for those with alcohol or other drug abuse problems.[32] The services generally offered include:

- Alcohol and/or drug abuse
- Stress and emotional disorders
- Grieving
- Marital and family problems
- Legal counseling
- Smoking cessation and weight reduction
- Retirement counseling
- Outplacement counseling
- HIV/AIDS education and support groups
- Health risk screening
- Financial counseling[33]

Virtually all medium- to large-scale public employers have EAPs.[34] While some may establish EAPs as part of an effort to be a good and attractive employer, a common calculation is that it costs less to help a valued, experienced worker through some temporary difficulties than it does to hire and train replacements.[35]

Employees may initiate contact with an employee assistance office themselves, or a supervisor or manager can refer someone who shows symptoms of trouble. In many cases, the symptoms may stem from a combination of problems, such as marital difficulties and financial mismanagement or alcohol abuse and a gambling addiction. The first step for professionals in an employee assistance program is to diagnose the problem or problems, and then to prescribe treatment.

Employees who are participants in an EAP have the right to keep their ailments and their treatment confidential. Managers can sometimes find these privacy rights to be a source of frustration. Decisions about work schedules, the assignment of projects, and the use of temporary help depend on information about the implications of a treatment program. Providers of these services can let managers know what kinds of hours or work assignments are appropriate, but usually they cannot reveal the precise nature of the problems or the treatment.

Managers can tell an employee that he or she must seek medical or professional assistance and follow any prescribed treatment program in order to keep his or her job. The staff in an EAP can inform managers about whether or not an employee is cooperating and progressing satisfactorily, and the staff can provide estimates of when, if ever, the problems will be under control. EAPs are for rehabilitation, not termination. The latter can, however, be the outcome.[36]

Agencies can provide EAPs through a central office and/or through contracts with various health care, counseling, and financial services in the community. Only large-scale employers can afford to have their own employee assistance staff, and even then they may be supplemented with contractual arrangements with vendors. Contracts are the norm.

Wellness Programs

Wellness programs are preventive medicine. The intent here is to be proactive by encouraging employees to adopt a lifestyle of exercise, healthy eating, and stress reduction and therefore avoid the disruptions and costs of poor health and avoidable deaths. Insurance companies and the risk management pools established by smaller employers are often willing to underwrite the costs of wellness programs, thereby saving more expensive medical treatment later.[37] Some private sector employers require employees to be nonsmokers or to follow other healthy practices as a condition of employment. This is a rare practice and, for public employers, may be illegal unless directly and specifically job-related.

Wellness programs include education and awareness. Employees are informed or reminded about the importance of eating correctly and having good hygiene habits. Some of these efforts are general in nature, others may be tailored to the needs of specific employees. A popular topic for professional and managerial employees is stress management. These are programs that help individuals recognize and reduce their own stress.[38] Good eating, exercise, and other healthy habits help significantly to reduce stress. In addition, organizations can be structured and run to minimize stress on their employees. As with the importance of good health generally, organizational strategies tend to repeat what is often considered good management. Managers should make sure that employees know what their roles and responsibilities are and to develop opportunities to participate in organizational decision making.[39]

Another focus of wellness programs is physical exercise. Organizations have long sponsored sports teams among their employees. These are more a part of the human relations approach to organizations than they are examples of fitness programs because the major purpose of recreational teams is to foster organizational identity and pride in the employer. Fitness programs, on the other hand, are meant to include all employees and to be noncompetitive ways of maintaining health. They emphasize the benefits of doing aerobics, using weight and running machines, swimming, and jogging. In wellness programs, team sports like basketball and soccer tend to be pick-up activities rather than organized competition.

Large private companies sometime invest in facilities for their employees to participate in fitness programs, either directly at the worksite or through subsidizing membership in community clubs.[40] Government agencies and some nonprofit organizations risk political attacks when they pursue this same approach. Although there is general appreciation for the benefits of having employees who are healthy and fit, programs, facilities, and subsidized memberships are easily labeled as benefits that taxpayers and charitable donors should not have to fund.

Research indicates that those employees who participate in fitness programs and who use facilities are generally those who are most health-conscious and would find some way to work exercise routines into their lives, even without employer encouragement.[41] The most effective and the most acceptable wellness programs are those that are an integral part of an interventionist therapy that is part of an employee assistance program.[42] That would seem to be the top priority for managers seeking a healthier workforce. Even though making wellness programs and facilities generally available does not yield dramatic results, managers who are clever and committed enough to accomplish this will certainly gain some benefits and earn the gratitude of those employees who do participate.

FAMILY CARE

Family concerns and obligations can have a major impact on an employee's ability to get his or her job done.[43] This was noted in Chapter 11 and in the discussion of EAPs that help individuals deal with marital problems and with grieving. Another family circumstance that challenges employees is when a child, spouse, or older relative needs care. The federal Family and Medical Leave Act and similar state and local policies, discussed in Chapter 11, mandate that employers provide at least minimal amounts of leave for family needs.

Managers and employees can sometimes be very creative in arranging times and places for work in order to meet both job and family needs. **Flextime** is a term for allowing employees to vary their work schedule instead of using the traditional practice of requiring everyone to start and stop work at the same time. Employees in many jobs can alter their hours so they still do their work but leave early, leave late, and/or take a longer midday break so they can care for family members.[44] Similarly, **flexiplace**, the idea of doing work at home instead of at the office, is sometimes possible. Technological developments in electronic communications make flexiplace, or telecommuting, more feasible for some jobs now than it once was.

Managers and employees can be very creative in arranging times and places for work. For some jobs and some employees a regular early start or late finish may make sense, and schedules can be designed accordingly. Many professional and crafts jobs would allow for a **compressed workweek**, in which the employee works more than eight hours a day for one or more days, thereby completing the 40 hours each week outside the standard Monday through Friday framework. For some jobs, variation in schedule is possible on a daily basis. Managers in some agencies may find that they can better serve their customers by using flextime to extend the hours that the office is open, thus meeting the needs of individuals or businesses who find it difficult to go to the agency office during traditional, standard hours.

Another way in which employers help employees balance work and home obligations is in the provision of child care. The provision of child care at or near the worksite is ideal for many employees and employers. Transportation issues are obviously simplified. In addition, the inevitable call from a child care provider that requires a quick response and perhaps a trip to see the child is less disruptive if the service is provided at the worksite.[45] Other alternatives are to help employees locate child care services and perhaps include financial help for child care as an option in benefit plans. Given the general shortage of quality child care services, this kind of help is very valuable.

SUMMARY

Health and safety issues in personnel management are matters of public policy and of agency productivity. Public policy sets some minimal standards. Employers must make sure their employees are not subject to racial or sexual harassment. Although the regulations and standards of the federal Occupational Safety and Health Administration do not apply to government agencies, almost half of the states have committed their governments to comply, too. The federal Family and Medical Leave Act establishes an employment policy for the public and private sector that allows employees to take time off each year for family and health needs. The primary objective of these public policies is to provide basic standards for the health and safety of individuals in the workplace.

It is becoming commonplace for employers to respond to the needs of employees who are victims of violence or who are injured on the job or who are distracted by family problems. Many employers have gone beyond the legal mandates and provided employee assistance programs, wellness programs, paid leave for personal and family needs, and help with child care. Managers recognize that these programs contribute to productivity. Employees agree that these programs help make organizations attractive employers.

DISCUSSION QUESTIONS

1. Debate whether employers should pay for programs that address problems employees have that do not stem from their work or workplace.
2. Can managers ensure a workplace free of sexual harassment without violating individual privacy or without trying to end genuinely romantic relationships?

3. Do programs designed to help employees balance work and family needs inevitably create inequities for those employees without families?
4. What should managers do when they discover that one of their employees has HIV/AIDS?

Case Study:
Ensuring Supportive Work Environments

You are the manager of an agency in state government. Federal and state welfare reforms passed in 1996 and 1997 require welfare recipients to work. In order to make certain that jobs are available so these reforms can be implemented, you and other managers of state agencies have been instructed to fill vacancies whenever possible with welfare recipients. Accordingly, you have just offered a position as receptionist to Doris Brown.

Doris is a single parent of two children, ages 6 months and 2 years. She dropped out of high school when her first child was born and just recently earned her G.E.D. Doris has had three jobs previously, but only for periods of less than three months each. She was frequently late to work and sometimes did not go at all. The primary reason seems to be problems with her children. A neighbor provided care when she was at work, but the neighbor was not always reliable and last-minute arrangements sometimes had to be made. Also, although her older child does not have any chronic illness, he does get sick frequently.

One of your employees has informed you that several members of the staff are very upset with the appointment of Doris. They resent the process as one that in effect excluded people who are not on welfare, and they believe that welfare recipients are, with very few exceptions, people who are always trying to get something for nothing. Your informant fears that those opposed to this hire are likely to take out their feelings on Doris personally.

You recognize that receptionists are very vulnerable to the demands of other staff members. You can imagine a scenario where the receptionist is flooded with requests and demands from the staff and with a barrage of complaints about how she deals with the public, takes messages, makes appointments, and meets multiple deadlines. In short, there seems to be a strong possibility that Doris's co-workers will create a hostile working environment, one that may constitute racial and sexual harassment.

It is Wednesday afternoon. Doris is scheduled to begin work on Monday morning. You just received a message that she called and wants to talk with you about delaying her start because she has to take her oldest child to the doctor on Monday afternoon.

- What are your short-term and long-term concerns?
- What are your objectives?
- What will you do immediately?
- What are your more long-term strategies?

GLOSSARY

Compressed workweek A schedule in which employees work more than eight hours on some days in order to work fewer days in a week

Employee assistance programs A set of diagnostic, counseling, and therapeutic services offered by an employer to help employees address personal, financial, and other problems, regardless of whether they were caused by work or the work setting

Flexiplace Policy that allows employees to do some or all of their work at home; also known as telecommuting

Flextime Policy that allows employees to vary their work schedule from a standard workday or workweek

Hostile work environment A type of sexual or racial harassment in which supervisors and/or co-workers engage in repeated and unwanted gestures and activities that humiliate, deride, irritate, or otherwise mistreat one or more employees

Postie Name for an employee who takes out anger and frustration by being violent to co-workers. The term has its origins in a series of incidents involving disgruntled postal employees. This behavior is called going postal

Quid pro quo sexual harassment The type of harassment in which employment or an employment benefit is dependent on the granting of sexual favors

Wellness programs The provision of facilities, educational sessions, and activities designed to enable employees to have good general health

SOURCES

Seldon, Sally Coleman. (2003). Sexual harassment in the workplace. In S. W. Hays & R. C. Kearney, eds., *Public Personnel Administration: Problems and Prospects* (4th ed.). Englewood Cliffs, NJ: Prentice-Hall, 225–237.
Review of literature and issues on sexual harassment and a set of recommendations to managers.

Centers for Disease Control and Prevention, U.S. Department of Health and Human Services (1992). *Homicides in U.S. workplaces: A strategy for prevention and research.* Washington, DC: Government Printing Office.
A major report that brought attention to violence in work settings, including offices, and made recommendations for enhancing safety.

Erfurt, J. C., Foote, A., & Heirich, M. A. (1992). The cost-effectiveness of worksite wellness programs for hypertension control, weight loss, smoking cessation, and exercise. *Personnel Psychology* 42, 1 (January): 11–27.
A careful study and analysis of the value of employer wellness programs.

Green, G. M., & Baker, F. eds. (1991). *Work, health and productivity.* New York: Oxford University Press.
Essays that link health and safety issues to productivity and that offer prescriptions for improving workplace health and safety.

Kahn, Jeffrey P. & Langlieb, A. M. (2003). Mental health and productivity in the workplace: A handbook for organizations. San Francisco: Jossey Bass
A translation of research reports into lessons for managers about mental health issues.

Riccucci, Norma M. (2002). Managing diversity in public sector workforces. New York: Longman
A discussion of a broad spectrum of issues that managers face who are serious about having a productive, diverse workforce.

NOTES

1. Lloyd G. Nigro and William L. Waugh, Jr., "Violence in the American Workplace: Challenges to the Public Employer," *Public Administration Review* 56, no. 4 (July/August 1996): 326–333.

2. Frank Albers, "Preventive Measures Ease Workplace Violence," *PA Times* 19, no. 4 (April 1996): 2.

3. Consult the website of the federal Occupational Safety and Health Administration, www. osha. gov

4. Centers for Disease Control and Prevention, U.S. Department of Health and Human Services, *Homicides in U.S. Workplaces: A Strategy for Prevention and Research* (Washington, DC: Government Printing Office, 1992).

5. www. cdc. gov/ niosh/ violfs. html

6. Holly L. Howe, "Differences in Workplace Homicides by Sex, 1993," in Bureau of Labor Statistics, Department of Labor, *Fatal Workplace Injuries in 1994: A Collection of Data and Analysis* (Washington, DC: Government Printing Office, 1996), 22.

7. Felicity Barringer, "Postal Officials Examine System After Two Killings," *New York Times* (May 8, 1993), p. A7.

8. U.S. Department of Justice, *Violence and Theft in the Workplace* (Annapolis Junction, MD: Bureau of Justice Statistics Clearinghouse, 1994), 8–12.

9. Centers for Disease Control and Prevention, *Homicide in U.S. Workplaces*.

10. International Personnel Management Association, *Death in the Workplace* (Chicago: IPMA, 1996).

11. James S. Bowman and Christopher Jude Zigmond, "State Government Responses to Workplace Violence," *Public Personnel Management* 26, no. 2 (Summer 1997): 289–300.

12. Lloyd G. Nigro and William L. Waugh, Jr., "Local Government Responses to Workplace Violence," *Review of Public Personnel Administration* 18, no. 4 (Fall 1998): 5–17.

13. U.S. Merit Systems Protection Board, *Sexual Harassment in the Federal Workplace: Trends, Progress, Continuing Challenge* (Washington, DC: Government Printing Office, 1995), 33.

14. Merit System Review Board, *Accomplishing Our Mission: Results of the Merit System Principles Survey 2005*, www. mspb. gov

15. Bruce J. Eberhardt and Steven B. Moser, "Sexual Harassment in Small Government Units: An Investigation of Policies and Attitudes," *Public Personnel Management* 28, no. 3 (Fall 1999): 351–364.

16. Laura A. Reese and Karen E. Lindenberg, "Victimhood and the Implementation of Sexual Harassment Policy," *Review of Public Personnel Administration* 17, no. 1 (Winter 1997): 37–57.

17. See the ruling and discussion in *Burlington Industries* v. *Ellerth* (1998).

18. Thomas Li-Ping Tang and Stacie Leigh McCollum, "Sexual Harassment in the Workplace," *Public Personnel Management* 25, no. 1 (Spring 1996): 53–58.

19. U.S. Merit Systems Protection Board, *Sexual Harassment in the Federal Workplace*; Brian Stanko and Gerald J. Miller, "Sexual Harassment and Government Accountants: Anecdotal Evidence from the Profession," *Public Personnel Management* 25, no. 2 (Summer 1996): 219–236.

20. Jane H. Bayes and Rita Mae Kelly, "Managing Sexual Harassment in Public Employment," in Stephen W. Hays and Richard C. Kearney, eds., *Public Personnel Administration: Problems and Prospects*, 3rd ed. (Englewood Cliffs, NJ: Prentice-Hall, 1995), 217–231; S. L. Webb, *Sexual Harassment: Investigator's Manual* (Seattle: Premiere Publishing, Ltd., 1991).

21. Dennis L. Dresang and Paul J. Stuiber, "Sexual Harassment: Challenges for the Future," in Carolyn Ban and Norma M. Riccucci, eds., *Public Personnel Management: Current*

Concerns—Future Challenges (New York: Longman, 1991), 114–125; Robert E. Quinn, "Coping with Cupid: The Formation, Impact, and Management of Romantic Relations in Organizations," *Administrative Science Quarterly* 22, no. 1 (March 1977): 30–44; P. Horn and J. Horn, *Sex in the Office* (Reading, MA: Addison-Wesley, 1982).

22. Susan P. Baker, Ann H. Myers, and Gordon Smith, "Injury Prevention in the Workplace," in Gareth M. Green and Frank Baker, eds., *Work, Health, and Productivity* (New York: Oxford University Press, 1991), 86–99.

23. For a discussion of studies completed in the mid-1990s, see John Schwartz, "Secondhand Smoke Linked to Increased Heart Attack Rate," *Washington Post,* May 20, 1997.

24. Robert H. Elliott, "Contemporary Health Care Dilemmas and Public Personnel Management," in Hays and Kearney, eds., *Public Personnel Administration,* 267–268.

25. National Public Employer Labor Relations Association, *Newsletter* 8 (January 1986): 6.

26. D. H. Vaughn, "Smoking in the Workplace: A Management Perspective," *Employee Relations Law Journal* 18, no. 3 (Summer 1992): 123–139; F. D. Davenport, "The Legal Aspects of a Smoking Policy in the Workplace," *Industrial Management* (May/June 1989): 25–32.

27. K. B. Keeton, "AIDS-Related Attitudes Among Government Employees," Review of Public Personnel Administration 13, no. 2 (Spring 1993): 65–81.

28. James D. Slack, "The Americans with Disabilities Act and Reasonable Accommodations: The View from Persons with HIV/AIDS," *Policy Studies Journal* 29, 1 (Spring, 2002); R. H. Elliott and T. M. Wilson, "AIDS in the Workplace: Public Personnel Management and the Law," *Public Personnel Management* 16, no. 4 (Fall 1987): 209–219.

29. J. A. Johnson and W. J. Jones, "AIDS: Perspectives on Public Health, Policy, and Administration," *Public Administration Review* 51, no. 5 (September/October, 1991): 456–460.

30. James D. Slack, "AIDS and Disability Policy: How Can the Public Sector Prepare Itself?" in Ban and Riccucci, eds., *Public Personnel Management,* 139–154.

31. Pamela R. Johnson and Julie Indvik, "The Boomer Blues: Depression in the Workplace," *Public Personnel Management* 26, no. 3 (Fall 1997): 359–366.

32. Donald E. Klingner, Nancy G. O'Neill, and Mohamed Gamal Sabet, "Drug Testing in Public Agencies: Public Policy Issues and Managerial Responses," *Review of Public Personnel Administration* 10, no. 3 (Fall 1989): 3–68.

33. The Resource Survey, "79% of Companies have EAPs; Most Use Community Sources," *American Society for Human Resource Management/Resource* (April 1989): 2.

34. James D. Slack, "Chronic Health Challenges and the Public Workplace," in Norma M. Riccucci, ed., *Public Personnel Management: Current Concerns, Future Challenges*, 4th ed. (New York: Longman, 2006).

35. P. Stewart, "Investments in EAPs Pay Off," *Personnel Journal* 72, no. 1 (February 1993): 42–54; Fred Luthans and Robert Waldersee, "What Do We Really Know About EAPs?" *Human Resource Management* 28, no. 2 (Spring 1989): 385–401.

36. A. T. Johnson and N. O'Neill, "Employee Assistance Programs and the Troubled Employee," *Review of Public Personnel Administration* 9, no. 3 (Summer 1989): 66–80.

37. W. Wells, "Employee Wellness: TIAA-CREF's Rx for Good Living," *Personnel* 66, no. 1 (January 1989): 7–9.

38. Philip J. Dewe, "Examining the Nature of Work Stress: Individual Evaluations of Stressful Experiences and Coping," *Human Relations* 42, no. 7 (July 1989): 993–1013.

39. R. Weigel and S. Pinsky, "Managing Stress: A Model for the Human Resource Staff," *Personnel Administrator* (February 1982): 56–60; John M. Ivancevich and Michael T. Matteson, "Optimizing Human Resources: A Case for Preventive Health and Stress Management," *Organizational Dynamics* (Fall 1980): 4–25.

40. Jack N. Kondrasuk, "Corporate Physical Fitness Programs," *Personnel Administrator* (December 1984): 75–80.

41. Deborah L. Gebhardt and Carolyn E. Crump, "Employee Fitness and Wellness Programs in the Workplace," *American Psychologist* 45, no. 4 (Fall 1990): 262–272; David A. Harrison and Laurie Z. Liska, "Promoting Regular Exercise in Organizational Fitness Programs: Health-Related Differences in Motivational Building Blocks," *Personnel Psychology* 47, no. 1 (January 1994): 47–71.

42. John C. Erfurt, Andrea Foote, and Max A. Heirich, "The Cost-Effectiveness of Worksite Wellness Programs for Hypertension Control, Weight Loss, Smoking Cessation, and Exercise," *Personnel Psychology* 42, no. 1 (January 1992), 11–27.

43. Pamela R. Johnson and Julie Indvik, "The Organizational Benefits of Assisting Domestically Abused Employees," *Public Personnel Management* 28, no. 3 (Fall 1999): 236–374; Soonhee Kim, "Organizational Culture and New York State Employees' Work-Family Conflict: Gender Differences in Balancing Work and Family Responsibilities," *Review of Public Personnel Administration* 18, no. 2 (Spring 1998): 57–72.

44. Jon L. Pierce, John W. Newstrom, Randall B. Dunham, and Alison E. Barber, *Alternative Work Schedules* (Boston: Allyn and Bacon, 1989); Barbara S. Romzek, "Balancing Work and Nonwork Obligations," in Ban and Riccucci, eds., *Public Personnel Management*, 207–224.

45. Edward L. Suntrup, "Child-Care Delivery Systems in the Government Sector," *Review of Public Personnel Administration* 10, no. 1 (Fall 1989): 48–59.

Chapter 13

Discipline and Dismissal

A federal employee became angry with his supervisor, grabbed a baseball bat that someone brought for a picnic after work, and began beating his supervisor with the bat. The agency promptly fired the employee. The employee appealed the dismissal. After almost a year of hearings and arguments, the appeal board ruled that the agency had not given adequate notice of its intent to fire the employee and ordered that the employee be given eight months back pay and be reinstated in his former position—under the same supervisor![1]

Employees of an agency of a state government could not believe it when they learned their state's personnel board had just ordered that someone who had been fired for stealing equipment from the agency had to be reinstated in his old job. The employee had, over a period of several years, altered invoices, stolen expensive equipment, and sold that equipment to supplement his state salary. The available evidence was sufficient for the Internal Revenue Service to sustain a conviction for income tax evasion, but apparently did not meet the dismissal standards of the personnel board.

Anecdotes like these obviously do not create a positive image either of public employees or public personnel management. Although no personnel management system can be expected to screen out all potential crooks, insubordinates, and incompetents at the selection stage, it is hard to understand why, once those individuals have been identified, they cannot be dismissed. In the minds of many, civil service is synonymous with job security, regardless of job performance. Is it because managers lack the intent and courage to fire? Or, do rules and procedures tie the hands of managers? Is it easier to fire employees in nonprofit organizations?

LEARNING OBJECTIVES OF THIS CHAPTER

- Understand the distinctions between at will, contract, and indefinite status employment
- Know the different grounds, criteria, and procedures for disciplining employees
- Understand the appeals process available to employees who have been disciplined
- Know the restrictions on retaliation against employees who win appeals

HISTORICAL DEVELOPMENTS

Few public employees are, in fact, dismissed each year. Out of the two million federal civilian employees, between 0.2 and 0.4 percent are dismissed each year. In contrast, about 9 percent each year resign or retire.[2] Figures for state and local governments are comparable.

The founders of the merit system did not anticipate this pattern of so few dismissals. The Pendleton Act of 1883 provided that employees should not be dismissed because of political affiliation but did not go on to stipulate job security in the face of poor performance, rule violation, or the like. What in the mid-twentieth century was perceived as overprotection of employees to the detriment of management and accountability began as an imbalance that neglected employee rights. It was not, for example, until passage of the Lloyd-LaFollette Act of 1912 that a standard was established for the dismissal of federal civil servants. According to the act, federal employees can be removed or suspended without pay "only for such cause as will promote the efficiency of the service." This is a vague standard, but it established the basic principle that the burden of proof is on managers to show that dismissal is warranted.

Missing from the Lloyd-LaFollette Act was any procedure allowing employees to appeal a disciplinary action. In a sense, employees secured a right but no meaningful way of ensuring its application. The Veterans Preference Act of 1944 provided veterans with an appeal procedure and a right to reinstatement in their former job if, on appeal, it was determined that they were not dismissed for proper cause or according to proper procedure. Other employees could appeal dismissals, demotions, and suspensions, but the decisions of appeal boards were only advisory to the agencies. President John F. Kennedy, with the promulgation of Executive Orders 10987 and 10988 in 1962, extended to all federal civil servants the rights that veterans had enjoyed. The 1978 Civil Service Reform Act gave statutory status to these and related orders.

Most state and local governments established standards for dismissals and neutral appeal processes before the federal government. By the late 1930s, many states and large municipalities adopted codes that permit dismissal and demotion only when there is **just cause**. As is the case in the federal government, the employer shoulders the burden of proving that what the employee has or has not done is serious enough to warrant disciplinary action.

Standards specifying grounds for dismissal or other serious discipline were followed by procedures intended to ensure that employees knew their rights and had an opportunity to exercise them. These procedures, as sometimes happens in other areas of management, over time took on an importance and a life of their own. There is abundant anecdotal evidence about instances where the burdens of dismissing an employee are so great that managers have resorted to other ways of dealing with the situation. Some managers have hired additional staff to get needed work done and simply carried the nonproductive employee(s) without giving them any work. Other managers have reorganized their agencies, either to define a position out of existence—thereby allowing a nondisciplinary layoff—or to wrest authority from the unsatisfactory employee and give it to someone else. The problems managers face in dismissing employees, in other words, can present multiple burdens and costs to the agency.

An imbalance occurs when employees are favored to the detriment of agencies and when procedure overshadows purpose. This chapter explains how this imbalance emerged and goes on to describe efforts begun in the late 1970s to provide government managers with a meaningful opportunity to use discipline when appropriate without depriving employees of their rights to due process. Some of these efforts were based on an appreciation of the differences between discipline for improper behavior and action in response to low productivity. Other efforts revisited the distinctions between types of job security.

TYPES OF JOB SECURITY

Most individuals do not have the kind of **indefinite employment** that developed for civil service positions in government. The prevailing terms of service are **contractual** and **at will**. While most positions in government are civil service, some are for fixed terms (i.e., contractual), and some are at the pleasure of a senior official (i.e., at will). There are some notable and relatively recent exceptions. Georgia removed state employees from civil service and made them at will employees, effective in 1996. Florida soon followed with 16,300 of their positions in state government, and the federal government applied this principle when creating the Department of Homeland Security in 2002. For nonprofit (and profit) organizations, most employees are either at will or work on a contractual basis.

Employment contracts are usually for one year and typically renewed annually. Nonprofit and government agencies that get grants or contracts to complete certain projects will often hire employees for the duration of the project. Some organizations give multiyear contracts to long-term employees. The terms of contracts might be negotiated.

At will status means that the employer may terminate an individual's employment at any time. It is common to give someone two weeks (or a similar, rather short period) notice that their job is being terminated. The idea behind at will employment is that the employer does not have to have any reason—good or bad—to sever someone from the workforce. Generally, nonprofit organizations offer contracts to senior level managers and professionals and at will employment to others.

The basic descriptions of contractual and at will employment need to be qualified. Employers are not free to fire employees for any reason they like. There are some reasons that are unlawful.[3] For example, firings based on race, gender, religion, or national origin are prohibited. Likewise, nonprofit organizations (but not government agencies) are prohibited from firing someone because they are over 40 years old. It is illegal to terminate employees to avoid paying pensions or to punish them for testifying in court proceedings, blowing the whistle on illegal activity, organizing unions, or serving on a jury. In short, there are public policies designed to serve some general public purposes and to bestow certain individual rights that qualify the discretion available to managers terminating employees who serve at will or are in the midst of a contractual period. The restrictions on employment are found not only in federal laws and court rulings, but in the statutes of 44 states.[4]

Employee manuals or handbooks can also curtail the discretion of managers when disciplining and firing employees. Courts and state laws regard the statements in handbooks as a contract, although employers can sometimes evade promises about grounds for dismissal and appeal rights if they also have a written disclaimer somewhere in the document.[5] Contradictory statements are resolved by the disclaimer, or by issuing a revised handbook.

As will be explained in greater detail, government employers do have to meet the special demands of just cause when dismissing employees. Governments may not take people's property or liberty without good reason. This constitutional principle applies to the jobs of government employees. Nonprofit organizations do not have to meet this standard, but they do not have an unfettered right to terminate contracts or to dismiss at will employees. They can have good and bad reasons for what they do, but they cannot have illegal reasons.

WHY FIRE EMPLOYEES?

There are two basic reasons that are acceptable, legally and managerially, for dismissing employees: (1) the violation of a rule, policy, or procedure, and (2) unsatisfactory performance. These distinctions are not always made in statutes or contracts, but they nonetheless have important effects on how employees and disciplinary actions are handled.

Rule, Policy, or Procedural Violations

Violations of rules, policies, and procedures can be minor or major. Minor violations do not justify firing an employee unless those violations are committed frequently and after warnings that continued infractions will result in penalties. An employee who, without permission, does not report for work violates a rule in virtually every organization. A single incident of this nature may justify a warning or reprimand. Successive incidents, however, call for suspension without pay and even dismissal. On the other hand, most would agree that assaulting a supervisor with a baseball bat and stealing expensive equipment should result in immediate dismissal. Supervisors should not have to endure several beatings before getting rid of an employee! Box 13.1 lists examples of violations according to degrees of severity, based on a survey of common practices in public and private sector employment.

Table 13.1 illustrates progressive disciplinary steps usually taken in response to various rule violations by employees. Progressive discipline is not only a matter of good policy but is also necessary in most governmental jurisdictions if, on appeal, a manager's decisions are to be upheld. In personnel management, in other words, one must abide by the general principle of justice that the punishment must fit the crime.

Poor Performance

Sometimes, there is no crime to punish. At first blush, employees who cannot keep up with the duties and responsibilities of the job seem to deserve to be replaced just as much as the employees who beat their supervisor. Poor performance, however, could

---

BOX 13.1

**TYPES OF OFFENSES CAUSING DISMISSAL
ACTION IN ORDER OF PERCEIVED SEVERITY**

1. *Actions most frequently causing dismissal on first offense*

   Theft
   Falsifying employment record
   Possession of narcotics
   Possession of firearms or other weapons
   Fighting
   Criminal activity
   Intoxication at work

2. *Actions most frequently causing dismissal after second offense*

   Sleeping on the job
   Abusive or threatening language to supervisor (insubordination)
   Gambling

3. *Actions most frequently causing dismissal after third offense*

   Horseplay
   Leaving without permission

4. *Actions most frequently causing dismissal after fourth offense*

   Carelessness
   Chronic Absenteeism
   Unexcused absence
   Unexcused and excessive lateness

Source: Adapted from Bureau of National Affairs, *Employee Conduct and Discipline* (Washington, DC: Bureau of National Affairs, 1973), 6.

TABLE 13.1   TYPICAL PROGRESSION OF DISCIPLINARY ACTION FOR SAMPLE OFFENSES

Offense	First Offense	Second Offense	Third Offense	Fourth Offense
Theft	Discharge			
Sleeping on the job	Warning	Discharge		
Leaving without permission	Warning	Suspension	Discharge	
Unexcused absence	Warning	Warning	Suspension	Discharge

Source: Adapted from Bureau of National Affairs, *Employee Conduct and Discipline* (Washington, DC: Bureau of National Affairs, 1973), 6.

be the result of a number of different causes. It may be both more cost-effective and more humane to address those causes rather than to react to the poor performance itself.

The bottom line has to be that the job gets done. This, however, does not mean that all employees who cannot or do not do their job will be fired. When managers confront an employee who is not performing satisfactorily it is essential to identify the cause or causes for that performance.[6] Appropriate remedies, such as training or counseling, may be available, and discipline can be avoided. If there are no such remedies or if efforts to improve performance fail, then demotion or dismissal is necessary and justified.

These principles can be illustrated by discussing some of the frequent causes of poor performance and relating them to a hypothetical employee.

Personal Problems

Employees are not only members of an agency's workforce, they are also members of families, social and political groups, and private-sector economic entities. If Janet Jones, a civil engineer in a state's department of transportation, is turning in work late and with a number of miscalculations, an interview with her may well reveal that she is currently preoccupied with the trauma that often occurs when a person learns that a loved one is terminally ill. Disciplining Janet would not seem appropriate, and few would seriously consider such action in this situation. Instead, suggesting a vacation might be best. If she is giving care to the ill relative or partner, perhaps she should take advantage of the 1993 Family and Medical Leave Act. Some professional counseling could be appropriate for Ms. Jones.[7] It may be possible to assign her less demanding tasks, at least on a temporary basis.

A more creative and sensitive response than initiating disciplinary action can be better both for the employee and the agency. A manager might be better off waiting for a good employee to adjust to a disruptive personal situation than replacing that employee and incurring the time and financial expenditures to select and train a new one. Harsh reactions are, in addition, likely to lower morale among other employees. They will probably identify with the misfortunes of the employee rather than the arbitrary standards of a manager.

On the other hand, it is essential to recognize when personal problems are not being resolved and continue to affect work performance adversely. If Janet's family problem were deteriorating marital relations, rather than someone's terminal illness, the same kinds of reactions—vacation, new assignments, counseling—may help her resolve the situation and return to a satisfactory level of productivity. She may not, however, be able to resolve her personal problems. In that case, progressive action, with warnings, suspension, a demotion if that is possible and appropriate, and finally dismissal, may be proper and necessary.

Alcohol and Drug Abuse

Alcohol and drug abuse present other examples of when counseling and assistance are appropriate initial responses and, if not effective, discipline, including dismissal, may be necessary. A number of employers, recognizing the frequency of alcohol and drug abuse problems and the costs to employees and the agency, have established formal, identifiable assistance programs.[8]

The state government of Massachusetts uses an approach that follows a standard model. Supervisors receive training in the procedures and structure of the program and in the detection of symptoms of alcohol and drug abuse. Employees are informed about the employee assistance program (EAP) through notices and during new employee orientation. If a supervisor suspects an employee is having an alcohol or drug abuse problem, the supervisor sends that employee to an office for counseling and perhaps diagnosis and treatment. Employees can also refer themselves to this office. Once employees begin counseling and treatment, the details of their participation are kept confidential, except for guidelines that may be given to a supervisor when work responsibilities become part of the prescribed therapy. Also, a supervisor who regards continued unsatisfactory work performance as warranting disciplinary action can secure information on whether an employee faithfully participated in the prescribed program. EAPs were discussed in Chapter 12.

As in the case of family problems, counseling and professional help may not be effective. At some point, managers may have to fulfill their responsibility to the organization and the general public by terminating or demoting the employee. It is invariably difficult to know when that point has been reached. It is difficult, as well, to add to someone's problems by disciplining the person. Nonetheless, it may be necessary.

Sexual Harassment

Janet Jones, the civil engineer whose performance has suddenly deteriorated, may have a different problem. Her poor performance may be due to sexual harassment. Her work environment, in other words, may cause the personal problem. Women who must endure verbal abuse in the form of ridicule and who are referred to by four-letter words understandably lose the concentration and enthusiasm necessary for quality work performance. This situation is obviously worse when the abuse includes demands for sexual favors or actual sexual assault.

Clearly, if sexual harassment is Janet's problem, then the disciplinary action should be aimed not at Janet but at the individual or individuals doing the harassing. Sexual harassment involves issues unique to other instances that call for disciplinary action. A more detailed discussion of sexual harassment appeared in Chapter 12.

Competence

Janet Jones may, of course, not be suffering from a personal problem at all. It may be that she has not kept up with developments within her profession. If that is true, then training rather than dismissal is probably the best response. It may be that the hypothetical department of transportation has acquired a mission that is somewhat different but has not reorganized to accomplish the new responsibilities. Janet may be one of a number of employees who has been assigned a combination of duties and responsibilities that is not easily fulfilled. Her work performance may be a symptom of an organizational rather than an individual problem.

These possibilities point away from discipline and dismissal, but they, too, may simply be a prelude to dismissal. Janet may, despite training opportunities, be unable to keep up with her profession. Perhaps this means she should be demoted. That, in turn, assumes the agency has a position to which she could be demoted and still make a worthwhile contribution. If the agency must reorganize in order to assume new responsibilities, the new structure may not include a position for someone with the knowledge, skills, and abilities of Janet Jones.

The world is complex, and dismissing employees is no panacea. A variety of factors can cause poor performance. In fact, in many individual cases there is more than one factor. Janet Jones could have a personal, family problem that is precipitating a drug abuse problem, and she could simultaneously be falling behind with the technological developments in the field of civil engineering. Janet Jones could also be lazy and incompetent. The mistake could have been to hire her in the first place. Managers must assess each situation carefully, sensitively, and creatively.

Managers can design **performance improvement plans** for employees who are having difficulties getting their work done. These plans can serve as an effective way of addressing performance problems, regardless of the cause or causes, and as a way of generating documentation that can support discipline or dismissal if that is necessary. A performance improvement plan establishes specific, attainable goals and objectives that the employee must meet by a specific time and delineates any training or treatment programs that the employee is expected to complete, if such programs are relevant. Employees are more closely supervised when they are in such a plan and they are evaluated more frequently so that everyone has a good idea of the progress being made.

It is important to have grounds for placing an employee on a performance improvement plan. If there is no justification and the employee eventually gets fired, the manager is at risk of being charged with engineering a **constructive discharge.** This term refers to a situation where a manager predetermines that he or she is going to dismiss a particular employee and then sets unreasonable objectives and aggressively and intently supervises that employee to generate documentation to be used to justify the discharge. In short, the manager is setting the employee up to fail. Constructive discharges typically do not withstand judicial scrutiny if they are challenged.

Managers must remember that their primary responsibility must be to keep the agency running as effectively and efficiently as possible. The act to dismiss is weighted in favor of agency interests; the procedures required to take this action favor employee rights.

DISCIPLINARY PROCESSES

Due Process

The right of public employees to due process when they are the subject of serious disciplinary action is relatively new. Prior to 1972, the U.S. Supreme Court applied the **doctrine of privilege** to public employees. According to this doctrine, individuals were expected to regard employment in the public sector as an honor—as an opportunity to serve. Government workers had to accept the terms and conditions of employment provided by their employers even if these terms deprived employees of some of the constitutional protections other citizens enjoyed. The Court was particularly adamant that public employees who were dismissed or demoted had no constitutional right to hearings or appeals or other procedural protections. These rights were available only if the employer specifically provided them.

The Court established a new standard for itself with two rulings in 1972: *Board of Regents* v. *Roth* and *Perry* v. *Sinderman*. The new standard became known as the **doctrine of substantial interest**. In the first case, David Roth, who was hired as an instructor on a one-year contract, claimed that the University of Wisconsin–Whitewater had deprived him of his constitutional rights when it did not renew his contract and refused to explain why or to allow him to appeal the action. Roth argued that the Fourteenth Amendment to the U.S. Constitution provides that agencies of state governments may not deprive someone of life, liberty, and property without due process. Roth said the Court needed to expand the traditional definition of property to include jobs because they were functional equivalents to land and equipment as a source of wealth in modern economies. Roth went on to reason that liberty should include reputation as an employee because a bad reputation could keep one from moving to another employer. He argued that when the campus administration refused to renew his contract and refused to provide any reasons for the action, his professional reputation was tarnished, and he no longer had the liberty to seek similar employment in an unfettered manner.

The Court accepted Roth's reasoning but came to a different conclusion. The Court agreed that employment involved the kinds of liberty and property interests that Roth identified. The Court said that where such "substantial interests" exist there must be due process protections. However, the Court did not see the existence of such interests where a one-year contract was the basis for employment. The property was only promised for one year and the expiration of a contract does not threaten liberty or reputation.

In *Perry* v. *Sindermann,* the Court had opportunity to apply the doctrine of substantial interest articulated in the *Roth* decision. Robert Sindermann had been an employee of Odessa Junior College for four years and previously worked two years at the University of Texas and four years at San Antonio Junior College. Although Odessa Junior College did not have a formal tenure system, Sindermann felt that because he had been "employed as a teacher in the state college and university system for seven years or more" he qualified for "some form of job tenure."[9]

When he was told his employment had been terminated but not provided with reasons for the action or a chance to appeal the decision, the Court reasoned he was deprived of liberty and property without due process. The Court ordered that the College have a hearing to determine whether Sindermann should be dismissed. After the hearing, the College reinstated Sinderman as a member of its faculty.

It is important to note that the doctrine of substantial interest is based on a provision of the Constitution that limits what government can do to individuals. Thus, this doctrine does not apply to nonprofit organizations or to private-sector employers. It only applies to governments as employers.

Several years after the *Roth* and *Perry* decisions, the Court made it clear that it would use a somewhat restrictive definition of liberty and property interests.

In *Bishop* v. *Wood* (1976), the Court did not set aside the dismissal of a police officer despite the fact that his employer refused to arrange a hearing. The Court based this ruling on its reading of city regulations, which did not appear to provide city employees with a right to be retained. There was, in other words, no property interest. Thus, if jurisdictions do not provide in their laws for job security for public employees, then the Court may be reluctant to find a substantial property interest. The employee, in such situations, would have to show a threat to a liberty interest, that is, a reputation and record that will prevent one from securing employment somewhere.[10]

The Court expressed in *Bishop* v. *Wood* its desire to minimize its own involvement in personnel management:

> The federal court is not the appropriate forum in which to review the multitude of personnel decisions that are made by public agencies. We must accept the harsh fact that numerous individual mistakes are inevitable in the day-to-day administration of our affairs. . . . The Due Process clause of the Fourteenth Amendment is not a guarantee against incorrect or ill-advised personnel decisions.[11]

Most jurisdictions do, in fact, provide in their laws and regulations for employee job security. It is common for governments to require that dismissal and other serious discipline occur within the framework of due process. Also, in virtually all instances where collective bargaining is allowed, contract provisions include the right to due process whenever disciplinary action is taken.

According to due process, employees must:

1. Be informed of why an action is being taken against them
2. Be given the right to question the evidence and/or witnesses used to support the disciplinary action
3. Have the opportunity to appeal management's decision

Some statutes and collective bargaining agreements restrict the scope of due process rights, especially the right of appeal, by specifying certain circumstances under which an individual would be disqualified from securing or retaining a position in government. The most common bases for nonappealable disqualifications are being convicted in a criminal court of a felony or not complying with requirements that government employees must be residents of the community.

Appeal Processes

Usually there are four basic steps employees must follow when they want to appeal a firing or other serious disciplinary action. Some jurisdictions and organizations specify more steps than others.[12] Ideally, the number of steps is enough to facilitate communication within an agency about who is being disciplined and why. Also, it is important to allow for a quick resolution of the dispute. Generally, if an employee is not satisfied after two appeals, both the agency and the employee are better served by getting a final resolution. Little is served by forcing employees to move up every rung of an organizational ladder with their appeal. The four steps follow.

1. Informal conference with immediate supervisor. Although this step stresses the need for an informal discussion between employees being disciplined and their supervisor, the step itself is formally recognized and usually recorded in notes or a memorandum. Informality is needed initially to open communication and perhaps get a change in supervisory action and/or the kind of understanding that will end the appeal right away.

2. Formal, written appeal to immediate supervisor.   If an employee is not satisfied after step 1, then he or she files a written appeal, specifying what he or she is unhappy about and why. The immediate supervisor then responds in writing to this appeal.

3. Formal, written appeal to agency head.   This step facilitates communication within the agency, and, importantly, allows the agency head to set and/or rearticulate agency policy by ruling on appeals from supervisory decisions.

4. Formal, written appeal to personnel board, arbitrator, or other third party.   Some jurisdictions specify that agency head decisions on some or all appeals are final, but most provide for appeals outside the agency to a personnel board/civil service commission, hearing examiner, or arbitrator. Collective bargaining pacts invariably provide for arbitration. Until the 1978 Civil Service Reform Act, the final appeal body in the federal government was the Civil Service Commission. This commission was also expected to act as the personnel management arm of the president, and thus could hardly be regarded as a neutral third party.[13] The 1978 legislation separated the appeals process from the personnel management operations. It established the Merit Systems Protection Board for the former and the Office of Personnel Management for the latter. Both for symbolic as well as substantive purposes, the neutral third-party identity of the final appeals body is important.

In many jurisdictions, the appeal mechanisms available to employees have been more like a maze than the rather simple four-step model just presented.[14] Before reforms in the late 1970s, it was not uncommon to have separate appeals systems for agency rules, for the merit system, for equal employment opportunity policies, for union contract provisions, and for unemployment and worker's compensation. Confusion reigned in even simple disciplinary cases, where employees had to determine the category of offense for which they were being penalized and then file the appeal through that channel. Most cases are not simple, however.

A majority of cases involve more than one issue. One might have, for example, a Latino employed as a mechanic for a state's department of natural resources who is being demoted and transferred involuntarily from the central headquarters motor pool to a regional office. The disciplinary charges state that he repeatedly violated department safety regulations concerning the use and care of tools, he accumulated a record of excessive, unexcused absences, and his work occasionally was faulty and had to be done over. The violation of department safety rules is appealable to the agency head, but no further. The collective bargaining contract negotiated by his union covers demotions and transfers and the allegations of unexcused absences and unsatisfactory work performance. Our mechanic might contend that the selection process did not treat him fairly in recent competition for a promotional appointment; this would be under the jurisdiction of the state's director of personnel. As a Latino, he can charge discriminatory treatment and gain access to the Equal Employment Opportunity appeals process. Which appeal route should he choose? There are usually prohibitions against pursuing more than one route simultaneously, although it is possible to pursue an alternative route if unsuccessful in an initial appeal.

An important consideration in deciding which of several available appeal routes to pursue is the set of time limits attached to each route. To facilitate resolution of disputes, appeals systems include deadlines. Step 2 in the model presented earlier, for example, may have to occur within ten days of Step 1, and Step 3 within ten days of Step 2. If the department of natural resources employee thinks that his best chance is to allege discrimination, but then loses in that forum, he may have missed the deadlines for pursuing some or all of the other appeal options.

Typically, the longest time periods are used in equal employment opportunity appeals and the shortest in collective bargaining agreements. When part-time citizen boards, like personnel boards or civil service commissions, hear appeals, time limits are treated as guidelines. Typically, these bodies have considerable backlogs, sometimes requiring waits of over a year.

In 2007 the U.S. Supreme Court reversed lower court decisions on a pay discrimination case because of deadlines. In *Ledbetter* v. *Goodyear*, a key issue was whether the beginning of a pattern of pay discrimination determined when the clock started ticking on the 180-day time limit to sue or whether each time pay was set constituted the start of the clock. Lilly Ledbetter was able to convince lower courts that Goodyear consistently paid her low wages because she was a woman. But a divided Supreme Court accepted Goodyear's argument and ruled against Ledbetter because she did not file her case 180 days after the discriminatory treatment began.

When a dismissal is in the appeals process, the agency manager must decide whether to keep the employee on the job, hold the job vacant, or hire a replacement. Keeping the employee on the job can cause morale problems and be very disruptive to an agency's activities. Likewise, holding a position vacant pending the appeal and thereby increasing the workload of other employees is not desirable.

In *Sampson* v. *Murray* (1974), the U.S. Supreme Court ruled that it is not necessary to keep an employee on the job while an appeal is pending unless the employee can show irreparable harm. The Court further ruled that loss of pay does not constitute irreparable harm unless there are no provisions for a back-pay award if the employee wins. Back-pay awards can be expensive and, in any case, the process of reinstating employees after they win an appeal is uncomfortable and disruptive at best. Nonetheless, reinstatement and back pay are usually preferred to keeping a dismissed employee on the job pending an appeal or holding a job vacant during an appeal.

In short, both employees and employers have an interest in as simple and expeditious an appeals process as possible. A confusing maze of possible appeal routes can lead to missed deadlines and miscalculations about the best course to pursue. Overlapping jurisdictions among appeals bodies tend to divert attention from matters of justice to issues over turf. Lengthy and cumbersome processes are disruptive to agencies and can have the effect of making any decision too late to be meaningful to employees.[15]

Personnel management reform efforts of the late 1970s included provisions to simplify and expedite appeals. Single routes of appeal, regardless of the bases for disciplinary actions, were not possible where there are collective bargaining agreements.

Discrimination, agency rules, personnel director regulations, and unsatisfactory performance can, on the other hand, be merged into a single system. The special concerns of discrimination can be accommodated by allowing review of the record by a separate body, and decisions could be made through the common appeals system. In other words, the department of natural resources mechanic could pursue those issues covered under the collective bargaining contract through the process provided in that contract (probably contact immediate supervisor to agency head to arbitrator) while at the same time pursuing all other issues through the common appeals process (immediate supervisor to agency head to personnel board/commission or examiner). If this employee is not satisfied with the personnel board/commission decision and thinks that he is the victim of ethnic discrimination, then he can ask the equal employment opportunity body to review the case. Their review is not based on a new and independent investigation and set of hearings; instead, the ruling is based on the record that has already accumulated. Figure 13.1 illustrates the appeal routes.

The courts are, of course, available for further appeal, although they generally do not take appeals from government bodies unless there are constitutional issues involved or if there are charges of procedural violations. Courts have been directed by legislators not to overturn a ruling when there have been procedural mistakes unless those mistakes can be shown to have had harmful effects.

An important feature of the reforms of the late 1970s was the discretion provided to government personnel boards/commissions and examiners to amend disciplinary actions. Prior to these reforms, most public sector appeal bodies had to either accept or reject the action taken against an employee. An appeal body that believed a government employee should be disciplined but thought that dismissal was too harsh would either have to accept that harsh penalty or overturn the entirety of the

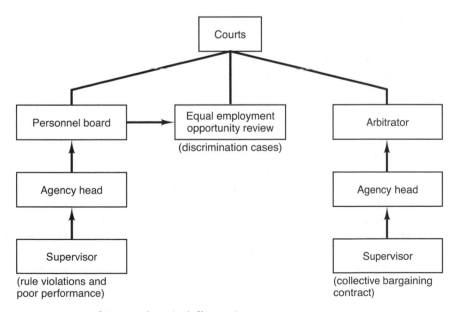

FIGURE 13.1   Appeal Routes for Disciplinary Cases.

supervisor's action. With discretion to amend, the appeals body can direct a suspension or a demotion instead of dismissal. This not only assigns a more appropriate penalty but also leaves open the possibility of harsher action if the employee does not improve.

An appeals board or arbitrator who amends a discipline must nonetheless resolve the conflict between a manager and an employee. An amendment cannot include, in other words, a decision that the employee must try harder and the manager must give more direction. That is too vague to be implemented and there is no resolution about whether or not discipline is warranted. Likewise, a decision cannot be to place the employee on probation instead of firing or demoting them. First, remember that probation is part of the selection process and not, in employment, a form of discipline. Also, probation continues rather than resolves the basic disagreement about whether a manager is exercising direction and discretion appropriately. An appeals board or arbitrator cannot be the manager. It can only judge whether a manager is justified in meting out discipline.

A way of illustrating and summarizing the points made here is briefly to describe the appeals process the federal civil service reforms established in 1978. That process follows the pattern common to the many state and local governments that modernized their personnel systems in the 1970s and 1980s.

Federal Appeals Process

If a manager in a federal agency is going to discipline an employee by suspending him or her without pay for 14 or more days, demoting him or her, or firing the employee, the manager must give notice of the action 30 days before the action is to take effect. This allows time for formal and informal discussions between the employee and the immediate supervisor. If the employee is not satisfied with the explanations or results of these discussions, he or she may appeal to the agency head. The employee can appeal orally or in writing, and he or she may have representation by a lawyer. If the agency deems it appropriate, there may be a formal hearing. Management must respond to the employee's appeal within ten days.

Employees can appeal agency decisions to the U.S. Merit Systems Protection Board (MSPB). The MSPB has set a 90-day limit for itself to render a decision, and it has, with few exceptions, kept to that limit. The MSPB assigns the case to one of its staff or to an administrative law judge, who schedules a formal hearing and then makes a determination. This decision can be reviewed and revised or overturned by the full MSPB on its own motion or at the request of the employee, the agency manager, or the director of the Office of Personnel Management. Decisions of the MSPB are appealable to circuit courts or, if pay is involved, to the Court of Claims.

Many of the horror stories about frustrated efforts to discipline an employee are based on the theme that procedure is more important than substance. The case cited at the beginning of this chapter, in which the dismissal of someone who physically assaulted a supervisor was reversed on appeal because the agency did not give sufficient notice of its intent to dismiss, illustrates an emphasis on procedure at the expense of reason and justice.

During its first two years of operation, the MSPB reversed agency disciplinary actions because the procedure previously outlined was not followed. The MSPB, however, reversed agencies' decisions because of procedural violations considerably less often than did its predecessor. Whereas in 1977 and 1978 the Civil Service Commission reversed 15 percent of the actions of agency managers because of procedural violations, similar reversals by the MSPB have been only 4 percent. The 1978 Civil Service Reform Act provides that the MSPB must use the **test of harmful effects** when reversing a decision because of procedural mistakes. In other words, the board must make a reversal only if the procedural mistake caused some harm that otherwise would not have occurred. If the error did not have any ill effects, then it should be ignored.

With the decrease in reversals on procedural grounds came an increase in the percentage of cases reversed on a consideration of their merit. As a result, there was no net increase or decrease in the number of cases reversed. A sampling of 1,000 cases before the 1978 reforms and 1,000 cases after shows that 15 percent were reversed on procedural grounds and 10 percent on merit before the change, and 4 percent on procedure, and 20 percent on merit after the change.[16] Although from this standpoint neither employees nor managers gain, it is more satisfying to everyone when a case can be considered and disposed of on its merits. The purpose of due process is to ensure justice, not frustrate it.

STANDARDS FOR DISCIPLINARY ACTION

The 1978 Civil Service Reform Act also recognized the need to balance employee rights and agency needs by requiring that standards be met to justify serious disciplinary action against employees. The act makes a distinction between action taken because of unsatisfactory performance and action because of rule violations. In both situations, the burden of proof is on the employer, but the definition of sufficient proof for cases of rule violations is more demanding than for cases of unsatisfactory performance.

For discipline based on rule violation, agency managers must have the support of a preponderance of evidence, whereas for unsatisfactory performance, there must be substantial evidence. Evidence managers need in both circumstances include documentation of employee behaviors, performance evaluations, written communication with a problem employee detailing the concerns and expectations, and the records of any performance improvement plan, as previously discussed. A **preponderance of evidence** applies a balance test. If the evidence of the employer outweighs the evidence of the employee, the employer prevails. A tie or an imbalance in favor of the employee means the employee prevails. The standard of **substantial evidence** is a less demanding standard for the employer. It does not utilize a balance analogy but rather requires the employer to show that there are job-related reasons for the decision to discipline. The employer, in other words, must be prepared to counter a charge that the action is arbitrary and capricious.

There are two basic justifications for this distinction in standards. The first relates to the need to protect the constitutional rights of individual employees. As the Supreme Court agreed in *Board of Regents* v. *Roth,* employees have a liberty interest in their ability to seek other employment. If employees are dismissed because they violate work rules, steal, fight, and so forth, the ability to secure future employment is likely to be impaired. An employee who violates rules in one setting is arguably at risk of violating rules in other settings, too. Because of the seriousness of the implications of dismissal on these grounds, managers must meet the preponderance of evidence test in supporting their action.

In contrast, when employees are dismissed because they cannot perform satisfactorily in a particular job, or even in a category of jobs, employees are not seriously disadvantaged in competing for a wide variety of other jobs. An employee who has been fired because he or she has not been able to keep up with developments in the field of civil engineering, for example, may suffer personal trauma as he or she seeks to redefine career plans. Someone in this situation, however, is not prevented from securing the training needed to become a landscape architect, computer programmer, musician, travel consultant, or a wide variety of other positions. Although the individual's initial career objectives are destroyed, liberty interests are not threatened.

The second justification for the distinction between poor performance and rule violations is based on the ability to measure. One should be able to provide convincing evidence where there are rule violations. Performance, as pointed out in Chapter 9, is sometimes very difficult to measure. Cases of a civil engineer who does not report for work and an employee who beats a supervisor with a baseball bat can be documented. It is more difficult to measure and to identify civil engineers who are no longer creative or who are not fully current in their profession. A lesser standard of supporting evidence is appropriate not only because there is no serious threat to liberty interests, but also because for many public sector jobs the problems of measurement would make it almost impossible to meet any standard other than substantial evidence.

Mixed cases of rule violations and poor performance are, of course, likely. In such cases, standards for proof are likewise mixed. On appeal, mixed cases can be only partially upheld and disciplinary action accordingly amended. A manager who intended to fire someone for both rule violations and poor performance, for example, but cannot provide a preponderance of evidence to show that rules have been violated, may be told to suspend the employee without pay for a certain period of time and require that the employee complete a training program. This is likely to be more appropriate and satisfactory than rejecting all disciplinary action.

SEXUAL HARASSMENT

Sexual harassment is a separate category of discipline for two reasons: (1) the employer has a responsibility to provide a work setting for employees that is free of sexual harassment, and (2) the personally sensitive character of sexual harassment requires that special steps be taken to keep victims from being further victimized. The nature of sexual harassment was discussed in Chapter 12. The concern here is with the process for disciplining employees who harass others.

Victims of sexual harassment are understandably sometimes reluctant to appear in a visible and adversarial manner to lodge a complaint. Not only are the issues private and sensitive, but victims fear the risk of putting themselves through hassles and trouble that may bring no relief and perhaps make the situation even worse.[17]

Consequently, the disciplinary steps have been modified so that confidentiality can be maintained. The modifications are as follows:

1. Employers are obliged under Equal Employment Opportunity Commission (EEOC) guidelines to designate a central person/office to whom reports of sexual harassment can be made, both to avoid forcing employees to go through their supervisor (who may be the person doing the harassing) and to allow employers to fulfill their general responsibilities in this area.
2. The identity of employees making reports can be kept confidential.[18]

Managers must investigate reports of sexual harassment and determine what, if any, action is appropriate. It may be that a forceful, general reminder will put a halt to the harassment. Perhaps the solution is a reassignment of duties or transfer of some personnel so that the parties involved will no longer have to work together. If this is the strategy, managers need to be careful not to make the victim bear the burden of the changes, thereby being mistreated even further.

If disciplinary action against the perpetrators is taken, the person or persons charged have, of course, the same rights to due process as in any other case. The victim may have to come forward at that point. The investigation may have identified other victims and more evidence so that the individual who lodged the initial complaint may feel less vulnerable, but testimony by that victim may still be essential. It is also possible that an employer can defend the disciplinary action without the testimony of some or all of the victims. In any case, it is important to remember that the dynamics in a sexual harassment disciplinary matter are fundamentally between the employer and the accused employee(s)—not between the victim and the harasser.[19]

RETALIATION

Managers are bound to discipline some employees and then have their actions reversed. In such situations, it is critical that managers not retaliate or appear to retaliate against employees who win appeals. Likewise, it is inappropriate for there to be the substance or appearance of retaliation who lodge appeals and lose. Personnel boards, arbitrators, and courts are especially intolerant of retaliation. In essence, this means that employees who appeal disciplinary actions secure special protections. Managers, on the other hand, lose any marginal benefit of the doubt they might otherwise have. The safest position for managers is clearly to bend over backward to avoid taking any actions against the employee unless they have clear evidence of rule violation or unsatisfactory performance.

SUMMARY

The system and standards described here are based on principles of fairness, reasonableness, and logic. Some charge that the application of these principles has led to too much job security for public employees, at the sacrifice of efficient government service. Changes in law seem to have little impact. The number of federal employees dismissed immediately after the 1978 Carter Civil Service Reforms was lower than before the reforms. In part, this can be explained by the lack of understanding of the new standards and processes throughout the federal government and by delays in establishing performance evaluation systems that might be used to support dismissals. In part, the general resistance to the reforms among employees may be a factor.

A major additional explanation, however, lay with the tendency of people, managers and supervisors included, to avoid unpleasant, confrontational situations. The prospect of bringing employees into an office to tell them they are fired causes considerable stress. The knowledge that even with the most efficient appeals system, dismissing employees is going to require many unpleasant hours preparing for hearings and defending oneself is enough to make most managers either ignore the consequences of having a problem employee or search for some other way of dealing with the situation.

All this is not to say that attention does not need to be paid to formal appeals processes and criteria. Formal systems allow those who wish to act the opportunity to do so. Formal criteria provide at least a means of communicating what is expected to employees and their supervisors. Systems for disciplining employees are an affirmation of the liberty interests of employees, the public policies limiting managerial discretion in contract and at will employment, the concomitant right to due process and to fair treatment, and the recognition of the legitimacy of the public's expectation for good and competent service from government agencies and nonprofit organizations. Dismissal and discipline are not the answers for every problem, but it is a responsibility of managers to determine when these are appropriate actions and to proceed fairly and effectively.

DISCUSSION QUESTIONS

1. Why might a manager be reluctant to bring disciplinary action against an employee?
2. Compare the differences and similarities of indefinite employment, contract employment, and at will employment.
3. What are the differences and similarities of a performance improvement plan and a constructive discharge?
4. What are the differences in how managers must proceed if they are considering taking action against an employee for each of the following:
   - Poor performance
   - Violation of work rules
   - Sexual harassment
5. Do multiple routes of appeal favor employees, managers, or neither?

Appeal of Employee Dismissal Exercise

Assume the role of a hearing examiner assigned to decide an appeal from I. M. Angree, a social worker who has been fired from his job with the Normal County Department of Human Welfare. Your decision will stand unless your employer, the County Personnel Commission, reviews and revises it. You can uphold the agency's dismissal action, reverse that action and order reinstatement of Mr. Angree, or stipulate that there be some other punishment.

A standard format for decisions of this nature is to first determine the facts on which the decision is based and then to issue the decision. The first part is already provided. What remains is for you to decide whether the facts support dismissal or some other action and to explain the reasons for your decision.

Findings of Fact

Mr. I. M. Angree is a Social Worker 2, who was employed by the Normal County Department of Human Welfare. He is an African American and, until his dismissal, had been an employee with the department for seven years. His performance evaluations for the first six years consistently ranked him as "highly satisfactory" and "outstanding," the two highest ratings.

On September 1, last year, I. M. Angree injured his back while on the job. The injury occurred as Mr. Angree carried a wheelchair-bound client up a flight of stairs so that the client could get to Mr. Angree's office. The elevator in the building was not operating at the time. Work rules state that if individuals with disabilities need to be carried because physical facilities do not allow access, two or more employees must do the lifting.

Mr. Angree reported the injury to his supervisor, Ms. Donna Bosse, on the morning of September 2. He admitted carrying the client by himself and breaking a work rule. Ms. Bosse granted Mr. Angree's request for a two-week sick leave.

When Mr. Angree returned to work on September 17, his work performance was not as high as it had been before the injury. Not as much work was completed and a backlog of casework and administrative assignments developed. Ms. Bosse received complaints from other social workers, clerical employees, and clients that Mr. Angree was short-tempered in his behavior. On October 15, Ms. Bosse had a conference with Mr. Angree and discussed his performance with him. He explained that he was still suffering pain and discomfort from the back injury. Ms. Bosse suggested that Mr. Angree consult with a doctor.

There was no noticeable improvement in Mr. Angree's performance, and on November 7, Ms. Bosse had another conference with Mr. Angree. She asked if he had seen a doctor about his back. He said he had not because he thought he was improving. Ms. Bosse expressed concern about the deterioration in Mr. Angree's quality of work.

By December 1, Mr. Angree's backlog of work continued to accumulate and criticism of his harshness and anger continued. In addition, Mr. Angree began arriving late for work almost every day, and he left work early on the three preceding workdays. December 1 was the regularly scheduled time for Mr. Angree's annual performance evaluation. The problems of the previous three months were noted in the evaluation and he was rated overall as "satisfactory." During the discussion about performance evaluation, Mr. Angree indicated that he continued to have back problems and that he was also having marital problems. He said he was so upset about the latter that he did not pursue medical treatment for his back.

Ms. Bosse warned Mr. Angree that he would have to resolve his personal problems and improve his work performance. She explained that the agency could not continue to receive so many complaints, and it was not fair to other workers to let his work accumulate. Mr. Angree became frustrated and hostile and stormed out of the office. As he left, he reminded Ms. Bosse that the start of all the problems was an injury he sustained when helping someone. He expressed a wish for more understanding under the circumstances.

During the next six weeks, Mr. Angree's work remained at the same level. On January 17, Ms. Bosse sent Mr. Angree a letter warning him that if there were no improvements within the next 30 days, she would begin disciplinary action. Mr. Angree conferred with two other African-American employees in the department to confirm whether co-workers and clients were lodging complaints about him. They responded that they were not aware of any complaints. Mr. Angree confronted Ms. Bosse with this information on January 20. She indicated that the complaints were all verbal, and she showed him notes she had kept when complaints were made. Mr. Angree said he doubted the veracity of the complaints and the notes.

On February 20, Mr. Angree received notice that he was suspended without pay for two weeks. At the end of this period, he returned to work and was given notice that he would be dismissed if his work did not improve within one month. On April 9, Ms. Bosse notified Mr. Angree that he was dismissed, effective April 20.

Mr. Angree is appealing this dismissal to Ms. Bosse and to the Secretary of the Department of Human Welfare. He argues that his work performance has suffered not because of malice or negligence on his part but as a result of discomfort due to his injury. He further contends that the mandates to improve his performance were vague and ambiguous. He alleges that the arbitrary treatment he has received is because of racial discrimination. He demands reinstatement, back pay, and attorney's fees.

Judgment

Decide whether the facts support the agency's dismissal action or call for some other action. Explain the reasons for your judgment and submit your statement to your class instructor.

GLOSSARY

At will employment A status of employment in which the employee may be terminated at any time by the employer

Constructive discharge A plan of establishing unrealistic goals and objectives and accumulating unusual and excessive documentation in order to dismiss a particular employee

Contractual employment Terms of employment that specify a specific length of time in which an employee is guaranteed work, usually conditioned on satisfactory performance

Doctrine of privilege Legal philosophy that public employment is an honor and opportunity and public employees do not have due process protections for their jobs

Doctrine of substantial interest Legal philosophy that public employees have liberty and property interests in their jobs that entitle them to due process should their jobs be taken away

Indefinite employment A guarantee to an employee that they will have a job as long as the employer needs to have the duties and responsibilities performed by the employee and as long as there are not grounds for dismissal for just cause

Just cause Principle that a disciplinary action must be taken only for a significant job-related reason

Performance improvement plan An individualized program for an employee who is encountering job performance problems that sets attainable goals and objectives, methods for improvement, and deadlines

Preponderance of evidence A standard of proof in which the party with the most persuasive evidence wins

Substantial evidence A standard of proof in which managers need to support disciplinary action with a job-related reason

Test of harmful effects Principle that violations of procedures should not be grounds for overturning the managerial discipline of an employee unless the violation(s) caused substantive effects

SOURCES

Daley, D. (1993). Formal disciplinary procedures and conflict resolution remedies. *Public Personnel Management* 22, 1: 12–22.
  A review of disciplinary procedures in the public sector.

Deitsch, C., & Dilts, D. (1990). *The Arbitration of Rights in the Public Sector.* New York: Quorum Books.
  Historical and legal discussion of grievance arbitration in governments.

Robinson, R. K., et al. (1993). Sexual harassment in the workplace: A review of the legal rights and responsibilities of all parties. *Public Personnel Management* 22, 1: 123–135.
  Essay that includes legal discussion of how managers should respond to complaints of sexual harassment.

Rollinson, D., & Hook, C. (1996). Supervisor and manager styles in handling discipline and grievance. *Personnel Review* 25, 4: 38–59.
  A review of approaches managers have taken towards troublesome employees.

NOTES

1. General Accounting Office, *A Management Concern: How to Deal with the Nonproductive Federal Employee* (Washington, DC: Government Printing Office, 1978), 42.
2. U.S. Merit Systems Protection Board, *Annual Report for Fiscal Year 1997* (Washington, DC: Government Printing Office, 1998) or www.access.gpo.gov/mspb
3. Cynthia L. Estlund, "Wrongful Discharge Protections in an At-will World," Texas Law Review 74 (1996): 1655–1692.
4. Max Schanzenbach, "Exceptions to Employment At Will: Raising Firing Costs or Enforcing Life-cycle Contracts?" *American Law & Economics Review* 5 (2003): 470–504.
5. Bureau of National Affairs, *Labor Relations Reporter* (2004), 505:51.
6. Steven Hays, "Employee Discipline and Removal: Coping with Job Security," in Steven W. Hays and Richard C. Kearney, eds., *Public Personnel Administration: Problems and Prospects*, 3rd ed. (Englewood Cliffs, NJ: Prentice-Hall, 1995); Richard Kearney and Frank White, "Behaviorally Anchored Disciplinary Scales (BADS): A New Approach to Discipline," *Public Personnel Management* 17, no. 3 (Fall 1988): 341–350.

7. Arthur T. Johnson and Nancy O'Neill, "Employee Assistance Programs and the Troubled Employee in the Public Sector Workplace," *Review of Public Personnel Administration* 9, no. 2 (Summer 1989): 61–73.

8. Donald E. Klingner, Nancy G. O'Neill, and Mohamed Gamal Sabet, "Drug Testing in Public Agencies: Public Policy Issues and Managerial Responses," *Review of Public Personnel Administration* 10, no. 3 (Fall 1989): 1–17; Frank J. Thompson, Norma M. Riccucci, and Carolyn Ban, "Biological Testing and Personnel Policy: Drugs and the Federal Workplace," in Carolyn Ban and Norma M. Riccucci, eds., *Public Personnel Management: Current Concerns–Future Challenges* (New York: Longman, 1991), 156–172.

9. Cornell University Law School, *Perry v. Sindermann* 408 U.S. 593 (1972) http:/ /www. law. cornell. edu/ supct/ html/ historics/ USSC_CR_0408_0593_ZO. html

10. D. Daley, "Formal Disciplinary Procedures and Conflict Resolution Remedies," *Public Personnel Management* 22, no. 1 (Spring 1993): 12–22; Deborah D. Goldman, "Due Process and Public Personnel Management," *Review of Public Personnel Administration* 2, no. 1 (Fall 1981): 19–28.

11. *Bishop v. Wood*, 426 U.S. 321 (1976).

12. M. Gordon and S. Miller, "Grievances: A Review of Research and Practice," *Personnel Psychology* 37 (Spring 1984): 117–141; Robert White, "State Grievances and Appeals Systems: A Survey," *Public Personnel Management* 10, no. 3 (Fall 1981): 313–322.

13. Robert Vaughn, *The Spoiled System: A Call for Civil Service Reform* (Washington, DC: Public Interest Group, 1972).

14. C. Deitsch and D. Dilts, *The Arbitration of Rights Disputes in the Public Sector* (New York: Quorum Books, 1990); Joseph Kroslov and Robert M. Peters, "Grievance Arbitration in State and Local Government: A Survey," *Arbitration Journal* 25 (1970): 196–203.

15. George W. Bohlander, "Public Sector Independent Grievance Systems: Methods and Procedures," *Public Personnel Management* 18, no. 3 (Fall 1989): 339–354.

16. Carolyn Ban, Edie N. Goldenberg, and Toni Marzotto, "Firing the Unproductive Employee: Will Civil Service Reform Make a Difference?" *Review of Public Personnel Administration* 2, no. 2 (Spring 1982): 87–100.

17. Bureau of National Affairs, *Sexual Harassment and Labor Relations: A BNA Special Report* (Washington, DC: Bureau of National Affairs, 1991); Robert H. Faley, "Sexual Harassment: Critical Review of Legal Cases with General Principles and Preventive Measures," *Personnel Psychology* 35, no. 3 (Fall 1982): 583–600.

18. Equal Employment Opportunity Commission, Document 1604, *Guidelines on Discrimination Because of Sex: Sexual Harassment* (Washington, DC: Government Printing Office, 1978). See also Robert K. Robinson et al., "Sexual Harassment in the Workplace: A Review of the Legal Rights and Responsibilities of All Parties," *Public Personnel Management* 22, no. 1 (Spring 1993): 123–135.

19. Richard W. Crockett and Julie A. Gilmere, "Retaliation: Agency Theory and Gaps in the Law," *Public Personnel Management* 28, no. 1 (Spring 1999): 39–50.

Chapter 14

Compensation

Politics is involved in compensation more than in any other dimension of public personnel management. Citizens and the officials they elect relate to compensation issues more easily than others. Members of the public have a difficult time tracing their tax payments to submarines, nursing homes, and prisons. They have almost no problem, however, conceptualizing how their taxes become the income of a government official. The annual raises of public employees as a whole and the specific salaries of individual top officials are visible and often controversial. Inside government, employees are very concerned about how much they make, how much others make, and what political and personal games need to be played in order to get wage increases.

Similarly, top officials of nonprofit organizations are vulnerable to criticism and loss of support when their salaries are considered excessive. The Internal Revenue Service is mindful of the possibility of an organization registering as a nonprofit and then violating the spirit and letter of the law by translating what is essentially profit into the personal income of executive directors and their staff. The public intuitively reacts negatively when they learn that what they consider a charitable or religious organization is paying generous salaries or providing perks to board members and senior management.

Public attention has a general effect of capping salaries. But there are other determinants of the level and structure of compensation in governments and nonprofit organizations. These agencies tend to keep their salaries roughly even with those of other employers. Managers are concerned that salary differences reflect the hierarchical positions employees hold within an agency. Employees and their families count on wages keeping pace with the cost of living. A concern for fairness argues for the removal of discriminatory determinants of compensation. In short, pay is important and the policies that determine general and individual compensation levels are diverse and sometimes contradictory.

LEARNING OBJECTIVES OF THIS CHAPTER

- Understand compensation policy issues, regarding both general levels of salaries as well as the ranges for specific occupations, and pay of specific individuals
- Understand the principles of comparable worth or pay equity
- Know about efforts to link pay and job performance

- Know about the forms in which compensation is provided, that is, salary, vacations, health insurance, retirement programs, and other benefits
- Know the techniques and approaches used to calculate and set both general and individual salary level
- Be able to conduct pay surveys

THE PRINCIPLES OF COMPENSATION

Compensation is integral to personnel management. There are four key principles that guide compensation policies.

1. Compensation must be at a high enough level to *attract* good people. All of the efforts to have an effective recruitment plan and a valid selection process can be for naught if the compensation is so low it discourages good candidates from applying for or from accepting a position.
2. The distribution of salaries and benefits within the agency must be perceived as *equitable* in order to retain good employees. The perception of equity depends on more than whether those doing the same job are getting paid the same. This concern also includes how salaries recognize different levels of skill and responsibility, service with the organization, hazardous duty, and the like.
3. Compensation systems are expected to *motivate* employees to apply their full talents and energy to their work. Most commonly, this is taken to mean that the most productive employees will be rewarded in a special way for their distinguished work. As pointed out in Chapter 5, employees differ fundamentally in their orientation to work. Professionals and many paraprofessionals can get more satisfaction out of accomplishments in their job than in other benefits attached to employment. Nonprofit organizations and public service positions appeal to an altruistic set of values for some people—very important as a form of nonpecuniary compensation for volunteers. Nonetheless, monetary compensation is still important to motivate employees.
4. Compensation must be within the employer's *ability to pay*. Determining that in the private sector involves projections of sales and comparisons of assets to liabilities. For governments, a key calculation is the level of taxation that is politically possible. Nonprofit organizations rely heavily on grants and contributions for their capacity to meet payrolls.

Governments also recognize another principle when setting compensation for their employees: *social equity*. Attention must be paid to the level of compensation for certain jobs. In the 1960s, the major concern was the wages paid for jobs that African Americans typically filled in certain parts of the United States. In the 1980s and 1990s, the issue was to correct the social practice of paying low wages for work women traditionally did. This concern has been phrased as paying equal wages for work that, although not exactly alike, is comparable—for example, a secretary (traditionally female job) and a stock clerk (traditionally male job).

Pay and Performance

The jury is still out. There has been a considerable amount of research devoted to the question of how compensation affects employees' performance, and the evidence has been submitted. However, there is no consensus on how to interpret it.

To a great extent, the debates reflect disagreements in organization theory over how to use pay to make employees productive. Frederick Taylor and the scientific management adherents were convinced that paying employees on a piecework basis—for every chair built the worker was paid a set amount—was the best system to use.[1] The human relations school that dominated during the 1930s and 1940s focused on issues other than compensation. Pay was not regarded as an effective incentive for increased productivity.[2] Abraham Maslow and Frederick Herzberg developed need theories emphasizing the link between motivation and the particular needs of individual employees. Pay is critical to meet the most fundamental level of Maslow's hierarchy of needs.[3] According to Herzberg, pay can be a source of dissatisfaction, but it is unlikely to be a positive source of satisfaction or an inducement to increased effort.[4] A 1996 study demonstrated that an agency with high pay and excellent benefits nonetheless had low morale and high turnover problems. Career structures were more important than pay.[5]

Research since the 1960s has led to the emergence of a more optimistic view of the role that compensation might play in motivating excellence from employees. This view is articulated in **expectancy theory**. Employee perceptions are of key importance in expectancy theory. There are three elements to the theory:

1. Expectancy. Employee beliefs about the relationship between effort and performance. Employees must feel that by trying harder or doing something different they can improve their performance.

2. Instrumentality. Employee perceptions about the relationship between performance and rewards. There must be a belief that better performance will result in higher compensation.

3. Valences. Employee values attached to the reward. Employees must regard the higher compensation or other reward as valuable enough to warrant the extra effort to improve performance.

The work of Victor H. Vroom provides major support for this theory.[6] His is not the only relevant research, however. A number of other scholars have confirmed parts of the expectancy theory sequence and the theory as a whole.[7]

The major missing element from expectancy theory is the social setting within which employees work. Their perceptions about the relationships between effort, performance, and pay do not emerge in a vacuum. Social interaction among employees plays a major role in the calculations individuals make about whether more effort and better performance are worth it. Social interaction is also important as a determinant of conflict, and a common reaction to organizational conflict is resistance to the achievement of organizational goals and lower productivity.

Equity theory, developed by Stacy Adams, observes that employees compare each other's performance and level of compensation.[8] In order for there to be a positive relationship between pay and performance, employees must perceive that pay levels correspond with the usefulness of various contributions employees make.[9] The combination of expectancy theory and equity theory, with supporting research, in short, provides a basis for policies and procedures that might establish compensation systems that encourage high levels of performance and pursue the principle of fairness.[10]

Comparable Worth/Pay Equity

The efforts to eliminate race and gender discrimination include providing similar compensation for individuals doing similar work. Two policies apply this general concern: (1) equal pay for equal work and (2) equal pay for work of comparable value.

The federal Equal Pay Act of 1963 makes the principle of **equal pay for equal work** the law of the land. Employers—private, nonprofit, and public—must pay employees at the same rate if they are doing the same work. The standards for comparison under this act are rather narrow.[11] Employees must be working for the same employer, work under the same working conditions, and perform identical or almost identical jobs, requiring similar skills, efforts, and responsibilities. A male social worker and a female social worker, under this act, must be paid the same. Likewise, a male teacher and a female teacher, and a male firefighter and a female firefighter, must be paid the same wages. Differences in pay can be justified only when one or more of the following "affirmative defenses," as they are referred to in the act, apply:

1. Seniority system
2. Merit system
3. Productivity
4. Some factor other than gender

In other words, a male third-grade teacher may be paid more than a woman working in the same school district and at the same grade level if the man has more seniority. A female social worker may be paid more than a man in the same agency and same position if she has better performance evaluations.

The concern about equal pay for comparable, but different, work—known as **comparable worth** or **pay equity**—stems from social practices of identifying certain jobs with either males or females. Even after 25 years of laws banning discrimination in hiring, women constituted 98.8 percent of the workforce in secretarial positions and 96.8 percent of those who were nurses. In contrast, 98.7 percent of carpenters were men, as were 97.1 percent of engineers.[12]

Not only are certain jobs stereotyped as occupied by men or women, but also the salaries for traditionally female jobs are lower than their male counterparts. There are a variety of reasons given for the discrepancy between traditionally male and female jobs. Many labor economists regard clerical, nurse, waitress, librarian, elementary-school teacher, and so forth as jobs where the supply of workers exceeds the demand—thus, low wages.[13] This argument fails dramatically when applied to nurses, waitresses, and clericals, whose salaries remain low despite chronic shortages.

The law of supply and demand is not the only determinant of salaries. Social customs also play an important role. When typewriters were invented and the federal government decided to hire women to operate these new machines, it decided to pay them half of what it was paying male clerks. Likewise, when the federal government decided to hire women as librarians—a virtually all-male profession until the twentieth century—it set the pay at about half that for men. These decisions were based primarily on assumptions about the role of women in families and their limited need for compensation. Women were assumed to be either married and supplementing their husband's salary or single and just supporting themselves. Men, on the other hand, were assumed to be breadwinners for families. Thus, women supposedly did not need as much money as did men. (A similar need justification was used for supporting low wages paid to children prior to the enactment of child labor laws.)

Need continues to be a factor in wage setting because the cost of living and inflation are considered. It is, however, no longer accepted practice to judge the need of a whole class of people based on traditional societal roles. Likewise, employers rarely consider the financial obligations of individual employees in setting their salaries.

Nonetheless, the legacy of historic decisions to designate certain jobs as women's jobs and to pay those jobs at lower rates than if men had filled them continues to affect general salary schedules. Employers typically make the same type of wage adjustment from year to year for all of the positions in an organization. Everyone gets about the same percentage increase, for example, without changing the relative position of jobs in the salary system. Thus, clericals remain below male jobs of similar levels of skill and responsibility. Nurses and librarians remain below professions that men predominantly fill.

Efforts began in the 1980s to adjust the salaries of jobs women traditionally fill to get rid of the legacy of past discrimination. As economist Heidi Hartmann put it, the objective is to get the pay for these occupations to their true market value.[14] No one seriously proposes that government set wages for the entire society in order to eliminate discriminatory practices. Instead, the focus was employer specific, and the goal was to achieve pay equity within organizations.

There is a common misunderstanding that the analysis of gender- and race-based salary inequities is to select a job that women traditionally fill and then subjectively to select a job that seems to have similar responsibilities or skill requirements that men traditionally fill and compare the salaries of the two jobs. Such job-to-job comparisons would violate virtually every basic principle of sound research. Some researchers prefer to use the term pay equity instead of comparable worth because it helps avoid a misunderstanding of the methodology.

The mechanism for determining the amount of adjustments necessary for an employer to correct for past practices is the quantitative job evaluation system described in Chapter 8.[15] As explained in that chapter, job evaluation systems have been designed to analyze a wide variety of jobs and to rank them according to a common yardstick. The ranking has traditionally been used to determine pay for jobs for which an employer cannot get guidance from the market, either because the job is unique or because an employer is the major employer for a particular occupation.[16] In order to avoid incorporating any biases built into the general market, employers can similarly use current job evaluation rankings and not their own or anyone else's past practices to set wages for jobs that women traditionally fill.

In other words, benchmark jobs that are not female-dominated would be tied to market rates, since past practices of discrimination are not germane. Then the internal market of an organization could set the salaries of female-dominated jobs; that is, pay would be set by how, according to job evaluation, they relate to the benchmark jobs tied to the external market. For example, the external market would set the salary for accountants in a city government, and the job evaluation analysis would set salaries for clericals and librarians. If the job evaluation points for accountant positions totaled 90 points, for librarian 100 points, and for clericals 70 points, then the librarian salary should be set somewhat above that for the accountants, with the clericals below the accountants. (Obviously there would be more precise guidance if one had the full array of jobs with their evaluation points on the one hand and, for the male-dominated jobs, external market comparisons on the other hand.)

Studies of gender- and race-based pay disparity have found that the gap between female- and male-dominated jobs in the same employing organization is usually between 11 and 17 percent. The cost of eliminating this gap is typically only 3 to 4 percent of total payroll costs (wages and benefits for the entire workforce).[17] The state of Iowa implemented its full pay equity plan in a single day. The more common pattern has been to phase in the adjustments over a three- to five-year period.[18]

Nonprofit organizations and many local governments have too small a workforce to conduct a sophisticated and valid study of gender- and race-based inequities. In response to this limitation, local governments in Minnesota made adjustments based on an analysis of relevant studies done for other employers. This approach is not only practical, but it recognizes the kind of market and social forces affecting pay in the kind of positions that these governments fill.

As with the adoption of child labor laws, minimum wage laws, the Fair Labor Standards Act, and other employment and antidiscrimination policies, pay equity has encountered political and legal battles. The first major struggle was in San Jose, California, where it took a strike by public employees in 1981 to get the city to correct gender-based pay inequities that were identified in a study that, in fact, the city itself had commissioned. The state of Washington, similarly, refused to act on the results of its own study and wound up in the courts, finally agreeing in 1987 to an out-of-court settlement to correct the disparities that had been identified. Wisconsin, North Carolina, Florida, and other states encountered heated battles. In the 1984 presidential campaign, both parties included positions on comparable worth in their platforms.[19]

The adoption of pay equity policies has not always generated controversy. Many major cities and the states of Minnesota, Iowa, and, to a lesser extent, New York, adopted pay equity policies without major controversy. Their approaches were to make adjustments through the regular salary setting and collective bargaining processes, rather than through a major political or policy initiative. Personnel professionals, through the International Personnel Management Association, have advocated pay equity as part of sound and proper personnel management policy.

FORMS OF COMPENSATION

Uppermost in a discussion of compensation is wages. Because of the general concerns with health care in the United States and with the retirement of baby boomers, compensation in the form of benefits such as health insurance and pensions has gained visibility. Other important benefits include vacations, child care, and personal leave. Benefits typically constitute almost 30 percent of some employees' total compensation. Wages and benefits have features that are critical both for an understanding of compensation and a capacity to accomplish management goals through compensation.

Wage Structures

Until the twentieth century, it was common to set wages for each employee individually. There was no system either for paying the same wages to employees doing the same work or for determining pay increases for incumbent employees. It was not uncommon for clerks in different agencies of the same government or organization to be paid highly divergent wages, nor even for clerks in the same office to be paid differently. As pointed out in Chapter 8, in large part the adoption of position classification systems was in response to this situation. Now, almost to a fault, position classifications drive compensation. With few exceptions, each classification is allocated to a set level of pay. Expressed another way, wages are structured primarily according to classifications rather than to individuals, performance, or other factors.

Pay Rate
A **pay rate** is a fixed amount that is attached to a particular job or position classification. The principle behind a pay rate emphasizes that a job is worth only a certain amount to an employer, regardless of the skills, experience, or enthusiasm any employee might bring to that job. Pay rates are usually expressed on an hourly basis and apply primarily to a limited number of craft positions like plumber, electrician, and carpenter.

Pay Range
The basic structure of most compensation systems is the **pay range** or grade. Each job classification is attached to a salary range, with a minimum, a maximum, and a midpoint or median. Salary ranges can be expressed on an hourly, weekly, monthly, or yearly basis. Although the general principle is to set an appropriate salary range for every job classification, few jurisdictions, in fact, proceed in this way. If there were as many salary ranges as job classifications, most organizations would have hundreds of salary ranges. Instead, a more manageable number of salary ranges is established and then classifications are allocated to these ranges.

The distance between the minimum and maximum salaries in each range varies. Generally, the lower the level of the salary range, the narrower the difference between the top and bottom of the range. Lower-level jobs tend to be more routinized and predictable, thus one can be more specific about their salary. Managerial and professional positions, on the other hand, can vary considerably, and, especially if there is a desire to recognize performance, the salary ranges are broad enough to accommodate these differences. Most compensation specialists suggest a 25 to 35 percent spread for lower-level positions and a 50 percent spread for senior positions. Thus, a park maintenance worker might expect to be in a weekly salary range of from $164 to $220, whereas the manager of the parks department would expect a salary anywhere from $443 to $740 per week.

Pay Step

But how does an employee move from the minimum to the maximum of the range? Each pay range is usually divided into several increments, known as **pay steps**. A step increase is usually about 5 percent. Thus, as Table 14.1 illustrates, the first increase that a park maintenance worker could expect would be from $164 to $172 per week. The manager, if hired at the minimum of the range, would move from $433 to $455. Because of the broader range for the manager, there are more steps in the range (12, instead of seven).

Movement from one step to another depends on the policies of the employer. It is very common to increase employees' salaries when they successfully pass the probationary period. Thus, movement from Step 1 to Step 2 is dependent on movement from probationary to permanent or indefinite status. Step increases after this are based on length of service and/or performance. For some agencies, there is automatic progression from the bottom to the top of the range, without any regard for the level of performance. The park maintenance worker, for example, would move up a step every year, or perhaps a half-step every nine to 12 months, and eventually reach the top of the range. Some agencies have automatic progression to the midpoint of the range and then performance-based increases thereafter. Another pattern is to have a half step for performance and a half step for longevity. A few employers base all increases on performance. Some have one system for managerial employees and another system for other employees. In short, the variations possible are considerable.

Broad Banding

A number of state governments and other employers are creating rather large pay ranges, without steps. This is known as **broad banding** or **pay banding**. The major advantage is to provide agency managers with more flexibility and discretion in setting pay for their employees. States that have gone to broad banding have done this primarily for professional positions, like attorneys. Instead of having separate salary ranges for Accountant 1, Accountant 2 and Accountant 3, for example, all three levels of accountants would share the same range, which would generally span from the minimum of the old Accountant 1 to the maximum of the old Accountant 3. The federal government tried this approach in a limited experiment in 1979,[20] and in 1997 the Commerce Department received approval to switch over 3,000 employees to a broad-band system. The Commerce Department still has ranges for entry, developmental, expert, and managerial levels in each occupation, but managers have considerable discretion in determining individual raises and starting salaries, rather than having to work within predetermined steps. Broad banding works particularly

TABLE 14.1 PAY RANGES AND STEPS FOR PARK EMPLOYEES (WEEKLY SALARIES IN DOLLARS)											
	1	2	3	4	5	6	7	8	9	10	11	12
Park maintenance worker	164	172	180	190	200	209	220	—	—	—	—	—
Park manager	433	455	477	501	526	552	580	609	640	672	705	740

well in professional and paraprofessional jobs and where there are the use of teams in the organization. The concern is that managerial discretion will allow favoritism and a general push to get employees in the upper part of the pay range.[21]

Pay Schedule

The relationships between various pay ranges are determined by organizational and career structures, as well as influenced by general compensation policies such as being competitive with other employers and following comparable worth principles. Public jurisdictions have had anywhere from four to 60 pay ranges, and thus pay schedules can be relatively simple or complex.

In its simplest form, a **pay schedule** orders the ranges from the lowest to the highest. There is an unwritten rule that pay ranges be numbered consecutively, beginning with the lowest range. Also, it is common that there is some overlap between the high end of one pay range and the low end of the next range. Generally, the overlap will be no more than one-third of either range and thus can mean that any overlap be confined to two ranges. These are, it should be stressed, guidelines, and there may be circumstances in a particular jurisdiction for ignoring them. Figure 14.1 illustrates the structure of a pay schedule.

Large employers are likely to have more than a single pay schedule. These are likely to be grouped according to occupations or, where there is collective bargaining, according to bargaining units. Sometimes letters are used as a code to denote

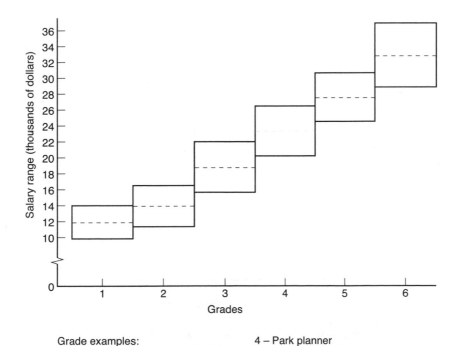

Grade examples:
1 – Park maintenance worker
2 – Park equipment repair person
4 – Park planner
5 – Personnel manager
6 – Park director

FIGURE 14.1 Salary Structure.

which occupational group or groups are included in a given pay schedule. Thus, an employee who is a prison guard may be in a salary range Human Services 4 (HS–4) and a social worker may be in HS–7. A payroll clerk, on the other hand, may be in salary range Fiscal Services 2 (FS–2) and an accountant in FS–6. The federal government has separate pay schedules for the military, public corporations like the U.S. Post Office and the Tennessee Valley Authority, the Foreign Service, and regular civilian agencies.

Some employers have a nonintegrated pay schedule instead of multiple integrated pay schedules like those just described. A nonintegrated schedule orders ranges from lowest to highest, but there are no rules or formulas for relationships or overlap. Instead, each pay range is assigned to a given occupation or cluster of jobs and then keyed to wages paid by other employers for similar jobs.[22] Figure 14.2 presents an example of a nonintegrated pay schedule.

Benefits

The use of nonwage benefits to compensate employees began, in a major way, during World War II. As a wartime measure, severe limits were placed on salary increases. Thus, in order to increase rewards to employees, companies had to rely on insurance, vacations, and the like. Since their inception, benefits have become a major part of

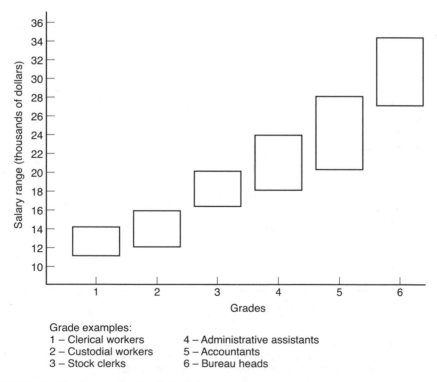

Grade examples:
1 – Clerical workers   4 – Administrative assistants
2 – Custodial workers   5 – Accountants
3 – Stock clerks   6 – Bureau heads

FIGURE 14.2   Nonintegrated Pay Schedule.

total employee compensation. As pointed out earlier, it is not unusual for 30 percent of compensation to consist of benefits.[23]

Some benefits offer major advantages to employers. Retirement costs are usually not due immediately, and some benefits such as vacations and holidays do not require any dollar outlay. Employees are advantaged in that some benefits represent compensation that is not subject to taxation and some benefits, like insurance, are far less expensive because they are getting them as members of a group.

The types of benefits that can be provided are limited only by one's imagination and political acceptability. Some private-sector employees may remember fondly and appreciatively the group tour to an amusement park that their employer provided, but they would regard a similar use of their tax dollars or charitable contributions for the benefit of employees as scandalous.

There are some fairly standard benefits. Almost all employers provide vacation for their employees, as well as sick leave and leave for jury duty, National Guard duty, and family emergencies. Moreover, 76 percent of all workers have a group life insurance policy through their work, and 72 percent have health insurance that covers them and members of their family for illness and injury, regardless of whether the illness or injury is contracted on the job. Some benefits are mandated and funded through employer contributions. These programs include Social Security, unemployment compensation, and workers' compensation.[24] Discussion of the major types of benefits begins with the most expensive: retirement programs and health insurance.

Retirement Programs

More than 90 percent of public employees are covered by retirement plans, whereas less than half of the employees in the private sector have this coverage.[25] Private-sector and nonprofit agency employees rely more heavily on Social Security. In fact, up until 1983, governments had a choice that other employers did not, that is, whether or not to participate in the Social Security system. The federal government itself had not participated. One part of the proposals to increase the financial health of the Social Security system that Congress passed in 1983 was to include all new federal employees and to remove the option state governments had to particiapte or not.

There are two other important contrasts between public and private-sector, including nonprofit, retirement plans. The private-sector plans are regulated under the Employee Retirement Income Security Act of 1974, which aims at ensuring the fiscal soundness of pension plans. The public sector is not regulated. Most government programs are partially funded by assets held in retirement plans and partially funded by current revenues. A few are on a pay-as-you-go basis.[26]

The major purpose of retirement plans, of course, is to provide an income to employees after they are no longer working. The concept of **replacement ratio** is used to measure the difference between what an employee was making while still on the job and what is provided in a retirement program. A replacement ratio of 100 exists when in real terms (that is, adjusting for inflation) an individual is receiving as much from a pension as he or she was making at the point of retirement.

Almost all public retirement plans are defined benefit programs, which means that the level of benefits is established by a formula that includes, typically, years of service, amount contributed by the employee, and an average of the salary of either the last three or the highest three years. Although many state and local governments began their retirement plans as supplements to Social Security income, there is no attempt to integrate the level of Social Security benefits with the defined benefit formula. It is common for nonprofit employers to integrate their plans with Social Security. As a result, nongovernment plans almost always have a replacement ratio of 100 or close to it; most public jurisdictions that participate in Social Security have replacement ratios higher than 100, although state and local governments that did not participate in Social Security before 1983 have ratios less than 100.[27]

The combined effects of the pending baby boomer retirements and the lack of regulation or self-discipline are prompting concerns about the funding of government retirement plans. Exacerbating the potential problems is the rapid rise in health care costs, which are typically included in retirement benefits. Governments and employees have contributed over the years to special retirement funds that are kept separate from annual budgets and invested in stocks and bonds. Anticipating a shortfall in their ability to pay promised retirement benefits, managers of the investments in some states have put retirement money into hedge funds, which are high return, but also high risk. The California Public Employees' Retirement System, the larges pension fund in the country, initially invested $50 billion in hedge funds in 2002, and since then has added another $12 billion annually. Virginia's public retirement fund began putting money in hedge funds in 2003 and Montana in 2007. Some states, recognizing the high risks, have avoided this step, but nonetheless remain concerned about the rise in costs on the horizon.

Nonprofit organizations do not usually have retirement programs that they provide to their employees. Instead, they counsel employees to have their own individual savings programs. Nonprofit employees are typically included in the Social Security system.

Health Insurance

The cost of health care as well as the cost of health insurance to employers has soared steadily from the mid–1970s through the first decade of the twenty-first century. Health care in the United States has risen faster than the general cost of living, usually at double digit rates every year. The rise in health insurance premiums has at times led to a cut in take-home pay for employees, even when total compensation increases. Employees are paying more of the premium costs and having to accept cuts in benefits and to forego choosing their own physicians in favor of group managed care plans. While it is still far better to get health insurance through a group, such as employees, this benefit is not as robust as it once was.[28]

Educational Opportunities

Opportunities to pursue one's education can be regarded as part of the employee development efforts (discussed in Chapter 11) and as part of employee benefits. The latter is particularly true when an agency does not insist that an educational program be directly relevant to the job an employee is currently doing. Even with this requirement, facilitating an employee's career advancement is an important and valued personal benefit.[29] In addition to tuition reimbursement, this benefit can be provided through time off or flexible hours to attend classes and reimbursement for books.

Time Off

More than 7 percent of national payroll costs is allocated to compensating employees for time they are not working. Almost three-quarters of this is for vacations.[30] The common pattern is for all employees to get at least one week of vacation each year, and then as employees accumulate seniority they get more vacation time, up to a maximum of four weeks. Some jurisdictions allow employees to carry unused vacation time from one year over to the next year. There are also some employers that allow employees to get extra pay in lieu of vacation time. There are usually limits to these options. One reason for providing vacation time is to provide relaxation and diversion that might rejuvenate employees. Not only is this purpose not served when vacations are not taken, but supervisors can have a more complicated schedule to arrange when an employee finally takes an extended vacation.

Chapter 12 discussed an employee's time off from the perspective of individual and family needs. Included in that discussion was the concept of collapsing the various categories of excused leaves into one.

Cafeteria-Style Benefits

Beginning in the mid-1970s, employers began introducing a cafeteria approach to benefits, whereby employees could construct their own benefit package from a wide array of options.[31]

Usually, there is a core set of benefits for all employees. Law might mandate some of these, such as workers' compensation, unemployment compensation, and Social Security. Other core benefits, such as basic medical insurance and retirement, may require full group participation in order to pool risks, be viable financially, and make costs low enough so that it is a meaningful benefit.

The optional benefits in a cafeteria plan are priced separately, and employees are informed about the budget that they have. The total value of the benefit package may vary with the time that the employee has been with the agency. Employees may then choose, for example, from such options as dental insurance, life insurance, longer vacations, tax-deferred annuities, parking privileges, and child care. As needs change, employees can change benefits. Insurance coverage for pregnancies and provision for child care are important at one age, whereas tax-deferred annuities and extra vacations may be more important at another.

Implications for income taxes have been an important consideration in the establishment of benefits generally and in **cafeteria-style benefits** particularly. If income can be provided in a way that avoids taxes, it is obviously more valuable than if it is taxable. It would be better for an employee to forego $500 in salary in order to get an employer to provide a parking space, than for the employee to get the $500, pay 15 to 45 percent in taxes and Social Security on that amount, and then still have to pay $500 to a private lot for parking.

The Internal Revenue Service has placed some limits on cafeteria-style benefit programs. First, if a nontaxable benefit is taken in lieu of pay or some other taxable income, then the value of that benefit is taxable. The $500 parking privilege, in other words, is best taken in lieu of dental insurance or extra time off than in lieu of salary. Second, the cafeteria options must be available to all employees, except as collective-bargaining agreements may provide otherwise. This ruling is aimed particularly at discriminating in favor of highly paid employees. Tax-deferred annuities, more exten-sive insurance coverage, and the like are sometimes more valuable and practical options for the highly paid than for other employees. In the public sector, where management is generally not paid as well as in the private sector, it is tempting to use cafeteria-style benefits to attract top talent. The selective availability of options is not, however, an approach that can be used.

The Tax Reform Act of 1986 made changes to Section 125 of the Internal Revenue Service Code, which regulates cafeteria plans, to allow for the inclusion of flexible spending accounts (FSAs). Under this provision, employees may each year place a por-tion of their taxable income in a tax-exempt account from which they can reimburse themselves for medical expenses, health insurance premiums, and expenses that are normally eligible for dependent care tax credits. These accounts reduce an employee's tax liability by the amount that is set aside. There is a risk because if any funds remain in this account at year's end, they are lost to the employee and go to the federal gov-ernment. This use-it-or-lose-it provision deters some from establishing FSAs and make some employees very cautious about how much they deposit in the account.

There are administrative costs to providing cafeteria-style benefits. These costs, without computer technology, can be prohibitive. With the use of computer programs that have been developed, the operation of this approach is both feasible and relatively inexpensive. The major cost, as with almost any innovation, is the initial installation. Typically, the introduction of cafeteria-style benefit programs begins with a survey of employees to determine the options they value most. Then the various benefits are priced, the core benefits are established, and the options and employee limits are defined.[32] Edward E. Lawler, III, a widely recognized expert in compensation, is con-vinced the costs are good investments. His review of studies done on cafeteria-style benefits has led him to conclude that this approach "can increase employee percep-tions of the value of their pay package and also increase their pay satisfaction, improv-ing organizational effectiveness by decreasing absenteeism and turnover and generally allowing the organization to attract a more competent workforce."[33]

Initially, unions were opposed to the cafeteria approach on the grounds that the level and forms of benefits was a subject of bargaining and should not be determined on an individual basis between each employee and the employer. Since the early 1980s, however, unions have regarded this approach more positively and have found ways of integrating it into the collective bargaining process.

Part-time Employees

Employment, compensation, and benefits have traditionally been based on the assumption that employees worked full time. With job sharing, permanent part-time work, seasonal jobs, and short-term projects all emerging as permanent features of the employment landscape for nonprofit organizations and for governments, this assumption has to be set aside. The policies of some agencies have been to make temporary and some part-time employees ineligible for benefits. Their compensation consisted of wages and mandated benefits, like Social Security, workers' compen-sation, and, in some cases, unemployment compensation. Temporary employees who are on projects lasting two or three years and part-time employees who anticipate working indefinitely on a part-time basis are increasingly being given benefits. They get ill, need vacations, and will retire, just like other employees.

Once a decision is made to provide benefits to these employees, the issue is whether to adjust the benefits to the status of employment. Some of these issues are easy to resolve. Vacation, sick leave, and time off generally can be prorated according to the percentage of time worked. If a beginning full-time employee has 40 hours of vacation, then a half-time employee can have 20 hours of vacation. Likewise, retirement contributions and benefits can be linked to the amount of time worked. Other benefits, however, are not easily reduced or divided. It is not practical to prorate health insurance benefits. It may, on the other hand, be possible to adjust employee contributions to health insurance costs so that part-time employees pay proportionately more than full-time employees. In part, these decisions are financial, designed to put all benefits on a sound basis. In part, these are policy decisions, articulating a commitment to the social and managerial value of temporary and part-time employment.

SETTING LEVELS OF COMPENSATION

Determining how many dollars to assign to pay ranges, steps, and benefits is a dynamic process. In some instances this is done within the context of collective bargaining, discussed in the next chapter. In others, this is done within budget and personnel management processes and involves nonprofit boards or government executives and legislatures.

The determination of an individual employee's salary occurs at both a structural and an individual level. Dollar amounts must be established for the top and bottom of each pay range, and, using the percentage increase that is relevant, the value of each step in the ranges must be calculated. In addition, there must be a process and a set of criteria for setting the salary of each employee.

Structural Issues of Compensation

Pay Ranges

To set pay for the compensation scheme as a whole, it is necessary to have completed job analyses and position classifications, to have identified compensable factors, and to have information on what other employers are paying similar types of employees. Job analysis and position classification are the subjects of Chapter 8. The allocation of classifications into pay ranges is a critical step in the application of the comparable worth principle, as previously discussed.[34]

Once salary ranges and jobs have been linked, the assignment of dollar amounts to the minimum and maximum positions on the salary ranges is done by determining what other employers are paying for positions similar to benchmark jobs that are not ones in which government is the major employer and ones that are not traditionally female-dominated. The Department of Labor collects and provides information on compensation levels used in private businesses, nonprofit organizations and government bodies. In addition, some employers conduct a salary survey of employers within their geographic area, or—more likely—contract with a consultant to do this study. The steps and calculations used in salary surveys are explained in the exercise appended to this chapter.

Cost of Living and Base Adjustments

Periodically, jurisdictions adjust all salaries in order to recognize increased inflation and costs of living. Formal cost of living adjustments (COLAs) are tied to the federal Consumer Price Index or to some other indicator of the economy. This is sometimes done on an automatic basis every three, six, or 12 months. The commitment to keep pace with some index is, however, often a risk that governments are unwilling to take.

Government revenues and nonprofit organizational income are only partially tied to inflation and activity in the general economy, and there is no guarantee that there will be enough money in the treasury to pay for the adjustments. Instead, the common pattern is for these employers to make yearly or biannual salary adjustments that are influenced by the state of the economy but also take other factors into consideration. Other factors that determine the level of these rates are the agency's ability to pay, policy decisions about equity, and judgments about what is acceptable to a board or to elected officials.

Base adjustments in salaries are usually done on an across-the-board basis, that is, everyone has their salary increased by the same percent. In some systems, however, the percentage increase is applied to the lowest salary and then a formula that may take into account longevity or some other factor is applied to adjust salaries throughout the system. Although the usual expectation is for an increase in salary, during harsh economic times the discussion may be about decreases. An examination of strategies for reducing salaries is included at the end of this chapter.

Minimum Wages

In 1974 the federal government attempted to set minimum standards that state and local governments had to follow in compensating their employees. Congress passed a law that would have required state and local governments to abide by the Fair Labor Standards Act (FLSA), which regulates private employers. This act sets a minimum wage and also specifies a maximum number of hours employees can work. The latter would have caused some problems with fire departments, because the time firefighters spend sleeping in fire stations would have counted toward the maximum number of hours worked. The 1974 law was set aside. In 1976 the U.S. Supreme Court, in *National League of Cities* v. *Usery,* ruled that Congress acted unconstitutionally and infringed on state and local sovereignty. In *Garcia* v. *San Antonio* (1985), however, the Court reversed itself and ruled that the Fair Labor Standards Act does apply to state and local governments. Congress made some modifications in the FLSA to respond to local government concerns, but the basic requirements of the act are now embedded in the compensation practices of state and local governments. Minimum wage laws, of state governments and the federal government, do apply to nonprofit organizations.

Hiring Above the Minimum

Decision rules begin with the hiring process. Although recruitment notices typically provide information about the salary range, not just the minimum salary, the usual decision rule dictates that new employees will be hired at the minimum salary. There are, however, opportunities for exceptions. Most organizations have a special procedure that managers can use for requesting permission to hire someone at a salary above the minimum of the range. The justification might be the level of competing offers or unusual education or experience that the individual might have.

Individual Pay Levels

In general, it is common practice to avoid making decisions when determining the pay of individual employees. Rather than bargain with individuals about their worth to the organization and rather than make judgments about an employee's performance, there is a preference for self-implementing decision rules that determine what an employee will earn from one year to the next. Employees do not want their compensation affected by someone's judgment, even if they could get higher raises with a positive judgment. Managers prefer systems that do not ask them to make a choice about salary increases for their employees. Where a choice is required, managers and supervisors tend to select across-the-board increases.[35]

Longevity

Longevity is an important operative rule in setting individual employee salaries. Once employed, it is common for an employee to move through a pay range on the basis of having performed satisfactorily for the required period of time at one step before moving to the next. Not moving to the next step would usually be regarded as a disciplinary action and, at least under most collective bargaining agreements, would be subject to the grievance process. Moving, on the other hand, does not require improvement in performances, evidence of exceptional contribution, or anything other than a record of satisfactory performance. Systems like this typically do not allow an employee to advance more than one step at a time. Performance, in short, is not a factor except in an unusually negative way.

Performance

Despite the general reluctance of managers to make distinctions among employees that might result in differences in compensation, and despite the reluctance of employees to have their compensation linked to assessments of their performance, there is widespread agreement that performance should be a factor. This was a theme in the literature reviewed earlier in this chapter. After reviewing studies of failures of attempts to link pay to performance, W. Clay Hamner itemized major obstacles. The list included the employee's failure to perceive pay as linked to performance, performance evaluation systems regarded as biased, supervisors more concerned with morale and satisfaction than with performance and productivity, and a low level of trust and openness between employees and supervisors. Nonetheless, Hamner remains convinced of the soundness of the principle of relating pay to performance and confident that all of the obstacles can be overcome.[36]

Individuals are likely to differ in their optimism that better communication within the organization, more thorough performance evaluation systems, better training for supervisors, and more meaningful rewards for superior performance are likely to make a merit pay system work as it should. The intuitive soundness and reasonableness of the concept will nonetheless continue to prompt efforts to make it work.

The federal government has had a particularly frustrating time trying to establish a performance-based pay system. A major feature of the 1978 Civil Service Reform

Act was the replacement in the GS–13, GS–14, and GS–15 ranks of the traditional compensation system, which emphasized seniority or longevity, with one recognizing and rewarding exceptional performance. The implementation was delayed until 1981 so that performance evaluation systems could be put in place. Then, however, the president and Congress were not disposed to fund the merit plan fully. Also, the performance evaluations failed to make meaningful distinctions among employees. As a result, some managers began receiving less pay than significant numbers of those they supervised.[37] Former Representative Mary Rose Oakar, an expert in the House of Representatives on the federal civil service, condemned the performance-based pay system and called for change.

In 1984 Congress passed legislation providing for the Performance Management and Recognition System (PMRS). This approach required that employees be rated at one of five levels, with the middle level being satisfactory. Employees had to be rated at satisfactory or above in order to receive a full general pay increase. Those rated as fully successful, highly successful, or outstanding were also eligible for a step increase if they were not at the maximum level of their pay range and were qualified for a performance bonus, which depended on their performance evaluation. The PMRS restricted agencies to spending no more than 1.5 percent of their payroll for all performance awards.

Reviews of the PMRS were not encouraging. Most employees were rated as outstanding or highly successful and PMRS merit increases became automatic, much like the system for salary adjustments prior to the 1978 Civil Service Reform Act. The crucial link between pay and performance is hard for either researchers or employees to see.[38]

In 1997 the federal government began, on a limited basis, several programs linking pay to performance. Part of the broad-banding project in the Commerce Department discussed above is a program in which managers within the agency could reward employees for superb performance with bonuses of up to $10,000. The bonuses are lump-sum payments that do not affect base salaries.

The Department of Defense developed the Acquisition Workforce Demonstration Project in July 1998, which places up to 50,000 acquisition professionals in broad pay bands. Managers meet each year with individual employees to discuss their contributions to the department. If managers believe employees have exceeded their respective contribution expectations, then raises are granted. The project is conceptually similar to management by objectives, discussed in Chapter 9.

As part of the implementation of the 1993 National Performance Review recommendations, agencies are defining performance objectives and developing measures of performance. By mid–1977, nine agencies had been designated as Performance-Based Organizations (PBOs). The designation frees the agency from many of the rules and routines of the federal government and links a portion of the agency manager's pay to the performance of the organization as a whole.

The Total Quality Management philosophy supports linking the pay of all team or organizational members, not just the agency manager or chief executive officer, to the performance of the team or organization as a whole. This is known as **gain sharing** or **success sharing**. A demonstration project at McClellan Air Force Base in California is one of the few public-sector attempts to use group rewards for group performance.

Evaluations of these are mixed, but in any case probably premature. More experience will yield more conclusive lessons.[39]

Compensation in the public sector is still determined primarily by position classification, job evaluation, seniority, and across-the-board adjustments.[40] Nonetheless, there is continued support for the principle of performance-based pay. The federal government in the late 1990s has supported specific experiments and projects. State governments, according to a 1997 survey, acknowledge problems with implementing pay for performance, but continue to struggle and make adaptations.[41]

Competence

Qualifications can be another determinant of individual pay.[42] This is sometimes referred to as competency-based pay. Teachers in public schools typically are paid in part according to what degrees they have, how many post-graduate credits they have earned, and how many years they have taught. Similarly, a feature of the Department of Defense project for acquisitions professionals is to base an individual's pay in part on his or her qualifications. Some regard competency-based pay as a form of performance pay. It more directly, however, addresses an important ingredient of performance, but not performance itself. As discussed in Chapter 5, performance and productivity depend on effort and on working conditions as well as on skills and qualifications.

CUTTING PAY

The economic difficulties of the early 1980s and again 20 years later were a dramatic reminder that one should not assume that increases in salary are automatic or inevitable. Nonprofit organizations had to cope with cuts in donations and grants. State and local governments, under strictures to balance their budgets and faced with lower than expected revenues, found that they had to cut, among other items, personnel costs. The first and most common reaction to this need is to curtail any hiring activity and save money by coping with funded but vacant positions. That was not always sufficient, and jurisdictions had to devise even more painful measures.

Layoffs, of course, are one way of responding to revenue shortfalls. Another strategy is to decrease the salaries of the current workforce. This can be done by paying employees less than they had been making and still requiring them to work as many hours and be as productive as they had been. Sometimes it is not legally possible to do this. Collective bargaining contracts typically rule out this option. Legalities aside, it may not be prudent to pursue this course of action.

Instead, agencies can cut back on the hours that employees work. Mandating that all employees take an unpaid vacation can save considerable money in most jurisdictions. Given some of the more painful alternatives, employee dissatisfaction is relatively low with this option. Another relatively painless option is to delay scheduled pay increases. Employees can still look forward to the increase and the new base salaries can be used in calculating further increases, but the solvency of the agency can be salvaged by waiting to implement announced wage increases.

SUMMARY

Compensation is a matter of vital importance to employees, taxpayers, board members, and elected officials. It is a matter of policy and political significance, as well as key to management. As with other aspects of public personnel management, there are a variety of conflicting principles and pressures that must be accommodated. More than other aspects of public personnel management, this takes place in a highly visible setting. Care and systematic approaches are essential not only to do the job well, but to provide assurances that salaries are not being set arbitrarily or based on favoritism or prejudice.

A long-standing issue pursued by researchers and policy makers is how to construct a pay system that prompts worker productivity. There are many approaches that have intuitive appeal but in fact seem to generate more conflict and dissatisfaction than productivity. Some of the setbacks appear related to general traits of organizations. Despite disappointments and obstacles, efforts continue to identify pay policies and procedures that are fair, affordable, and provide productivity incentives.

DISCUSSION QUESTIONS

1. Why are market forces (in particular, the compensation paid by other employers for jobs similar to those in a government agency or nonprofit organization) not always useful determinants of pay?
2. There continues to be considerable intuitive appeal for linking pay to performance. Why is this not a common compensation practice in governments and nonprofits?
3. What would you like to be included in a cafeteria-style benefit plan? Would you anticipate finding some benefits more useful than others depending on your personal circumstances?
4. How would you define a fair compensation policy? Can you envision alternative definitions of fairness?

Conducting a Pay Survey Exercise

One of the factors that must be included in a pay plan is the level of compensation other employers in the community are paying employees who do work similar to that done in a particular government agency or nonprofit organization. Although some relevant information is available from the national surveys conducted by the Office of Personnel Management and the Bureau of Labor Statistics, one can periodically conduct pay surveys of selected employers in the community as a way of identifying market rates.

PREPARING THE SURVEY INSTRUMENT

Identify key job classes.   It is not possible to include every job found in a particular organization in a survey. Key jobs need to be identified as the focus of the questions that will be posed in the survey. A job class can be regarded as key if it satisfies at least some of the following criteria:

1. It includes a substantial number of employees.
2. It includes a substantial number of employees in the firm or organization participating in the survey.
3. It is a field in which there is a shortage of qualified individuals, and thus employers are competing for applicants.

For purposes of this exercise, if an organization in the community has a position similar to the one you analyzed for Chapter 8, use that as the focus of your survey. If there is no reasonable counterpart, use a familiar clerical, custodial worker, accountant, or other position that is common in public, nonprofit, and private organizations.

Describe the jobs included in the survey.   A brief, accurate description of the key job classes that will allow an employer to identify counterparts is essential to the quality of the data collected by the survey. Job titles can sometimes be misleading. Existing job descriptions may have to be rewritten to communicate more effectively or in a more concise manner with other employers.

Select employers to be included in the survey.   The local public library and the Internet are likely to be good sources of employers in the community. Lists are usually available from employment services, banks, chambers of commerce, and licensing agencies. Those employers selected should, of course, have jobs similar to the key jobs and have a relatively large workforce. Small businesses may pay low noncompetitive wages but are sometimes included in the survey both for balance and as a way of maintaining good public relations with the smaller firms.

There are no commonly accepted rules for how many employers should be included. More important than numbers is the similarity of the jobs.

For purposes of this exercise, select two or three employers with positions similar to the one you are using.

List salient questions.   The questions should anticipate the kinds of compensation decisions that the organization will have to make. These questions will be about salaries and benefits, and typically will include:

1. Number of employees in the job class
2. Number of hours in the workweek
3. Minimum and maximum, if any, of pay range
4. Average salary
5. Number of pay rates, if any
6. Required length of time one must serve before advancing to another step
7. Cost of health insurance to employer and employee
8. Major benefits of health insurance
9. Cost and benefits of life insurance
10. Cost and benefits of retirement program
11. Number of paid holidays
12. Number of days of paid sick leave

13. Number of paid vacation days
14. Number of other paid days off
15. Merit pay provisions

Collecting the Data

The most effective way of collecting this information is by personal interview. This should be done via a personal visit, rather than by telephone.

Frequently, all of the needed information is not readily available. If the employer feels uncomfortable or not confident about providing information from memory, a list of questions can be left. Usually, this needs to be followed by another visit.

Some employers will not provide compensation information unless they are assured of its confidentiality.

Presenting the Data

Information collected through the survey is presented separately for each job class, although benefits are presented collectively if employers provide the same benefits for all their employees.

A commonly used calculation in presenting salary data is the weighted average pay. Completing the following steps makes that calculation:

1. For each employer, multiply the number of employees by their average pay, being certain that the average pay is based on the same unit of time—either pay per hour or pay per 40-hour workweek.
2. Add the results of the first step.
3. Divide the sum from Step 2 by the total number of employees reported for all employers.

It is usually very difficult to summarize in any simple way the benefits that various employers pay. There are subtle but important differences in health insurance. Seniority and other individual traits have a different impact on benefits, depending on the employer. There are two ways that are used to convey these data. One is to present the data for a limited number of types of employees (based on seniority, level of pay, occupation, etc.). The other is to calculate the percentage of either total compensation or of salary that each benefit represents and use that as a basis for comparisons.

Using the Data

Except when an organization is committed to paying a certain class of jobs at the prevailing rate in the community, the pay survey data are a source of information that affects the assignment of money amounts to pay ranges, but they are not the only influence and concern. Prevailing wage rates are most common for blue-collar jobs.

The practice in many agencies that conduct salary surveys is to arrange key job classes in the hierarchical order that represents their value to the jurisdiction and then to attach the survey data to these classes. Job classes that were not included in the survey are then assigned dollar figures that provide a link between the key classes included in the survey. To avoid incorporating the societal practice of paying discriminatory wages to those in jobs traditionally filled by women, job classes occupied predominantly (more than 70 percent) by women should not be included in salary surveys. These jobs, like others for which there are no good market data, should be assigned pay ranges that are appropriate for their respective job evaluation points.

This then provides a first draft or outline from which other work and decisions can proceed. With the framework provided by the survey data, decisions can be made about whether the organization should be more or less generous, whether comparable worth concerns are being accommodated, and what might be done to incorporate a merit pay system. The survey information is not the final word, but it is very instrumental in arriving at the final word.

GLOSSARY

Broad banding The consolidation of classifications, pay steps, and pay ranges for a particular occupational category in order to create a larger range and more flexibility for movement within the range of jobs and pay levels

Cafeteria-style benefits Program that allows employees to select from among a variety of benefits as part of their compensation rather than providing all benefits to each employee

Comparable worth Principle that pay should be equal within an organization for jobs that are similar in difficulty, responsibility, and the like even though different in tasks

Equal pay for equal work Principle that pay should be the same for individuals doing the same job within the same organization, unless justified by performance, seniority, or some factor other than gender

Equity theory Links compensation and performance based on comparisons employees make among themselves about the relationships between work and rewards

Expectancy theory Links compensation and performance based on employee perceptions about what they have to do to get valued rewards

Gain sharing Bonuses given as rewards to each member of a team or group when the team or groups meet or exceed a performance objective

Pay banding Another term for broad banding

Pay equity Another term for comparable worth

Pay range An amount of compensation, with a set minimum and maximum, that varies for a job depending on such factors as longevity, productivity, or qualifications

Pay rate An amount of compensation for a specific job that does not vary according to seniority, productivity, or other factors

Pay schedule A hierarchical ordering of pay ranges

Pay step A specific level of compensation within a pay range

Replacement ratio The relationship between payments from a retirement program and the compensation an individual would be making if still working in the job from which he or she retired

Success sharing Another term for gain sharing

SOURCES

DeCenzo, D. A., & Holoviak, S. J. (1990). *Employee benefits.* Englewood Cliffs, NJ: Prentice-Hall.
   General description and discussion of the various types of benefits paid to employees.

Evans, S. M., & Nelson, B. J. (1989). *Wage justice.* Chicago: University of Chicago Press.
Discussion and analysis of sex-based pay inequities and comparable worth.

Lawler, E. E. (1990). *Strategic pay.* San Francisco: Jossey-Bass.
An interpretation of the linkages between compensation and motivation.

Risher, H. (1997). *New strategies for public pay.* San Francisco: Jossey-Bass.
Description and discussion of approaches in governments to link compensation to performance.

NOTES

1. Frederick Taylor, *The Principles of Scientific Management* (New York: Harper and Row, 1945).
2. E. J. Roethlisberger and W. J. Dickson, *Management and the Worker* (Cambridge, MA: Harvard University Press, 1939).
3. Abraham H. Maslow, *Motivation and Personality* (New York: Harper & Row, 1954).
4. F. Herzberg, B. Mausner, and B. Snyderman, *The Motivation to Work* (New York: Wiley, 1959); F. Herzberg, "One More Time: How Do You Motivate Employees?" *Harvard Business Review* 46, no. 1 (January–March 1968): 53–62.
5. William M. Leavitt, "High Pay and Low Morale-Can High Pay, Excellent Benefits, Job Security, and Low Job Satisfaction Coexist in a Public Agency?" *Public Personnel Management* 25, no. 3 (Fall 1996): 333–342.
6. Victor H. Vroom, *Work and Motivation* (New York: Wiley, 1964).
7. Edward E. Lawler, Strategic Pay (San Francisco: Jossey-Bass, 1990); J. W. Atkinson, *An Introduction to Motivation* (New York: Van Nostrand, 1964); J. M. Ivancevich, A. D. Szelagyi, and M. J. Wallace, *Organizational Behavior and Performance* (Belmont, CA: Goodyear, 1977).
8. J. S. Adams, "Toward an Understanding of Inequity," *Journal of Abnormal and Social Psychology* 67 (1963): 425–427; J. S. Adams, "Inequity in Social Exchange", in L. Berkowitz, ed., *Advances in Experimental Social Psychology* (New York: Academic Press, 1965).
9. K. Dow Scott, Steven E. Markham, and Michael J. Vest, "The Influence of a Merit Pay Guide Chart on Employee Attitudes Toward Pay at a Transit Authority," *Public Personnel Management* 25, no. 1 (Spring 1996): 103–118.
10. G. Stephen Taylor and Michael J. Vest, "Pay Comparisons and Pay Satisfaction Among Public Sector Employees," *Public Personnel Management* 21, no. 4 (Winter 1992): 445–454.
11. Suzanne M. Crampton, John W. Hodge, and Jitendra M. Mishra, "The Equal Pay Act: The First 30 Years," *Public Personnel Management* 26, no. 3 (Fall 1997): 335–344; Linda S. Hartenian and Nancy Brown Johnson, "Establishing the Reliability and Validity of Wage Surveys," *Public Personnel Management* 20, no. 3 (Fall 1991): 367–384.
12. Elaine Sorenson, "The Wage Effects of Occupational Sex Composition: A Review and New Findings," in Anne Hill and Mark R. Killingsworth, eds., *Comparable Worth: Analyses and Evidence* (Ithaca, NY: Cornell University ILR Press, 1989).
13. George Hildebrand, "The Market System," in Robert Liverhash, ed., *Comparable Worth: Issues and Alternatives* (Washington, DC: Equal Employment Advisory Council, 1980); Henry J. Aaron and M. Lougy Cameron, *The Comparable Worth Controversy* (Washington, DC: Brookings Institution, 1986).
14. Heidi I. Hartmann, "The Case for Comparable Worth", in Phyllis Schlafly, ed., *Equal Pay for Unequal Work: A Conference on Comparable Worth* (Washington, DC: Eagle Forum, 1983), 11.

15. Richard W. Scholl and Elizabeth A. Cooper, "The Use of Job Evaluation to Eliminate Gender Based Pay Differentials," *Public Personnel Management* 20, no. 1 (Spring 1991): 1–18; Jonathan Tompkins, "Comparable Worth and Job Evaluation Validity," *Public Administration Review* 47 (May/June 1987): 254–258; General Accounting Office, *Options for Conducting a Pay Equity Study of Federal Pay and Classification Systems* (Washington, DC: Government Printing Office, 1985); Donald J. Treiman and Heidi I. Hartmann, eds., Women, Work, and Wages: *Equal Pay for Jobs of Equal Value* (Washington, DC: National Academy Press, 1981).

16. Bernadette M. Racicot, Dennis Doverspike, Jeffrey S. Hornsby, and Neil M.A. Hauenstein, "Job Grade and Labor Market Information Effects on Simulated Compensation Decisions," *Public Personnel Management* 25, no. 3 (Fall 1996): 343–350.

17. Gregory B. Lewis, "Continuing Progress Toward Racial and Gender Pay Equality in the Federal Service," *Review of Public Personnel Administration* 18, no. 2 (Spring 1998): 41–56.

18. Frances C. Hunter, *Equal Pay for Comparable Worth: The Working Woman's Issue of the Eighties* (New York: Praeger, 1986), 190–205; C. Chi, "Comparable Worth in State Government: Trends and Issues," *Political Studies Review* 5, no. 4 (May 1986): 800–814; Alice H. Cook, "Pay Equity: Theory and Implementation" in Carolyn Ban and Norma Riccucci, eds., *Public Personnel Management: Current Concerns-Future Challenges* (New York: Longman, 1991), 100–113.

19. Sara M. Evans and Barbara J. Nelson, *Wage Justice* (Chicago: University of Chicago Press, 1989); B. S. Steel and N. P. Lovrich, Jr., "Comparable Worth: The Problematic Politicization of a Public Personnel Issue," *Public Personnel Management* 16, no. 1 (Spring 1987): 23–36.

20. Carolyn Ban, "The Navy Demonstration Project: An Experiment in Experimentation," in Carolyn Ban and Norma M. Riccucci, eds., *Public Personnel Management: Current Concerns-Future Challenges* (New York: Longman, 1991), 31–41.

21. David Hofrichter, "Broadbanding: A Second Generation Approach," *Compensation and Benefits Review* 25 (September-October 1993): 53–58.

22. Robert J. Trudel, "Principles of Pay Administration," in Harold Suskin, ed., *Job Evaluation and Pay Administration in the Public Sector* (Chicago: International Personnel Management Association, 1977), 267–269.

23. Dennis M. Daley, "An Overview of Benefits for the Public Sector," *Review of Public Personnel Administration* 18, no. 3 (Summer 1998): 5–22.

24. Stephen C. Caulfield, "Benefits in a Changing Workforce," *Employee Benefits Journal* (December 1990): 19–24; David A. DeCenzo and Stephen J. Holoviak, *Employee Benefits* (Englewood Cliffs, NJ: Prentice-Hall, 1990).

25. A. Deutchman, "The Great Pension Robbery," *Forbes* 125, no. 1 (1992): 76–78.

26. M. S. Melbinger, "The Possibility of Federal Regulation of State and Local Government Retirement Plans," *Employee Benefits Journal* 17, no. 4 (1992): 23–27; William N. Thompson, "Public Pension Plans: The Need for Scrutiny and Control," *Public Personnel Management* 6, no. 4 (July/August 1977): 203–224.

27. Blair Testin, "1990 Comparative Study of Major Public Employee Retirement Systems," in M. J. Brzezinski, ed., *Public Employee Benefit Plans-1991* (Brookfield, WI: International Foundation of Employee Benefit Plans, 1992), 102–136; P. Zorn, "A Survey of State Retirement Systems Covering General Employees and Teachers," *Government Finance Review* 6, no. 5 (1990): 25–29.

28. Perry Moore, "Health Care Cost Containment in Large American Cities," *Public Personnel Management* 18 (Spring 1989): 87–100; Thomas P. Burke and Rita S. Jain, "Trends in Employer-Provided Health Care Benefits," *Monthly Labor Review* 112, no. 2 (1991): 24–30.

29. Helen Weems Daley and Ronald D. Sylvia, "A Quasi-Experimental Evaluation of Tuition Reimbursement in Municipal Government," *Review of Public Personnel Administration* 1, no. 2 (Spring 1981): 18.

30. A.N. Nash and S. J. Carrol, Jr., "Supplemental Compensation," in Herbert G. Henemann, III, and Donald P. Schwab, eds., *Perspectives on Personnel/Human Resource Management* (Homewood, IL: Richard D. Irwin, 1978), 224.

31. Ronald W. Perry and N. Joseph Cayer, "Cafeteria-Style Health Plans in Municipal Government," *Public Personnel Management* 28, no. 1 (Spring 1999): 107–118.

32. William B. Werther, Jr., "Flexible Compensation Evaluated," *California Management Review* 19 (1976): 40–46; Roger Thompson, "Switching to Flexible Benefits," *Nations Business* 79 (1991): 95–99.

33. Edward E. Lawler, III, "New Approaches to Pay: Innovations that Work," in Henemann and Schwab, *Perspectives,* 226–233; Lawler, *Strategic Pay*.

34. Helen Remick, "The Comparable Worth Controversy," *Public Personnel Management* 10 (Winter, 1981): 373–377.

35. James L. Perry, "Linking Pay to Performance: The Controversy Continues," and Mark W. Huddleston, "The Senior Executive Service: Problems and Prospects for Reform," in Carolyn Ban and Norma Riccucci, eds., *Public Personnel Management: Current Concerns—Future Challenges* (New York: Longman, 1991), 73–86 and 175–189.

36. National Research Council, *Pay for Performance: Evaluating Performance Appraisal and Merit Pay* (Washington, DC: National Academy Press, 1991); James L. Perry, Beth Ann Petrakis, and Theodore K. Miller, "Federal Merit Pay, Round II: An Analysis of the Performance Management and Recognition System," *Public Administration Review* 49 (January/February 1989): 29–37.

37. Jane L. Pearce and James L. Perry, "Federal Merit Pay: A Longitudinal Analysis," *Public Administration Review* 43, no. 2 (May/June 1983): 315–325.

38. Perry, Petrakis, and Miller, "Federal Merit Pay, Round II: An Analysis of the Performance Management and Recognition System," 34–36.

39. Howard Risher, *New Strategies for Public Pay* (San Francisco: Jossey-Bass, 1997).

40. Howard Risher, "Are Public Employers Ready for a 'New Pay' Program?" *Public Personnel Management* 28, no. 3 (Fall 1999): 323–344.

41. J. Edward Kellough and Sally Coleman Selden, "Pay for Performance Systems in State Government: Perceptions of State Agency Personnel Managers," *Review of Public Personnel Administration* 17, no. 1 (Winter 1997): 5–21.

42. James R. Thompson and Charles W. LeHew, "Skill-Based Pay as Organizational Innovation," *Review of Public Personnel Administration* 20, no. 1 (Winter 2000): 20–40.

Chapter 15

Collective Bargaining

A major objective of personnel management is to foster agency productivity. A general reasoning underlying the personnel management functions discussed thus far purports that if an organization anticipates its needs for personnel in a timely and accurate way, structures its tasks in accordance with technological and organizational needs, identifies and hires competent people, conducts and uses evaluations of employee performance, trains and develops employees, and compensates workers in ways that are perceived as fair and rewarding performance, then the organization's workforce will be productive and the organization will accomplish its goals. All of this is logical and at least partially supported by empirical evidence. There is, however, one major caveat: Conflict between employees and supervisors detracts from the productivity increases that could be attained through these efforts.

This chapter explains a major approach toward dealing with organizational conflict. That approach is to bargain a contract that resolves some issues such as wages and work rules and provides a process for resolving the many ongoing, inevitable disputes between management and workers.

ORGANIZATIONAL CONFLICT AND COLLECTIVE BARGAINING

Conflict is inevitable and ubiquitous in organizations. That is the conclusion of sociologists of organizations.[1] Ralf Dahrendorf, whose theories here are seminal,[2] noted that authority is a basic variable in social conflict and a basic feature of organizations. Divisions emerge between workers and bosses, with the former—sometimes informally—banding together for self-protection from supervisory activities and protest against managerial demands. A manifestation of this conflict is lower productivity. Workers do not work as hard or as enthusiastically as they could; shortcuts are devised; minor rule infractions are the norm. For those who have worked in an organization, as a supervisor or as one being supervised, all of this will readily sound familiar.

There are a variety of approaches that have been used to mitigate or eliminate conflict in organizations. Supervisors are sent to training courses to learn how to deal effectively with their employees. Employees are organized into teams and invited to work with, not against, managers. The physical environment where employees work is made pleasant with plants, music, and pastel-colored walls. These are all improvements that, at least for a short period of time, are appreciated. However, they do not get at the central issue in the conflict between managers and workers—a difference in power.

One way that employees try to offset the power and authority of management is through anonymous group conflict.[3] Without leadership or structure, employees implicitly agree on the rate at which they will work and the rules they will fully obey. There are no explicit discussions or agreements. Informal understandings govern. Employees appear physically at the office on time (not early) and then spend an hour organizing the work on their desks, reading the newspaper, and sipping coffee. Memos and reports are adequate, but they do not include all available information and details. The lack of creative suggestions in the reports may be more a sign of protest or indifference than of incompetence. The pace of work is a bit more furious when supervisors are in the office than when they are not present. It is conflict that managers find difficult to deal with because of its informal, anonymous nature. There is no leader to punish or persuade, no structure through which to communicate. Workers, on the other hand, find this kind of conflict frustrating because, although it makes a point, it does not resolve anything.

One way in which managers deal with conflict is to use the techniques of participatory management. Management by objectives and Total Quality Management (TQM) are types of participatory management.[4] These approaches have limitations because they are management controlled and management oriented and quickly—if not from the start—lose credibility with workers.[5] Indeed, the intent of these techniques sometimes is to avoid employee unionization, where employees have a more equal, powerful footing.

Collective bargaining is another way of handling organizational conflict. Collective bargaining does not deny conflict, and it does not end conflict. It does, however, resolve and manage conflict. Issues of disagreement are brought to the bargaining table and, at least for the duration of the contract, settled. In the day-to-day relationships between supervisors and employees, a process exists whereby employees can, through their union leaders, raise an objection and get a response. The response is not guaranteed to be to the employee's liking. Collective bargaining does not work just to the employee's advantage. In fact, the major public employee union for state and local employees (other than teachers), the American Federation of State, County and Municipal Employees, was started at the initiative of senior managers in Wisconsin state government as a way of managing conflict between employees and their supervisors.

THE EMERGENCE OF PUBLIC SECTOR BARGAINING

As in the private sector, the first to unionize in government were laborers and mechanics. Blue-collar workers in naval shipyards and federal arsenals organized themselves in the 1830s. Postal workers unionized in the 1880s. Little other activity occurred prior to the twentieth century.

Then there was the infamous police strike in Boston in 1919. Police in Boston were working an average of 87 hours per week. Police stations were incredibly unsanitary and infested with rats. The salary range was $1,100 to $1,600 per year—at the poverty level. Salary increases were rare, and when they occurred, they were below the rise in the cost of living. It is no wonder that police organized and, when they were unable to bargain a settlement, they went on strike.

When they struck, however, thieves and hoodlums had a field day. Calvin Coolidge, then governor of Massachusetts, reacted harshly. The State Guard was called to restore order, Governor Coolidge assumed control over the police department, striking officers were dismissed, order was restored, and Coolidge received acclaim that carried him into the vice presidency and presidency of the United States. The effect on collective bargaining among government employees was chilling.[6]

Except for the unionization of the Tennessee Valley Authority employees in the 1930s—a special case in many ways—there was practically no activity for almost 50 years. During the 1960s and 1970s, however, there was a spurt of union growth in the public sector. Between 1953 and 1975, as union membership in the private sector declined from one-fourth to one-fifth the total number of employees, union membership in the public sector grew from less than one-tenth to over one-third.

Despite the extent of collective bargaining in the public sector, there is no standardization of processes or rights as there is for the private sector. Private employers and employees, including those in nonprofit organizations, are covered under the National Labor Relations Act (NLRA), which defines unfair labor practices, scope of bargaining, procedures for resolving an impasse, and the like. The National Labor Relations Board, which is a quasi-judicial body that implements and enforces the NLRA, does not have jurisdiction over government employment.

State and Local Governments

Activity leading to the current status of collective bargaining began in Wisconsin. In 1932, Arnold Zander, head of the Wisconsin State Employees Association, founded the **American Federation of State, County, and Municipal Employees (AFSCME)**. The American Federation of Labor in 1936 chartered AFSCME, and by the 1940s the union had over 700 local organizations active throughout the country.[7] Public employees did not, however, have an explicit, legal right to unionize and the aftermath of the Boston police strike did not encourage illegal action. In 1959, however, at the instigation of personnel managers in local governments and AFSCME officials, the Wisconsin state legislature passed a bill requiring local governments to bargain with their employees if the employees organized.

Wisconsin also pioneered when, in 1967, state employees were granted the right to bargain. Initially, state employees could bargain on only a few issues. Effective in 1971, however, the subjects that could be brought to the negotiating table were extended to include compensation, transfers, and virtually anything other than agency missions, position classifications, and the selection process.

Other states soon followed. By 1982, 37 states provided the right of public employees to bargain the conditions of their employment. Most did this through statutes. Some, like Illinois, did so through an executive order. Michigan and California, which have constitutional clauses prohibiting collective bargaining by public employees, agree to meet and confer with their employees. Technically, meet-and-confer agreements are not binding, but advisory only. Nonetheless, these states regard their bargaining seriously and their agreements are treated as binding. Kansas and Missouri also have a meet-and-confer process, but this is treated as a step short of serious and binding collective bargaining.

The Federal Government

The federal government is not a leader in the field of public employee bargaining. The federal government has been a latecomer and from 2002 to 2007 took steps to withdraw collective bargaining rights from some of its employees. Perhaps more important, it has allowed bargaining on a very narrow range of issues. The first serious move to let federal employees organize and negotiate was when President John F. Kennedy, fulfilling a campaign promise, issued Executive Order 10988 in 1962. That order stated that employees could bargain collectively over the establishment of a grievance procedure and over a few personnel policy issues but not anything dealing with compensation. Prior to this order, each federal agency set its own policies on employee unionization. The Department of the Interior, the Government Printing Office, the Post Office, and the Alaska Railroad were the only agencies where significant bargaining was occurring. President Kennedy maintained a departmental focus to the structure and processes of unionization in the federal government.

President Richard Nixon, acting on a report provided to him by President Lyndon B. Johnson as he left the White House, improved the processes by simplifying the steps for a union to get recognition as a bargaining agent and by providing for binding arbitration when the parties reach an impasse. President Jimmy Carter included the essence of the Kennedy and Nixon Executive Orders in his Civil Service Reform Act of 1978, thus making collective bargaining statutory. The Federal Labor Relations Authority (FLRA) was established to certify unions as bargaining agents and to provide mediation and arbitration services. President George W. Bush argued that national security concerns trumped rights to unionize and severely limited collective bargaining in several agencies, most notably the Department of Homeland Security and Department of Defense.[8]

Despite the statutory base of collective bargaining since 1978, the federal government still participates in collective bargaining in a very limited way. Bargaining cannot include compensation issues, layoff policies, and a number of other critical matters. Congress, unlike legislative bodies in other jurisdictions, does not play a role in the collective bargaining process. The patterns of experiences that inform this chapter come primarily from state and local governments.

There are several concerns that affect the establishment of bargaining units. There is concern that employees in the same unit be doing work similar enough so that they might reasonably be covered under the same contract. Contracts include provisions about work rules, overtime pay, working conditions, and the like. To include employees whose circumstances vary widely complicates both the negotiation and administration of contracts.

Another concern is size. A large bargaining unit can, simply because of its numbers, have more power than either management or unions feel is desirable. A large unit can dominate the process. It can hold management hostage, and it can effectively determine the terms of settlement for the other unions. Dominance over the content of the settlement is particularly likely in compensation issues. If a large bargaining unit agrees to an increase in compensation of 5 percent, that union is not likely to allow management to settle on 6 percent raises with another union. Legally, of course, the large union can do little. But it takes little imagination to envision the probable kinds of protests and pressures. In effect, 5 percent becomes the ceiling.

Finally, employers are concerned that there not be too many bargaining units. With a large number of bargaining units, management could be negotiating constantly. Sometimes the only feasible way of negotiating where there are large numbers is for unions to form coalitions and bargain a number of contracts simultaneously. Management's concern with the number of bargaining units goes beyond the time that might be consumed in reaching settlements. There could be a whipsaw effect, where unions try to outdo one another in winning concessions. In the process, management would find itself under enormous pressure continually to escalate the benefits offered.

The two common ways of defining bargaining units are by occupational groupings and administrative departments. The latter, used in the federal government and in states including Minnesota and Washington, have the virtue of establishing work rules and other provisions according to the agency's mission. The disadvantage to this approach is that it is difficult to maintain equity within occupational groups, such as clericals, accountants, and attorneys, that cross departmental lines. Using administrative divisions to define bargaining units also leads to a large number of units. Minnesota, for example, has 138 bargaining units and Washington has 117.

The states of Massachusetts, Hawaii, and Wisconsin provide examples where bargaining units are defined according to occupations. A common pattern is to have separate bargaining units for clerical employees, building trades and crafts, blue-collar workers, technicians, security, and public safety officers. In addition, there are professional categories, such as legal, fiscal services, social services, education, and engineering.

Organizations differ about what relationship first-line supervisors should have to collective bargaining. Some jurisdictions (Maryland, Oregon, and Connecticut) do not allow supervisors to unionize at all. Municipalities frequently place first-line supervisors in the same unit as the employees they supervise. This is also the pattern in Maine, New Hampshire, and New Jersey. Still others (Hawaii, Minnesota, Massachusetts, and New York) allow supervisors to bargain, but insist that they be in units separate from the workers they supervise and that they be represented by a different union from the one representing their subordinates. Pennsylvania negotiates with supervisors on a meet-and-confer basis. There is no consensus on what pattern works best or even on the criteria to be used for defining best.

Managers are not allowed to unionize, although it is not uncommon for managers to form an association and perhaps even hire staff and an attorney to represent their views to nonprofit boards, legislative bodies, and chief elected officials. The definition of who is a manager is sometimes arbitrary, defined by a position title or a salary level.

Another group of employees not allowed to unionize is **confidential employees**. These are employees at all levels who are closely involved in collective bargaining for management. Personal secretaries to agency heads and clerical employees who work for management involved in collective bargaining are included. Many personnel officers and certain attorneys are also regarded as confidential.

Administrative Agency

Even with very specific language in a statute providing for collective bargaining in government, there will be confusion and conflict over how to proceed. A common source of confusion, for example, is what bargaining unit, if any, is most appropriate for a particular position. Unions suspect managers of expanding the use of confidential positions beyond what was intended just to keep unions from growing. Unions also fight with one another. A union representing clerical workers may argue that particular payroll officers are in fact doing so much filing and other clerical tasks that they should be in the clerical bargaining unit rather than the fiscal administration bargaining unit. These are not disputes that can be resolved at the bargaining table. They must be on the agenda of some separate, quasi-judicial body.

The federal National Labor Relations Board resolves these disputes for nonprofit organizations, as well as private businesses. In the federal government, the relevant agency is the FLRA. This authority consists of three members appointed by the president and confirmed by the Senate for staggered five-year terms. They can only be removed for cause. Most states and local governments use the National Labor Relations Board model and have established an independent agency to handle these issues. Some states, including Nebraska, Pennsylvania, and Florida, use their civil service commission or their department of labor for administering their collective bargaining laws. Florida, Hawaii, and Iowa are examples of jurisdictions that have a separate, independent body just for public employee collective bargaining. Wisconsin's Employment Relations Commission has jurisdiction over private- and public-sector labor relations, but the NLRB preempts so many of the private-sector cases that most of the work is actually public sector.

Certification

The agencies administering collective bargaining laws are responsible for the **certification** of a union as the recognized bargaining agent for a group of employees. This involves monitoring the petition of a union to represent a group of employees and supervising the elections to determine whether there is the required support from the employees. Each jurisdiction has its own criteria for certifying a union as a bargaining agent for a particular group of employees. Usually, at least 30 percent of the employees in a bargaining unit must sign a petition saying that they want to participate in collective bargaining. Once this petition is filed and judged to be valid, elections are held. A majority of those voting in a bargaining unit must favor being represented by a particular union in order for that union to be certified as the bargaining agent for all employees. There can be a change in the bargaining agent by decertifying one union through a negative vote or through a charge that the union has violated some provision of the law. Then another election can be held. A failure of any union to secure majority support in most cases means simply that no one will be certified and there will be no collective bargaining.

Negotiable Issues

As the parties prepare for and begin the negotiating process, questions often emerge about whether a particular issue can be regarded as a subject for bargaining. The **scope of bargaining** is defined and discussed below. A major part of the workload of any agency administering collective bargaining laws is to resolve disputes about what must be bargained, what may be bargained, and what cannot be bargained.

Good-Faith Bargaining

A less frequent but very important function of labor relations commissions and boards during the bargaining process is to act on complaints that one of the parties is not bargaining in good faith. A fundamental precept of the collective bargaining process mandates that both sides come to the table prepared to give and take to reach a settlement (i.e., to engage in **good-faith bargaining**). A union that wants to go on strike in order to demonstrate that it is a determined and militant organization is vulnerable to a bad-faith bargaining charge. Similarly, if management comes to the table with a single offer and does not budge at all from it, then they are vulnerable.

Impasse

When the parties to the negotiating table are at an **impasse**, a third and neutral party is usually necessary to get the two adversaries to reach a settlement. Impasse resolution is discussed in more detail later. Whatever the options and procedures are in a particular jurisdiction for resolving impasses, an agency for administering them is necessary. In some states, such as Wisconsin, this agency is the same one that certifies bargaining agents and resolves disputes over bargainable issues and unfair labor practices. In other states, such as Connecticut, there are separate agencies. The State Board of Labor Relations is in charge of certifying bargaining agents, determining whether issues are bargainable, and judging unfair labor practice charges. The State Board of Arbitration and Mediation participates in the resolution of impasses.

SCOPE OF BARGAINING

The scope of bargaining refers to those subjects that can be brought to the negotiating table. Usually a distinction is made between mandatory subjects of bargaining—those subjects that must be negotiated if either side raises them; permissive—those subjects that may, if the parties agree, be negotiated; and prohibited—those subjects that may not be brought to the bargaining table. Prohibited subjects of bargaining typically have to be resolved through a legislative process or even a constitutional amendment.

Although most states specify in statute which subjects are in the mandatory, permissive, and prohibited categories, some have very general statutory language and categorize subjects virtually on a case-by-case basis. In either circumstance, there is a need for some way to resolve disputes over whether or not the parties must, may, or may not bargain on a particular issue. A common example is when employee workload is bargainable, but agency mission and policy are not. The size of classes can be viewed as workload by the teachers who have to instruct the students and grade their work. It can also be viewed by a school board or school administration as policy, based on their reading of research about what size provides the most effective learning experience for the students. The policy might also be a judgment about the best possible mix between effective pedagogy and efficient allocation of resources. Similar relationships exist between workload and policy in social work, policing, and the operation of correctional and mental health institutions. The parties may be able to agree on how to categorize these cases. They may even negotiate on what subjects to include in bargaining. If, however, they cannot agree, then they have to bring the case before the commission or agency that administers the collective bargaining law.

Narrow Scope of Bargaining

When specifying the scope of issues that may or may not be brought to the bargaining table, some jurisdictions have chosen to restrict negotiations to just a few items. In the federal government, for example, there can be bargaining only on the following subjects:

- Work scheduling
- Work clothes
- Working safety
- Policies for promotion, training, and discipline
- Grievance procedures
- Union security

Typically, if there is any bargaining at all, it will be on working conditions (which include items like rest periods and parking facilities), grievance procedures, and union security (which includes whether union officials can use working time, office bulletin boards, and the like to conduct union business). There is, as illustrated in Table 15.1, a scale that is generally followed when moving from a narrow to a broad scope of bargaining.

Part of narrowing the scope of bargaining is the identification of prohibited subjects of negotiation. The list in the federal government includes compensation, layoffs, the selection process, and agency missions. In almost all instances in the public sector, two subjects may not be brought to the negotiating table:

- The criteria and process for selecting new employees
- Agency missions

The former protects the merit system. Nonprofit organizations do not share the concern of protecting civil service, of course. There is no common pattern among nonprofits defining the scope of bargaining.

TABLE 15.1 SCOPE OF BARGAINING FOR SELECTED STATES					
Bargainable Issues	**Delaware**	**Florida**	**Minnesota**	**Pennsylvania**	**New York**
Working conditions	X	X	X	X	X
Grievance procedure	X	X	X	X	X
Union activities and facilities at work place	X	X	X	X	X
Layoffs	X	X	X	X	X
Transfers	X	X		X	X
Promotions		X	X	X	
Wages		X	X	X	X
Vacations, days off		X	X	X	X
Insurance			X	X	X
Assignment of classifications to salary ranges			X		X
Retirement				X	X
Productivity				X	X

The intent of prohibiting negotiation on the missions of government agencies is to preserve the essence of the democratic system. Elected representatives, not government employees, are supposed to determine what government does. Even in the best situations, this principle is not always easy to uphold, but it would clearly be in jeopardy if unions and managers, not representatives of the electorate, established policies and priorities.

Whether or not there are statutory prohibitions that specify which subjects are not negotiable, a standard clause in collective bargaining agreements is one that articulates management rights. An example of such a clause is as follows:

> The Union recognizes the prerogatives of the Employer to operate and manage its affairs in all respects in accordance with its responsibility and powers or authority which the Employer has not officially abridged, delegated, or modified by this Agreement, and such powers or authority are retained by the Employer. These management rights include, but are not limited to the following: The rights to plan, direct, and control the operation of the workforce, determine the size and composition of the workforce, to hire, to lay off, to discipline or discharge for just cause, to establish and enforce reasonable rules of conduct, to introduce new or improved methods of operation, to contract out work, to determine and uniformly enforce minimum standards of performance, all of which shall be in compliance with and subject to the provisions of this Agreement.

Note that later in the agreement these rights may be subject to particular processes or criteria, unless statutory language prohibits even that. When layoffs occur, for example, they may have to be done in order of least seniority. When a jurisdiction decides they must contract with a firm or with employees not a part of the jurisdiction, there may have to be consultation with the union. Nonetheless, the jurisdiction can decide that there will be layoffs and work will be contracted out.

When the scope of bargaining is narrow, there is not necessarily low intensity of conflict or little interest in the bargaining process. Tempers flare and impasses occur when there are few items to discuss, just as when there are many. Some, in fact, argue that a narrow scope can lead to more intense conflict. General discontent and frustration can be focused on a few seemingly insignificant but bargainable issues.[15]

A narrow scope of bargaining can lead to inefficiency. Limiting bargainable issues can have the illusion of preserving traditional administrative and legislative processes for various aspects of public personnel management. In reality, however, the unions might be able to seek benefits in a fragmented way. They bargain some issues; they lobby for others in the legislative arena or with boards, commissions, and elected chief executives.

Broad Scope of Bargaining

When the scope of bargaining is expanded beyond the minimum issues, the range of what can be included is limited only by what is specifically prohibited. Including compensation represents a major threshold. Moreover, compensation issues illustrate dramatically the inefficiencies and dangers of limiting the scope of bargaining and fragmenting the decision-making process. Where, for example, compensation bargaining includes only salaries and time off, unions can go to legislatures or boards for retirement and insurance benefits and then secure a rather generous total compensation package.[16]

Bargaining Retirement

One compensation issue that is frequently not bargainable is retirement. It is feared that the parties will take advantage of the delayed costs of retirement programs and trade items requiring immediate expenditure of funds for generous retirement benefits that the jurisdiction may eventually regret. On the other hand, pensions are, as pointed out in the previous chapter, a major part of compensation, and it may be far better to treat retirement as part of the total compensation package than to separate it.

Bargaining Classification

Position classification represents another compensation-related item that is sometimes deleted from the list of bargainable issues. Position classifications are involved in both the selection process and in compensation. Some jurisdictions do not bargain anything related to classifications in an effort to retain the integrity of the merit system. Others prohibit bargaining over the assignment of duties and responsibilities to a position and over the establishment of qualification standards and examination processes for the position, but they do allow bargaining on the assignment of the position to a classification and the allocation of the classification to a salary range. Bargaining the allocation of classifications to salary ranges risks ranking jobs on some basis other than job evaluation points. This threatens adherence to pay equity principles.

Bargaining Agency Shop

Another issue of bargaining that raises some controversy is the establishment of an **agency shop**. An agency shop or fair-share agreement is where all employees that a union represents must pay union dues, even if they are not formally union members. The argument for agency shops holds that employees in a particular bargaining unit are covered under the negotiated settlement and benefit from its clauses, regardless of whether they are members of the union. These employees should not be free riders. They should contribute to union expenses just like anyone else who benefits from union activities. The opposing argument is based on the individuals' right to associate or not associate with whomever they wish. In *Abood* v. *Detroit Board of Education* (1977), the U.S. Supreme Court dealt in part with this issue. The major concern of this case was an objection an employee raised who was not a union member but who, in an agency shop, was contributing to political activities with which he disagreed. The Court ruled there was nothing illegal or unconstitutional about an agency shop, per se, but that unions engaging in political activities had to identify those expenses and charge nonmembers only for their share of the expenses of negotiating and administering a contract.

Productivity Bargaining

In the mid-1970s, employers and unions began what is known as productivity bargaining. These agreements included a quid pro quo provision in which if a particular change was made and a savings in expenditures realized, then the workers would receive an extra benefit or bonus. Management usually takes the lead in productivity bargaining. They have information from organizational or TQM analyses or human resource planning that identify areas where savings might be achieved. Typically, the full development of the ideas and the monitoring of the efforts are done by joint labor-management committees or in quality management teams.[17]

Privatization

Public employee unions have objected to the expansion of contracting out. In part, unions object to the loss or potential loss of public employee jobs. In part, unions take issue with the assumption that the private sector could do the work of government better and cheaper than government.[18]

Unions have sought, not always successfully, to participate in decisions about outsourcing—or at least to be notified when government intends to contract out for services. Some unions have been able to include in their contracts authority to veto any contracts with adverse implications for current employees. Another clause that unions seek ensures continued employment for current workers if a government agency becomes a corporation or is managed by a private firm. More commonly, however, privatization is a management right beyond the reach of union negotiators.

BARGAINING PROCESS

It is difficult to convey the drama and the subtleties of the negotiation process. A major purpose of the exercise included in this chapter is to provide some idea of what happens when union and management try to agree on a contract. The exercise is a role play in which the collective bargaining process is simulated. The purpose of the discussion here is to outline some general principles that apply to the structure and dynamics of the bargaining process.

The Negotiators

The selection of union negotiators is frequently specified in the union's charter or bylaws. Typically, the union will send a team of representatives who have been elected from among the membership. Some unions structure their elections in order to achieve a certain balance of occupations, agencies, regions, and the like. Unions usually have a full-time staffperson who either is the chief negotiator or an advisor to the chief negotiator that the union selects. That staffperson often has a support staff of researchers and lawyers. Large unions have a year-round staff. Smaller unions may secure help from their national organization or a professional labor negotiator who is hired specifically to bargain a given contract. The chief negotiator, whether professional staff or union official, directs the team and is the only spokesperson for the union during negotiations.

Management follows a less consistent pattern. Some organizations have a department or part of a department that has as its sole responsibility the negotiation and administration of labor contracts. Some organizations have added this responsibility to the work of personnel departments. Smaller governmental units and nonprofit agencies expect their executives to negotiate or, in many instances, they hire a professional negotiator, a hired gun, to secure a contract. In almost all cases, management, like union, uses a team, not just a single person or office. The management team, however, is appointed, not elected. The usual representation includes a personnel manager, an attorney, a budget analyst, and managers from the affected agency or agencies.

A useful concept in understanding the dynamics of collective bargaining is "organizational boundary role."[19] A negotiator, whether union or management, operates at the juncture of the organization they represent and the negotiating table. This is represented in Figure 15.1. Being a negotiator involves a role conflict. On the one hand, negotiators define success as reaching agreement. On the other hand, negotiators must define success as getting what their side wants.

The resolution of the role conflict will depend in part on the negotiator's internal pressures and expectations, in part on the messages received from the organization being represented, and in part on the behavior of the other negotiator or negotiators. If, for example, a school board hires a professional negotiator from a nearby community to bargain with a union, and if the board is not clear about what it wants in a contract—either because of vagueness or internal strife—then the negotiator is likely to emphasize getting an agreement over getting a particular set of clauses. In this situation, there is distance between negotiators and the organization they represent. Negotiators are probably going to use past contracts that they negotiated as guidance for the content of the contract.

Distance from management is exaggerated here because of the so-called hired gun in the situation that has been hypothesized. A labor relations director or personnel manager may also emphasize getting a contract instead of getting a particular

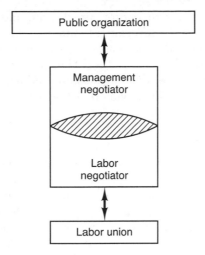

FIGURE 15.1   Boundary Role Structure.
Source: Adapted from James L. Perry and Harold L. Angle, "The Politics of Organizational Boundary Roles in Public Sector Collective Bargaining." Paper presented at Midwest Political Science Association Meeting, Chicago, IL, April 20–22, 1978. By permission of the authors.

contract, but their familiarity with and their commitment to their organization can temper that tendency. On the other hand, a set of firm demands imposed on a negotiator is likely to have an impact on the way in which the role conflict is resolved and the content of the final settlement. Figure 15.2 summarizes the major possible configurations.

Conflict can occur within both unions and management. Factions develop in unions that vie for leadership. Units in an organization compete with one another for

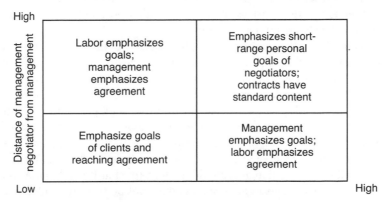

FIGURE 15.2   Boundary Role Distance and Bargaining Outcomes
Source: Adapted from James L. Perry and Harold L. Angle, "The Politics of Organizational Boundary Roles in Public Sector Collective Bargaining." Paper presented at Midwest Political Science Association Meeting, Chicago, IL, April 20–22, 1978. By permission of the authors.

budgetary and personnel resources, for jurisdiction, and for general attention. Negotiators, in contrast, may be adversaries but they are in the same profession. The career paths of both union and management negotiators frequently bring an individual from one side of the table to the other. Thus, the concepts of organizational boundary roles and distance between organization and negotiator provide relevant guides in understanding negotiations and predicting outcomes.

Strategies and Tactics

Generally, negotiations begin with the union making the initial presentation of what it is seeking in the contract. Invariably, despite the inevitable protestations to the contrary, the initial demands by the union are more than they hope to get. The task of management, in part, is to determine or guess which items on the union's list are there for trading purposes and which are there as requirements for securing agreement to a contract.

With few exceptions, when collective bargaining began, the pattern of management participation was simply to determine which of the union demands it could grant. There was no meaningful effort to provide counter demands by management. Now it is common that negotiators for government employers arrive at the initial negotiating session with a list of demands by management. Unions, then, have the same task of trying to determine which of the demands are basic and dead serious and which are there to be abandoned as concessions.

In some state and local governments, some or all of the bargaining sessions are open to the public. When the initial session is public, the tendency is to posture even more dramatically than usual. Sometimes preposterous statements are made as the chief negotiators present their cases. Management will be characterized as a group of fat cats who are violating the public trust and expecting employees of good will and faith to work for next to nothing. Unions will be painted as selfish and lazy, with no regard for the burdens that taxpayers shoulder and with concern only for benefits and not for service. Veterans to negotiations are either bored or entertained by these histrionics. They certainly do not take them seriously.

Games and dramatics continue throughout the process. Negotiators mix table pounding and stubbornness with compliments and gestures to be accommodating. Bargaining teams strategize about when to walk out of the room in a huff: it may be early on; it may be just as an agreement is in reach as an effort to extract one more concession. Union leaders will negotiate around the clock just before meeting with their members in order to use bags under their eyes, disheveled hair, and raspy voices to make an impression of how hard they are working. Managers will publicly wring their hands and fret about the lack of available funds and the inevitable degeneration of services if the union gets anything close to what it is asking. A union may take a vote to authorize its leaders to call a strike—not because the union necessarily wants to go on strike or thinks that negotiations warrant it, but rather to strengthen the position of union negotiators.

As an agreement is being reached, management must be concerned with costs. Both sides come armed with computers and calculators. As proposals are made, the direct and indirect costs are estimated. Examples of direct costs are wages, insurance premiums, retirement contributions, vacations, new tools, uniform allowances, improved facilities, educational reimbursements, and use of official time for union activities. Indirect costs include the administration of the grievance procedure, collection of union dues and fair-share payments, provision of facilities for union activities and notices, and extra steps in the process of contracting out for services.

Although it is management's responsibility to project the costs of various features of an agreement, unions also participate in this process.[20] In part, this is an aspect of the adversarial nature of collective bargaining—one rarely accepts at face value what the other side says. In part, too, the union may find it useful to provide costing information as a way of getting some of the benefits it is seeking. As Neil W. Chamberlain and Donald E. Cullen point out,

> It is part of each party's job of persuasion to convince the other that the costs of agreeing are actually lower and those of disagreeing actually higher than the other may have estimated, thereby moving the other's "final" position. There have been numerous instances in which a union has become convinced, in the course of negotiations, that management could not give what the union genuinely expected to make its "last-ditch" demand and in which managements have been persuaded of the reasonableness of sums which they considered grossly unreasonable on first entering into negotiations.[21]

When, after sometimes months of negotiation and posturing and conflict, the negotiators make a bleary-eyed joint appearance to announce agreement and embrace one another in joy, they seem either like very forgiving souls or individuals with short memories. The joy may be genuine. It may be because the negotiations are over, rather than that each party is thrilled with the contents of the agreement. It may, as well, be a transition to the ratification stage—that point at which those who have been in organizational boundary roles assure their respective clients their interests have been well served, or served as well as possible under the circumstances.

Ratification

Unions follow a fairly standard and common procedure for accepting or rejecting the agreement reached at the negotiating table. That procedure is to submit the agreement to union members for a vote. Most unions require approval by a simple majority of those voting. There is no opportunity to amend the agreement in this process. The choice is simply to accept or reject.

Ratification by government employers involves legislative bodies—state legislatures, city councils, school boards, county boards, and the like. Management ratification in nonprofit organizations usually involves board approval. In some government jurisdictions, such as Hawaii, the only issue for ratification is the cost of the settlement. In most other jurisdictions, ratification includes substantive matters (like work rules) as well as cost items. Contracts supersede statutes, ordinances, and rules that may conflict with them, and thus ratification is akin to establishing personnel policies.

Legislative bodies in some jurisdictions, particularly large ones, delegate ratification authority to a committee. Others treat ratification just like any other legislative action. There is, however, one important caveat: the proposed agreement cannot be amended. Like the union, management must either accept or reject the negotiated contract. If amendments are needed, they must be agreed on jointly by union and management.

This raises an issue of fundamental importance. The discussion up to this point has made the assumption that one can simply transfer the bilateral negotiating model from the private sector to the public. This has been the assumption on which public-sector bargaining has been based. Yet, there are more than two parties that play a role in the public sector. There is the union, the executive management, and the legislature. As long as legislative bodies are willing to rubber stamp what union and management negotiators agree to, the two-party collective bargaining model works. As soon as legislative bodies assert their right to play a more meaningful role, then the two-party model does not apply.

Legislators have been dissuaded from playing an active role in collective bargaining in part because legislative bodies tend to be too deliberative and some-what unwieldy for participating in negotiations with another body. In a few instances, legislatures have refused to approve a proposed settlement. The states of Pennsylvania, Wisconsin, Minnesota, and Oregon have all experienced this. And in all instances, both management and union representatives were outraged. They acted as if the legislature had overstepped its proper role. These disapprovals did disrupt the normal scenario of collective bargaining, but the legislatures did not, of course, act inappropriately. How can legislative bodies best be accommodated in the collective bargaining process? This question remains unresolved.

IMPASSE RESOLUTION

What happens when the parties cannot agree on the terms of a contract? The choices are to continue working without a contract and trying to reach a settlement, to strike against the employer (if it is a union), or to lock out employees (if it is management). In governments, the option of striking has been a source of great debate. The option of a lockout has not seriously been considered.

The union argument for striking is fairly straightforward. The power that unions have in the adversarial model of collective bargaining is the ability to withhold labor from an employer. If labor cannot be withheld, then unions are toothless tigers.

The arguments against strikes by public employees are more complex and mul-tifaceted. A philosophical position holds that government is the sovereign being of the people, and no one has the right to thwart or debilitate that sovereign being. Public employees are supposed to be committed to serving the public, and this commitment is supposed to supersede any individual interest that government employees might have.

A practically oriented position against public-sector strikes notes the peculiar nature of government as an employer. It is a monopoly supplier in many of the services it provides, and citizens must rely on government for essential services, like police and fire protection and refuse collection. It would seem to follow from this observation that strikes by public employees cannot be tolerated if society is to continue functioning. This was at least part of the rationale behind the reaction to the Boston police strike of 1919.

With a few exceptions, strikes in the public sector are illegal. Despite this and despite the arguments prohibiting strikes by government employees, strikes still occur. When frustrated over the inability to reach an agreement, public-sector employees follow the example of their private-sector counterparts. Public employee unions have gone on strike and paid whatever penalties in fines and jail terms were imposed. More commonly, unions insist that part of the settlement in the aftermath of an illegal strike includes no penalties. There were few strikes, just as there was not much unionization, prior to the mid–1960s. Most of the strikes, just like most of the unionization, have been by teachers. Public employee strikes reached a peak in 1979, when there were 593; teachers and municipal employees staged 536 of these. Throughout the 1980s and 1990s, the number of strikes declined to about 300 per year. In part, unions responded to a general antigovernment sentiment and a low level of public tolerance for public employee militancy.

There are ways of responding to an impasse other than going off the job. Striking usually is, in fact, the last step, taken when other measures have failed. The first step is **mediation**. A neutral, third party is brought in to chair the negotiating sessions and to work informally with each party, trying to identify where common ground and bases for an agreement exist. Mediators also serve an important symbolic function, providing evidence to workers and managers that their negotiators are fighting hard for them.[22] Mediators provide a face-saving way for antagonists to come to an agreement.[23]

Another approach to resolving an impasse in negotiations is referred to as **fact finding**. Actually, this is a misnomer. A fact finder does not engage in an effort to find or discover facts. A fact finder listens to the positions of both sides, much like a mediator, and then formally and publicly makes a recommendation for a settlement. The effectiveness of a fact finder depends on the reasonableness of the recommended settlement and on the public pressure that is placed on both sides to accept the recommendation. The most common and important criterion that fact finders use are comparability with similar workers employed in other organizations and changes in the cost of living.

Arbitration is another option for the resolution of impasses. Under this alternative, an arbitrator or panel of arbitrators reviews the positions of the two sides and then provides a contract that both parties are committed to accept. **Interest arbitration** is when this process establishes a contract. **Grievance arbitration** refers to the use of this process for the enforcement of an existing contract.

Seventeen states use binding arbitration for employees providing essential services, such as police and fire protection. These jurisdictions do not want any strikes, legal or illegal, in essential service areas, so they want to be sure they have some way of resolving an impasse in negotiations. An arbitrator's decision is, no matter how unpalatable in parts, generally preferable to a work stoppage, at least to one of the parties. The result has been very few strikes.

There are two types of binding arbitration. One allows arbitrators to pick and choose from the proposals or demands of the two parties and to do some creative work on their own constructing a contract.[24] The other requires both sides to provide their last best offer and then mandates the arbitrator to choose one of those offers.

The arbitrator may not make any amendments to either of those offers. State statutes instruct arbitrators on the general criteria (e.g., ability of the jurisdiction to pay and comparable wages in a community or region) to use in selecting an offer.

The last-best-offer variety retains for the negotiating parties the most meaningful role possible in the decision-making process, thus meeting a concern of some that an arbitrator should not set public policy. The last-best-offer alternative also provides a strong incentive to both parties to be reasonable. If one party has even one outlandish provision, that party risks having the arbitrator reject its entire set of proposals.

State supreme courts in Colorado, California, South Dakota, and Utah have ruled that binding arbitration is unconstitutional. Ten other states have state supreme court decisions upholding the constitutionality of binding arbitration. After Colorado received the ruling of its court, it passed a law that uses a popular referendum to settle impasses. Voters, rather than arbitrators, choose between the contract proposal that the union and management both offer.

IMPLEMENTING CONTRACT PROVISIONS

Cleverness can nullify a loss at the bargaining table. Clumsiness can nullify a gain at the bargaining table. Collective bargaining agreements establish personnel management policies for the employees and supervisors covered under the contract. As with any other set of policies, actual effects will depend on implementation. Supervisors and employees can ignore or twist contract provisions in ways to sabotage the intent of policy makers. Implementation can also be fraught with inefficiencies and unintentional errors, thereby frustrating efforts to achieve stated goals.[25]

The drama of the process of negotiating a collective bargaining agreement attracts attention. Although less visible, contract administration is not uninteresting and it obviously is not unimportant.

Communication

For a contract to be effective, employees and managers must know what it provides. News conferences announcing agreement at the conclusion of negotiations are not sufficient for getting the word out. Nor is it effective to print enough copies of the contract for everyone to have a personal copy. News conferences are held and contracts are distributed, but those organizations that administer their contracts with the least amount of conflict and confusion go beyond these steps. One step is to translate the contract into ordinary English. Legal prose is necessary, but it has its place. Its place does not include informing employees and managers about the rules and policies they must follow.

Steward and Supervisor Training

Although general communications are necessary, the most important and effective communication is that directed at the union steward and the first-line supervisor. Those are the officials who have direct contact with employees. Stewards work with the employees; supervisors do, as well, and in addition they are the first representation of management that employees meet.

Some jurisdictions use teams drawn from those involved in negotiating the contract to train first-line supervisors and union stewards. Joint training efforts have the side benefit that both sides involved can learn how the other is interpreting the contract and have an opportunity to discuss and perhaps resolve differences over how the contract should be administered.[26] In a general review of studies of training for contract administration, Milton Derber found widespread agreement on the importance of this training.[27]

There may, of course, be circumstances when joint union-management training is not desired. As pointed out earlier, coming to an agreement at the bargaining table does not mean an end to conflict. In part, the contract provides a framework and arena for the ongoing adversarial relationship; in part, the contract can be part of an overall strategy for either or both of the parties. A union that wants to get a strict transfer by seniority rule may, as an apparent trade-off, agree to a transfer provision that seems to give management discretion but is complex and vulnerable to grievances. The consideration of transfers might include requirements for posting notices, reviewing qualifications, considering different categories of employees in different sequences, and the like. The language might be vague and ambiguous in places. Then, the union might want to instruct its officers to watch carefully each time there is a transfer and grieve every potential violation of the contract. By overloading the grievance system with complaints about transfers, the union would be setting the stage for the next round of negotiations, in which it would point out the attractions of a simple transfer-by-seniority principle.

Contract Clarification

Just as a settlement does not necessarily mean the end of conflict, neither does it mean the end of negotiations. During the period of the contract, there is constant communication and negotiation between management and the union. There may have been language that neither side meant to be vague or confusing and that needs to be clarified in a memorandum or some other document. There almost inevitably are specific instances that are not anticipated at the bargaining table and need to be resolved.

In order to dispose of these situations in a consistent and effective manner, union and management need not only to work with one another but also to coordinate internally. Structures that already exist for organizational communication and activity are usually adequate for labor-contract administration as well.

The parties involved cannot, of course, always resolve disputes. A fundamental feature of every contract is a grievance process. This process is essential for contract administration.

Labor-Management Cooperation

Since the early 1990s, union and management leaders in almost 50 jurisdictions have formed formal teams to try to resolve problems in the middle of a contract period.[28] While there is some hope that this might generate a cooperative spirit that might replace adversarial relations in contract negotiation, the major objective is to address specific issues and to resolve these outside the formal negotiating process. The term for this approach is Labor-Management Cooperation.

The procedures and techniques in Labor-Management Cooperation are similar to those in TQM, but done within the context of union and management relations. Typically, union and management provide an equal number of team members and there are co-leaders, one from each side. Facilitators convene the teams and get them to focus on a specific issue, like high turnover, frequent tardiness, cumbersome or unsafe work procedures, and unsatisfied customers. Team members then examine relevant data and information, consider options and, hopefully, form a consensus on a resolution. Depending on the resolution, there may be a need for budget approval, a change in contract language, or action by an elected official.

While problems have been solved through this process, the basic relationship between labor and management continues.[29] Specific issue resolution has not altered the fundamentally adversarial nature of union and management relations.

GRIEVANCE AND ARBITRATION

Whether out of intent or ignorance, provisions of the contract are likely to be violated. When these violations are brought to the attention of the offender and are not addressed satisfactorily through informal means, then a more formal procedure must be used.

The grievance process that is a part of collective bargaining is similar to the appeal process used in disciplinary cases under civil service systems, as described in Chapter 13. The steps in the grievance provisions of the contract appended to the exercise in this chapter are very much like the steps in an appeal process. To review, Step 1 is an oral discussion of the matter between the employee and/or the union steward and the first-line supervisor. Step 2 is a written appeal of the supervisor's decision to the department head. Step 3 is an appeal to a central committee or official in charge of personnel and/or labor relations. If, finally, the issue is not resolved satisfactorily by the top personnel official, then Step 4, binding arbitration, is taken.

In addition to the grievance process provided by the contract, unionized employees may pursue appeals through civil service processes (if they are civil service employees, of course) and through employment discrimination processes.[30] According to the usual arrangement, if a subject, such as transfer or sexual harassment, is included both in the contract and in civil service and/or equal opportunity rules, then the grievance procedure in the contract is used. If the subject is not included in the contract, then union, like nonrepresented employees, use the civil service or equal opportunity appeal process. Cases that involve a mixture of issues can be disposed of in more than one of the processes. These arrangements do not have the beauty of simplicity, but they do provide for conflict resolution.

Scope of Process

Grievance procedures frequently cover a broad range of issues. Disciplinary cases constitute the largest single category, but they are only 20 percent of the total number of cases handled each year.[31] Other cases range from grievances over work assignments to the availability of parking spaces.

Two competing theories seek to define the scope of grievable issues. One, which the U.S. Supreme Court articulated in *United Steelworkers* v. *Warrior and Gulf Navigation Co.* (1960), states that an issue is grievable unless it is specifically excluded. This was a private-sector case and most clearly applies to nonprofit organizations. Although the courts have not made any definitive ruling, most public jurisdictions and public sector arbitrators adhere to another perspective, known as the **residual rights theory**. According to this view, the employer retains as a management right any subject that is not a part of the collective bargaining agreement, and only issues explicitly covered in a contract are grievable.[32]

Selection of an Arbitrator

Contracts usually provide for a specific process. A very common pattern is to get a list of five or seven names from a source like the American Arbitration Association, a state equivalent to the National Labor Relations Board, or the Federal Mediation and Conciliation Service. Then, union and management take turns striking one name from the list until one name remains: That is the name of the arbitrator.

Some arbitrators are avoided because they submit bills for extravagant expenses. Some are selected or avoided because they get identified with a particular position. Government managers in one region had great fun and considerable success because they did not, as unions had expected, strike the name of an arbitrator who had long been involved in a local socialist party. This individual's socialist philosophy made him an advocate of tax-supported, free medical services for everyone and, thus, an opponent of health insurance as a benefit for employees. Any grievance that included an issue of health insurance was one that unions, much to their surprise, lost. Once union officials noticed the pattern, they used their own pens to strike his name when it appeared on selection lists.

Arbitration Decision

As in civil service appeals, when a grievance goes to arbitration, the deliberations occur in a courtroom fashion. Witnesses present testimony under oath and are subject to cross-examination. Written documents can be formally entered into the record as exhibits. A written record is kept of the proceedings, often by using a court reporter. Evidentiary rules are relaxed, but what is presented must be relevant and supported.

A major criterion used by arbitrators in deciding cases is the intent of the negotiators. Where this is not clear from the contract itself, arbitrators allow evidence that indicates the intent. Sometimes, of course, negotiators have not addressed a particular issue or could not agree on unambiguous language. If possible, arbitrators base their decision on past practices of the agency or the jurisdiction. When this cannot be done, the decision will reflect the arbitrator's own judgment about what is common practice or what is fair. Courts typically uphold arbitration decisions as long as arbitrators act within the bounds of their authority and in accordance with proper procedures.

THE IMPACTS OF COLLECTIVE BARGAINING

Are unions good or bad? That is a question that can evoke intense feelings. Good and bad are in the eyes of the beholder and, in any case, it is necessary to be more specific. Rather than trying to make a summary judgment, it is more useful to evaluate the impact of unionization in terms of good for what and good for whom.

Compensation

A natural expectation of employees and a natural fear of budget officers is that unionization leads to higher levels of compensation. The evidence on the relationship between collective bargaining and compensation, however, is mixed and inconclusive. It certainly does not confirm either the worst fears of budget officers or the highest hopes of workers.

One review of relevant studies concluded that unionization, in the public and private sectors, can generally be credited with achieving a 5 to 15 percent increase in compensation for represented employees.[33] But, having stated this conclusion, the researchers shared their worries about the defensibility of that conclusion. Most studies focus on a particular occupation, like firefighters,[34] or a particular community, like Los Angeles.[35] Moreover, not all studies indicate a positive relationship between unions and wage increases. One study actually found that unions led to salary declines.[36]

The U.S. General Accounting Office, in a report issued in 1983, concluded that those federal employees who have been able to bargain wages have done relatively well. In the period 1975 to 1980, postal employees fared the best. They received a 53.7 percent increase in their pay. Other federal workers who bargained compensation received a 46.2 percent increase, whereas those unable to bargain salary were given a 34.4 percent increase.[37] All employees received less than the 57.4 percent increase in the Consumer Price Index over the period covered in the study. The same pattern continued throughout the 1990s, although the gap between the Consumer Price Index increases and federal salary increases was even greater.

David Stanley's examination of municipalities in the late 1960s and early 1970s led to inconclusive results.[38] Daniel J. B. Mitchell's analysis of aggregate data collected by the Bureau of Labor Statistics and the U.S. Bureau of Economic Analysis was also inconclusive.[39] As Mitchell pointed out, there are a variety of forces that determine compensation. Factors like the general condition of the economy and an employee's place in the hierarchy of the organization are far more important than whether or not there is collective bargaining over compensation. The general policy of most employers is to keep their wages comparable to what similar workers are getting elsewhere. This takes some of the sting out of union activities and complicates research to determine the effects of unions on compensation. Unions may have an impact in specific situations, but there is not a general pattern that can be detected.

Supervision and Management

Collective bargaining is, as pointed out, an approach to conflict within organizations. With collective bargaining, employees do not have to confront management as single individuals. They have a grievance process, and they have the right to union representation and assistance.

Managerial decision making is more complex because of collective bargaining. Supervisors have to be conscious of contract provisions, and they have to be sensitive to the possibility that if they violate a clause in the contract, they may have a grievance filed against them. Whereas supervisors had been able to make decisions on their own or in consultation with other supervisors or managers, they now have to consult, formally and informally, with union officials.

The changes collective bargaining have prompted in supervision and management need not be cast in a negative or compliance perspective. Better management should lead to better organizational performance and higher employee morale. In their study of public transit systems, James Perry and Harold Angle found empirical support for these linkages.[40]

Merit System

Public employee unions are not hiring halls, and they have not been interested in playing this role. Statutorily prohibiting negotiations on the selection process assures the right of government to employ individuals of its choice, regardless of union policies and preferences. The value of preserving this right for government employers helps maintain the merit system tradition.

Whereas the selection process for initial hiring has been kept separate from the collective bargaining process, some jurisdictions have agreed to provisions for transfers and/or promotions that make the area of connection between the merit system and unionization a subject of concern. A major concern is the preservation of a balance between the right of an employee to expect to transfer to a more desirable working environment and a manager's need to be certain that an office has a congenial and competent staff. Similarly, both the right of an employee to expect promotional opportunities and the need of a government employer to seek new talents and perspectives are at issue. It is obviously difficult to establish or maintain a balance between competing objectives when transfers and promotions occur almost entirely by seniority.

There are some approaches that meet the needs of both employer and employee more satisfactorily than selection by seniority. One is to limit the number of transfers that can occur with any single vacancy, say, no more than two or three. The transfers allow employee mobility, whereas the limit on transfers permits managers to select on the basis of their needs. Another approach, which provides more discretion to appointing authorities, only requires notification of vacancies to current employees so that they might apply for them, through transfer, promotion, or competition. Because employees usually know more about their organization than outsiders, employees often have a competitive advantage. Ensuring employees of the chance to compete, however, does not ensure their selection.

Political Activity

Employee unions are political actors: They lobby; they endorse candidates; they provide financial support and volunteer labor for causes and candidates whom they favor. Employee unions are regarded as an important power in most communities. In local elections, candidates prize the endorsement and support of employee unions. Firefighters and teachers, in particular, have acquired reputations as effective campaign workers and valuable allies. As pointed out in Chapter 3, public employees are more likely than other members of the citizenry to vote and participate in politics. Government workers tend to have a high level of knowledge about politics, and they have a personal interest in the outcome of elections. That personal interest is no longer a matter of whether or not they will have a government job, but rather about the status of their programs and the identity of their bosses.

Some fear a scenario in which public employees control all phases of our political system. There are, however, too many political actors in the U.S. political system for public employee unions to be a dominant force that could not be dislodged by other groups unwilling to pay the costs of public employee victories. The taxpayer revolts of the 1980s and antigovernment sentiment of the 1990s illustrate the limited influence of public employee unions, not their dominance.

Diversity

Unions have been some of the most avid and effective opponents of efforts to achieve equal employment opportunities for minorities and women. In the public sector, this has been especially true among police officers and firefighters. Unions have fought the alteration of requirements that screened out women and minorities.

There are traditional principles upheld by unions that are major obstacles to the achievement of diversity in the workforce. These principles are based not necessarily on opposition to diversification, but on distrust of the capacity of supervisors and managers to exercise discretion fairly. Seniority is the most visible and notable of these principles.

On the other hand, affirmative action advocates can utilize union organizations to accomplish their goals. Especially when bargaining units are organized in ways that allow women and minorities to mobilize, unions can become integral parts of the struggle against discrimination. Unions have, for example, played a major role in getting pay equity policies adopted.

This point applies particularly to women because they have been clustered in jobs that are stereotyped and "reserved" for them. Bargaining units organized according to occupation, in other words, provide the potential for women to resolve affirmative action conflicts through collective bargaining. If clericals, nurses, or aides in female institutions are all in the same bargaining unit, they can insist that their contracts include provisions for educational and training opportunities that advance them into traditionally male jobs, rather than just train them to do their current job better. They can include provisions covering sexual harassment.

Productivity

Unions are frequently identified with protecting their workers from change and maintaining the status quo. There are many examples of unions resisting change and acting as obstacles to improved productivity. There have been, on the other hand, examples since the mid–1970s of agreements between union and management to improve productivity. An element of suspicion and distrust is to be expected, and unions will undoubtedly continue to regard one of their mandates to be the avoidance of layoffs and loss of jobs. Nevertheless, there are enough experiences to indicate that this position of unions does not mean that management must give up on productivity improvement. Moreover, the management rights clauses of contracts and statutes provide government employers with the responsibility for and the latitude to pursue productivity concerns.

At the outset of the discussion of collective bargaining, the point was made that conflict between supervisors and employees was responsible for a lack of productivity among workers. One way of protesting supervision and distasteful work rules was to engage in minor rule violation, cut corners, and work at a minimal rate. With the resolution of conflict provided by collective bargaining and the aven ues for protesting in ways other than lower productivity, it is expected that workers will work more intensely and effectively. Collective bargaining would, no doubt, continue regardless of whether this expectation was met.

SUMMARY

Employee unions and collective bargaining have emerged as integral parts of personnel management systems. Wages, working conditions, work rules, and other dimensions of personnel management are set at a bargaining table, not just in the chambers of a legislative body or a nonprofit board. The administration of the contract is as much a part of managerial and supervisory duties and responsibilities as the implementation of civil service laws and other employment policies.

The process is adversarial, but it is in response to existing conflict. That conflict exists at the bargaining table during negotiation and in offices as the contract is being implemented. Likewise, conflict resolution occurs at the bargaining table and at the workplace.

The impacts of collective bargaining are mixed and uncertain, but it is fair to say that the worst fears have not been confirmed and the highest hopes have not been realized. The essence of the merit system has remained intact. Diversification of the workforce has been both hampered and assisted. Wages have and have not been increased as a result of unionization. The debates and resistance that met the introduction of collective bargaining are still evident in some quarters, but, on the whole, collective bargaining has been accepted as a feature of personnel management in government agencies and nonprofit organizations. Some have even welcomed it.

DISCUSSION QUESTIONS

1. Are relations between unions and management inherently adversarial or are there ways in which the two can join in a cooperative partnership?
2. What are the advantages and disadvantages of managers relying on a firm or individual contractor, rather than an agency employee, to negotiate with employee unions? Under what circumstances, if any, would you favor the hired gun approach?

3. If you were an agency manager, how would you prepare for contract negotiations? How would you be certain the management negotiating team knew of and pursued your concerns?
4. Should public employees be allowed to go on strike?

Collective Bargaining Exercise

This exercise is a role play designed to give participants an understanding of the collective bargaining process in the public sector. Basic information is provided for the context in which the bargaining occurs and for specific roles. As in an actual situation, the personalities, creativity, and imagination of individual participants provide the rest of the necessary ingredients.

THE SETTING

This simulation takes place in Mediumville, a city of about 210,000 people. The community is fairly diversified. It is the location of an undergraduate college, has three industries, and is the home of a major insurance company. The local economy is a microcosm of the national economy. Last year's rate of inflation was 2 percent, this year's is 3 percent, and most predictions for next year are for 3 percent again. There are more than the usual uncertainties about city revenues. Both the state and federal governments are considering cuts in aid to cities that could reduce city revenues by one-third. Property taxes in the community are somewhat below the average for the state, but taxpayers are nonetheless concerned about drastic increases.

The community's political composition is also diversified. There is an active group concerned with women's issues. There is a substantial Chicano community of about 10 percent of the population. A coalition of conservative religious groups has been campaigning against abortion, pornography, and the refusal of the school system to have Christmas programs.

The city bargains with six different unions. Three of the unions are in the middle of two-year contracts. Those contracts include wage increases of 5 percent each year. Three other unions are currently bargaining. One is a blue-collar union, which is demanding a 9 percent salary increase. The average salary of blue-collar workers is $29,000 per year. Another union, representing bus drivers, is asking for a 10 percent increase per year for each of the next two years. The average salary for bus drivers is $34,000.

The third union—the focus of this role play exercise—represents clerical employees. The average salary of clericals is $24,000. The pay ranges currently in effect for the blue-collar, clerical, and bus driver unions are presented later, with salary range 1 allocated to clericals, 2 to blue collar workers, and 3 to bus drivers. There are 350 blue-collar workers, 175 bus drivers, and 1,000 clerical employees. In each instance, the distribution of employees is one-tenth of the work force in each of the first two steps of the salary range, one-fifth in Step 3, two-fifths in Step 4, and one-fifth in Step 5.

While negotiations are being conducted, the city council is deliberating about a proposed ordinance to prohibit abortions in any medical facility within the city's limits. Medical facilities are defined as hospitals, clinics, and doctors' offices. The penalty would be a fine and the revocation of permission to provide any further health services. Abortions are defined to include all abortions, regardless of circumstances.

An abridgement of the existing contract for the clericals is appended to this exercise. Standard clauses not likely to be involved in negotiations have been omitted.

Elections for union leaders are scheduled for next year. Elections for the city council and mayor are scheduled as the last step in this exercise.

PROCEDURE

The instructor will assign roles and set deadlines. The sequence of activities is as follows:

1. Simultaneously, the city council will begin deliberating on the antiabortion proposal, and the management and labor negotiating teams will prepare for bargaining by drawing up their positions and discussing strategies. The scope of bargaining is like that presented for the state of New York in Table 15.2. The city council will continue to deliberate on the antiabortion proposal throughout the rest of the exercise, or until they resolve it. They will have to ratify the final settlement and should make whatever arrangements for getting that on their agenda that seem appropriate.

The proponent of the antiabortion measure is the Anti-Abortion Club (AAC). It is opposed by the Women's Interest Group (WIG), which includes pro-choice as one cause in a general effort to improve the lot of women in society. These groups and general citizens should seek access to the city council and/or the collective bargaining process to express their views as best they can throughout the exercise.

2. Negotiations begin first with the union's presentation and then a response and/or presentation by management. After these initial presentations, discussions and bargaining on each item should take place. Recesses for caucusing may occur whenever desired.

As agreement is reached on each item, the chief negotiator on each side should initialize the wording.

3. If there is an impasse, there is a mediator available and that mediator can, on request, act as an arbitrator. If there is an impasse and the parties agree on binding

| TABLE 15.2 | PAY RANGES (DOLLARS) |

Salary Range	Steps				
	1	2	3	4	5
1	19,360	21,180	23,000	24,820	26,640
2	20,980	23,115	25,250	29,385	32,520
3	23,170	26,480	29,700	33,010	36,320

arbitration, state law requires that the arbitrator select from the last best offers presented by each side.

If binding arbitration is not invoked, the agreement must be ratified by a majority vote by union members and a majority of the city council. A failure to ratify sends negotiators back to the bargaining table.

4. All members of the city council and the mayor must immediately run for reelection. They, for purposes of this exercise, will not have opponents. Members of the class will vote yes or no for each official. The votes cast for the abortion proposal and the contract shall be public information. The mayor should be identified with the majority in the abortion case and with the settlement in collective bargaining.

DESCRIPTION OF ROLES

Participants should read only the role assigned to them. These descriptions emphasize the formal character of the role and provide some guidelines about the values and personality assigned to the role. Although these guidelines should be adhered to in order to let the entire exercise run as it is designed, individuals should not feel constrained. As mentioned, creativity and innovation are important, too.

The instructor will assign individuals who are not assigned a role to be members of AAC, WIG, or the general public.

Mayor.   This is your second four-year term as mayor. You enjoy considerable support throughout the community, due in part to your attractive personal style and in part to your ability to meet the most essential needs of various groups in the community. Your plans are to serve another four-year term and then to run for a seat in the U.S. Congress. As a politician, you wish the abortion issue would go away but recognize that it will not and that it provokes intense feelings. You personally think that the pro-choice arguments are the most persuasive. Regarding collective bargaining, you are concerned about the uncertainty of funding for next year and fear political repercussions of any sizable tax increase.

President of the City Council.   You are a highly respected lawyer in the community and have been elected to the city council and to the presidency of that body because of your reputation as a moderate and as someone who is good at settling disagreements among different groups. You personally do not oppose abortions but respect the views of those who do consider abortions as equivalent to murder. The city budget officer is a neighbor and close friend and has sensitized you to the element of uncertainty in the city's finances. This has made you nervous about the possibility of generous wage settlements with the unions.

City Council Member (A).   You are the proponent of the antiabortion proposal. You are a member of a fundamentalist Christian church, and you are generally conservative politically. One of your closest friends has a daughter who, without her parents' knowledge, had an abortion at one of the city's hospitals. This has traumatized your friend and, in part, this experience has prompted your proposal.

City Council Member (B).   You are a worker in one of the city's major industries. You are very active in your own union and generally supportive of collective bargaining and the status of workers. Abortion is not high on your list of concerns, although you recognize that others feel very intensely about it.

City Council Member (C).   You are the owner of a small business in the central part of the city. You are fiscally conservative, but you have not formed any strong opinion on the abortion issue. You take a great deal of pride in the community, and you are concerned about avoiding conflict and division.

City Council Member (D).   You are a Chicano and a liberal generally, although as a Catholic you oppose abortions on moral grounds. You are not particularly sympathetic to cries by the majority of taxpayers that they are paying too much. You do, however, recognize them as a political force.

City Personnel Manager.   You have been appointed to the negotiating team because of your expertise in personnel management and in order to maintain as much consistency and compatibility as possible between the unionized employees and the nonrepresented. The nonrepresented are about 35 percent of all city employees. You have been in the personnel management profession for almost 20 years, in both the public and private sectors. You support the principle of collective bargaining in government, but you prefer a structure where labor relations and traditional civil service are under the same director. This position makes you a rival to the labor relations director. You serve at the pleasure of the mayor.

City Labor Relations Director and Chief Negotiator.   You have been involved in public sector negotiations ever since receiving your master's degree in public administration 12 years ago. You serve at the pleasure of the mayor and thus far you have maintained good relations with both the mayor and the city council. Your personal aspirations are to move to a larger jurisdiction within the next few years. You enjoy your work, and you have established the kind of record that in all probability will generate more challenging opportunities.

City Budget Officer.   You are on the negotiating team because of your expertise on the city's finances. Your concerns are, of course, to keep the costs of any settlement as low as possible. You have been through negotiations before, and you have become very sensitive to the effects that a settlement with one union can have on negotiations with other unions. You are also aware of and frustrated by the uncertainties that you face regarding how much money the city will have during the next couple of years. Uncertainty has always been a factor, but the deliberations at the federal and state level about cuts in aid have made the level of uncertainty higher than ever. You serve at the pleasure of the mayor.

City Director of the Department of Administration.   The mayor has appointed you to the negotiating team because your department is the largest employer of clericals and because, as the mayor's former campaign manager, you enjoy a close relationship with the mayor. Given your interest in administration and politics, you are expected to bring a good balancing perspective to the negotiations. Your agency has not been regarded as a good working environment for clericals, and you expect some of the hostility common to negotiations to be directed at you. The major problem, as far as you can tell, has been poor supervision, causing conflict, hostility, and a higher than usual turnover rate.

City Director of the Department of Transportation. The mayor has appointed you to the negotiating team because your department is one of the largest and because the mayor would like to have some continuity in the bargaining with the various unions. Bus drivers are also negotiating a contract this year. You are a professional civil servant. You have served as director of the department of transportation for five years, and you would like to retain this position until your retirement four years from now. You serve at the pleasure of the mayor.

Union Executive Director and Chief Negotiator. You are a full-time staff person for the AFSCME local involved in this negotiation. You also serve the bus drivers and two of the unions not involved in negotiations at this time. You have been the executive director here since the beginning of unionization, eight years ago. You would like to move to a larger city or to a position working with state employees, and have set yourself a two-year deadline for doing this.

Union President. You are a secretary in the department of human services and rank-and-file members have elected you to your position. As president, you are a member of the negotiating team. You were elected to the presidency when clericals first unionized eight years ago and have been in office ever since then. You plan to run for reelection next year, and you have heard that the secretary-treasurer is thinking of challenging you. You are somewhat puzzled by this, because the wages and benefits of clericals have improved noticeably since unionization.

Union Vice President. You are a secretary in the parks department and rank-and-file members have elected you to your position. As vice president, you are a member of the negotiating team. You initially resisted the move to unionize clerical workers but became convinced that this was inevitable and that it might indeed improve working conditions and wages. You were elected to your position primarily because of the respect you command from other clericals who had the same initial misgivings as you did. You will be retiring in one year.

Union Secretary-Treasurer. You are a secretary in the assessor's office and rank-and-file members have elected you to your position. As secretary-treasurer, you are a member of the negotiating team. You are seriously considering running for the presidency. A prime motive is your concern that the current president is not militant enough in pressing for the needs not only of clericals but of women.

Union Member of Bargaining Team (A). You are a secretary in the department of administration and you have been elected by rank-and-file members to be on the negotiating team. You have been elected primarily because of your identification with the comparable worth cause. You have been a member of the union ever since it began organizing in the city, and you are convinced that the most effective way of achieving comparable worth is through the collective bargaining process.

Union Member of Bargaining Team (B).   You are a receptionist and typist in the parks department, and you have been elected by rank-and-file members to be on the negotiating team. Your best friend, who worked in the department of administration, just quit her job because she could no longer stand the sexual harassment to which she had been subjected. She has the mixture of anger and guilt feelings that are common in such situations. You are angry.

Union Member of Bargaining Team (C).   You are a secretary in the department of transportation, and you have been elected by rank-and-file members to be on the negotiating team. You are a member of the Chicano community. Your concerns include securing a reasonable wage increase and getting educational and training opportunities for all union members but especially minorities.

President of Anti-Abortion Club.   You are the head and chief spokesperson of a conservative, religiously based group that opposes abortion on moral grounds. Because of the conviction that life begins at conception, you regard abortion as murder and are therefore intense about your cause. Your group includes men and women and, although generally conservative, is basically concerned about the issue of abortion.

President of Women's Interest Group.   You are the head and chief spokesperson of a liberal women's group. Your concerns include choice regarding reproduction, equal pay for comparable worth, sexual harassment, and the entry of women into jobs traditionally held by men. You have been elected as head primarily because you are articulate and firm without being abrasive.

Mediator-Arbitrator.   You are a professional mediator-arbitrator, currently working for a state agency that provides mediators and arbitrators to local governments. You hope to move eventually to the National Labor Relations Board or to become a professional negotiator for either unions or employers. Your job here is first to be certain that the parties are bargaining in good faith. Then you should try and determine where the parties are in basic agreement and what the "bottom line" is of each party. As mediator you should suggest proposals and compromises where appropriate. Stress the desirability of the two parties reaching their own accord, without going to arbitration. Remember not to get identified with either side and thereby lose your effectiveness. As arbitrator, you must, without making any changes, select the entire set of proposals submitted by one of the two parties.

AGREEMENT BETWEEN CITY OF MEDIUMVILLE AND CLERICAL UNION, AFSCME, AFL-CIO

This agreement made and entered into pursuant to the provisions of Section 111.11 Pennsylvania Statutes by and between the City of Mediumville, hereinafter referred to as the employer, and the clerical union as representatives of clerical employees employed by the City of Mediumville, hereinafter referred to as the union or employee, Witnesseth:

[Management rights and union recognition and security clauses not included]

GRIEVANCE AND ARBITRATION PROCEDURE

Grievances shall be processed in the following manner: (Time limits set forth shall be exclusive of Saturdays, Sundays, and holidays.)

Step 1.   The employee and/or the steward shall take the grievance up orally with the employee's first line of supervision outside of the bargaining unit within ten days of their knowledge of the occurrence of the event. The supervisor shall attempt to make a mutually satisfactory adjustment, and, in any event, shall be required to give an answer within ten days.

Step 2.   The grievance shall be considered settled in Step 1 unless within ten days after the supervisor's answer is due the grievance is reduced to writing and presented to the department head. The department head shall respond to the grievance in writing within ten days.

Step 3.   The grievance shall be considered settled in Step 2 unless within ten days from the date of the department head's written answer or last date due the grievance is presented in writing to the personnel committee. The personnel committee shall respond in writing to the union steward, grievance committee, or union representative (with a copy to the president of the union) within ten days.

Step 4.   If a union or employee grievance is not settled at the third step, either party may take the matter to arbitration.

ARBITRATION

(a) The arbitrator shall, if possible, be mutually agreed upon by the parties. If agreement on the arbitrator is not reached within ten days after the date of the notice requesting arbitration or if the parties do not agree upon a method of selecting an arbitrator within ten days, then the Pennsylvania Employment Relations Board shall be requested to submit a panel of five arbitrators. The parties shall alternately strike names until one remains and the party requesting arbitration shall be the first to strike a name. Each party shall pay one-half of the cost of the arbitrator.

(b) The arbitrator shall have the authority to determine issues concerning the interpretation and application of all articles or sections of this agreement. He or she shall have no authority to change any part; however, he or she may make recommendations for changes when in his or her opinion such changes would add clarity which might avoid future disagreement.

(c) The written decision of the arbitrator, in conformity with his or her jurisdiction, shall be final and binding upon both parties but shall not constitute a binding precedent in connection with future negotiations.

Discipline, Suspension, Discharge.   Employees shall not be disciplined, suspended, or discharged without good cause. A suspension shall not exceed 30 days. Written notice of the suspension, discipline, or discharge and the reason or reasons for the action shall be sent to the employee with a copy to the Union within 24 hours.

Interdepartmental Transfers.   Those employees wishing to transfer to another department within their same job classification shall file an application for such transfer with the personnel manager designating which department(s) they wish to transfer to. Such transfer applicants shall be given first consideration by the appointing authority for their possible transfer to the position being filled by order of their seniority.

Layoffs.   The employer shall have the right to reduce the number of jobs in any classification and/or department because of shortage of funds, lack of work, or because of a change in organization or duties. Employees whose jobs have become eliminated shall have the right to bump any junior employee in their classification and/or in their pay range or classifications in pay ranges below—provided they are qualified and can demonstrate their ability to do the junior employee's job. Such junior employees who have lost their positions as a result of a bump, shall have the right to exercise their seniority in the same manner as if their job had been eliminated.

Recall from Layoff.   Employees shall be recalled from layoff in accordance with their seniority to jobs for which they are qualified. The employer shall not employ any new employees or temporary or part-time employees in positions for which there exist a qualified employee on the layoff list.

Compensation.   Employees shall be paid in accordance with the following scale (based on an annual salary for a full-time employee):

Step 1: $19,360

Step 2: $21,180

Step 3: $23,000

Step 4: $24,820

Step 5: $26,640

Employees shall be hired at no less than the first or minimum step and shall be advanced to the second step effective upon the completion of 1,040 hours (six months, full-time) of work. Employees shall thereafter be advanced one step for each additional 2 ,080 hours of work, until they reach the maximum, unless at least 30 days prior to the scheduled time for an increase the department head notifies the employee in writing that the increment increase is being denied. The written denial shall give the reasons thereof and shall be grievable.

Paid Holidays.

The following are determined to be holidays:

January 1

Memorial Day (last Monday in May)

July 4

Labor Day (first Monday in September)

Thanksgiving Day (fourth Thursday of November)

December 24

December 25

December 31

Whenever any of said holidays shall fall on Saturday or Sunday, the succeeding Monday shall be the holiday.

Vacation. All employees covered by this agreement shall earn annual paid vacation according to the following schedule:

1st year through 7th year: 80 hours of vacation

8th year through 14th year: 120 hours of vacation

15th year through 22nd year: 160 hours of vacation

23rd year and thereafter: 200 hours of vacation

Sick Leave with Pay. All full-time employees covered by this agreement shall be granted sick leave with pay at the rate of four hours of sick leave for each 160 hours worked. The accumulation of sick leave days shall not exceed 96 hours per year, and sick leave may not be carried over from one year to the next.

Educational Programs. It shall be the policy of the parties to this agreement to develop training and educational programs. Such programs shall be designed to improve the skills of employees relative to the jobs they currently perform. Any such training or educational programs as are developed shall be at the mutual consent of the parties.

GLOSSARY

Agency shop Arrangement where all employees that are covered by a union contract must pay union dues, even if they do not belong to the union

American Federation of State, County and Municipal Employees (AFSCME) The largest public employee union in the country representing employees other than teachers

Arbitration Process in which a third, neutral party provides a binding settlement of a dispute (See grievance arbitration and interest arbitration.)

Bargaining unit The category of employees within an organization that are grouped together for collective bargaining purposes

Certification The process of determining that employees want to be represented by a particular union

Confidential employees Individuals who may not be included in a collective bargaining agreement or a union because their responsibilities involve working with managers in contract negotiation

Fact finding An approach to resolve an impasse that relies on a proposed settlement offered by a third, neutral party. The proposal is advisory

Good-faith bargaining A requirement that applies to both union and management that parties genuinely engage in the give-and-take of negotiations

Grievance arbitration Arbitration used to settle a disagreement about how to apply or administer a contract

Impasse A stage in which there appears to be no grounds for movement in negotiation toward an agreement

Interest arbitration Arbitration used to settle an impasse in negotiating a contract

Mediation Effort to resolve an impasse that uses a neutral third party to work informally to help the parties reach agreement. The mediator plays an advisory role

Ratification The adoption by union members and by management of the contract negotiated by their representatives

Residual rights theory Principle that anything not explicitly included in a contract is a management right. This is the prevailing approach in the public sector

Scope of bargaining The issues that must or that may be negotiated between union and management. Issues are categorized as mandatory, permissive and prohibited subjects of bargaining

SOURCES

Bureau of National Affairs. (1992). *Basic patterns in union Contracts.* Washington, DC: Bureau of National Affairs.
Survey of existing contracts with analysis of frequent patterns.

Follett, M. P. (1949) *Freedom and co-ordination.* London: Management Publications Trust.
Classic statement of the perspective that conflict between management and workers is inherent and can be managed, but not eliminated.

Kearney, R. C. (1992). *Labor relations in the public sector.* New York: Marcel Dekker.
A general review and discussion of unions and bargaining in the public sector.

Reeves, T. Zane (2006) The demise of public employee unionism? in Norma M. Riccucci, ed., *Public personnel management: Current concerns, future challenges* (4ᵗʰ ed.). New York: Longman
A brief, but lucid review of the history of public employee unions.

Russel, F. (1975). *A city in terror, 1919: The Boston police strike.* New York: Viking.
Account of the police strike that affected public sector collective bargaining for almost the next half-century.

NOTES

1. Peter M. Blau and W. R. Scott, *Formal Organizations* (San Francisco: Chandler, 1962); Reinhard Bendix, *Work and Authority in Industry* (New York: Harper and Row, 1963).
2. Ralf Dahrendorf, *Class and Conflict in Industrial Society* (Stanford: Stanford University Press, 1959).
3. Mary Parker Follett, *Freedom and Co-ordination* (London: Management Publications Trust, 1949). For an example from outside the United States, see David K. Leonard, *Reaching the Peasant Farmer* (Chicago: University of Chicago Press, 1977), 64–80.

4. Peter F. Drucker, *The Practice of Management* (New York: Harper & Row, 1954); George L. Morrisey, *Management by Objectives and Results in the Public Sector* (Reading, MA: Addison-Wesley, 1976); J. C. Abegglen, *The Japanese Factory: Aspects of Its Social Organization* (Glencoe, IL: Free Press, 1958); Steven Cohen and Ronald Brand, *Total Quality Management in Government* (San Francisco: Jossey-Bass, 1993).

5. J. Armshaw, D. G. Carnevale, and B. Waltuck, "Cooperating for Quality: Union-Management Partnership in the U.S. Department of Labor," *Review of Public Personnel Administration* 13, no. 2 (Spring 1993): 25–47; Richard C. Kearney and Stephen W. Hays, "Labor-Management Relations and Participative Decision Making: Toward a New Paradigm," *Public Administration Review* 54 (January/February 1994): 44–52.

6. Francis Russel, *A City in Terror, 1919: The Boston Police Strike* (New York: Viking, 1975).

7. Ronald C. Kent, AFSCME: *A Brief Labor History* (Madison, WI: AFSCME, 2003).

8. T. Zane Reeves, "The Demise of Public Employee Unionism?" in Norma M. Riccucci, ed., *Public Personnel Management: Current Concerns, Future Challenges*, 4th ed. (New York: Longman, 2006).

9. Joseph B. Mosca and Steven Pressman, "Unions in the 21st Century," *Public Personnel Management* 24, no. 2 (Summer 1995): 159–166.

10. Leo Kramer, *Labor's Paradox* (New York: Wiley, 1962), 27.

11. Michael T. Leibig and Wendy L. Kahn, *Public Employee Organizing and the Law* (Washington, DC: Bureau of National Affairs, 1987); Paul E. Gerhart, "The Emergence of Collective Bargaining in Local Government," *Public Personnel Management* 9, no. 4 (Fall 1980): 287–295.

12. Hugh O'Neill, "The Growth of Municipal Employee Unions," in Robert H. Connery and William Farr, eds., *Unionization of Municipal Employees* (New York: Academy of Political Science, 1970), 3–4; Jim Seroka, "The Determinant of Public Employee Union Growth," *Review of Public Personnel Administration* 5, no. 2 (Spring 1985): 5–20.

13. Joan Pynes, "Human Resource Management in Nonprofit Organizations," in Riccucci, ed., *Public Personnel Management*.

14. Jennifer C. Berkshire, "Nonprofit Groups Turn to Unions to Organize Workers and Collaborate on Common Causes," *The Chronicle of Philanthropy* (2002) www.philanthropy.com/jobs/2002

15. R. G. Brown and T. L. Rhodes, "Public Employee Bargaining Under Prohibitive Legislation: Some Unanticipated Consequences," *Journal of Collective Negotiations* 20, no. 1 (1991): 23–30; Bernard Ingster, "Themes and Issues—An Afterword," in Walter J. Gershenfeld, J. Joseph Lowenberg, and Bernard Ingster, *Scope of Public-Sector Bargaining* (Lexington, MA: Lexington Books, 1977), 207.

16. William H. Holley and Kenneth M. Jennings, *The Labor Relations Process* (Chicago: Dryden, 1994); Bureau of National Affairs, *Basic Patterns in Union Contracts* (Washington, DC: Bureau of National Affairs, 1992).

17. W. N. Cooke, "Product Quality Improvement Through Employee Participation: The Effects of Unionization and Joint Union-Management Administration," *Industrial and Labor Relations Review* 46 (October 1992): 119–134; Dianne R. Layden, "Productivity and Productivity Bargaining: The Environmental Context," *Public Personnel Management* 9, no. 4 (Fall 1980): 244–256.

18. Donald F. Kettl, Sharing Power: *Public Governance and Private Markets* (Washington, DC: Brookings Institution, 1993).

19. R. L. Kahn, D. M. Wolfe, R. P. Quinn, J. D. Snoek, and R. A. Rosenthal, *Organizational Stress: Studies in Role Conflict and Ambiguity* (New York: Wiley, 1964); D. Katz and R. L. Kahn, *The Social Psychology of Organizations* (New York: Wiley, 1966).

20. David E. Northup, "Management's Cost in Public-Sector Collective Bargaining," *Public Personnel Management* 5, no. 5 (September/October 1976): 328–334.

21. Neil W. Chamberlain and Donald E. Cullen, *The Labor Sector* (New York: McGraw Hill, 1971), 233. See also Richard C. Kearney, *Labor Relations in the Public Sector* (New York: Marcel Dekker, 1992).

22. Patrice Mareschal, "Providing High Quality Mediation: Insights from the Federal Mediation and Conciliation Service," *Review of Public Personnel Administration*, 18, no. 4 (Fall 1998): 55–67.

23. Susan R. Quinn, Debbie Bell, John Wells, "Interest-Based Negotiation: A Case Study," *Public Personnel Management* 26, no. 4 (Winter 1997): 529–534.

24. Gregory G. Dell'Omo, "Capturing Arbitrator Decision Policies Under a Public Sector Interest Arbitration Statute," *Review of Public Personnel Administration* 10, no. 2 (Spring 1990): 19–38.

25. Eugene Bardach, *The Implementation Game: What Happens After a Bill Becomes Law* (Cambridge, MA: MIT Press, 1977); Jeffrey L. Pressman and Aaron B. Wildavsky, *Implementation* (Berkeley: University of California Press, 1973); Donald S. Van Meter and Carl E. Van Horn, "The Policy Implementation Process: A Conceptual Framework," *Administration and Society* 6 (February 1975); George C. Edwards, III, *Implementing Public Policy* (Washington, DC: Congressional Quarterly, 1980).

26. Donald P. Crane, "Patterns of Labor-Management Cooperation," *Employer Responsibilities and Rights Journal* 5, no. 4 (1992): 1–11; and D. Carnevale, "Federal Service 2000: Staff Training and Labor-Management Cooperation," *International Journal of Public Administration* 16, no. 6 (1993): 865–887.

27. Milton Derber, "Management Organization for Collective Bargaining in the Public Sector," in Benjamin Aaron, Joseph R. Grodin, and James L. Stern, eds., *Public-Sector Bargaining* (Washington, DC: Bureau of National Affairs, 1979), 109–112. See also, John F. Burton, Jr. "Local Government Bargaining and Management Structure," in David Lewin et al., eds., *Public Sector Labor Relations: Analysis and Readings* (Sun Lakes, AZ: Thomas Horton and Daughters, 1981).

28. Report of the U.S. Secretary of Labor's Task Force on Excellence in State and Local Government Through Labor Management Cooperation (May, 1996). U.S. Government Printing Office, Washington, D.C.

29. Jon Brok, ed. "Labor-Management Cooperation—Special Issue," *Public Personnel Management* 27, no. 1 (Spring 1998): 1–102.

30. George W. Bohlander, "Public Sector Independent Grievance Systems: Methods and Procedures," *Public Personnel Management* 18, no. 3 (Fall 1989): 339–354.

31. Debra J. Mesch. "Grievance Arbitration in the Public Sector," *Review of Public Personnel Administration* 15, no. 4 (Fall 1995): 22–36.

32. Harry Graham, "Arbitration Results in the Public Sector," *Public Personnel Management* 11, no. 2 (Summer 1982): 112. See also Mario F. Bognanno and Charles J. Coleman, *Labor Arbitration in America: The Profession and Practice* (New York: Praeger, 1992); Paul F. Gerhart and Donald P. Crane, "Wrongful Dismissal: Arbitration and the Law," *Arbitration Journal* 48, no. 2 (1993): 56–68.

33. David T. Methe and James L. Perry, "The Impacts of Public-Sector Bargaining on Local Government Operations: A Review of Research." Paper presented at Annual Meeting of American Society for Public Administration, Baltimore, April 1–5, 1979.

34. R. G. Ehrenberg, "Municipal Government Structures, Unionization, and the Wages of Firefighters," Industrial and Labor Relations Review 27, no. 1 (October 1973): 36–48.

35. W. Fogel and D. Lewin, "Wage Determination in the Public Sector," *Industrial and Labor Relations Review* 27, no. 3 (April 1974): 391–404.

36. D. Lewin and J. H. Keith, "Managerial Responses to Perceived Labor Shortages," *Criminology* 14, no. 1 (May 1976): 65–93.

37. General Accounting Office, *Comparison of Collectively Bargained and Administratively Set Pay Rates for Federal Employees*, Document No. FPCD 82–49 (Washington, DC: Government Printing Office, 1983).

38. David T. Stanley, *Managing Local Government Under Union Pressure* (Washington, DC: Brookings Institution, 1972).

39. Daniel J. B. Mitchell, "The Impact of Collective Bargaining on Compensation in the Public Sector," in Benjamin Aaron, et al., *Public Sector Bargaining*, 118–149.

40. James L. Perry and Harold L. Angle, "Collective Bargaining and Organizational Performance," *Policy Science* (1983): 1–25.

Chapter 16

Summary and Conclusions

Personnel management was once driven by a vision. Over 100 years ago, in 1883, the Pendleton Act was passed and reformers dreamed of governments hiring individuals on the basis of their respective merit rather than on their political identity. True, part of the intent behind the establishment of the merit system was to deprive political machines of the patronage so essential to their existence. Major actors in the reform movement aimed to weaken the political power of newly immigrant communities and to retain supremacy for English-speaking whites. Part of the fervor of the reform movement, however, arose from those once active in the effort to abolish slavery. The abolitionists saw the merit system as another way to secure individual freedoms.

Patronage received a staggering blow. Merit-based civil service systems were a major factor in the demise of political machines. But full individual freedom and dignity has proven to be a more elusive goal.

The emphasis at the beginning of the twentieth century was on making administration, including personnel management, in and outside of government, scientific in order to maximize productivity. The scientific management approach—supported in the public sector by Woodrow Wilson's assertion that politics and administration could and should be separated—searched for the single best way of accomplishing tasks and then routinizing work. Employees were valued for their ability to conform to work rules, not for their creativity or compassion. Personnel managers did clerical work and saw their role primarily as preventing spoils and corruption, rather than as pursuing a more positively defined goal. Agency managers determined the rules and routines that defined work and then monitored their staff to be certain everyone did their assigned tasks.

Changes in the workforce and in the scope of government activity and nonprofit organizations made the clerical features of public personnel management increasingly inappropriate and irrelevant. Work was less routine and more professional. Classification systems based on the scientific management, assembly-line school of thought no longer fit. The workforce grew beyond what could be handled by traditional styles of management. Workers organized to demand better treatment and better conditions of employment. Ethnic minorities, women, people with disabilities, and the elderly mobilized to have greater access to societal resources. Their demands included equal access to professional and managerial opportunities. Computer technology presented opportunities and challenges. The public demanded more services and more problem solving.

THE CONTEMPORARY VISION OF PERSONNEL MANAGEMENT IN GOVERNMENT AGENCIES AND NONPROFIT ORGANIZATIONS

From the mid-1970s to the early 1980s, personnel management experienced another surge of reform. A new vision emerged to provide direction. Whereas the major goal of the Pendleton Act was to prevent something (i.e., patronage), the major goal of the Carter Civil Service Reform Act was to accomplish something (i.e., a competent, accountable, and diverse workforce).

Individual employees won new rights. Largely to combat gender and race discrimination, the emphasis on defining employee rights and restrictions and on judging applicants and employees is on job-relatedness. Personal lifestyles are not the matter of concern and regulation they once were. There is a rich diversity within the workforce, and social representation is valued and pursued.

Organizations have placed more emphasis on career planning, educational and training opportunities, and internal transfers and promotions. There is a greater understanding of the ways in which personal and work tensions can interact. Employee assistance programs (EAPs) to deal with alcohol and drug abuse, mental health, and emotional distress are replacing the assumptions that all work problems reflect laziness, incompetence, and indiscipline.

A significant number of state governments and the federal government established a general category of senior managers and provide a program of career mobility opportunities, training, and monetary incentives to meet the special needs and interests of these officials. Civil service laws have been modified to recognize that personnel management is policy-oriented and that it is an art as well as a science.

The slogan, "Let managers manage," has been embodied in many of the reforms adopted since the mid-1970s. The number of candidates certified for appointment has been expanded to give greater choice. Human resource planning incorporates the designs of agency managers. A wide array of options is available for rewarding high achievers and for working with low performers.

The reform proposals that provide the vision and the framework of contemporary public personnel management are still being implemented. In addition, there are new concerns and challenges.

The 1980s were not kind to government in general and they were not conducive to achieving the vision of civil service reformers in particular. Popular sentiment was more antigovernment than usual. More emphasis was placed on privatization and avoiding government than on improving government. Recessions and taxpayer revolts prompted legislatures, governors, and presidents to withhold resources needed for incentive pay, employee development, and EAPs. The commitment to remedying the effects of past discrimination was threatened by divisive forces, fears, and misunderstandings. These factors led to an incomplete implementation of some reforms and to an initiation of others.

The 1990s began with some renewed optimism and dedication. The prestigious commission headed by Paul Volcker called forcefully for an end to bureaucrat bashing.[1] The Volcker Commission went on to specify what steps needed to be taken to reinvigorate the public service. A commission headed by former Mississippi Governor William P. Winter echoed the same themes for state and local governments.[2]

Throughout his term, President George H. W. Bush showed appreciation and respect for government employees and refused to join the naysayers. The Reinventing Government reform theme of President Bill Clinton emphasized and tried to build on what government agencies and public employees can do, rather than assuming government cannot be improved.[3]

If organizations are to do their jobs well, they must have human resources of high quality and they must be good employers. Personnel management cannot be an afterthought. As pointed out at the beginning of this book, personnel management is based on a number of public values and is charged with the pursuit of a number of policy objectives. The last part of this book has discussed techniques and processes, but always in the context of policies.

The different values and policies could be presented as dilemmas for agency managers, but only if differences are taken to extremes. A more useful and realistic approach is to see the managerial, organizational, employee, democratic, and professional perspectives embodied in personnel management as a rich blend of values. The protection of employee rights can and must be provided while at the same time employees are expected and enabled to do their jobs well. The achievement of a diverse workforce does not inevitably lead to lower levels of competence. In fact, as pointed out in Chapter 4, a major effect of the 1964 Civil Rights Act has been to emphasize job-relatedness in selecting and evaluating employees.

Whereas the blend of values and objectives is basic, the configuration of personnel management is dynamic. Technological and sociological changes provide new capacities and new challenges. The baby boomer retirements clearly present both challenges and opportunities. The shortage of skilled and experienced workers will force organizations to find new ways of defining jobs and fulfilling their missions. Young people will have to assume high levels of responsibility more quickly than workers in other generations. At the same time, changes in gender roles and in families will heighten the importance of work-family balance issues. New mixtures of government agencies and nonprofit organizations are serving individuals and communities. The partnerships and the rivalries between these institutions will alter job designs and allow for more options and inter-organizational mobility for those in careers in public service. Whatever the specific challenges and opportunities, one trusts that human resource management in government agencies and nonprofit organizations will continue to be pursued with both competence and vision.

NOTES

1. National Commission on the Public Service, *Leadership for America: Rebuilding the Public Services* (Lexington, MA: Lexington Books, 1989), 1–10.
2. National Commission on the State and Local Public Service, Frank J. Thompson, ed., *Revitalizing State and Local Public Service: Strengthening Performance, Accountability, and Citizen Confidence* (San Francisco: Jossey-Bass, 1993).
3. David Osborne and Ted Gaebler, Reinventing Government: How the Entrepreneurial Spirit Is Transforming the Public Sector (Reading, MA: Addison-Wesley, 1992); National Performance Review, *From Red Tape to Results: Creating a Government that Works Better and Costs Less* (Washington, DC: National Performance Review, 1993).

Appendix

General Sources in Personnel Management

For those who want to pursue additional sources and reference to keep up with developments in the field, the two major journals in the profession are *Public Personnel Management* and *Review of Public Personnel Administration*. The latter is a journal begun in 1981. The International Personnel Management Association, the professional association of public personnel managers, publishes the former journal. The IPMA publishes a very useful newsletter and a number of books and pamphlets.

The online address for the IPMA home page is www.ipma-hr.org.

Other relevant journals are *Public Administration Review, Personnel Journal, Labor Law Journal,* and the *Journal of Applied Psychology.*

The U.S. Office of Personnel Management has published a number of handbooks, guides, and research reports. The home page addresses of the OPM and other relevant federal agencies are:

Office of Personnel Management: www.opm.gov/
U.S. Merit Systems Protection Board: www.access.gpo.gov/mspb/
Equal Employment Opportunity Commission: www.eeoc.gov/
Bureau of Labor Statistics: www.statistics.bls.gov/

Government Executive is a commercial journal written for managers in the public sector, especially the federal government. It is accessible online at www.govexec. com/. In addition, the Bureau of National Affairs, a private commercial organization, publishes a series of reports and studies on personnel, labor relations, and equal employment issues. It has a home page: www.bna.com/.

There are a number of online services that provide access to court cases, including those cited in this text. One such service is FindLaw Internet Legal Resources, and its address is www.findlaw.com/.

Universities increasingly are offering courses and programs designed to prepare individuals for management in nonprofit organizations. In addition, there are a number of organizations that specialize in nonprofit management, including the Urban Institute (www.urban.org) and the Center for Nonprofit Management (www.cnmsocal.org).

Index